CREATING INDIGENOUS PROPERTY

Power, Rights, and Relationships

While colonial imposition of the Canadian legal order has undermined Indigenous law, creating gaps and sometimes distortions, Indigenous peoples have taken up the challenge of rebuilding their laws, governance, and economies. Indigenous conceptions of land and property are central to this project.

Creating Indigenous Property identifies how contemporary Indigenous conceptions of property are rooted in and informed by their societally specific norms, meanings, and ethics. Through detailed analysis, the authors illustrate that unexamined and unresolved contradictions between the historic and the present have created powerful competing versions of Indigenous law, legal authorities, and practices that reverberate through Indigenous communities, including relationships to land and non-human life forms, responsibilities to one another, environmental decisions, and wealth distribution. *Creating Indigenous Property* identifies the ways that Indigenous discourses, processes, and institutions can empower the use of Indigenous law and explores the conditions under which Canadian and Indigenous legal orders can productively co-exist.

ANGELA CAMERON is the Shirley Greenberg Chair and associate professor in the Faculty of Law at the University of Ottawa.

SARI GRABEN is assistant professor in the Department of Law and Business in the Ted Rogers School of Management, Ryerson University.

VAL NAPOLEON is the Law Foundation Professor of Aboriginal Justice and Governance at the University of Victoria.

Creating Indigenous Property

Power, Rights, and Relationships

EDITED BY ANGELA CAMERON,
SARI GRABEN, AND VAL NAPOLEON

UNIVERSITY OF TORONTO PRESS
Toronto Buffalo London

© University of Toronto Press 2020
Toronto Buffalo London
utorontopress.com
Printed in Canada

ISBN 978-1-4875-0545-5 (cloth)   ISBN 978-1-4875-3213-0 (EPUB)
ISBN 978-1-4875-2382-4 (paper)   ISBN 978-1-4875-3211-6 (PDF)

Library and Archives Canada Cataloguing in Publication

Title: Creating Indigenous property : power, rights, and relationships / edited
    by Angela Cameron, Sari Graben, and Val Napoleon.
Names: Cameron, Angela (Angela Jane), editor. | Graben, Sari, 1975– editor. |
    Napoleon, Val, 1956– editor.
Description: Includes bibliographical references.
Identifiers: Canadiana (print) 20200195123 | Canadiana (ebook)
    20200195190 | ISBN 9781487505455 (hardcover) | ISBN 9781487523824
    (softcover) | ISBN 9781487532116 (PDF) | ISBN 9781487532130 (EPUB)
Subjects: LCSH: Indigenous peoples – Land tenure – Canada. | LCSH: Land
    tenure – Law and legislation – Canada. | LCSH: Land titles – Canada. |
    LCSH: Land use – Canada. | LCSH: Real property – Canada. | LCSH:
    Indigenous peoples – Legal status, laws, etc. – Canada. | CSH: Native
    peoples – Canada – Claims. | CSH: Aboriginal title – Canada.
Classification: LCC E98.L3 C74 2020 | DDC 333.2–dc23

This book has been published with the help of a grant from the Federation
for the Humanities and Social Sciences, through the Awards to Scholarly
Publications Program, using funds provided by the Social Sciences and
Humanities Research Council of Canada.

University of Toronto Press acknowledges the financial assistance to its
publishing program of the Canada Council for the Arts and the Ontario Arts
Council, an agency of the Government of Ontario.

Canada Council   Conseil des Arts
for the Arts   du Canada

ONTARIO ARTS COUNCIL
CONSEIL DES ARTS DE L'ONTARIO
an Ontario government agency
un organisme du gouvernement de l'Ontario

Funded by the   Financé par le
Government   gouvernement
of Canada   du Canada

Canada

MIX
Paper from
responsible sources
FSC® C016245

Contents

Preface

Our world feels increasingly divided. This could be the result of social media, Russian intervention, or perhaps the backlash of those accustomed to the benefits of unearned privilege who are now threatened by substantive equality. Whatever the cause, public discourse about Indigenous peoples and our rights is not immune to the rise of the politics of division. In this context, we might wonder how to build community among people who hold differing views, aspirations, and norms. How do we facilitate productive dialogue across increasingly disparate perspectives?

My experience is that these discussions are often mired in debates about outcomes. Which laws and policies will produce better outcomes? The implication is that outcomes can serve as the measure by which to judge the merits of various laws, and therefore the merits of the norms that underlie those laws. I have witnessed this approach while teaching Indigenous and Aboriginal legal issues within mandatory law school courses. Some students want to engage in a critical assessment of Indigenous laws by comparing the outcomes produced by Indigenous laws to those produced by Western laws. They argue that Western laws – and the values that inform them – have generated a level of socio-economic security and a standard of living that far surpass anything achieved by Indigenous laws and cultures.

It can be difficult to see the flaw in this approach, especially when the outcomes are articulated at a sufficiently general level of abstraction. After all, who doesn't want better health, education, or socio-economic outcomes for Indigenous peoples? Even the common rebuttal – that the achievements of Western laws and culture are questionable, given that Indigenous communities have been largely excluded from the wealth generated by these laws – still engages the debate at the level of outcomes. Of course, debates about outcomes can be productive, such as when a discussant offers previously unavailable empirical data to demonstrate that a desired outcome is more likely to follow from a particular law. But a basic precondition for the success of such debates is a shared set of norms held by the discussants. If the discussants disagree about the most fundamental norms underlying the premises of each side's argument, no argument about the benefits of the expected outcomes – supported by empirical evidence or otherwise – will be persuasive.

When discussants focus on outcomes without first establishing a shared set of norms, the debate tends to operate within a Western, liberal framework, and the norms underpinning that framework go unquestioned and can even become characterized as pragmatism or common sense. But if the laws of an Indigenous nation are based on fundamentally different norms, then those Indigenous laws will inevitably *fail to cohere with* – or from a Western perspective, will *fall short of* – the outcomes valued by liberalism.

Scholarship advocating for the privatization of Indigenous lands sometimes falls into this trap by pointing towards what are assumed to be desirable outcomes, such as increased economic development, wealth, access to capital, equity, investor confidence, and stability. The norms that underpin these outcomes are the norms of liberalism and capitalism.

Arguments that are premised on these liberal assumptions to the exclusion of Indigenous laws and the norms that underpin those pose a question: Why these particular outcomes? From within a liberal perspective, the kinds of outcomes mentioned above – increased economic development, wealth, and access to capital – seem obvious and even unquestionable. But from the perspective of at least some Indigenous nations, these outcomes are at best unsupported and at worst undesirable. Of course, supporting the well-being of Indigenous people is laudable, but for many Indigenous peoples, this cannot be done at the expense of other fundamental values and norms.

To begin to facilitate understanding between those who hold competing perspectives, the analysis needs to be directed not towards outcomes but in the other direction, towards the norms that underpin our laws. This book undertakes this vital work. It makes explicit what is often left implicit by identifying the ways in which privatization arguments rest upon characterizations of land as a commodity and the neoliberal discourse of market efficiency. It counters these assumptions by offering robust discussions of Indigenous laws, including their underlying assumptions and norms, and it demonstrates the implications for the privatization debate. At the same time, the analyses presented within this collection eschew simplistic, monolithic characterizations of Indigenous law by recognizing both the diversity across various Indigenous legal orders and the sometimes conflicting norms that pertain to land held within Indigenous communities. In so doing, this book acknowledges that some Indigenous legal orders can accommodate some forms of privatization. The result is a sophisticated and nuanced investigation of the privatization of Indigenous lands.

This collection is an essential resource for law and policymakers from both Indigenous and non-Indigenous communities. It provides guidance on facilitating shared understandings about the privatization debate, as opposed to further entrenching incongruent positions. For those who seek to move beyond the politics of division and to engage in genuine and productive dialogue, this book is indispensable.

Karen Drake
Associate Professor
Osgoode Hall Law School, York University

CREATING INDIGENOUS PROPERTY

Power, Rights, and Relationships

Introduction: The Role of Indigenous Law in the Privatization of Lands

ANGELA CAMERON, SARI GRABEN, AND
VAL NAPOLEON

There is a move afoot in Canada towards the privatization of Indigenous[1] lands.[2] This move is striking, given the centrality of lands to Indigenous laws[3] and legal orders, as well as to overall economic and social flourishing. But what is privatization?[4] While widely used across many discourses, what is meant by *privatization* varies. Privatization is often defined as "the transfer of an ongoing business or service from

1 We use the terms *Indigenous, Aboriginal*, and *First Nation* throughout.
    • *Indigenous* is the common international term and we use it here, especially when we want to move away from the language of Canadian courts and government policy.
    • *First Nation* is the term used in most current government legislation, and many communities have adopted this language when describing themselves. We use *First Nation* when it is more appropriate to do so.
    • *Aboriginal* is the language of the *Canadian Constitution Act, 1982*, the courts, and government, and we use this language when necessary.
2 Australia is also proposing a move to privatization. See Joyce Green, ed., *Indivisible: Indigenous Human Rights* (Halifax: Fernwood Publishing, 2014), 34.
3 We are using the term *Indigenous laws* to refer to laws deriving from historic and contemporary Indigenous societies. This is in preference to the former common language of customary laws. The distinction of Indigenous is not useful where the majority of the population and the state are Indigenous, as in South Africa and many other parts of the world (e.g., Tonga and the South Pacific generally). And given that custom is one source of Indigenous law, along with other sources of law such as deliberative law, positive law, natural law, and sacred law, it is also inaccurate. See John Borrows, *Canada's Indigenous Constitution* (Toronto: University of Toronto Press, 2010), chapter 2. The term *customary* has also come to be regarded as negative by Indigenous people because it suggests Indigenous law is simple and undeveloped, as compared to other more complex conceptions of law.
4 David Clapham, *Housing Privatization in Western Europe* (Santa Barbara, CA: Greenwood Publishing Group, 1996), 3.

government control and ownership to the private sector."[5] However, there is no bright line between what is public and what is private, especially when concerning Indigenous peoples and their lands. For our purposes and to set the stage for the chapters that follow, privatization is used here to capture the replacement of services on Indigenous lands and ownership of those lands by governments with individuals or organizations owned and controlled by individuals.

In Canada, most privatization took place between 1980 to the mid-1990s with the sale of extensive federally and provincially owned assets organized as corporate-like entities (e.g., CNR, Air Canada, etc.).[6] While revenue from these sales was a large impetus, privatization reflects a particular logic within neoliberalism.[7] According to this logic, it is the market, not public governments, that makes the most efficient, and therefore profitable, decisions. The resulting trend was the massive devolution of government services (e.g., social welfare) and entities involving natural resources, transportation, and telecommunications.[8] In addition to the sale of public assets, privatization introduced a "market discipline" into service delivery and to encourage private sector investment (and market growth).[9]

All of this is supported and advanced through the Western school of law and economics, which applies a particular economic (i.e., capitalist) theory to law in order to frame the aspirations, interpretations, and applications of law, as well as to limit its role. The underlying assumption of Western law and economics is that the market is more efficient than the courts[10] and so should drive social and economic ordering. In Western law, property, along with contracts and torts, is classified as private in that the legal transactions take place between individuals or private entities. Private law defines the rights and duties of individuals

---

5   Anthony E. Boardman and Aidan R. Vining, "A Review and Assessment of Privatization in Canada," *SPP Research Papers* 5, no. 4 (2012): 2, https://www.policyschool.ca/wp-content/uploads/2016/03/boardman-vining-privatization.pdf.

6   Boardman and Vining, "Review and Assessment of Privatization," 4.

7   Isabel Altamirano-Jiménez argues that there is a "grid of neoliberal intelligibility" that is reshaping Indigeneity, gender, nature (land), and the market according to neoliberal precepts. We adopt Altamirano-Jiménez's definition of neoliberalism in this introduction as "an economic project involving deregulation, privatisation, individualisation and transformation of the state-citizen relationship" but also "practices, knowledge and ways of inhabiting the world that emphasize the market, individual rationality and the responsibility of entrepreneurial subjects." Isabel Altamirano-Jiménez, *Indigenous Encounters with Neoliberalism: Place, Women, and the Environment in Canada and Mexico* (Vancouver: UBC Press, 2013), 2 and 5.

8   Boardman and Vining, "Review and Assessment of Privatization," 5.

9   Clapham, *Housing Privatization*, 6.

10 Paul H. Rubin, "Law and Economics," (n.d.), Library of Economics and Liberty, http://www.econlib.org/library/Enc/LawandEconomics.html.

and private entities in relation to one another. It stands in contrast to public law, which establishes the powers and responsibilities of governments, defines the rights and duties of individuals in relation to governments, and governs relations between and among nations.[11] The central player in private property is conceived as a private autonomous individual or private entity operating in a sphere that is outside the public.[12] However, the state remains a part of every dispute. After all, private law is law, so it necessarily involves government, and to assert a private claim against another is to direct this demand through the state. In other words, there is very little in law that is "private" if we mean that it is treated as of no interest to the wider community.

The logics of market efficiency are a major factor in what is now called the privatization of Indigenous lands. This is evident in the claims about the wealth-generating merits of private property made by Indigenous and non-Indigenous people, and by government. But there are many contradictions and thorny issues when it comes to Indigenous peoples and their lands, including what is private and what is public in Indigenous law. Indigenous societies have law and public legal institutions through which law, including land law, operates.[13]

All of this is further complicated by the range of ways that Indigenous lands actually have been privatized with a range of bounded systems that limit who the "private" is in regards to ownership on reserves and in modern agreement or treaty lands. For example, underlying title of fee simple can remain with the Indigenous group, or alternatively, only community members can hold fee simple under some regimes. In contrast, the Nisga'a Lisims government has opened up their lands as estates in fee simple, and these may be owned by non-Nisga'a people.[14]

Indigenous peoples obviously had historic functioning economies[15] that land was absolutely central to, but it was not commodified in

---

11 John C.P. Goldberg, "Introduction: Pragmatism and Private Law," *Harvard Law Review* 125 (2012): 1640.

12 For well-developed arguments that counter this characterization, see Jennifer Nedelsky, *Law's Relations: A Relational Theory of Self, Autonomy, and Law* (Oxford: Oxford University Press, 2011), 19.

13 See Jeremy Webber, "The Public-Law Dimension of Indigenous Property Rights," in *The Proposed Nordic Saami Convention: National and International Dimensions of Indigenous Property Rights*, ed. Nigel Bankes and Timo Koivurova (Oxford: Hart, 2013), 79; Val Napoleon, "Thinking about Indigenous Legal Orders," rev., in *Dialogues on Human Rights and Legal Pluralism*, ed. Colleen Shepard and Kirsten Anker, Ius Gentium Series (New York: Springer, 2012), 229.

14 See Graben and Morey, this volume.

15 See, for example, Shalene Jobin, "Cree Economic Relations, Governance, and Critical Indigenous Political Economy in Resistance to Settler-Colonial Logics" (PhD diss., University of Alberta, 2014).

the way it developed for Western societies. It is helpful to think of Indigenous societies as having historic economic orders as well as contemporary economies that are deeply enmeshed with the world today. Today's Indigenous economies are the result of colonial history: small land bases that until very recently were entirely controlled by the federal government, capitalism, extensive Aboriginal rights and title litigation, and creeping neoliberal ideology. To varying degrees today's Indigenous economies are still rooted in and informed by their historic economic roots through societally specific norms, meanings, and ethics. As a consequence, there are often contradictions and conflicts within Indigenous communities about relationships to land and non-human life forms, about responsibilities to one another, about environmental decisions, and about wealth distribution. There are many variables, with some Indigenous communities having great economic success while others struggle in the grip of poverty. A more positive take is that these issues are live and they matter deeply to Indigenous people. There are no quick fixes. Rather, there are tensions that must be navigated every day in Indigenous community life.

The question that runs through many of the debates both within Indigenous communities and among academics, is whether the move towards privatization is a manifestation of the negative forces of neoliberalism and capitalism at work, or an economic engine that Indigenous peoples can and should take advantage of to rectify the ongoing effects of colonization. As Egan and Place[16] argue, a move to privatization can be variously characterized, either as a continuation of a colonial enterprise, or as a potential mechanism that will allow Indigenous nations to develop their own social and economic agendas. There are Indigenous supporters on both sides of this debate.[17]

This book explores some of these debates, with a focus on the role of Indigenous law in answering key questions. In some chapters, these turns to privatization are fully explicated and explored,[18] while other chapters probe important theoretical questions underlying the

---

16 Brian Egan and Jessica Place, "Minding the Gaps: Property, Geography, and Indigenous Peoples in Canada," *Geoforum* 44 (2013): 136.

17 Others optimistically see privatization as a hybrid of these two trends. Egan and Place, "Minding the Gaps," 136.

18 See chapters in this volume on the Nisga'a (Graben and Morey), matrimonial property on reserve (Morin), the impact of historical privatization on the Island Hul'qumi'num peoples (Morales and Thom), and international examples of privatization (Odumosu).

privatization debate.[19] Arguments in support of privatization often assume with certainty that Indigenous laws governing land and resource use will cease to exist just because the land is privatized. There is, therefore, a need for more complex conversations that identify and debunk this assumption.

This volume raises important questions about the role of Indigenous law before, during, and after privatization. Indigenous law may present a unique challenge to the privatization of Indigenous lands, as it is underpinned by a profoundly different theoretical and societal model of property, which, at least in its historic form, does not easily co-exist with private property models of today. However, each contribution to this volume considers historic legal institutions and law in relation to present-day Indigenous legal institutions and law. They illustrate that unexamined and unresolved contradictions between the historic and the present have created powerful competing versions of Indigenous law, legal authorities, and practices that reverberate through Indigenous communities, economic planning, and political goals. These contradictions can generate conflict, which, if not accounted for or managed, can result in dysfunctional paralysis.

We collectively argue that any move towards privatization must assume that Indigenous law will play a role. First, the power to generate Indigenous law is protected by section 35 of the *Constitution Act, 1982*, as an inherent Indigenous right.[20] Second, Indigenous law is embedded in the common law via the *Indian Act* in such areas as custom election codes,[21] in the *First Nations Land Management Act*,[22] and in recent matrimonial property legislation.[23] Finally, and most importantly, for many Indigenous people living in Canada, Indigenous laws and legal orders *are* the law.[24] The dichotomous approaches to economy, land ownership and use, culture and theory between privatization models and some

---

19 See Napoleon and Snyder, this volume, and Kermoal and Carter, this volume.

20 *Tsilhqot'in Nation v British Columbia*, 2014 SCC 44, paras 34 and 35.

21 The minister can, at their request, remove an *Indian Act* band from the election requirements of s 74 of the *Indian Act*.

22 SC 1999 s 24.

23 *Family Homes on Reserves and Matrimonial Interests or Rights Act (FHRMIRA)*, SC 2013, c 20.

24 See, for instance, Napoleon, "Thinking about Indigenous Legal Orders"; John Borrows, *Canada's Indigenous Constitution* (Toronto: University of Toronto Press, 2010); Richard Overstall, "Encountering the Spirit in the Land: 'Property' in a Kinship-Based Legal Order," in *Despotic Dominion: Property Rights in British Settler Societies*, ed. John P.S. McLaren, A.R. Buck, and Nancy E. Wright, 22–49 (Vancouver: UBC Press, 2005).

forms of Indigenous law will arguably position those who abide by the precepts of Indigenous law at odds with the legislative and political agenda of privatization. However, much of the privatization debate stands erroneously on an incomplete and inadequate comprehension of Indigenous law, particularly laws governing lands, ownership, and management.[25]

Erroneous assumptions are the consequence of the deliberate denial of Indigenous land laws, except as absolutely necessary to enable settlement through treaties. However, Canadian courts have also perpetuated the incomplete representation of Indigenous land law. As Jeremy Webber has argued, Indigenous land rights are respected as proprietary, but not as deriving from and operating through the Indigenous political and legal orders that created them.[26] The problem is that "rights are intrinsically bound up with the legal order by which they have been defined and according to which they are interpreted, adjusted and deployed."[27] Webber advocates for a broader understanding of Indigenous land rights that includes an effective incorporation of the public law dimension and Indigenous legal institutions into the actual framing and operation of those rights.[28] For our purposes, Webber's insights mean that consideration of Indigenous land laws and issues of privatization requires contextualizing them within specific Indigenous legal and political orders, and their corresponding public law institutions.

According to the SCC, "Aboriginal title confers ownership rights ... including: the right to decide how the land will be used; the right of enjoyment and occupancy of the land; the right to possess the land; the right to the economic benefits of the land; and the right to pro-actively use and manage the land."[29] Here the recognition of Aboriginal title in Canadian law sets out what Indigenous peoples can do on their land, but not the actual property rights that they hold according to Indigenous law. So at least initially, the basis of Aboriginal title is that Indigenous peoples owned their land according to their laws, but what does

---

25 This argument is further developed in Val Napoleon, "Tsilhqot'in Law of Consent," in special issue, ed. Joshua Nichols, special issue, *UBC Law Review* 15 (2015): 873. See also Morales and Thom, this volume.

26 Webber, "Public-Law Dimension," 79.

27 Webber, "Public-Law Dimension," 79.

28 Webber, "Public-Law Dimension," 98–102. Webber was writing before the SCC released its *Tsilhqot'in* judgment, and only time, along with continued Tsilhqot'in legal and political activism, will tell whether it is possible for Tsilhqot'in land rights to exist as proprietary in their own right, as opposed to being subsumed and redefined by Canadian law.

29 *Tsilhqot'in Nation v British Columbia*, 2014 SCC 44, para 73.

not get transported into Canadian law are the Indigenous governing and legal institutions through which that land was owned and managed both through time and today.[30]

Why does this matter? Because there is a pervading assumption that all Indigenous lands were held communally,[31] and some Indigenous societies *did* organize their land relationships more or less along these lines. However, other Indigenous societies have laws governing forms of land ownership, use, access, inheritance, trespass, liability, transfers, life interests, economic and political obligations, and definitions of private and public, as well as those who view land as a relation rather than an object of ownership.[32] Hence, the privatization debate must develop specificity according to each Indigenous legal order, rather than perpetuating a fictitious binary between communally and privately held lands.

While we take it as a given that Indigenous law will be drawn upon in debates over land and the terms of its ownership, there is a cautionary note to factor into our expectations. Indigenous communities do not live in isolation from Canadian law or the political, economic, and social forces that surround them. And, as Indigenous law was always a result of its time and created by the serious and sustained engagement[33] of every generation before European settlement, it is a result of its time today. This means that engagement with Indigenous law must move to thoughtful rebuilding. Building on work by Friedland and Napoleon, contributors to this volume have been guided by two questions: (1) What are the terms for thoughtful rebuilding with communities? and (2) What are the intellectual processes in each Indigenous society that historically enabled people to deal with and account for change?[34]

---

30 Webber, "Public-Law Dimension," 83. See also Morales and Thom, this volume; and Gordon Christie, "Who Makes Decisions over Aboriginal Title Land," *UBC Law Journal* 48 (2015): 743.

31 See, for instance, *Manitoba Metis Federation Inc v Canada (Attorney General)* 2013 SCC 14, in which the Supreme Court relies on the assumption that Indigenous lands were always held communally to deny the land claims of the Metis people, who engaged in individual landholding.

32 For a description of the earliest settlement of Gitksan land, see Neil J. Sterritt, Susan Marsden, Robert Galois, Peter Grant, and Richard Overstall, *Tribal Boundaries in the Nass Watershed* (Vancouver: UBC Press, 1998). For a description of Gitksan land laws, see Val Napoleon, "Ayook: Gitksan Legal Order and Legal Theory" (PhD diss., University of Victoria, 2009).

33 Jutta Brunnée and Stephen J. Toope, *Legitimacy and Legality in International Law: An Interactional Account* (Cambridge: Cambridge University Press, 2011), 355.

34 Hadley Friedland and Val Napoleon, "Gathering the Threads: Indigenous Legal Methodology," *Lakehead Law Journal* 1 (2015): 17.

As the diversity of viewpoints provided by authors to this volume illustrate, the answers to these overriding questions and the research generated by them are emergent and exploratory. The authors can therefore be read in relation to each other and, to this end, do make associations with and comparisons to other authors explicit. However, their dialogue will often relate to differences in focus, rather than explicit differences between them on these two questions.

I. Legal and Social Changes in Canada: Three Forms of Privatization of Indigenous Lands

We propose that there are three main forms of privatization, either proposed or already happening on Indigenous lands: legislated privatization of real property on-reserve or on treaty lands, legislative reform of matrimonial property on-reserve, and a catch-all category of more subtle moves towards an ideology of privatization. The first category reflects a movement to define parts of reserves or contemporary treaty lands in fee simple through federal legislation or modern land claim agreements.[35] The second category reflects a suite of federal legislative reforms that purportedly aim to balance collectively held property rights against private interests. The third category includes trends such as *Indian Act* bands or First Nations negotiating various agreements[36] directly with multinational corporations for resource extraction on their historic territories as a supplement to, or instead of, accessing land claim, treaty negotiation, or title litigation with the Crown. This trend also includes individual *Indian Act* First Nations' participation in and support of infrastructure such as oil and gas pipelines on their historic territories. In some cases both the reforms themselves and their impacts are nascent.

The following section describes each of these privatization trends, outlining any legal reforms, the main arguments for and against each trend, and examines the role of Indigenous law in defining property.

---

35 See, for instance, the Algonquins of Ontario ("Preliminary Draft Agreement-in-Principle," http://tanakiwin.com/our-treaty-negotiations/preliminary-draft-agreement-in-principle), the Tsawwassen Nation ("Treaty and Constitution," http://tsawwassenfirstnation.com/governance-overview/treaty-and-constitution/), and the Nisga'a Nation ("Nisga'a Final Agreement," http://www.nisgaalisims.ca/nisgaa-final-agreement).

36 Ginger Gibson and Ciaran O'Faircheallaigh, *IBA Community Toolkit: Negotiation and Implementation of Impact and Benefit Agreements*, Walter & Duncan Gordon Foundation, March 2010, http://www.afoa.ca/afoadocs/L3/L3a%20-%20IBA_toolkit_March_2010_low_resolution.pdf.

A. The Privatization of Reserves, Title, and Treaty Lands

Under section 91 (24) of the *Constitution Act, 1867*,[37] Parliament claims jurisdiction over "Indians and lands reserved for the Indians." Pursuant to the powers claimed under the *Constitution Act, 1867*, Parliament first passed the *Indian Act*[38] in 1867, which purported to give the federal government authority over most land management on reserve lands.

Under this landholding system, legal title to reserve lands is held by the Crown rather than Indigenous individuals or collectivities living on or using the lands. The lands are inalienable, and the exclusive right to occupy and use the land by Indigenous peoples is held collectively. Land on reserves cannot be mortgaged or be seized in a legal judgment. Only the minister of Aboriginal affairs and northern development can allow a land transaction under the *Indian Act*.

While this authority was frequently exercised in direct ways,[39] the *Indian Act* also created, and maintains, a system for democratic elections on reserve lands of an Indigenous governing body with limited powers called an "Indian band." The *Indian Act* devolves some powers over land distribution to the band. While the right to use all reserve land is held collectively by the Indigenous community, the band can grant individuals allotments (often formalized in certificates of possession), conferring on the individual the exclusive right to "lawful possession" of land or housing. The legal title to the land, however, remains with the Crown.

Both the *Indian Act* itself, and the land management system contained within have long been the subject of criticism, from many quarters.[40]

Post–*Indian Act* land reform is relatively recent in Canada. In response to calls for reform from some First Nations, the federal government passed *The First Nations Land Management Act* in 1999.[41] The act permits *Indian Act* bands to develop individual land ownership laws that

---

37 *Constitution Act, 1867* (UK), 30 & 31 Vict., c 3.

38 RSC 1985, c I-5.

39 See J.W. Daschuk, *Clearing the Plains: Disease, Politics of Starvation and the Loss of Aboriginal Life* (Regina: University of Regina Press, 2013), 98.

40 For example, the *Indian Act* (including its current iteration) discriminates against Indigenous women, denying them and their offspring status under the *Act*, because of their sex. See FAFIA-AFAI, "Update on Bill S-3," 6 June 2017, http://fafia-afai.org/en/update-on-bill-s-3-check-out-the-letters-sent-out-to-federal-ministers/.

41 SC 1999, c 24. Other federal reforms intended to boost economic prosperity include the now repealed *First Nations Property Tax Act* (1988), the *First Nations Commercial and Industrial Development Act* SC 2005, c 53, and *the First Nations Fiscal Management Act* SC 2005, c 9.

had previously been dictated by the federal government. The rationale behind the Act was that giving First Nations more control, with support from the federal government, would enhance economic growth for the First Nation.[42] That same year the Nisga'a Nation signed a contemporary treaty or land claim agreement with the governments of British Columbia and Canada, taking expanded forms of legal control over a portion of their historic territory, and defining those lands as fee simple.[43] Several other First Nations across British Columbia, the Yukon, the Northwest Territories, and Nunavut subsequently did the same. While each land claim agreement differs slightly in how fee simple is described or is expected to operate in relation to other governmental powers, they all describe the lands or parts thereof as estates in fee simple. The most recent occurrence arose in the recent case of *Tsilhqot'in Nation v British Columbia*. In this case the SCC conferred the first recognition of Aboriginal title on the Tsilhqot'in and highlighted what it saw as similarities between the incidents of Aboriginal title and that of fee simple. In doing so, the Court used proprietary frames as a means to settle disputes over land and resource use.

In 2006 the federal government launched a policy initiative for privatization of on-reserve property across Canada. The call for re-designating reserve lands as fee simple was clearly articulated by some Indigenous individuals and groups, in partnership with the newly elected Conservative federal government.[44] The First Nations Property Ownership Initiative (FNPO)[45] was launched, led by the First Nations Tax Commission (FNTC)[46] and financially supported by the federal government. On the basis of their consultative process the FNPO recommended that *Indian*

---

42 Thomas Isaac, "The First Nations Land Management Act and Third Party Interests," *Alberta Law Review* 42 (2004–5): 1047.

43 Graben and Morey, this volume. In 2009 the Nisga'a Nation passed a law allowing members to take title to their real property in fee simple.

44 For discussion of the alliance of political actors that has consolidated support for fee simple estates on reserves, see Shiri Pasternak, "How Capitalism Will Save Colonialism: The Privatization of Reserve Lands in Canada," *Antipode* 47, no. 1 (2015): 183–7.

45 "Background on the First Nations Property Ownership Initiative," First Nations Tax Commission, https://fntc.ca/en/background-on-the-first-nations-property-ownership-initiative/.

46 First Nations Tax Commission, https://fntc.ca/en/home/. The First Nations Tax Commission was created, via the First Nations Fiscal Management Act, by the federal government. According to their website they are "a shared-governance First Nation public institution that supports First Nation taxation under the First Nations Fiscal Management Act and under section 83 of the Indian Act."

Act bands be given the choice (requiring a majority vote of all members) to take fee simple title in the lands formerly held as reserve lands. These lands would be recorded in a Torrens-style registry, where title could be transferred to any individual.[47] The proposal suggests passing a piece of federal legislation, tentatively called the *First Nations Property Ownership Act*, in order to facilitate the transition in property holding.

1. THE ARGUMENTS FOR PRIVATIZING INDIGENOUS PROPERTY

Land privatization is supported in Canada by an alliance of political and academic proponents that share neoliberal preconceptions about the role of property in economic development and who seek to reorder land management along those lines. The proposed legislation by the FNPO is based closely on a proposal outlined by academics Tom Flanagan, André Le Dressay, and Christopher Alcantraz in their book *Beyond the Indian Act: Restoring Indigenous Property Rights*.[48] The foreword is written by Manny Jules. FNPO's proposal is also gaining some traction in mainstream Canadian law and policy.[49] Moreover, ideas that echo the FNPO's proposal circulate in the mainstream media.[50]

Proponents of land reform argue that privatization of this kind will have economic and social benefits for Indigenous communities, whose socio-economic disparities are a direct consequence of the failure of the market for private investment on First Nations lands.[51] According to the FNPO, adopting a Torrens-style registry where First Nations and individuals can hold land in fee simple will have striking benefits[52] These include an improved market for reserve land and investment on reserve, thereby allowing First Nations to earn equity from their land, resolve

---

47 FNPO, "Creating Opportunities for Wealth and Prosperity," https://ilti.ca/en/welcome-to-ilti/.

48 Tom Flanagan, André Le Dressay, and Christopher Alcantara, *Beyond the Indian Act: Restoring Aboriginal Property Rights* (Montreal and Kingston: McGill-Queen's University Press, 2010).

49 Canada, Office of the Auditor General, "Programs for First Nations on Reserve," in *Status Report of the Auditor General of Canada* (Ottawa: OAG, 2011), 21.

50 Kevin Libin, "Rethinking the Reserve Problems of Governance," *National Post*, 8 February 2008.

51 Fiscal Realities Economists, "Making Markets Work on First Nation Lands: The Role of the Land Title System in Reducing Transaction Costs" (prepared for the First Nations Tax Commission, April 2009), 1.

52 Fiscal Realities Economists, "The Role of Land Title in Developing First Nations Economics and Government" (March 2007) (presented to the Indian Taxation Advisory Board and DIAND), 16, http://sp.fng.ca/fntc/fntcweb/land_title_and_developing_fn_economies_.pdf. The FNPO proposes a slightly modified system based on that used by the Nisga'a nation. See Graben, this volume.

matrimonial property and estate matters, introduce speed, efficiency, and certainty of transactions, and encourage trade and innovation.[53] At a social level, supporters of privatization claim it will support First Nations governance and rights, help reduce socio-economic disparities, assist communities to escape poverty and dependency, and to develop confidence and behaviours of independence and self-reliance.[54]

The arguments are premised on "trickle-down" economic theories that collective prosperity will come from increased private investment in Indigenous-owned real property.[55] Indigenous land holding, certificates of possession, and leases are all seen as economically inefficient and therefore "counter-economic" to obtaining financing and securitization.[56] This is grounded in classic private property theories, which view the importance of the free market, individualism, freedom of alienation, and right to exclude others as the building blocks of a free, democratic, and thriving Western liberal democracy. Moreover, First Nations who opt for individual titling would maintain some form of governance jurisdiction over the land, regardless of who held fee simple title.[57]

2. THE ARGUMENTS AGAINST PRIVATIZING INDIGENOUS PROPERTY

Detractors of privatization share concerns about the negative economic and social implications of privately titling communal lands. The Assembly of First Nations (AFN) passed a resolution in 2010, rejecting fee simple landholding generally, and the proposed legislation.[58] The AFN Chiefs-in-Assembly rejected the proposed legislation for several reasons, including that it contradicts constitutional protections of land and treaty rights, and that a fee simple title system imperils the authoritative requirement that First Nations hold their lands in trust for future generations.

---

53 For discussion of proposed costs and benefits, see Sari Graben, "Lessons for Indigenous Property Reform: From Membership to Ownership on Nisga'a Lands," *UBC Law Review* 47 (2014): 399.

54 Fiscal Realities Economists, "Making Markets Work," 4.

55 See Fiscal Realities Economists, "The Role of Land Title"; Fiscal Realities Economists, "Making Markets Work." These works rely heavily on liberal economists and political theorists such as Hernando De Soto and Terry Anderson.

56 Fiscal Realities Economists, "Making Markets Work," 10.

57 FNPO, "Creating Opportunities for Wealth and Prosperity," 2.

58 Bill Curry, "Idea of Land Ownership on Reserves Gets Mixed Reviews Assembly of First Nations," *Globe and Mail*, 15 December 2011, https://www.theglobeandmail.com/news/politics/idea-of-private-land-ownership-on-reserves-gets-mixed-reviews/article4197114/.

Academic critiques of the proposed privatization of on-reserve property are multi-pronged and multidisciplinary. First, critics note that such a strong reliance on a particular version of capitalist economics as a theoretical basis for privatization implies a hierarchy of world views – one in which European notions of property prevail. Rather than perceive private land rights as emancipatory, its critics situate it in discourses and technologies of dispossession that have impinged upon Indigenous land use since first contact. Those who are critical of private property are often painted as confined to archaic forms of traditionalism.[59] However, at the heart of this critique is recognition of differences in legal and philosophical notions of property. Non-Indigenous notions assume rationalized decision-making based on individual autonomy and self-fulfilment, alienability, use, and commodification. In contrast, Indigenous notions draw from each Indigenous society's history and organization of political and legal orders, and in some cases Indigenous world views. These theoretical and historical differences confound homogenization and generate tensions that are not understood by proponents of privatization.

Sarah Morales and Brian Thom illustrate this tension in their chapter, through a discussion of the continuing relevance of Hul'qumi'num peoples' law and, in particular, the governing principle of sharing. They argue that though Indigenous property law continues to inform Island Hul'qumi'num peoples' legal orders, conventional Canadian property law casts a long shadow on the legal landscape, making it difficult for these principles to be seen and exercised. In order to reveal such *shadowing*, they show differences between Hul'qumi'num peoples' property laws and Western concepts of property in matters related to the determination of legal persons that can constitute property relations, what objects receive the attention of property relations, and how rights, duties, obligations, and remedies are allocated to particular individuals or societal organizations. However, they also show in what ways Western property law has concealed – and at times transformed – these laws and practices. Interestingly, Morales and Thom argue that it is the resilience of social institutions premised on these principles that continue to confound state practices and aspirations to "normalize" property rights and gain economic certainly over the land.

---

59 Jessica Dempsey, Kevin Gould, and Juanita Sundberg, "Changing Land Tenure, Defining Subjects: Neoliberalism and Property Regimes on Native Reserves," in *Rethinking the Great White North: Race, Nature and the Historical Geographies of Whiteness in Canada*, ed. Andrew Baldwin, Laura Cameron, and Audrey Kobayashi (Vancouver: UBC Press, 2011), 24.

Identification of how European concepts of property have been used in the past also raises serious concerns with future privatization. In the past, common and civil law property regimes have been instrumental in dispossessing Indigenous peoples of their historic territories. There is little disagreement that Canada's sovereign claim to jurisdiction and underlying title, supported through legislation and jurisprudence, is premised on a complete disregard for the legal fact that Indigenous people held underlying title, jurisdiction, and sovereignty prior to European contact.[60] Indigenous use or its supposed non-use lay at the heart of Canada's claim. Pam Palmater,[61] Jessica Dempsey et al.,[62] and Cole Harris[63] have each pointed to the role of Lockean discourse in justifying state ownership and control of Indigenous lands. The seizure of Indigenous properties was historically rooted in the Western idea that Indigenous people were not appropriately "using" the land for economic development – an argument that echoes today in pro-privatization positions. While the doctrine of *terra nullius* has been repudiated, the subordination of Indigenous jurisdiction and underlying title to that of the Crown remains in legal effect. This alchemy, as Borrows puts it, is justified by perceptions of non-use.[64]

Current manifestations of preclusion are subtler insofar as they use state law to create opportunities for capitalist enterprise that can potentially benefit Indigenous peoples, but only if Indigenous landowners adopt the legal technologies of liberal capitalism and their normative underpinnings. These technologies are varied but share an orientation to exploiting the capital value of land. They include the designation of land as fee simple through legislation or contemporary land claims, as well as the negotiation of compensatory contracts that recognize the commodification of the land in accordance with Western private law. However, they also include the more mundane use of regulation and regulatory regimes that rationalize land and resource development such as land use planning and environmental assessment. These

---

60   Michael Asch, *Home and Native Land: Aboriginal Rights and the Canadian Constitution* (Toronto: Methuen Publications, 1984).

61   Pamela Palmater, "Opportunity or Temptation? Plans for Private Property on Reserves Could Cost First Nations Their Independence," *Literary Review of Canada* (April 2010): 2.

62   Dempsey et al., "Changing Land Tenure."

63   Cole Harris, "How Did Colonialism Dispossess? Comments from an Edge of Empire," *Annals of the Association of American Geographers* 94 (2004): 165–82.

64   John Borrows, "Sovereignty's Alchemy: An Analysis of Delgamuukw v British Columbia," *Osgoode Hall Law Journal* 37 (1999): 537.

regimes individually and collectively reorganize Indigenous property to be available for use in resource development.

Critics of these technologies note that the preclusion of Indigenous conceptions of property under contemporary practices occurs in two ways. The first is that the use of the fee simple estate presumes radical title and therefore affirms state sovereignty rather than challenge it. Christian Morey and Sari Graben apply this critique in their chapter on the *Tsilhqot'in* decision. They argue that the net effect of changes brought about by the decision is to bring Indigenous title conceptually closer to the position assigned to private property-owners in the liberal framework. While the court is attempting to rectify the disadvantage of Aboriginal titleholders relative to other property owners, it is important to identify in what ways the shift to privatization privileges Crown authority and precludes the use of Aboriginal title as a form of communal ownership and control. Actions of Indigenous peoples pursuant to Aboriginal title, thus conceived, will have detrimental effects on more expansive claims. Indigenous peoples may contest the right of the state to exercise its authority over lands in principle, but willing participation affirms and legitimizes state authority over their territory. The state remains authorized to exercise its jurisdiction over the use of land for large-scale projects, irrespective of Indigenous ownership or control over regulation.

Moreover, this criticism of fee simple contains a more fundamental concern that Indigenous conceptions of property are precluded by the use of monolithic concepts of property. The monikers of ownership undermine the ability of Indigenous peoples to define land in accordance with Indigenous legal traditions or values that are infused with notions of stewardship and relations. Shalene Jobin's discussion of market citizenship in chapter 2 illustrates this dilemma with preclusion. Jobin's critique of negotiated governance reveals it as a site in which the struggle over defining Indigenous property is increasingly settled in favour of the Canadian government, which seeks to streamline the incidents of ownership and erase sui generis differences through treaties. Jobin illustrates how the effort directly affects the spaces in which Indigenous laws could arise, ultimately altering Indigeneity. In chapter 5 Richard Daly illustrates how certain discourses regarding state taxation have obscured Indigenous interpretations of individual and community responsibility to levy and pay taxes. He argues that we should address Indigenous peoples' perspective that they have been operating with a complex system of sharing at the local level that involves the calculation of reciprocity. This would recognize that goods and services given or "paid" publicly sanction a kin-based form of ownership and community membership. Sarah Morales and Brian Thom argue that that in exercising self-determination, Indigenous peoples must not be strictly limited to a precise mirroring of the Canadian state forms of property relations. In exploring the ways in which the common law flattens and oversimplifies Island Hul'qumi'num people's property laws, they demonstrate preclusion in a concrete and specific example of conflict.

An alternative critique of privatization has focused on the ways in which the potential benefits of privatization will be distributed between communities and among community members. Sarah Carter and Nathalie Kermoal address the issue of distribution and dispossession from securitizing land in their chapter about property rights on reserve. Through their study of privatization of St Peter's Reserve in 1907, they question the universality of the claim that private ownership will create wealth, as well as the motivations of its proponents. They instead point out inequality in distribution within and between First Nations communities, depending upon the location of particular Indigenous lands and the increased risk borne by those communities in high-demand areas. Unlike De Soto's simplified promise that the benefits of property ownership will accrue when the trapped or dead value of land is unlocked, wealth creation is contingent on other factors. More importantly, their study illustrates that investment creates risks that secured parties will seize assets or seek compensation for loss so high that retaining lands becomes prohibitive for First Nation communities.

Baxter identifies the use of property as a popular trope used in the Idle No More movement. He argues that the property model of Aboriginal title (versus territory) continues to function as a legal technology of consensus that can contribute to forging broad coalitions of allied actors and movements. This underscores the power of received legal interpretations to support direct action but also problematically constrains new understandings around which new mobilizations and publics might organize.

Concerns with distribution also encompass concerns that the economic benefit or social damage caused by privatization would be unequal along gender lines.[65] This concern is often paired with close

---

65 For instance, Linda Archibald and Mary Crnkovich have written about women and self-government negotiations within the Nisga'a land claim settlement, and Gail Whiteman et al. more generally about public/private partnership mining projects in Canada's North. Archibald Crnkovich and Mary Crnkovich, "If Gender Mattered: A Case Study of Inuit Women, Land Claims and the Voisey Bay's Nickel

attention to the role of Indigenous laws and legal orders in structuring relations and therefore goes beyond questions of allocation.[66] In their chapter in this volume, Napoleon and Snyder use critical Indigenous feminist theory to address gendered marginalization and real property on reserve. Using community case studies along with an analysis of legislative frameworks, housing practices and policies, land codes, debt, and histories, they illustrate the ways in which both the old and new matrimonial property regimes have ignored Indigenous legal traditions and failed to take account of feminist critiques. Rather than forward solutions that advocate for the allocation of property to women, they introduce a possible Tsimshian property theory that has internalized these critiques in relation to generating feminist Indigenous property law.

Tenille Brown undertakes a related task to Napoleon and Snyder in chapter 10, where she addresses the negative, gendered effects of privatization when engaged with the legal pluralist reality of Swazi law and custom. Brown's chapter illustrates that the privatization experiences in Indigenous communities should be perceived and analysed as microcosms of a global trend and the enormous body of literature that critiques and advocates land privatization around the world. She notes the prominent role Western feminist critique has played in framing the constitutional equality claims of women in Swaziland. However, the continuing prominence of Swazi law and custom has meant that the application of legislated rights is fluid, with a resulting negative impact on women's land security.

While an in-depth review of the international privatization scholarship is beyond the capacity of this book, recurring experiences signal how privatization of Indigenous lands has a global context. What Brown, Napoleon, and Snyder illustrate is that communal land systems contain complex and interlocking rights, in which the rights of individuals are tied intimately to the collectively held land system that

---

Project" (Status of Women Canada, 1999); and William Hipwell, Katy Mamen, Viviane Weitzner, and Gail Whiteman, "Aboriginal Peoples and Mining in Canada: Consultation, Participation and Prospects for Change," Working Discussion Paper (North-South Institute, 2002); Ann Varley, "Gender and Property Formalisation: Conventional and Alternative Approaches," *World Development* 35 (2007): 1739.

66 This is central to the discussion of Altamirano-Jiménez, *Indigenous Encounters with Neoliberalism*. The importance of gender in economic planning is discussed by Patricia Muñoz Cabrera, *Intersecting Violences: Poverty and Violence against Women in Latin America* (Central America Women's Network, 2010), https://www.academia.edu/4774037/Intersecting_Violences_Poverty_and_Violence_against_Women_in_Latin_America.

emphasizes community responsibility as a cultural identifier. Change in this context requires more than layering Western rights on top of Indigenous laws. It requires that Indigenous laws internalize bespoke critiques and that state law internalize Indigenous laws that contain those critiques.

3. THE REFORM OF MATRIMONIAL PROPERTY ON-RESERVES

If land titling is the clearest example of privatization, the creation of matrimonial regimes offers a less obvious but impactful one. The creation of matrimonial property regimes on reserves aims to address the need of Indigenous women for stable and just allocations. However, in doing so, these regimes affect how property is used to address relations between community members as well as relations with the state. Just as there is nothing apolitical about the distribution and allocation of matrimonial property in any circumstance, on reserve it remains entangled in gendered allocations as well as colonial practices regarding membership and use. What is problematic about legislative solutions is that they often pit individual and collective rights against one another, rather than in relation to each other and thereby limit the capacity to think about Indigenous lawmaking differently – to think about it as an opportunity to allow modernity to reference customs and traditions that ground community relations.

Because of the constitutional division of powers between the provincial and federal governments, the division of matrimonial[67] property protections and options available to Canadians living off-reserve were not available to those living on-reserve.[68] The negative, gendered impacts of this legislative disparity have been the subject of three separate parliamentary committees,[69] and much critical

---

67 In this case "matrimonial" also usually refers to non-married couples in common-law conjugal relationships, including same-sex couples.
68 *Derrickson v Derrickson*, [1986] 1 SCR 285.
69 In 2003 the Senate Standing Committee on Human Rights recommended that the *Indian Act* be amended: *A Hard Bed to Lie In: Matrimonial Real Property on Reserve*, http://www.parl.gc.ca/37/2/parlbus/commbus/senate/com-e/huma-e/rep-e/rep08nov03-e.pdf. In 2005 the Standing Committee on Aboriginal Affairs and Northern Development of the House of Commons heard many witnesses on this issue and released a report: *Walking Arm-in-Arm to Resolve the Issue of On-Reserve Matrimonial Real Property*, https://www.ourcommons.ca/Content/Committee/381/AANO/Reports/RP1906551/aanorp05/aanorp05-e.pdf. In 2005 the Senate Standing Committee on Human Rights released another report urging the House of Commons to take action: http://www.parl.gc.ca/38/1/parlbus/commbus/senate/com-e/huma-e/rep-e/rep17may05-e.htm. In 2011 the Senate

commentary.[70] *The Family Homes on Reserves and Matrimonial Interests or Rights Act (FHRMIRA)*[71] was enacted in 2013 to close a legislative gap for people living on-reserve.[72] The Act allows First Nations to make their own laws concerning matrimonial property on-reserve and sets out a series of federal rules that apply until First Nations draft their own laws. The Act allows for the division of "interests and rights" rather than only real property held by married (and in some circumstances common-law) spouses upon separation. These rights and interests might include a right to exclusive occupation of a home, or the right to a portion of rental or lease income. This is intended to allow the title to remain with the First Nation, while equally distributing any interests in the property accrued during a relationship.

The *FHRMIRA* is not strictly a form of privatization, as title and control are intended to rest with the First Nation under the *Indian Act* landholding regime. Privatizing on-reserve lands through the matrimonial property regime is also not a clearly stated objective of the Act. However, the *FHRMIRA* attempts to balance communally held on-reserve

---

Standing Committee on Human Rights released a short report asking the minister responsible to put a centre of excellence in place to assist First Nations who wish to draft custom codes under the new legislation, http://www.parl.gc.ca/Content/ SEN/Committee/403/huma/rep/rep03jun10-e.htm. The centre for excellence has since been created: Centre of Excellence for Matrimonial Real Property, http:// www.coemrp.ca/.

70 Jacinta Ruru, "Finding Solutions for the Legislative Gaps in Determining Rights to the Family Home on Colonially Defined Indigenous Lands," *UBC Law Review* 41 (2008): 315–48; Jo-Anne Fiske, "Political Status of Native Indian Women: Contradictory Implications of Canadian State Policy," in *In the Days of Our Grandmothers: A Reader in Aboriginal Women's History in Canada*, ed. Mary-Ellen Kelm and Lorna Townsend (Toronto: University of Toronto Press 2006), 336; Sharon D. McIvor, "The Indian Act as Patriarchal Control of Women," *Aboriginal Women's Law Journal* 1, no. 1 (1994): 70; Mary Ellen Turpel-Lafond, "Patriarchy and Paternalism: The Legacy of the Canadian State for First Nation Women," in *Women and the Canadian State*, ed. Caroline Andrew and Sanda Rodgers (Montreal and Kingston: McGill-Queen's University Press, 1997), 70; Christopher Alcantara, "Indian Women and the Division of Matrimonial Real Property on Canadian Indian Reserves," *Canadian Journal of Women and the Law* 18, no. 2 (2006): 513; Wendy Cornet and Allison Lendor, "Discussion Paper: Matrimonial Real Property on Reserve," Indian and Northern Affairs Canada (2002), https://www.aadnc-aandc.gc.ca/eng/1100100032571/11001 00032573.

71 SC 2013, c 20.

72 For a full history of the various times this legislation was introduced to the House of Commons, see Morin (this volume); and Ashley Smith, "Bill C-47: The Answer or the Continuance of Inequity for the First Nations of Canada," *Canadian Family Law Quarterly* 29 (2010): 47.

property rights with individual rights to interests accrued during matrimonial relationships, in particular the rights of individual women and their children. Critics have argued that in some instances, this balance is not struck clearly in favour of collectively held property rights.[73] The regime has, therefore, been the subject of critiques that dovetail with those of privatization, and its role in perpetuating rather than alleviating the legacies of colonization. The new property regime is also closely tied to debates about the role of Indigenous law in Indigenous communities, especially in relation to gender inequality. Critics have noted that the *FHRMIRA* is one part of a suite of federal legislative reforms, including the *First Nation Land Management Act*, that underpin broader moves to privatization of on-reserve property.[74]

It is important to note that many scholars and activists have reacted positively to the *FHRMIRA* in its current form. For instance, Cree scholar Mary-Ellen Turpel-Lafond, amongst the first and most vocal critics of the legislative gap,[75] stated, "The bill is a promising step to protect victims of domestic violence on-reserve and permits some form of asset division when relationships break down."[76] She notes that with appropriate resources and measures to ensure access to the courts, the legislation has the potential to address many of the problems created by a lack of federal regulation on-reserve in this area.[77] The Congress of Indigenous Peoples[78] endorsed the legislation with

73 For example, Canada, Senate, Hearing for the Standing Committee on Human Rights, 40th Parl, 3rd Sess, (31 May 2010) at 37 (Christopher Devlin and Gaylene Schellenberg, Canadian Bar Association).

74 Canada, Senate, Hearing for the Standing Committee on Human Rights, 40th Parl, 3rd Sess, (5 May 2010) at 45 (Shining Turtle, chief, Anishinabek Nation). Pam Palmater notes that the *FHRMIRA* was one of five pieces of major legislative change that affected Indigenous peoples being pushed through the Senate and House of Commons at the same time. Canada, Senate, Hearing for the Standing Committee on Human Rights, 40th Parl, 4th Sess, (5 May 2010) at 38 (Pamela D. Palmater, chair, Centre for Study of Indigenous Governance, Department of Politics and Public Administration, Ryerson University).

75 Mary Ellen Turpel-Lafond, "Home/Land," *Canadian Journal of Family Law* 10 (1991): 17. Few changes were made following her testimony. Canada, Senate, Hearing for the Standing Committee on Human Rights, 41st Parl, 1st Sess, (28 Nov 2011) at 18 (Mary Ellen Turpel-Lafond, as an individual).

76 Canada, Senate, Hearing for the Standing Committee on Human Rights, 41st Parl, 1st Sess, (28 Nov 2011) at 18 (Mary Ellen Turpel-Lafond, as an individual).

77 Canada, Senate, Hearing for the Standing Committee on Human Rights, 41st Parl, 1st Sess, (28 Nov 2011) at 20 (Mary Ellen Turpel-Lafond, as an individual).

78 CAP represents all off-reserve status and non-status Indians, Métis, and Southern Inuit Aboriginal People. See Congress of Aboriginal People, http://abo-peoples. org/our-mission/.

no reservations.[79] Taking a comparative approach, Maori scholar Jacinta Ruru sees the *FHRMIRA* as a better path to self-government and self-determination for First Nations than has been put in place by the state for Indigenous populations in Aotearoa/New Zealand in respect to matrimonial properly.[80]

Nonetheless, commentators claim the Act fails to adequately support Indigenous law and sovereignty in two important ways.[81] First, "the proposed legislation is based on a delegated law-making authority model."[82] Rather than explicitly recognize Indigenous laws and jurisdiction within its text, it treats the ability of First Nations to pass custom codes as delegated from the federal government.[83] Mi'kmaq scholar Pam Palmater points out that the *FHRMIRA* is ambiguous about some particularly important aspects of Indigenous sovereignty over their diminishing land base. It allows non-Indigenous people to hold life interests in on-reserve property,[84] and the Act does not explicitly protect the special status of on-reserve property under the *Indian Act* or section 35 constitutional questions such as title and treaty.[85]

Second, many have noted that while the standardized legislation of matrimonial property in part II is intended to be temporary, without money and capacity building, First Nations will not be able to draft and

---

79 Canada, Senate, Hearing for the Standing Committee on Human Rights, 40th Parl, 3rd Sess, (31 May 2010) at 25 (Betty Ann Lavallée, national chief, Congress of Aboriginal Peoples).

80 Ruru, "Finding Solutions for the Legislative Gaps," 345.

81 Canada, Senate, Hearing for the Standing Committee on Human Rights, 40th Parl, 3rd Sess, (31 May 2010) at 8 (Jody Wilson-Raybould, regional chief, British Columbia, Assembly of First Nations); Canada, Senate, Hearing for the Standing Committee on Human Rights, 40th Parl, 3rd Sess, (31 May 2010) at 40 (Mary Eberts); and Smith, "Bill C-47," 62.

82 Canada, Senate, Hearing for the Standing Committee on Human Rights, 40th Parl, 3rd Sess, (31 May 2010) at 13 (Jeannette Corbiere Lavell, president, Native Women's Association).

83 Hearing for the Standing Committee on Human Rights, 41st Parl, 1st Sess, (28 November 2011) at 41 (Mary Eberts, former Arial F. Sallows Chair in Human Rights, College of Law, University of Saskatchewan).

84 S. 20(1) *FHRMIRA*.

85 Dr Palamter suggested at the Senate hearing that the Act be amended to "include a section in the preamble that specifically acknowledges First Nations jurisdiction over property and civil rights in their communities, consistent with section 35 of the Constitution Act." Canada, Senate, Hearing for the Standing Committee on Human Rights, 40th Parl, 4th Sess, (5 May 2010) at 39 (Pamela D. Palmater, chair, Centre for Study of Indigenous Governance, Department of Politics and Public Administration, Ryerson University).

implement their own law.[86] At this point, implementation of the Act does not allow for direct funding to First Nations who wish to draw up laws,[87] but the Centre for Excellence for Matrimonial Real Property was established to provide assistance to First Nations wishing to develop a law.[88] The Act does not include any extra or specialized legal aid.[89] The Act and on-reserve property generally is a highly specialized and complex area of law, and most lawyers who can accept legal aid do not have the capacity to do this kind of application.[90] This is exacerbated by the fact that there are many unanswered questions about how the *FHRMIRA* will interact with other legislation such as the *FNLMP*, and constitutional rights such as title, and about the ability of Canadian judges to adequately deal with such disputes arriving in their courts.[91] Moreover, a nearly universal commentary on the *FHRMIRA* has been its failure to mandate increased housing on-reserve. Nearly every critical approach to the legislation points out that allowing one party in a matrimonial dispute to take exclusive possession of the matrimonial home in a context where there is simply no other housing is bound to exacerbate rather than alleviate gendered inequality, violence, and other legacies of colonization. Without a parallel commitment to new housing on-reserve, NWAC calls the *FHRMIRA* a partial fix. They ask

---

86   Canada, Senate, Hearing for the Standing Committee on Human Rights, 40th Parl, 3rd Sess, (31 May 2010) at 69 (Christopher Devlin and Gaylene Schellenberg, Canadian Bar Association); and Canada, Senate, Hearing for the Standing Committee on Human Rights, 40th Parl, 4th Sess, (5 May 2010) at 38 (Pamela D. Palmater, chair, Centre for Study of Indigenous Governance, Department of Politics and Public Administration, Ryerson University).

87   Concerns about the *FHRMIRA* prompted the Blood Band, a Blackfoot nation in Alberta, to launch a constitutional challenge against the Act one day before the part one provisions came into effect, mandating a set of federal laws for First Nations that did not have their own custom codes in place. *The Blood Band v Canada* 2014 FC 1225.

88   The Centre of Excellence for Matrimonial Real Property, hosted by the National Aboriginal Lands Managers Association, is an arm's-length First Nation organization that will assist First Nation communities in developing their own matrimonial real property laws and will provide research on alternative dispute resolution mechanisms. The centre will focus on disseminating knowledge to First Nation individuals, communities, and organizations to assist them in understanding and implementing the *Act*. *See* https://www.coemrp.ca.

89   Canada, Senate, Hearing for the Standing Committee on Human Rights, 40th Parl, 3rd Sess, (31 May 2010) at 42 (Mary Eberts).

90   Canada, Senate, Hearing for the Standing Committee on Human Rights, 40th Parl, 3rd Sess, (31 May 2010) at 77 (Christopher Devlin and Gaylene Schellenberg, Canadian Bar Association).

91   Smith, "Bill C-47," 73.

for a more holistic approach that would include increased housing stock, violence prevention, and other supports.[92]

While these have been the central concerns with the new legislation, one issue that has not yet been raised in the discussion of matrimonial real property on-reserve is the construct of the family in relation to law. In the Western discourse, this debate corresponds with the categorization of property as private, which effectively created the home as male controlled enclaves that were sacrosanct and essentially immune from public interference.[93] While this history changed the private domain of the family from being subject to male authority, its remnants remain.[94] All of this has been extensively documented elsewhere but has yet to be given the same kind of critical treatment is how historical conceptions of the family and corresponding private/public divides were and are conceived for Indigenous peoples and Indigenous law.

In contrast, contributions to this book highlight the continuing relevance of the way Indigenous societies historically operated through decentralized institutions. For example, law operated through a range of kinship networks, which for the Indigenous peoples in northwest British Columbia included matrilineal families, matrilineal and patrilineal extended families, clans, larger clan alliances, at a broader societal level, and on an inter-societal level with neighbouring peoples.[95] Individuals, including women, were legal agents born of their mother's house group, which served as a locator and term of reference for territorial interests along with social and economic obligations and rights. Protections and liabilities operated by locating the individual as an agent within one's house group, and the house group is the collective legal agent with other house groups and beyond. A duality also operated where an individual's father's house group was responsible and liable for injuries sustained by or perpetrated by the individual.

Tsimshian peoples no longer reside in longhouses and, for the most part, live as nuclear families. However, Napoleon and Snyder identify

---

92 Canada, Senate, Hearing for the Standing Committee on Human Rights, 40th Parl, 3rd Sess, (31 May 2010) at 12 (Jeannette Corbiere Lavell, president, Native Women's Association of Canada).

93 Susan B. Boyd, "Can Law Challenge the Public/Private Divide? Women, Work, and Family," *Windsor Yearbook of Access to Justice* 15 (1996): 161–85.

94 Angela Cameron, "Restoring Women: Community and Legal Responses to Violence against Women in Opposite-Sex Intimate Relationships" (PhD diss., University of Victoria, 2012), https://dspace.library.uvic.ca/bitstream/handle/1828/3947/Cameron_Angela_phd_2012.pdf?sequence=1&isAllowed=y.

95 See Napoleon and Snyder, this volume. Also see Napoleon, "Ayook."

that the ethics and legal obligations regarding family, kinship, and community still continue in some form in Tsimshian family and community life. For example, historic Tsimshian family and family home were not private. Despite many changes in how people manage themselves, family, extended families, and communities are involved to varying extents with legal responses to harm and injuries.[96] Napoleon and Snyder argue that it is the identification of those responses as law and creating the Indigenous institutions necessary to implement the law that will bring the healthy reformation of matrimonial property on reserves. Their work represents an effort to find useful ways to examine and respond to these issues. As Jeannette Corbiere Lavell has stated, "In the twenty-first century we deserve legislative solutions that do not pit individual and collective rights against one another but, rather, work to complement the unique set of rights that Indigenous women and their families hold, both as individuals and as members of collectives, referring back to our customs and traditions."[97]

Napoleon and Snyder posit that applying a relational lens to Indigenous property theory will enable definition of Indigenous property that resides "within the collective itself" while at the same time, provide protection against the collective.[98] This steps away from situating property rights against individual rights of equality, individual freedom, or collective freedom. Instead, what becomes possible is "ongoing collective formulation of individual rights in a political culture that respects both democratic decision making and individual freedom and that recognizes the need to sustain the inevitable tension between them."[99] From this perspective, the task in rethinking Indigenous property is, as Nedelsky suggests, to examine ways to maintain the necessary tension between the individual rights of a property holder along with the collective rights of the Indigenous community or larger society, as well as to look for collective legal processes through which individual rights are understood and arranged.

The need for Indigenous institutions sets the stage for the discussion of band council powers by Michel Morin in chapter 7. He uses a positivist approach to Indigenous law to identify how bands have long exercised powers, albeit limited, over land allocation in ways that

---

96   Friedland and Napoleon, "Gathering the Threads."
97   Canada, Senate, Hearing for the Standing Committee on Human Rights, 40th Parl, 3rd Sess, (31 May 2010) at 12 (Jeannette Corbiere Lavell, president, Native Women's Association of Canada).
98   Nedelsky, Law's Relations, 95.
99   Nedelsky, Law's Relations, 96.

affect matrimonial property and that these powers continue to affect the distribution of property under new legislation, such as *FHRMIRA*. Exploring how parties to litigation, band councils, and the courts have used customary and legislated possession of reserve lands, he examines how issues concerning matrimonial property play out on reserves when different sources of rights to occupy or possess lands are considered. Moreover, he identifies the future relevance of band councils as sites for lawmaking.

The contribution of these authors highlights the fact that Indigenous communities are exploring options for dispute resolution including Canadian courts, therapeutic or integrated courts, tribunals, general community-based programs, and specific Indigenous law. Many communities have already implemented tribunals and community-based programs, and are some are drawing on their legal traditions. However, Indigenous peoples may decide that historic family, extended family, and Indigenous law have no place in today's matrimonial real property arrangements. It will take some time yet to assess their outcomes, as well as to more fully comprehend the efficacy and power dynamics in the arrangements between Indigenous and Canadian law.

B. Contracting and Privatization

The last and perhaps most widespread trend to privatization of land arises from what collectively comes under the rubric of the private contract. This includes trends such as individual *Indian Act* bands negotiating IBAs or MOUs directly with corporations for resource extraction on their historic territories as a supplement to – or instead of – accessing land claim or title litigation with the Crown. This trend also includes individual *Indian Act* band or First Nation participation in, and support of infrastructures such as oil and gas pipelines on their historic territories, actualized through corporate structures and partnerships.

Generally, the power to contract for specific rights is constructed as one of the most powerful ways to exercise authority and control over objects in Western private law. Contract law assumes that negotiating parties exercise free will to contract and that rational actors will contract for a benefit. The capacity to determine use provides an owner with the opportunity to exchange land or resource use for a range of rights and entitlements that it would not otherwise be able to obtain. While financial compensation is the main object of exchange, parties to resource extraction regularly contract for the use of specific standards, deadlines, equipment, liabilities, accountabilities, monitoring, and oversight. The parties in this framework exercise authority over these objects through agreements that are backed by the enforcement mechanisms of the state.

The recent surge in the use of contracts to address development on Indigenous territories reflects the global recognition that IBAs, other types of revenue agreements, and related contractual mechanisms (process agreements, interim measures agreements, memorandums of understanding, and agreements in principle) are a part of the standard package of regulatory and benefit requirements associated with major natural resource development. The global use of IBAs reflects the wide-spread recognition that it is not socially acceptable for corporations to develop natural resources and resource infrastructure in a way that imposes local costs while benefits are enjoyed elsewhere. However, especially in Canada, IBAs are also nested within a regulatory frame-work that uses them to address legal obligations to Indigenous peoples. Contracts are therefore used as an important tool for preventing opposition to natural resource development projects on Indigenous lands and achieving regional economic development.

Given the ability of IBAs and other contracts to recognize, validate, and address Indigenous interests in lands, one might argue that Indigenous peoples can actualize their power over ownership through contracts. Terms that create equity ownership, financial participation and revenue sharing, employment quotas for local people, rights of first refusals for contracts, and the establishment of participatory governance committees that monitor and consult on projects suggest that Indigenous governments are able to use contracts to improve their oversight and benefit from projects.[100]

Moreover, if any legal tool seems capable of incorporating Indigenous laws and traditions, it is contract. There is a settled legal tradition in the common law to recognize and enforce whatever terms the parties agree to, including those laws that will determine disputes and the type of arbitral or decision-making bodies in which disputes will be litigated. This legal openness suggests that contracts are not only avenues for obtaining objects for exchange of importance to Indigenous peoples. Arguably they are also potential sites for Indigenous legal traditions – sites in which the relationship of the parties will be nested.

---

100 See, e.g., L. Galbraith, B. Bradshaw, and M.B. Rutherford, "Towards a New Supra-Regulatory Approach to Environmental Assessment in Northern Canada," *Impact Assessment and Project Appraisal* 25, no. 1 (2007): 27–41; Sari Graben, "Evaluating Stakeholder Participation in Sub-Arctic Co-Management: Administrative Rulemaking and Private Agreements," *Windsor Yearbook of Access to Justice* 29, no. 1 (2011): 195–221.

Yet if contracts hold the potential for a richer use for Indigenous legal traditions, a deeper analysis of the power dynamics at play in the negotiation and enforcement of contracts reveals that any power Indigenous peoples possess is actualized within very strict constraints. Rather than be able to use contracts to reflect a particular community's values or traditions, they are used to homogenize development. There are several reasons for these constraints, but generally they identify that where bargaining is limited, it is difficult to frame the Indigenous party as a rational individual actor operating within a generally equalized landscape of bargaining capacity that can be used to emancipate it.

Bargaining inequality arises because the negotiation of IBAs or resource revenue agreements on non-title land often occurs after proponents have made significant investments in exploration and permitting, and therefore against a background of inevitability. While the oil and gas legislation cannot supersede constitutional rights, including the duty to consult and accommodate, in Canada, IBAs often come after invasive exploration and licensing has been granted. For example, oil and gas legislation does not impose benefit requirements until after rights have been issued. As Caine and Krogman have noted, once such investments have been made, it is extremely difficult for government permitting agencies and Indigenous groups to slow the process or even stop it.[101] Therefore, where development occurs on treaty lands or on lands that are subject to unsettled claims, IBAs become a last option for influencing the flow of resources back to the community. This is especially the case where federal officials issue timelines and regulatory settings in which Indigenous peoples must make their claims.[102] Negotiations in this context are confined to mitigating any impacts or creating employment opportunities, rather than recognizing rights.[103]

Ibronke Odumosu-Ayanu's chapter on the Niger Delta illustrates how laws in Nigeria, which consolidated all land and resource ownership in the government, have affected the negotiating leverage of Niger Delta peoples. The use of contracts in these circumstances illuminates that it is problematic to assume that the parties are contracting for clear

---

101 Ken Caine and Naomi Krogman, "Powerful or Just Plain Power-Full? A Power Analysis of Impact and Benefit Agreements in Canada's North," *Organization and Environment* 23, no. 1 (2010): 85.

102 For discussion on duty to consult, see Sari Graben and Abbey Sinclair, "Tribunal Administration and the Duty to Consult: A Study of the National Energy Board," *University of Toronto Law Journal* 65, no. 4 (2015): 382–433.

103 Ellen Bielawski, *Rogue Diamonds: Rush for Northern Riches on Dene Land* (Toronto: Douglas & McIntyre, 2003).

and certain rights and therefore problematic to assume that the parties are sufficiently empowered to negotiate in a way that is emancipatory. Much of this uncertainty arises because it is not entirely clear what ownership rights ground community entitlement to negotiate. In the Nigerian context, Odumosu-Ayanu identifies three legal innovations that could help legitimate community entitlements: trust law principles, industry agreements, and claims to Indigeneity. She advocates using these techniques to reconnect interests in lands to the peoples of the Niger Delta that the state sought to sever through legislation.

In Canada, proponents negotiate with communities who hold unrecognized rights pursuant to the Crown's duty to consult (either because title is contested or the meaning of treaty rights is unsettled). While the duty to consult is construed by the courts as a procedural entitlement, rather than a proprietary one, it certainly recognizes an Indigenous right to make use of resources and relates their entitlement to those of the Crown. Nonetheless, those rights do not preclude the Crown as owner of the same or ancillary resources from exercising its rights (i.e., to Crown land or subsurface resources). Nor do those rights preclude the Crown from effectively expropriating the land or resources of Indigenous peoples when the Crown chooses to create justifiable infringements that grant resource rights to third parties and reap the beneficial value from taxation and royalties for itself. Just as identified by Odumosu-Ayani, negotiations in this context are not easily characterized as emancipatory, since real property rights hinder the leverage of Indigenous peoples in negotiations.

The second criticism of contracts is that the terms purposefully aim to limit the capacity of Indigenous citizens to analyse, debate, and advocate against the terms agreed to by Indigenous governments. Confidentiality clauses, stability clauses, non-compliance clauses, and the use of pro forma terms limit the potential for contracts to be used to creatively incorporate standards and values of the community.

Confidentiality clauses restrict the communication of the details or content of the IBAs to anyone who is not a beneficiary. Stability clauses prohibit legislation that will alter the value of the investment. Non-compliance clauses prohibit Indigenous governments from undertaking action that would delay or object to a development. While both communities and industry advocate for confidentiality, there is no transparent communication or outside discussion about what was achieved for the community, and no capacity to compare or learn from comparative experiences. Similarly, non-compliance clauses prevent the use of public and regulatory mechanisms to ensure oversight. While non-compliance clauses are probably unenforceable against individual Indigenous

citizens, in variations on this clause the Indigenous government indem-
nifies the proponent for any loss suffered. This collective penalty creates a social disincentive for individuals to organize and use democratic
processes should they disagree with government or proponent actions
at any stage in the development.

Concerns with contract terms that limit transparency raise questions
about how the law has separated the use of private contracts from their
use as a site for Indigenous law. As Napoleon has argued elsewhere,

> If we understand law, including Indigenous law, to be a public collab-
> orative process through which legitimacy is created, how are we to un-
> derstand the characterization of IBAs as private? Are they private only
> insofar as Canadian law in that they do not involve state governments,
> but still are governed by public state law? Since Indigenous governments
> are negotiating IBAs, can they still be considered private insofar as Indig-
> enous law? If IBAs are somehow considered private and perhaps located
> outside of Indigenous law, what might be the consequence of taking issues
> of paramount importance to Indigenous peoples out of their public legal
> processes? Does this place IBAs beyond the reach of Indigenous processes
> of legitimacy, beyond accountability, and lawfulness? Does this strengthen
> or undermine Indigenous legal traditions and their efficacy?[104]

The issues of transparency and confidentiality also trouble the creation of Indigenous law. For example, if we asked how an IBA might be
drafted according to Cree law, it requires us to think about the required
Cree legalities that might inform the drafting of a Cree impact benefit
agreement.[105] Arguably, if IBAs concern Cree lands or resources, then
they should be a matter of public Cree law and as such are not private.
The next question from a Cree legal perspective is whether IBAs fulfil the public requirements of Cree law, particularly if there are limitations to transparency and confidentiality requirements. In other words,
while IBAs might well be public in that they involve Cree government,
do constraints to transparency and confidentiality terms render them
unlawful? These are the kinds of questions that can be answered only
in the application of Indigenous law from an internal perspective – and
hence the need for a resurgence of Indigenous law with enough scope
for disagreement, reasoning, and argumentation.

---

104 Valerie Napoleon, "Indigenous Law and IBAs," in *Impact Benefit Agreements*, ed.
     Bartholemew Smallboy and Arielle Dylan (Toronto: University of Toronto Press,
     forthcoming).
105 Napoleon, "Indigenous Law and IBAs."

II. Indigenous Legal Traditions

What does the recognition of Indigenous legal traditions look like inside communities grappling with property rights? The uncomfortable answer is that it is not quite clear. As Ballantyne and Dobbin have noted, "Any series of property rights registration options must incorporate informal, traditional, or customary systems of property rights in land. Such traditional systems have arisen over many generations in response to a complex web of historical, social, and economic forces, and are ignored at the peril of any system which seeks to sweep them asunder."[106]

There are legitimate legal processes of deliberation and reasoning through which Indigenous communities have made and will continue to make hard decisions about lands, governance, and resources. Questions about Indigenous lands, privatization, matrimonial property, and the everyday disputes within Indigenous communities require that Indigenous legal processes be fully engaged, that their integrity be maintained, and that change is explicit, public, and accountable, at least within Indigenous communities.

It is in this developing context that the following chapters reveal tensions between competing philosophies regarding collective social, legal, economic, and political responsibilities and the liberally constructed autonomous individual. Ownership is conferred on individuated persons by state law, but Indigenous law premises ownership on those who constitute and are constituted by networks of relations.[107] Our preferred approach is to develop double vision – one that sees the individual, but also identifies one against the surrounding political and economic context. Further, we understand that a person's personal responsibility, as an agent, extends only to where his or her own power ends, and it is at this point that collective responsibility begins. As Jennifer Nedelsky writes, from "a relational view, the persons whose rights and well-being are at stake are constituted by their relationships such that it is only in the context of those relationships that one can understand how to foster their capacities, define and protect their rights, or promote their well-being."[108]

---

106 Brian Ballantyne and James Dobbin, *Options for Land Registration and Survey Systems on Aboriginal Lands in Canada (A Report Prepared for the Legal Surveys Division of Geomatics Canada* (2000), http://www.acls-aatc.ca/files/english/aboriginal/Ballantyne-Dobbin_report.pdf.
107 Nedelsky, *Law's Relations*, 19.
108 Nedelsky, *Law's Relations*, 121.

Indigenous law has been the focus of international study for decades, often under the rubric of customary law.[109] Nevertheless, our survey of the scholarship suggests that more research that explores the intellectual traditions and legal reasoning processes that comprise Indigenous law is needed. These are necessary for the effective management of societies, conflict, and governance. The categorization of Indigenous law only as customary limits its scope and often results in a focus on practices and rules.[110]

Consequently, with notable exceptions such as John Borrows,[111] David Milward,[112] Hadley Friedland,[113] and Matthew Fletcher,[114] among others, much of the literature about Indigenous law still reflects a very general way of thinking about Indigenous legal orders and law, and they tend to be more hortatory and philosophical. References to Indigenous law are usually liberally sprinkled throughout self-government agreements, land codes, constitutions, and other governing and program documents, but it is very difficult to see how Indigenous law would actually be practised and rigorously applied to contemporary

---

109 In Australia, extensive Indigenous law research has been conducted for over two decades. Still more Indigenous law research has been completed in South Africa, Papua New Guinea, Rwanda, Nigeria, New Zealand, Kenya, Ghana, and the United States.

110 For examples of research that focus more on legal practice than collaborative legal processes, see Minneh Kane, J. Oloka-Onyango, and Abdul Tejan-Cole, "Reassessing Customary Law Systems as a Vehicle for Providing Equitable Access to Justice for the Poor," (2005), http://siteresources.worldbank.org/INTRANETSO-CIALDEVELOPMENT/Resources/Kane.rev.pdf; Leila Chirayath, Caroline Sage, and Michael Woolcock, "Customary Law and Policy Reform: Engaging with the Plurality of Justice Systems," (2005), http://documents.worldbank.org/curated/en/675681468178176738/Customary-law-and-policy-reform-engaging-with-the-plurality-of-justice-systems; and Kathryn Trees, "Contemporary Issues Facing Customary Law and the General Legal System: Roebourne – A Case Study," Background Paper No. 6, Law Reform Commission of Western Australia (2004).

111 Borrows, *Canada's Indigenous Constitution*.

112 David Milward, *Aboriginal Justice and the Charter: Realizing a Culturally Sensitive Interpretation of Legal Rights in Canada* (Vancouver: UBC Press, 2012).

113 Hadley Friedland, "Reflective Frameworks Methods for Accessing, Understanding and Applying Indigenous Laws," *Indigenous Law Journal* 11, no. 1 (2012): 1; and Friedland, "The Wetiko (Windigo) Legal Principles: Responding to Harmful People in Cree, Anishinabek and Saulteaux Societies – Past, Present and Future Uses, with a Focus on Contemporary Violence and Child Victimization Concerns" (LLM thesis, University of Alberta, 2009).

114 Mathew Fletcher, "Rethinking Customary Law in Tribal Court Jurisprudence," Indigenous Law and Policy Centre Occasional Paper Series (2006).

issues and disputes. This simplification and separation of Indigenous law from practice and application in the real world has had an insidious effect on its development, rendering it into cultural remnants to be added on after the fact to state models of social, political, economic, or legal institutions.

Indigenous law inheres in each Indigenous society as a whole, forming legal orders that enable large groups of people to live together and to manage themselves accordingly.[115] The unfortunate reality is that many Indigenous political and legal institutions have been obscured, undermined, and damaged.[116] There are many internal contradictions and conflicts (as in other societies) that Indigenous groups must embrace and deal with in order to move beyond reacting to colonialism and to create social and political imaginaries beyond it.

If one understands Indigenous law as a collaborative construct that allows societies to manage themselves and derives from a particular cosmology and ontology, then one knows that Indigenous law cannot be easily codified into sets of rules for what to do and what not to do.[117] Instead, what should become apparent is that it is just as necessary to be critical and rigorous in the analysis of Indigenous legal orders and law as with any other legal system.[118]

For the purposes of how Indigenous law might be applied to real property, there is much to learn from the actual practice of Indigenous law. In other words, one can learn about Indigenous law in many ways, including from how people act on legal norms in their relationships and interactions, decision-making, and actions.[119] That being said, not

---

115   Napoleon and Friedland, "From Roots to Renaissance," in *Oxford Handbook of Criminal Law*, ed. Markus D. Dubber and Tatjana Hörnle (Oxford: Oxford University Press, 2014), 225.

116   For a discussion of these issues in an African context, see, generally, Gordon R. Woodman, "Legal Pluralism and the Search for Justice," *Journal of African Law* 40, no. 2 (1996): 152. Also see Napoleon and Friedland, "From Roots to Renaissance."

117   For a discussion about the theoretical dangers of essentializing law, see, generally, Brian Z. Tamanaha, "A Non-Essentialist Version of Legal Pluralism," *Journal of Law and Society* 27, no. 2 (2000): 296.

118   For a discussion about developing intercultural legal theory, see, generally, Christoph Eberhard, "Towards an Intercultural Legal Theory: The Dialogical Challenge," *Social and Legal Studies* 10, no. 2 (2001): 171.

119   Gordon Woodman advocates the need for extensive research into "practiced customary law." Woodman also suggests that such research be conducted in small localities rather than on a state basis. Gordon Woodman, "Customary Law in Common Law Systems," *IDS Bulletin* 32, no. 1 (2001): 28–34, https://core.ac.uk/download/pdf/43539808.pdf.

all contributors in the following chapters set out to identify Indigenous laws. Each uses distinct methods to identify whether state law is concomitant with the legal position adopted by Indigenous peoples. So whether those laws are broadly stated or specifically outlined in their chapters, Indigenous law underpins their analysis. However, each looks to the process by which Indigenous law is articulated and recognized by communities (writ large) as well as Indigenous, municipal, provincial, and federal governments.

Napoleon and Snyder use the four-phase Indigenous legal methodology developed by Friedland and Napoleon for the substantive articulation and restatement of Indigenous law. The phases of this Indigenous law methodology are (1) developing community-specific research questions; (2) analysing stories and cases; (3) creating a framework with a societal primer, synthesis, and preliminary legal theory; and (4) implementing, applying, and critically evaluating.[120] Since gender is central to their concern with Indigenous law and with property, questions about gender are an integral part of developing research questions and carrying out research projects.[121] Key to this methodology are the dual requirements for transparency of reasoning and interpretive processes, and the consistent citing of sources, be they interviews, discussion groups, or oral and written stories in order to foster respectful debate and engagement. Possible starting places for research questions might be:

- How did people in this legal order make decisions or resolve problems about where to live, access resources, and travel in their territories and beyond?
- How did people in this legal order resolve conflicts about living areas, access to resources, and travel in their territories and beyond?
- How did families respond to marriage (formal and informal), marriage break-ups, responsibilities to children, and separate living arrangements?

This methodology involves collecting publicly available stories, oral histories, and other materials that are relevant to the identified research

---

120 Friedland and Napoleon, "Gathering the Threads." Also see Napoleon and Friedland, "From Roots to Renaissance"; and Val Napoleon and Hadley Friedland, "An Inside Job: Engaging with Indigenous Legal Traditions through Stories" *McGill Law Journal* 61, no. 4 (2016), 739.
121 Emily Snyder, "Representations of Women in Cree Legal Educational Materials: An Indigenous Feminist Legal Theoretical Analysis" (PhD diss., University of Alberta, 2014).

question from each Indigenous community. There are also valuable resources that describe elements of historic Tsimshian property law, for example, such as Viola Garfield's research completed during the 1930s. Garfield's work describes property inheritance, individual and collective investments, building and location of plank longhouses, and allocation of living space. Using this work but also opening it up to critique and obtaining many versions of the same story produces a specific body of knowledge about a legal order synthesized into a framework that underlies legal processes, decision-makers, legal responses, obligations, substantive and procedural rights, and guiding principles. This restatement of law, in the form of a coherent and accessible legal synthesis, is developed in collaboration with the community and remains with the community for further use, application, and refinement. This methodology has been employed around the issues of harms and conflicts, and further partnerships will focus on Indigenous courts, marine management, and child welfare and family law.

Other methodologies also aim to practically articulate and restate specific areas of law that may be applied to today's legal issues. Indigenous legal scholars such as John Borrows are developing a linguistic and land-based learning.[122] The Mi'kmaq scholar James Youngblood Henderson has suggested that Indigenous legal traditions are best accessed in the context of language, stories, methods of communication, and styles of performance and discourse, because these are mediums that frame understanding and encode values.[123] Contributions by Jobin and Morales reflect this approach to identifying and applying Indigenous legal traditions.

While there is no agreed definition of customary law (just as there is no agreed definition of law generally), there is general agreement that "customary law is not restricted to the retrospective study of systems that no longer exist in their pure forms."[124] In other words, when considering Indigenous law, it is important to acknowledge that external forces and state law have affected Indigenous societies, and vice versa.

---

122 John Borrows, "Outsider Education: Indigenous Law and Land-Based Learning," *Windsor Yearbook of Access to Justice* 33, no. 1 (2016): 1.

123 J.Y. Henderson, *First Nations Jurisprudence and Aboriginal Rights: Defining the Just Society* (Saskatoon, SK: Native Law Centre of Canada, 2006), 127.

124 Scott Clark, *Aboriginal Customary Law: Literature Review* (prepared for the Public Inquiry into the Administration of Justice and Aboriginal People, 1990), 6. Also see, generally, Gordon Woodman, "Some Realism about Customary Law: The West African Experience," in *African Law and Legal Theory*, ed. Gordon R. Woodman and A.O. Obilade (New York: New York University Press, 1995), 145.

Thus, there are conceptual difficulties in imagining how law applies to reserves in particular, given that they do not derive from within Indigenous peoples' own legal orders and laws.[125] This perspective reveals an assumption of incommensurability that belies Indigenous law's ability to change or be applicable to everyday human problems. Indigenous communities have tried, sometimes successfully, to combine aspects of their Indigenous law within the federal *Indian Act* regime.[126]

In accordance with this line of thinking, Morin and Blanchette's method of identifying customary law, as forwarded by parties in litigation, does not purport to make definitive statements about the substance of the law. Rather, it identifies by-law making as one site in which customary law manifests. Baxter's discussion of how legal claims to territory are framed through direct action and political protest identifies how competing claims to interpret law arise in public sites.

Daly's ethnographic approach identifies principles of sharing and reciprocity in Aboriginal communities from actions in which individuals pay certain amounts or undertake certain tasks as a form of taxation. His process is to deconstruct the empirical, historical, and factual basis of twenty-first-century life and attempt to rebuild it. Daly achieves this by documenting and contextualizing the social and cultural structures, rules and discipline involved in actual Indigenous life – of the past and of today.[127]

Taken as a whole, the chapters to follow share our double vision – seeing Indigenous societies as having historic economic orders as well as contemporary economies that are deeply enmeshed with the world today. By identifying how contemporary Indigenous economies

---

125 For a discussion on the difficulties of comprehending law across cultures and recognizing one's own ideological baggage, see William P. Alford, "On the Limits of 'Grand Theory' in Comparative Law," *Washington Law Review* 61 (1986): 945.

126 For example, the Senate Standing Committee on Human Rights explains that there are five Ontario bands and two Alberta bands that explicitly allot reserve land according to "custom." They report, "Thirty-three other First Nations [i.e., bands] in Ontario, one in Alberta and two in Saskatchewan have a hybrid system which combines *Indian Act* Certificates of Possession and custom allotments. *A Hard Bed to Lie In: Matrimonial Real Property on Reserve*, interim report of the Standing Committee on Human Rights (November 2003), 24, https://sencanada.ca/Content/SEN/Committee/372/huma/rep/rep08nov03-e.pdf.

127 Val Napoleon, "Thinking about Indigenous Legal Orders" (Research paper for the National Centre for First Nations Governance, June 2007), http://www.fngovernance.org/ncfng_research/val_napoleon.pdf; Catherine Bell and Val Napoleon, eds., *First Nations Cultural Heritage and Law: Case Studies, Voices and Perspectives* (Vancouver, UBC Press, 2008).

are still rooted in and informed by their societally specific norms, meanings, and ethics, the contributors to this book have identified the contradictions and conflicts within Indigenous communities about relationships to land and non-human life forms, about responsibilities to one another, about environmental decisions, and about wealth distribution. Importantly, they also begin identifying the way that Indigenous discourses, processes, and institutions can empower the use of Indigenous law.

PART ONE

Indigenous Law in Practice

1 Housing on Reserve: Developing a Critical Indigenous Feminist Property Theory

VAL NAPOLEON AND EMILY SNYDER

I. Introduction

Paul Nadasdy has observed that in the negotiation of their land claim agreement, the Kluane First Nation in the Yukon "translate their complex reciprocal relationship with the land into an equally complex but very different language of 'property.'"[1] According to Indigenous political science scholar Glen Coulthard, the negotiation of land rights has reoriented "Indigenous struggle from one that was once deeply *informed* by the land as a system of reciprocal relations and obligations ... to a struggle that is now largely *for* land, understood here as some material resource to be exploited in the capital-accumulation process."[2] While Coulthard is not addressing reserve land, the questions concerning relationships to land, economies, and governance, along with competing legal orders, are the not-so-deep undercurrents beneath the property-on-reserve debate.[3] This larger political frame is usually ignored and replaced with debates about Indigenous property on reserve land that mainly start and remain inside unquestioned Western property constructs and ongoing colonial structures.

In a 2006 *Wall Street Journal* article, John Miller speculates, "Maybe we should give land back to the rez-dwellers, so that they may own

---

1 Paul Nadasdy, "'Property' and Aboriginal Land Claims in the Canadian Subarctic: Some Theoretical Considerations," *American Anthropologist* 1 (2002): 248, cited in Glen Coulthard, "From Wards of the State to Subjects of Recognition? Marx, Indigenous Peoples, and the Politics of Dispossession in Denendeh," in *Theorizing Native Studies*, ed. Audra Simpson and Andrea Smith (Durham, NC: Duke University Press, 2014), 86.
2 Nadasdy, "'Property.'"
3 See, e.g., John J. Miller, "The Projects on the Prairie," *Wall Street Journal*, 27 January 2006, http://www.wsj.com/articles/SB113833760164357997.

private property the way other Americans do."[4] According to Miller, poverty among "American Indians" is due to their inability to put up "reservation" land as collateral for personal mortgages and loans.[5] He argues that this is a major obstacle to American Indian economic development.[6] There is a similar mantra on the loose in Canada. It is in the form of the often quoted work of Hernando de Soto, who writes, "You need a property right before you can make money."[7] This narrative has been strongly advocated in Canada by Tom Flanagan,[8] among many others. For example, writing on behalf of the right-wing Canadian Taxpayers Federation, Richard Truscott extols the virtues of private property for Indigenous peoples: "Without a system of authentic individual property rights to activate the wealth of the land, fuel native entrepreneurship, and encourage investment, Indian reserves will remain Indian ghettos."[9] The neoliberal, colonial, heteropatriarchal structures that created and maintain these conditions of poverty to begin with are presented as a "solution."

We maintain that the relentless discourse about the "need" for private property is, as Coulthard so aptly describes, a facet of hierarchical economic, gendered, racialized, and state-power relationships.[10] What the vociferous assertions about private property fail to recognize is that if one accepts the private property premise, then one need not think any further about power or the ways that systemic forms of oppression such as colonialism, racism, and sexism circulate in law and economics. Instead, one can focus on the obstinate failure of most Indigenous people to buy into such an "obvious" quick fix. Nicholas Blomley rightfully observes, "Property discourse offers a dense and pungent set of social symbols, stories, and meanings" tied to judgments about

---

4 Miller, "Projects on the Prairie."

5 Miller, "Projects on the Prairie."

6 Miller, "Projects on the Prairie."

7 Hernando de Soto, *The Mystery of Capital* (New York: Basic Books, 2000), 6, cited in Clarence Nyce, *Masters in Our Own House: The Path to Prosperity – Report of the Think Tank on First Nations Wealth Creation* (Terrace, BC: Skeena Native Development Society, 2003), 64.

8 See, e.g., Tom Flanagan, Christopher Alcantara, and André Le Dressay, *Beyond the Indian Act: Restoring Aboriginal Property Rights* (Montreal and Kingston: McGill-Queen's University Press, 2010).

9 Richard Truscott, "Property Rights Are the Key to Indian Prosperity," Taxpayer.com, 29 July 2002, http://www.taxpayer.com/commentaries/property-rights-are-the-key-to-indian-prosperity.

10 Glen Coulthard, *Red Skin, White Masks: Rejecting the Colonial Politics of Recognition* (Minneapolis: University of Minnesota Press, 2014).

worth, morality, and nationhood.[11] For example, in frontier chronicles, one finds a consistent erasure of Indigenous peoples' presence, use, and relationships to land, and Canada is represented as a space that was in need of being settled and developed.[12] Contemporary property discourse similarly works to assert state property laws and Western private property regimes as superior and natural,[13] thus perpetuating colonial narratives about the inferiority of Indigenous peoples, their laws, and ideas regarding land and property ownership.[14]

Many writers have challenged the overly simplistic characterization of property and property rights that is proposed to and accepted by many Indigenous people. Too frequently "property" is imagined only as private property,[15] which stems from Western, liberal, capitalist ideologies. The Western conceptions and arrangements of property, specifically private property, are not going anywhere, and we do not take the position that there should be no private property. Rather, we argue that it must be problematized and that its unquestioned foundation and real material consequences must be laid bare, especially because of the way private property is consistently imposed as the way out of poverty for Indigenous peoples. The complexity of the issues we take up are reflected in several chapters in this collection; more specifically, Tenile Brown recommends to look to both customary and state law to deal with land and property inequality, and Shalene Jobin questions the impacts of institutional frameworks inherent to citizenship and market citizenship on Indigeneity. The private property approach is only one avenue, and we want to create space for other approaches, explorations, and ways to arrange the relationships between Indigenous peoples and land, including those drawn from Indigenous societies' legal traditions and land laws.

---

11 Nicholas Blomley, "Law, Property, and the Geography of Violence: The Frontier, the Survey, and the Grid," *Annals of the Association of American Geographers* 93 (2003): 122.
12 Blomley, "Law, Property, and the Geography of Violence," 124–5; Brian Egan and Jessica Place, "Minding the Gaps: Property, Geography, and Indigenous Peoples in Canada," *Geoforum* 44 (2013): 130–1.
13 Carol Rose, "Property as Storytelling: Perspectives from Game Theory, Narrative Theory, Feminist Theory," *Yale Journal of Law and the Humanities* 2 (1990): 53–4.
14 Egan and Place, "Minding the Gaps"; Jessica Dempsey, Kevin Gould, and Juanita Sundberg, "Changing Land Tenure, Defining Subjects: Neoliberalism and Property Regimes on Native Reserves," in *Rethinking the Great White North: Race, Nature and the Historical Geographies of Whiteness in Canada*, ed. L. Cameron, A. Baldwin, and A. Kobayashi (Vancouver: UBC Press, 2011), 233.
15 Margaret Davies, *Property: Meanings, Histories, Theories* (New York: Routledge-Cavendish, 2007), 14.

In section II we introduce a critical Indigenous feminist property theory, which we present to reflect on Indigenous property law. Next, in section III we present four Indigenous community case studies, along with an analysis of legislative frameworks, housing practices and policies, land codes, debt, and histories in order to identify similarities and differences in their experiences. Lastly, in sections IV and V we deconstruct the use of property and challenge its unexamined incorporation into Indigenous political and legal regimes. We identify potentially applicable Indigenous laws and raise questions for addressing gendered property issues on reserve. We explore and present a possible Tsimshian property theory and argue that all legal property theories, including those that are Indigenous, must be grounded in a substantive treatment of Indigenous law that allows for an internal perspective and rigorous critique and debate. In doing so, we provide constructive ways for Indigenous peoples to move forward to develop their own property theories.

II. Developing a Critical Indigenous Feminist Property Theory

A. Aims of the Theory

What work must a critical Indigenous feminist property theory do? While there should be many critical Indigenous property theories, does a critical Indigenous feminist property theory have to be articulated separately? We begin with the position that legal theories are necessary to reason through law in a way that moves beyond the legal technician level to examine law's overall function, aspirations, and normative commitments, and the health of law generally. While we take the position that all Indigenous property theories should include feminist perspectives, we sketch out a critical Indigenous feminist property theory here because the gendered nature of law is ignored and remains invisible and will be for some time yet. However one approaches developing these theories, the issues of Indigenous property are complex and far-reaching. Given this, the demands one can make of a critical theory of Indigenous property are many and they are tough.

Our approach is informed by critical legal theory and Indigenous feminist legal theory – applied to the specificities of property law. A critical Indigenous feminist property theory needs to account for Indigenous legal orders and state law, especially in the context of examining housing on reserve. While Michel Morin (in this collection), for example, provides important descriptions on the operation of the federal legislation regarding family homes on reserve, he does not take up

Indigenous law or a gendered analysis. Too often otherwise excellent Indigenous studies or Indigenous political science literature tends to focus on the very real problems created by the exercise of colonial law, and when references to Indigenous law are made, they are usually general, conflated in the language of governance, or described as ethics or values.[16] The result is an eclipsing of any space for discussing Indigenous law, critically or otherwise.

The field of critical legal theory comprises many competing perspectives. Since we are advocating an approach to resurgence and theorizing of Indigenous law that is attentive to power, our employment of critical legal theory attends to "both the beneficial and harmful aspects of law – both law's ability to further its purported goal of a just social order and its ability to fall away from that goal" or to distort those goals in ways that perpetuate oppression.[17] As we have argued elsewhere with John Borrows, gendered oppression can be perpetuated not only through state law, but also through Indigenous legal practices and interpretations of law – sometimes in the name of tradition, resurgence, and decolonization.[18] Not surprisingly, this tension between the promise of law and its potential for oppression is also alive within the construct of property itself, as Nicholas Blomley explains: "Property turns out to be a site for moral conflict and struggle. For activists, however, this struggle is not simply predicated on a condemnation of the negative side of property but a defense of property's potential and promise. This requires, of course, a reworking of what actually counts as property, such that the collective claim of local residents may also be acknowledged as 'property.'"[19]

It should be clear from our references to the scholarship of legal and political theorists that we are drawing on Western legal and political concepts and theories, as well as Indigenous legal scholarship and theory. What makes our proposed critical Indigenous feminist property theory unique is that it has to be able to apply to historic and contemporary Indigenous law and to state law. Given that Canada is multi-juridical – that is, the physical geographic space of Canada is

---

16 See, generally, Audra Simpson and Andrea Smith, eds., *Theorizing Native Studies* (Durham, NC: Duke University Press, 2014).

17 Jack M. Balkin, "Critical Legal Theory Today," in *On Philosophy in American Law*, ed. Francis J. Mootz III (Cambridge: Cambridge University Press, 2008), 65.

18 Emily Snyder, Val Napoleon, and John Borrows, "Gender and Violence: Drawing on Indigenous Legal Resources," *UBC Law Review* 48, no. 2 (2015): 593.

19 Nicholas Blomley, *Unsettling the City: Urban Land and the Politics of Property* (New York: Routledge, 2004), 103; in Davies, *Property*, 127.

filled with Indigenous legal orders operating simultaneously alongside civil law and common law, an Indigenous legal theory must account for and work with these overlapping legal orders.

B. Parameters of the Theory

Our goal with this chapter is to consider how Indigenous peoples might work towards the development of a critical Indigenous feminist property theory that can accommodate and make explicit the transformation of legal and political regimes for real property on reserve. It is crucial to be explicit about Indigenous laws and open to critical discussion and debate. Many questions need to be asked when developing a critical Indigenous feminist property theory. For example: What political ideology and assumptions are contained in ideas about property? What are the potential immediate and long-term social and political changes that may result from adopting Western property constructs? Do various property constructs further or inhibit the larger Indigenous political project, including the revitalization and rebuilding of Indigenous legal orders?

With all of the foregoing questions, the question of how property is gendered needs to be considered. For example, what gendered ideologies and assumptions are contained in ideas about property? In what ways are people affected differently by property practices because of gender? Too often discussions about gender are confined to "women's issues." However, we understand women's experiences, particularly Indigenous women's experiences with state law and Indigenous law, to operate far beyond issues such as matrimonial real property, status, and violence. Furthermore we contend that "women's issues" should be of concern to all gendered citizens and that men should take responsibility for challenging male privilege as it operates in any legal tradition. This propensity to consider women only in relation to "women's issues" is common in discussions about Indigenous laws. Moreover, thinking about gender should move beyond the gender binary of man/ woman and should include all gendered subjects.

We want to move beyond deconstructing property to instead offer a framework for creating another way through which to conceive and critique property. In doing so, we are not trying to go back in time to undo history or to return to some sort of "authentic" Indigenous notion of property. Glorifying and reifying romanticized interpretations of the past will not help to practically understand today's (or historical) lived realities, as such an approach negates the challenges that Indigenous societies, like all societies, face regarding conflict and power dynamics.

As such, we present eleven principles of a critical Indigenous feminist property theory.

First, a critical Indigenous feminist property theory begins with recognizing that Indigenous peoples had and have legal orders that have not gone anywhere, but exist, albeit in incomplete form, in Canada and elsewhere around the globe. Within the diversity of Indigenous legal orders are laws regarding the relationships between people, people and land, people and resources, and people and non-human life forms. As set out above, it is possible to substantively articulate and restate Indigenous law accessibly and coherently in the present day and to identify legal principles that may be applied to property on reserve. We suggest that a critical Indigenous feminist property theory must rest on this foundation.

Second, a useful critical Indigenous feminist property theory must include an acknowledgment that Indigenous law (as with all law) is not perfect or static, but at its best is legitimated by valid collaborative processes that can recognize human dignity and agency. These collaborative processes must be attentive to gendered and other systemic power imbalances that operate within settler and Indigenous contexts. Indigenous law is constituted by and constitutes the political forces in Indigenous society and its continuing efficacy and legitimacy in the face of everyday human contestations, requires ongoing critical challenge and critical analysis regarding gender, power and privilege, and wealth and class. The embrace of such challenge, no matter the methodology chosen to work with Indigenous law, requires the incorporation of two measures: (1) the transparency of legal interpretations and their underlying assumptions, and (2) the systematic referencing of the sources of legal knowledge so as to create spaces for informed debate, serious engagement, and shared public intellectual life.[20]

Third, measures or standards must be created to determine whether and how contemporary legal institutions and law undermine or maintain the historic legal order, and to generate critical conversations and informed decision-making about consequences, impacts, and necessity. To not engage in such conversations is to continue with the usually invisible undermining and possible distortion of Indigenous law and its potential efficacy in current application. A critical Indigenous feminist property theory must embrace and deal with the contradictions that have material consequences, including those that arise from

---

20 Hadley Friedland and Val Napoleon, "Gathering the Threads: Developing a Methodology for Researching and Rebuilding Indigenous Legal Traditions," *Lakehead Law Journal* 1, no. 1 (2015–16): 16.

conceptions of land on reserve and Western conceptions of private property. There are potential intellectual processes within Indigenous law to reason through and manage such tensions. In other words, the task is to find internal ways of legitimately reconciling the contradictions, or Indigenous law will continue to be broken and thereby diminished.

Fourth, one of the promises of law, especially in historic decentralized legal orders, is that full participation of individual and collective agents builds and rebuilds citizenries from the ground up through what James Tully calls civic practice.[21] He writes, "Civic empowerment and enchantment do not come from grand narratives of universal progress but from praxis – actual participation in civic activities with others where we become the citizens we can be."[22] Indeed, what can be more powerful in the restatement and renaissance of Indigenous law than the serious and sustained engagement with it that created law in the first place?[23] Civic participation must purposefully include women, people who are trans, and people with non-binary gender identities.

Fifth, as Borrows has effectively argued, that are a number of sources of Indigenous law[24] (as with all law) including, as Napoleon has argued elsewhere, everyday practice.[25] There are also ways that law and legal decisions are recorded as precedent and are expressed, including as explained earlier, in oral histories and stories, songs, dance, art, and performance. A critical Indigenous feminist property law theory should be grounded in and responsive to the ways that law is expressed and recorded, in order to generate a public, shared resource that will enable citizens to validate contemporary interpretations and challenge legal reasoning through legitimate and constructive processes. This theoretical approach is also attentive to ensuring that legal resources created and held by women and those with non-binary gender identities are valued and understood as integral to the vitality and usefulness of a legal order.

---

21 James Tully, *Public Philosophy in a New Key: Imperialism and Civic Freedom* (Cambridge: Cambridge University Press, 2008), 2:308.

22 Tully, *Public Philosophy*.

23 Jutta Brunnée and Stephen J. Toope, *Legitimacy and Legality in International Law* (Cambridge: Cambridge University Press, 2010), 8, discussing law in an international law context.

24 John Borrows, *Canada's Indigenous Constitution* (Toronto: University of Toronto Press, 2010).

25 Val Napoleon, Angela Cameron, Colette Arcand, and Dahti Scott, "Where Is the Law in Restorative Justice?" in *Aboriginal Self-Government*, ed. Yale Belanger, 3rd ed. (Saskatoon: Purich, 2008), 348. The sources of law that Borrows identifies include sacred law, natural law, deliberative law, positivistic law, and customary law.

Sixth, all law is constantly recreated, adapted, and refined through the engagement of citizens in everyday life. According to Borrows, the importance of such dynamism is that it allows the law to exist as a living tree, in the present as required by contemporary life and context.[26] The opposite of law as a living tree is what Borrows calls (ab)originalism or the retrospective treatment of law where original meanings and interpretations are sought from the past and brought forward in their entirety for application to present cases.[27] While Borrows is applying this analysis to Aboriginal and treaty rights, we contend that such an analytical approach is necessary for Indigenous law in order to prevent fundamentalist trends in Indigenous law – particularly where sexual orientation and sexism are concerned.[28] A critical Indigenous feminist property law theory should be alert to the possibility of fundamentalism when it is applied to the operation and theorizing of Indigenous law.

Seventh, as demonstrated in the short example of Tsimshian property theory below, law is an institution and is integral to other governing and administrative institutions, as with any society. Just as one cannot imagine the operation and management of Canadian law without the full gamut of institutions such as courts, law enforcement, legislative assemblies, and so on, it is just as important to consider historic and contemporary legal institutions through which Indigenous law operates. These Indigenous institutions, their arrangements, and functions are the form through which law is acted on – and this means that they are sites of power, authority, and potential exclusion. Questions about who is able to (and actually does) participate, about whose voices are heard, and where power is located are constantly necessary. Where property is concerned, there are important questions with material results about who makes decisions about when and where people can live, who has access to resources, among others, and these must not be allowed to become invisible. Communities are complex and they can be oppressive, as we have argued earlier. Therefore a critical Indigenous feminist property theory must be attuned and reflexive insofar as these power dynamics of inclusion and exclusion are concerned, especially in

---

26 John Borrows, "(Ab)originalism and Canada's Constitution," *Supreme Court Law Review* (2nd) 58 (2012): 353.

27 Borrows, "(Ab)originalism," 358.

28 Joyce Green, "Cultural and Ethnic Fundamentalism: The Mixed Potential for Identity, Liberation, and Oppression" (Scholar Series delivered at the Saskatchewan Institute of Public Policy, University of Regina, 18 November 2003), http://www.publications.gov.sk.ca/details.cfm?p=11972; see also Braden Hill, "Searching for Certainty in Purity: Indigenous Fundamentalism," *Nationalism and Ethnic Politics* 20, no. 1 (2014): 10.

the transformation of historic institutions and with the creation of new laws (i.e., the *First Nations Land Management Act* [*FNLMA*]).[29]

Eighth, we understand law and property as essentially relational. If we apply a relational lens to a critical Indigenous feminist property theory, then the definition of Indigenous property will "reside within the collective itself" while at the same time providing protection against the collective.[30] Here we rely on Nedelsky, who does not juxtapose property rights against individual rights of equality, individual freedom, or collective freedom. Rather, she argues for the "ongoing collective formulation of individual rights in a political culture that respects both democratic decision making and individual freedom and that recognizes the need to sustain the inevitable tension between them."[31] The task, then, for a critical feminist theory of Indigenous property is, as Nedelsky suggests, to examine ways to maintain the necessary tension between the individual rights of a property holder along with the collective rights of the community or larger society, as well as to look for collective processes through which individual rights are understood and arranged.[32]

Ninth, a critical Indigenous feminist property theory must be able to comprehend Indigenous legal orders in their entirety – complete with laws of force and all that they entail, and along with the future relationship between Indigenous law and Canadian law. Napoleon and Friedland have written about the importance of comprehending a legal order in its entirety, including its laws of force, which for Indigenous peoples have been monopolized by the state.[33] Even if laws of force are delegated to the criminal law of Canada (or other areas of law) conceptually, it is our position that a legal order is incomplete without them, and this perpetuates an incomplete understanding by the citizens of that legal order. Hence, the forced colonial delegation of laws of force must be explicitly factored into the efficacy of Indigenous law today in the management of property on reserve.

Tenth, historically, accountability in legal orders, such as the Tsimshian, was diffused through the entire legal order. Today, as a result of the fracturing of the larger legal orders, as described earlier, political and legal accountability has been undermined. The questions for

---

29 *First Nations Land Management Act*, SC 1999, c 24 [*FNLMA*].
30 Jennifer Nedelsky, *Law's Relations: A Relational Theory of Self, Autonomy, and Law* (Oxford: Oxford University Press, 2011), 95.
31 Nedelsky, *Law's Relations*, 96.
32 Nedelsky, *Law's Relations*, 96.
33 Val Napoleon and Hadley Friedland, "Indigenous Legal Traditions: Roots to Renaissance," in *Oxford Handbook on Criminal Law*, ed. Markus D. Dubber and Tatjana Hörnle, 225–47 (Oxford: Oxford University Press, 2014).

a critical Indigenous feminist property theory are about how such accountability is maintained today and whether there is an absence or gaps in accountability, and how might this might affect the management of property on reserve. A critical Indigenous feminist property theory is a way to explore the conditions that create conflicts and to consider strategies for more effective conflict management, despite the constraints created by colonial damage to historic legal orders.

Finally, Balkin has observed that critical legal theories should themselves be critically assessed.[34] We take this to mean that an effective critical Indigenous feminist property theory must be reflexive and understand that its value, as with law, is a political one, and while there are "demands that legal institutions and professional culture should work to restrain the arbitrary and unjust exercise of power ... we should build, preserve and protect legal and social institutions to that end."[35] A critical Indigenous feminist property theory, then, should seek to protect Indigenous legal and social institutions, while seeking to ensure that Indigenous law fulfils the promise of law.

C. Applying Critical Indigenous Feminist Property Theory

There are conceptual difficulties in imagining how Indigenous law applies to reserves in particular, given that they do not derive from within Indigenous peoples' own legal orders and laws. Giving up on Indigenous laws, though, on the premise of incommensurability, undermines the ability of Indigenous law to change or be applicable to everyday human problems. For the purposes of this chapter and the exploration of how Indigenous theory might be applied to real property on reserve (and potentially to other matters), there is much to learn from the actual practice of Indigenous law.[36] One can learn about Indigenous law in many ways, including from how people act on legal norms in their relationships and interactions, decision-making, and actions. Other analytical questions[37] that help to discern Indigenous law might include:

---

34 Balkin, "Critical Legal Theory Today," 75.
35 Balkin, "Critical Legal Theory Today," 75.
36 Napoleon et al., "Where Is the Law in Restorative Justice?" 348. See, e.g., Napoleon and Friedland, "From Roots to Renaissance," where Napoleon has previously dealt with incommensurability (239).
37 As a practice note, we are not suggesting that these analytical questions be posed to communities, but rather that they are applied to the structuring of the research and its findings.

- How have the legal order and laws developed over time?
- What do people recognize and treat as law through their social practices?[38]
- What are the intellectual and reasoning processes necessary for understanding and applying Indigenous law?
- What internal contradictions and tensions emerge?
- How was conflict managed historically? How have these practices changed? What are the implications of these changes for the group's internal power dynamics, relationships, and roles and responsibilities?
- What is the function of real property constructs in this legal order?

Ultimately, these inquiries inform how Indigenous law can be applied to the management of real property on reserve as well as to other human problems and community issues. More recently, Friedland and Napoleon developed a four-phase Indigenous legal methodology for the substantive articulation and restatement of Indigenous law.[39] The phases of this Indigenous law methodology are (1) development of community-specific research questions; (2) story/case analysis;[40] (3) creation of a framework with a societal primer, synthesis, and preliminary legal theory;[41] and (4) implementation, application, and critical evaluation.[42] Since ideally practice should inform theory, the Friedland-Napoleon methodology has promise for Indigenous communities that want to explore a practical and critical application of Indigenous law to questions about property on reserve. Key within this

---

38 See Brian Z. Tamanaha, "A Non-Essentialist Version of Legal Pluralism," *Journal of Law in Society* 27, no. 2 (2000): 319–20.

39 Friedland and Napoleon, "Gathering the Threads." See also Napoleon and Friedland, "From Roots to Renaissance"; Val Napoleon and Hadley Friedland, "An Inside Job: Engaging with Indigenous Legal Traditions through Stories," *McGill Law Journal* 64, no. 4 (2016): 725.

40 This phase involves collecting publicly available stories, oral histories, and other materials that are relevant to the identified research questions from each Indigenous community.

41 The very basic societal primer sets out the historic and contemporary political order and the social and legal structure, so that the logic and aspirations of the laws may be discerned. This phase also produces a specific body of law from each legal order synthesized into a framework of legal processes, decision makers, legal responses, obligations, substantive and procedural rights, and guiding principles. This restatement of law is developed in collaboration with the community and remains with the community for further use, application, and refinement.

42 Phase four involves the communities taking the synthesized body of law and applying it to the issues the communities have identified.

methodology are the dual requirements for transparency of reasoning and interpretive processes, and the consistent citing of sources, be they interviews, discussion groups, or oral and written stories, in order to foster respectful debate and engagement.[43]

Possible starting places for research questions related to property might be:

- How did people in this legal order make decisions or resolve problems about where to live, access resources, and travel in their territories and beyond?
- How did people in this legal order resolve conflicts about living areas, access to resources, and travel in their territories and beyond?
- How did families respond to marriage (formal and informal), marriage break-ups, responsibilities to children, and separate living arrangements?

Here we aim to focus on phase one, developing research questions, to demonstrate how gaps related to gender in research on Indigenous law and housing on reserve can start to be addressed with critical Indigenous feminist property theory. Since gender is central to our concern with Indigenous law and with property, questions about gender are an integral part of developing research questions and carrying out research projects.[44] Snyder argues that by gendering Indigenous laws (and legal research), the shift is from a focus on learning set rules based on the all too frequently universalized Indigenous male subject to a more dynamic focus on legal processes, reasoning, and interpretation – in a way that is attentive to power and gender.[45] Snyder suggests intertwining the following questions, for example, with the questions above:

- How do gendered power dynamics shape Indigenous legal interpretations?
- What are the Indigenous legal principles concerning gender?
- What assumptions are being made about the ways that gendered subjects engage with Indigenous law, and why?
- How are Indigenous laws gendered?

43 Napoleon and Friedland, "Inside Job."

44 Emily Snyder, *Gender, Power, and Representations of Cree Law* (Vancouver: UBC Press, 2018); see Snyder, "Indigenous Feminist Legal Theory," *Canadian Journal of Women and the Law* 26, no. 2 (2014): 365, for a discussion about Indigenous feminist legal theory.

45 Snyder, *Gender, Power, and Representations of Cree Law.*

- And specifically we are applying these questions to ask, How are Indigenous property laws gendered?[46]

III. Housing on Reserve: Community Case Studies

Four small Indigenous communities from northwestern British Columbia were selected for the case studies. The three communities of Metlakatla, located off the coast from Prince Rupert, and Kitselas and Kitsumkalum, located inland along the Skeena River, are part of the Tsimshian nation. The fourth community, Lheidli T'enneh, located in north central British Columbia near Prince George, is part of the Carrier (*Dakelh*) nation. It is noteworthy that the interviews were done in these communities in 2004, by Napoleon. The research was originally undertaken as the fieldwork portion of an earlier research project completed for the Law Commission of Canada. The aim of that research was to examine housing on reserve and the complexities of Indigenous property law. While gender was sometimes discussed, as illustrated below, it was not the focus of the interviews. However, the case studies are used here to illustrate the complexities of Indigenous property issues and the importance of robust Indigenous property theories, and to reflect on the importance of taking up gender in research on Indigenous property and land laws in all communities.

At the time the interviews were conducted, Lheidli T'enneh had already implemented its land management code under the *FNLMA*,[47] and Kitselas was still in the earlier stages of its land code development.[48] Metlakatla and Kitsumkalum were not considering development or implementation of a land code but were nonetheless dealing with the full range of complex and fraught issues relating to housing. A recent review of the four communities' websites, including telephone conversations with several of the key leaders, revealed few substantive changes to the original case study information.[49]

---

46 Emily Snyder, Lindsay Borrows, and Val Napoleon, with Hadley Friedland, *Mikomosis and the Wetiko: A Teaching Guide for Youth, Community, and Post-secondary Educators* (Victoria: Indigenous Law Research Unit, 2014), 20.

47 *Lheidli T'enneh Band Land Code* (2000, amended 2003) at s 28, http://www.lheidli.ca/Documents/LT_LandCode.pdf.

48 *Kitselas Reserve Lands Management Act*, 2005.

49 Interview of Steve Roberts, former chief of the Kitsumkalum First Nation, by Val Napoleon, June 2014; interview of Harold Leighton, former chief of the Metlakatla First Nation, by Val Napoleon, June 2014.

A. Shared Issues

Many First Nations struggle with debt, including housing-related debt. The defining feature of reserve land under the *Indian Act* is that it is communally held by the band,[50] and that individual band members have no right to the land, subject to certain exceptions.[51] Thus the general rule is that there is no individual possession in reserve lands unless there has been issued a Certificate of Possession (CP) (i.e., not ownership) to an Indian, pursuant to section 20 of the *Indian Act*.[52] The issue of custom allotments of land is highly political, because their creation lies in the gift by the band council. As a result, custom allotments can also be taken away under section 18(2) and under other sections without having clear and non-discretionary laws on compensation. This issue raises many questions, including whether a band council, since it has a fiduciary duty to the band,[53] ought to be allotting land to individuals, since that diminishes the property of the band as a whole – arguably, property that the band as a fiduciary should be protecting.[54] Further, if such an allotment is created, questions arise about the possible terms of band expropriation and about how any arising disputes are dealt with.

Although reserve land is communally held, housing plans vary from reserve to reserve. However, it is common for bands to borrow money through arrangements with Indigenous and Northern Affairs Canada (INAC) and the Canada Mortgage and Housing Corporation (CMHC)[55] to build houses on reserve. The recipient band member who obtains the house agrees to repay the band for the amount borrowed to build the

---

50 See *Indian Act*, RSC 1985, c I-5 (scheme under which reserve lands held in common are individuated at ss 20–8, 58).

51 *Joe v Findlay* (1981), 122 DLR (3d) 377 (BCCA). This proposition was affirmed at 380.

52 See Tom Flanagan and Christopher Alcantara, "Individual Property Rights on Canadian Indian Reserves," *Public Policy Sources* 60 (2002): 3. Some bands refuse to use the Certificate of Possession system for allotting band lands, while others use certificates for all land allotments at 7.

53 *Westbank Indian Band v Normand*, 1993 CarswellBC 902, [1993] BCWLD 2698 (BCSC).

54 *Fales v Wohlleben Estate*, [1977] 2 SCR 302, (*sub nom. Fales v Canada Permanent*) 70 DLR (3d) 257.

55 Canada Mortgage Housing Corporation, "Direct Lending" (2017), *First Nation Communities*, online: https://www.cmhc-schl.gc.ca/en/first-nation/financial -assistance/non-profit/direct-lending.cfm (site discontinued). "Band Councils or eligible sponsors have a choice to finance their project through Direct Lending with CMHC, with an Aboriginal Capital Corporation, where applicable, or through Approved Lenders."

house. The band holds the CP or interest in the house until the debt is paid in full, at which time a CP or other form of acknowledgment is issued to the member owner by the band. While many people refer to these housing debts as mortgages, they are in fact loans for which the band as a whole is liable. When band members fail to make their monthly payments, the band accrues the debt, which can extend to many millions of dollars. First Nations respond to the non-payment of members in a variety of ways.

Generally problems relating to real property on reserve are contextu- alized within a larger colonial and heteropatriarchal frame of structural power imbalances and economic disparity. Ongoing and sedimented conflicts have arisen from, among other things, disputes over land-use planning and zoning, resource use, surrender, leasing, expropriation, matrimonial property division, transfers, and inheritance.[56] This over- all situation has been compounded by many decades of bureaucratic obstacles and delays created by the *Indian Act*,[57] which have frustrated the local efforts of many First Nations (i.e., Indian bands) to manage reserve property.[58] However, added to the mix of conflicts are a number of much more practical and immediate considerations, including lim- ited reserve land bases, growing populations, limited housing, distance from the market economy, and deeply rooted social dysfunction.

While the current reserve system has created massive problems for Indigenous peoples – financial and otherwise – there are widely held assumptions that many of these problems are the result of bureaucratic ineptitude or lack of individual control over real property interests.[59]

---

56 Department of Indian Affairs and Northern Development, "Evaluation of DI- AND's Lands Management Program," by Beverly Clarkson, Project 94/16, 1997, Ihttp://dsp-psd.pwgsc.gc.ca/Collection/R3-4-1997E.pdf. In 1997 there were 614 Indian bands and 2,366 reserves totalling 2.7 million hectares at 2.

57 *Indian Act*, RSC 1985, c I-5.

58 The colonially created, elected entity called a band bears no relationship to the larger Indigenous society or to its own systems of governance, land ownership or manage- ment, law, or citizenship. However, the terms *Indian* and *band* will be used herein when referring to peoples or bands directly as per the *Indian Act*. The term *First Nation* is now more commonly employed instead of *Indian Band* and, where appropriate, this term will be used. The broader term *Aboriginal*, inclusive of Indian, Inuit, and Métis, will be used when references concern the *Canadian Constitution Act, 1982*. Otherwise, when not referring to a specific Indigenous society, in which case we will use their name (e.g., Cree), we will use the commonly accepted international term of Indigenous. See *Constitution Act, 1982* being Schedule B to the *Canada Act 1982* (UK), 1982, c 11.

59 See, e.g., Canada, Senate, Standing Senate Committee on Human Rights, *A Hard Bed to Lie In: Matrimonial Real Property on Reserve* (November 2003). These issues and conflicts, particularly those relating to marital property, have generated many reports and studies over the years.

In the interests of practically dealing with the real issues of economic disparity and development, and in response to the constraints regarding land management in the *Indian Act*, Indigenous peoples influenced the national agenda to create legislative initiatives such as the *FNLMA* and more recent legislation: the *Family Homes on Reserves and Matrimonial Interests or Rights Act*.[60] These legal mechanisms have created ways in which individuals can exercise control over real property interests on reserve – from maintaining basic restrictions on alienation of real property on reserve to allowing alienation under stringent circumstances.[61] Most of the *FNLMA* is directly related to drafting and implementing the reserve land codes. Title to reserve lands remains with the federal Crown and is "reserved" for Indians for the use and benefit of the band.[62]

The *FNLMA* does require participating First Nations to address matrimonial real property in a way that does not discriminate on the basis of gender. Those that have not enacted matrimonial real property codes will now fall under the regime of the *Family Homes on Reserves and Matrimonial Interests or Rights Act*.[63] However, this legislative change is also contested. As Egan and Place argue, there is broad agreement among Indigenous women about the need to address this property gap, which they see as resulting from the imposition of colonial laws and governance structures, but there are very different ideas about how they should be resolved.[64] For example, Joan Jack bluntly argues that the Act creates a slippery slope to privatizing reserve land that is "not about giving people rights, it's about money. Because there's no money coming from

---

60 *Family Homes on Reserves and Matrimonial Interests or Rights Act*, SC 2013, c 20.

61 See, e.g., *Métis Settlement Amendment Act*, SA 2004, c 25; *Tlicho Self-Government Agreement*, SC 2005, c 1. But see *Nisga'a Final Agreement Act*, RSBC 1999, for the recent property decisions reached by Nisga'a Lisims Government under the authority of this Act at c 2; *Nisga'a Final Agreement Act*, RSC 2000 c 7. Essentially, on October 2010, the legislative body of Nisga'a Lisims Government unanimously passed the *Nisga'a Land Title Act*, *Nisga'a Property Law Act*, *Nisga'a Law and Equity Act*, and the *Nisga'a Partition of Property Act*. This new legislation is described as complementing "the *Nisga'a Landholding Transition Act* which was enacted in 2009 and which gives Nisga'a citizens the opportunity to own their residential properties in fee simple." See the Nisga'a Lisims Government website, https://www.nisgaanation.ca. For analysis, see Sari Graben, "Lessons for Indigenous Property Reform: From Membership to Ownership on Nisga'a Lands," *University of British Columbia Law Review* 47, no. 2 (2014): 399.

62 "First nation land continues to be land reserved for the Indians within the meaning of the Class 24 of section 91 of the *Constitution Act, 1867*." FNMLA at s 5(c).

63 *FNMLA*.

64 Egan and Place, "Minding the Gaps," 135.

the federal government for housing for infrastructure. So therefore they need to turn everything into (private) land so people can borrow money from the bank, build a house, build a driveway and the government doesn't have to pay for anything.... It's about assimilation."[65]

The contradiction is that while much attention is paid to formal equality between men and women in determinations of property control, there are troubling questions about gender and power that lead others to contest reform.[66] Community experience therefore raises a shared set of questions: What are the substantive and ideological results of the matrimonial real property provisions that are implemented by the communities?[67] What is the relationship between decisions regarding matrimonial real property and the experience of violence and power imbalances at the local level?[68] Are decisions based strictly on formal equality equitable if there are larger issues of violence and marginalization (i.e., economic disparity between Indigenous women and men or political marginalization of Indigenous women) that are not addressed? A number of research reports are helpful here. For example, Linda Archibald and Mary Crnkovich consider gender in northern Labrador.[69] Here the authors investigate how gender issues are hidden in policies on land claims and environmental assessment, and how implementation of these policies affect Inuit women.[70] Among other things, Archibald and Crnkovich recommend conducting a gender-based analysis of the federal land claims policy

---

65 Melissa Ridgen, "New Matrimonial Property Laws a Slippery Slope to Reserve Land for Sale," *APTN Investigates*, 14 January 2014, https://aptnnews .ca/2014/01/24/new-matrimonial-property-laws-slippery-slope-reserve-land-sale/.

66 See, e.g., Native Women's Association of Canada, "Bill S-2: Family Homes on Reserves & Matrimonial Interests or Rights Act," news release, 21 November 2011; Assembly of First Nations, British Columbia Regional Chief Jody Wilson-Raybould, "Bill S-2: Family Homes on Reserves & Matrimonial Real Interests or Rights Act" (address to the House of Commons Standing Committee on the Status of Women, 2 May 2013), http://www.afn.ca/uploads/files/13-05-02_rc_jody _wilson-raybould_on_s-2.pdf.

67 See also Judith F. Sayers and Kelly A. MacDonald, "A Strong and Meaningful Role for First Nations Women in Governance," in *First Nations Women, Governance and the Indian Act: A Collection of Policy Research Papers* (Ottawa: Research Directorate, Status of Women Canada, 2001), 1.

68 Snyder, Napoleon, and Borrows, "Gender and Violence."

69 Linda Archibald and Mary Crnkovich, *If Gender Mattered: A Case Study of Inuit Women, Land Claims and the Voisey's Bay Nickel Project* (Ottawa: Research Directorate, Status of Women, 1999).

70 See especially Isabel Altamirano-Jiménez, *Indigenous Encounters with Neoliberalism Place, Women, and the Environment in Canada and Mexico* (Vancouver: UBC Press, 2013).

and self-government policy that would include full participation of Indigenous women's organizations.[71] Further, they recommend that a gender-based analysis be conducted of all concluded land claims agreements and the Canadian Environmental Assessment Agency guidelines.[72] These are the kinds of questions raised by the work of engaging seriously with Indigenous law and in the development of Indigenous property theories attentive to critical Indigenous feminist property theories.

B. An Introduction to the Tsimshian Nation

There is evidence of Tsimshian material culture dating back over 5,000 years, and Tsimshian oral histories record broad chronological periods since the last Ice Age.[73] Tsimshian society has been described as having "ranked social order, hierarchical villages, and seasonal coast-to-interior mobility."[74] The enormous Tsimshian territory can be divided into three regions: northern, southern, and interior.[75] Metlakatla, Kitselas, and Kitsumkalum are northern Tsimshian with a political, legal, and social structure consisting of four "clans" – matrilineal and exogamous descent groups who share a common history.[76] These clans are *Laxskiik* (Eagle), *Laxgibuu* (Wolf), *Gispwudwada* (Killer Whale), and *Ganhada* (Raven). Within the clans are extended family groupings called "houses"

---

71 Archibald and Crnkovich, *If Gender Mattered*.
72 Archibald and Crnkovich, *If Gender Mattered*.
73 See, generally, Andrew R.C. Martindale and Susan Marsden, "Defining the Middle Period (3500 BP to 1500 BP) in Tsimshian History through a Comparison of Archaeological and Oral Records," *BC Studies* 138, no. 9 (2003): 20. There are, however, archaeological artefacts dating back to 9,000 BP in the coastal areas of Alaska and northern British Columbia. Viola E. Garfield, *Tsimshian Clan and Society*, University of Washington Publications in Anthropology 7, no. 3 (1939): 167.
74 Martindale and Marsden, "Defining the Middle Period," 34. See David J.W. Archer, "Village Patterns and the Emergence of Ranked Society in the Prince Rupert Area," in *Perspectives in Northern Northwest Coast Prehistory*, ed. Jerome C. Cybulski, 203–22, Mercury Series, Archaeological Survey of Canada Paper 160 (Hull, QC: Canadian Museum of Civilization, 2001), for a discussion about the development of a royal class among the Tsimshian. See also Gary Coupland, Andrew R.C. Martindale, and Susan Marsden, "Does Resource Abundance Explain Local Group Rank among the Coast Tsimshian?" in Cybulski, *Perspectives on Northern Northwest Coast Prehistory*, 203, 223.
75 Martindale and Marsden, "Defining the Middle Period," 20.
76 As would be the case with any society, this basic representation of the Tsimshian society is provided at the risk of oversimplifying the highly complex nature developed over many thousands of years.

in English, each with a head chief and a number of sub-chiefs.[77] The individuals in the extended family groupings are considered members of their mother's house under the head chief's name. Each head chief's name covers a particular territory, which the house owns according to Tsimshian law and usually contains watersheds, valleys, and mountain-sides, and for some, coastal regions.[78] The number of houses in a line-age may vary over time, as houses divide and amalgamate in order to maintain their population bases and fulfil their responsibilities to their kinship networks and territories. While a chief's name and territorial connections remain, despite contractions and expansions of the house, the efforts and behaviours of that name-holder cause an increase or decrease in status.[79] These territorial connections are maintained even when a house's membership is depleted, and it is intentionally sub-sumed by a larger, closely aligned, and related house of the same clan; when the house membership again increases, it may divide along origi-nal house lines with its lineages and territories intact. Political alliances and strategic cooperation were vital within non-state and decentralized societies such as the Tsimshian, as there were no centralized authorities or bureaucracies designated to take up the responsibilities of law and governance. This is exemplified by Viola Garfield: "A chief is the social and ceremonial figurehead of the tribe, but has very little formalized political power. He has no control over the property or lives of his tribes-men, but exerts his authority mainly through the prestige of his position and his own personality. The cooperation of strong leaders in the tribe is necessary to any real extension of his power."[80]

While it appears that there were fewer women head chiefs among the Tsimshian and Nisga'a than with the Gitksan, there are exceptions, and there are accounts of women rising to exert strong influence in the

---

77 Martindale and Marsden, "Defining the Middle Period." In addition to the houses and clans in the Tsimshian kinship system, the northern Tsimshian have a social and political affiliation called a "tribe," which correlates with the winter village sites located in Metlakatla Pass and on Kaien Island. Tribal affiliation cuts across the clans and is determined by the residency of a member's forebears in one of the ten historical winter villages. In the 1840s the amalgamation of two of the tribes reduced the number to nine. The north coast Tsimshian tribes are the Giluts'aaw̓, Gitnadoiks, Ginax'angiik, Gispaxlo'ots, Gitando, Gitlaan, Gitsiis, Gitwilgyoots, and Gitzaxłaał.

78 Martindale and Marsden, "Defining the Middle Period," 20–1.

79 See, generally, Susan Marsden and Robert Galois, "The Tsimshian, the Hudson's Bay Company, and the Geopolitics of the Northwest Coast Fur Trade, 1787–1840," *Canadian Geographer* 39, no. 2 (1995): 169; Garfield, *Tsimshian Clan and Society*, 180.

80 Garfield, *Tsimshian Clan and Society*, 182; Jo-Anne Fiske, "Colonization and the Decline of Women's Status: The Tsimshian Case," *Feminist Studies* 17, no. 3 (1991): 509.

kinship system, which was formally recognized in the feast hall. For example, "When the feast was given the positions were held by a brother and sister, the latter being the sub-chief. She, however, had quite over-shadowed her weaker brother and was the real leader in tribal affairs. Not to offend her, the host had her name called simultaneously with that of the head chief."[81] However, Jo-Anne Fiske argues that a "careful read-ing of the written record, published and unpublished reveals serious flaws in the commonly held assumptions of male precedence in Tsim-shian society."[82] According to Fiske, the fur trade enhanced the "noble born males" to the detriment of their female counterparts and women's abilities to own and manage property, resulting in increased social and political prerogatives for men and new assumptions about male stew-ardship and access to resources, and male authority and leadership.[83]

House membership guides house members' participation in the Tsim-shian kinship system and permits their access to the house's territories and resources. In addition, each house member fulfils important mul-tiple roles with reciprocal responsibilities to the houses of their father, spouse, grandparents, and children's spouses.[84] Historically marriages were arranged with careful consideration given to territory adjacency and location, trade, and political alliances. Strong marriage alliances were necessary to maintain the fabric of Tsimshian society.[85]

Each person's placement in the kinship system also arranges access opportunities to the house territories of her or his other kin. In other words, while economic and political considerations were important to marriage, so was clan exogamy,[86] because it created a dual kinship structure around each person. This meant that while each person is born into her or his mother's house group, her or his father is always from a house group of a different clan, and both the father's side and mother's side have distinct responsibilities to the individual.[87] For instance, if a person is injured, the father's side is responsible for determining liabil-ity and compensation.[88] Arguably one result of this system may have

---

81 Garfield, *Tsimshian Clan and Society*, 217.
82 Fiske, "Colonization and the Decline of Women's Status," 530–51.
83 Fiske, "Colonization and the Decline of Women's Status," 530.
84 See, generally, Richard Daly, "Pure Gifts and Impure Thoughts" (paper presented at the Ninth International Conference on Hunting and Gathering Societies, Heriot-Watt University Edinburgh, 2002).
85 Susan Marsden, "Adawx, Spanaxnox, and the Geopolitics of the Tsimshian," *BC Studies* 135 (2002): 108.
86 Garfield, *Tsimshian Clan and Society*, 231.
87 Marsden, "Adawx, Spanaxnox, and the Geopolitics of the Tsimshian," 108.
88 See James Andrew McDonald, *People of the Robin* (Edmonton: University of Alberta Press, 2003), 45: "In particular, the father's side is responsible for helping the child through life's critical times, including birth and death."

been to break up male power blocks in pre-contact Tsimshian society, although Tsimshian oral histories (*adawx*) still have accounts of collective male sexist oppression and male violence.[89]

Each house owns an *adawx*, a formal, collective, intellectual and legal institution that contains the origins and migrations of the kinship groups to their current territories, their explorations, the covenants they established with the land, songs, crests, and names that result from the spiritual connection between people and their land.[90] The recounting of the *adawx* at pole-raising feasts is a public formal legal event, and accountability is ensured because a speaker's version may be challenged and amended according to Tsimshian civil procedure in the feast hall.[91]

James McDonald insightfully describes the Tsimshian feast as an instrument of knowledge that constructs social reality.[92] The feast is also a legal event, in that house authorities are confirmed, important decisions are formally witnessed for legal precedent and memory, and the legal obligations regarding land, resources, and social structure of the house groups are fulfilled.[93] In other words, "feasting can generate an orthodoxy about the social world, as well as the competencies needed to live in it,"[94] and furthermore, as an instrument of knowledge, the feast

1 works to build the type of implicit consensus Bourdieu refers to as a homogenization of people's understanding and knowledge about their heritage which allows heritage practices to be immediately intelligible, foreseeable and potentially taken for granted as the "way things are";
2 inculcates in its practitioners durable dispositions and competencies that enable them to act as Tsimshians;

---

89 See generally, George F. MacDonald and John C. Cove, *Tsimshian Narratives 2: Trade and Warfare* (Ottawa: Canadian Museum of Civilization, 1987).
90 Marsden, "Adawx, Spanaxnox, and the Geopolitics of the Tsimshian," 102–3.
91 For an example of such challenges, see Margaret Anderson and Marjorie Halpin, eds., *Potlatch at Gitsegukla: William Beynon's 1945 Field Notebooks* (Vancouver: UBC Press, 2000), 174.
92 James McDonald, "Building a Moral Community: Tsimshian Potlatching, Implicit Knowledge and Everyday Experiences," *Cultural Studies* 9, no. 1 (1995): 125.
93 For a more detailed explanation of the feast, see also Val Napoleon, "Ayook: Gitksan Legal Order, Law, and Legal Theory" (PhD diss., University of Victoria, 2009), 4–10). The Gitksan, Tsimshian, and Nisga'a are closely related peoples forming the Tsimshian linguistic group.
94 McDonald, "Building a Moral Community," 134.

3 provides principles for a practical logic that generates further appropriate practices in the same and different contexts.[95]

The Tsimshian legal order included extensive property laws, which included the relationships, ownership, access, and management of houses that people built and resided in. We return to these laws governing property in section V.

C. Recent Village Histories

The contemporary Tsimshian nation comprises seven Tsimshian villages (*galts'ap*).[96] There is extensive intermarriage between people from the different Tsimshian villages, as well as with the other northwest peoples – the Gitksan, Nisga'a, Haisla, Wet'suwet'en, and Haida. Historically Tsimshian people frequently moved from one village to another along marriage and family lines, and still do for employment and education.

The Tsimshian established early trade with Russia and perhaps Asia before the mid-1700s. Later, settlers, missionaries, traders, and Indian agents disrupted the Tsimshian kinship system, the feast system, and Tsimshian society generally. For example, in 1834 the trade centre settlement of Fort Simpson was built at present-day Lax Kw'Alaams (formerly called Port Simpson).[97] Another example is that of Methodist minister William Duncan, who began his missionary work at Fort Simpson in 1857, but in 1862 he and 350 of his followers moved to one of the old Tsimshian winter village sites at Metlakatla Pass to establish the present-day community of Metlakatla.[98] Thirty years later in 1887, dissatisfied with federal and provincial government policy, Duncan and over 800 of his followers again moved, this time further north to establish New Metlakatla in Alaska.[99]

---

95 McDonald, "Building a Moral Community," 134.
96 The other Tsimshian villages are Lax Kw'Alaams, Kitasoo, Gitga'at, and Kitkatla. All are located along the north coast with traditional inland territories.
97 Susan Marsden, Margaret Seguin Anderson, and Deanna Nyce, "Tsimshian," in *Aboriginal Peoples of Canada: A Short Introduction*, ed. Paul R. Magosci 269–70 (Toronto: University of Toronto Press, 2002).
98 See Garfield, *Tsimshian Clan and Society*, 333. In the same year, crews from ships visiting from Victoria introduced smallpox; an estimated 500 people died in Port Simpson, while in Metlakatla only five deaths were reported. Anecdotally, it is alleged that, while Duncan publicly attributed the low number of deaths in Metlakatla to faith, the reality was that he inoculated people in Metlakatla with smallpox vaccine.
99 Garfield, *Tsimshian Clan and Society*.

When Lax Kw'Alaams was established as a trade centre, the northern Tsimshian house chiefs relocated there in order to participate in the lucrative economic activity.[100] At the time of writing, as a consequence of the Lax Kw'Alaams relocation and the Duncan-led exodus to Alaska, the present-day community of Metlakatla no longer has any resident high chiefs. This leaves it in the unenviable position of being a Tsimshian village consisting only of house members. In other words, the authority for the territories owned by the house groups that Metlakatla residents are members of is located primarily in Lax Kw'Alaams. In pre-contact times this would have been an entirely untenable situation, given the reciprocal economic obligations between the house chiefs and the members.

Inland, Kitsumkalum and Kitselas were often called the Freshwater Tsimshian, because they remained inland throughout the year, rather than wintering at Metlakatla Pass on the coast.[101] They were also called Canyon Tsimshian, because they were located at the canyons on the Kitsumkalum and Skeena Rivers.[102] Archaeological and ethnographic evidence show that the Kitselas people have occupied the Kitselas Canyon area for at least 5,000 years.[103] In the 1870s the fishing industry drew many families from Kitsumkalum and Kitselas to work in the fish canneries on the north coast.[104] As the fishing industry slowed during the 1960s, many of the families returned to their communities near the small city of Terrace, British Columbia.[105]

In 1987 a formal feast was held in Kitsumkalum after what James McDonald describes as a "hiatus of more than fifty years."[106] During this potlatch ban, some feasting business such as transferring chiefs' names continued, but this was conducted through different activities such as funeral memorials and "little suppers."[107] Former elected chief Mel Bevan described how, in Kitselas, the Tsimshian business was conducted surreptitiously at night on a house-to-house basis to avoid repercussions from the Indian agent.[108] Since public

---

100 Marsden and Galois, "The Tsimshian."
101 McDonald, *People of the Robin*, 8–9.
102 McDonald, *People of the Robin*, 7.
103 McDonald, *People of the Robin*, 7.
104 See James McDonald, "Cultivating in the Northwest: Gleaning the Evidence from the Tsimshian," in *Keeping It Living: Traditions of Plant Use and Cultivation on the Northwest Coast of North America*, ed. Douglas Deur and Nancy Turner (Vancouver: UBC Press, 2005), 240.
105 McDonald, "Cultivating in the Northwest."
106 McDonald, "Building a Moral Community," 131.
107 McDonald, "Building a Moral Community," 132.
108 Interview of Mel Bevan by Val Napoleon, 30 August 2004, Kitselas Lands and Resources Office, Terrace, BC.

restoration of the feast, Kitsumkalum members have conducted an ongoing "community-wide" discussion about Tsimshian forms of political and social organization, and their possible revival. However, for many reasons, there is no agreement to reorganize the band council structure to reflect historic Tsimshian political institutions, and this remains an internal source of tension for Kitsumkalum as well as for the other Tsimshian communities.[109]

1. KITSUMKALUM, KITSELAS, AND METLAKATLA TODAY

Metlakatla, Kitselas, Kitsumkalum, and the other four Tsimshian communities are recognized as bands under the *Indian Act*.[110] The Tsimshian are engaged in the B.C. Treaty Commission's treaty negotiation process,[111] but there have been serious internal disagreements about the legitimacy and authority of the centralized political representative, the Tsimshian Tribal Council.[112]

Metlakatla is a thirty-minute ferry ride from the small port city of Prince Rupert, BC. About 300 band members reside in Metlakatla, while another 300 or so live in Prince Rupert.[113] The remaining Metlakatla band members reside elsewhere, mainly in Vancouver, Seattle, and on Vancouver Island. Metlakatla successfully manages a range of economic initiatives, and through its own development corporation there are a number of small, independent businesses operating in the community.

Kitsumkalum is located immediately to the west of Terrace, with over 600 members. About 200 members reside on reserve, with the rest

---

109 See, e.g., interview of Alex Bolton by Val Napoleon, 31 August 2004, Kitsumkalum Treaty Office, Kitsumkalum, BC; interview of Steve Roberts by Val Napoleon, 31 August 2004, Kitsumkalum Band Office, Kitsumkalum, BC.

110 The larger Tsimshian nation is divided into seven *Indian Act* bands, each with its own elected band council.

111 As of writing, there are only three treaty areas in British Columbia: (1) 1899 *Treaty 8* in the northeast corner, (2) the fourteen small 1850–4 Douglas Treaties on Vancouver Island, and most recently, (3) the recent 2000 *Nisga'a Treaty* in the northwest.

112 See *Tsimshian Tribal Council v Metlakatla Indian Band* 2005 BCSC 1186, 2005 Carswell BC 1962. For the Tsimshian bands, the treaty process has been a regular roller-coaster ride of conflict and litigation. For a brief period, a separate Tsimshian umbrella organization was formed in opposition to the Tsimshian Tribal Council leadership, but they were unable to secure funding or recognition from external governments. However, since the Tsimshian Tribal Council constitution and bylaws actually prohibited member bands from opting out, there was no point in forming an alternative organization. Given this, Metlakatla, Gitgaat, Kitselas, Kitasoo, Lax Kw'Alaams, and Kitsumkalum initiated a successful legal action to be reinstated within the Tsimshian Tribal Council.

113 See Metkalka First Nation, http://www.metlakatla.ca.

living throughout B.C.[114] As in historic times, members from Kitsumkalum are closely connected to other Tsimshian communities through marriage.[115] Kitsumkalum has very successful businesses on reserve, which generate local economic and employment opportunities.

Kitselas has over 700 members, of which over 300 reside on four of seven small separate reserves. Part of the Kitselas reserve is adjacent to the south of Terrace, and a newer housing development area is located about sixteen kilometres to the east, near the Kitselas Canyon (only four families live at the Endudoon Reserve, about twenty kilometres west of Terrace, B.C., and one family still lives at Zymoetz Reserve).[116]

D. An Introduction to the Lheidli T'enneh Nation

There is less ethnographic material available about the Lheidli T'enneh, which translates as "people from where the rivers flow together."[117] The Lheidli T'enneh community is part of the larger Carrier (*Dakelh*) Nation of about 15,000 people. The Carrier or Dakelh language is part of the northern Athapaskan linguistic group, a branch of a larger linguistic group that range from the Yukon and Northwest Territories to the southern United States.[118] "Songs and stories as old as any spoken history accompanied these covenants [original ties to the land affirmed in the *bah'lhats* (potlatch)] – equivalent to today's legal contracts. These songs and stories were also memoirs of the land. They articulated a harmony with the teachings of our long ago ancestors."[119]

---

114   Kitsumkalum First Nation, "Traditional Use Study: Project End Report," 12, Kitsumkalum Treaty Office, Kitsumkalum, BC.

115   Interview with Laura Miller by Val Napoleon, 31 August 2004, Kitsumkalum Band Office, Kitsumkalum, BC.

116   Kitselas First Nation, "Traditional Use Study," 12.

117   Lheidli T'enneh Band, "Historic Summary," 2000, 1, Lheidli T'enneh Lands and Resources Office, Prince George, BC. However, there are a lot more materials about language and children's stories. See, e.g., A.G. Morice, "Notes: Archaeological, Industrial and Sociological, on the Western Denes, with an Ethnographical Sketch of the Same," (1893) Transactions of the Canadian Institute at Session 1892–3; Morice, *The History of the Northern Interior of British Columbia: Formerly New Caledonia 1600–1880,* 2nd ed. (Toronto: William Briggs, 1904); Morice, *The Great Déné Race: Administration of "Anthrops"* (St Gabriel-Mödling, Austria: Press of the Mechitharistes, 1906); J.B. Munro, "Language, Legends and Lore of the Carrier Indians" (PhD diss., University of Ottawa, 1945).

118   Suzanne Gessner and Gunnar Ólafur Hansson, "Anti-Homophony Effects in Dakelh (Carrier) Valence Morphology" (paper delivered at the 30th Annual Meeting of the Berkeley Linguistics Society, University of California Berkeley, 2004).

119   Carrier-Sekani Tribal Council, "A History of the Dakelh: A Dakelh Story for the New Millennium," 1, http://www.cstc.bc.ca/Dakelh%20history.htm (site discontinued).

1. LHEIDLI T'ENNEH VILLAGE HISTORY

The Lheidli T'enneh have lived in their territories in central B.C. for over 15,000 years. Each extended family was responsible for a specific territory called a *keyoh*.[120] The central institution for conducting political, economic, and legal business was the *bah'lhats* (potlatch).[121] Seasonal villages were established throughout the territories along lakes and rivers. Trade was conducted with neighbouring groups such as the Sekani to the north and the Shuswap to the south. "No one knows for sure who was the first European in the area. However, many people believe it was Alexander MacKenzie as he would most likely have traveled through this area on his overland journey from the East Coast to West Coast in 1763. He was, indeed, the first non-Aboriginal person to cross the Rocky Mountains into Central British Columbia. Aboriginal people, had, of course, traveled this route before, for MacKenzie used them as guides to help determine the route."[122]

The North West Company arrived in 1805 and built a trading post by 1807 at the junction of the Fraser and Nechako (*Nee Incha Koh*) Rivers.[123] As in other parts of Canada, the combined factors of the fur trade, disease, and settlement had massive impacts on the Lheidli T'enneh people. One of the village sites was located in Prince George and became the Fort George Reserve. This reserve was surrendered in 1912, and people were forcibly moved to the current Lheidli T'enneh reserve locations of South Shelly and North Shelly.[124]

---

120 Lheidli T'enneh Band, "Historic Summary," 2.
121 Lheidli T'enneh Band, "Historic Summary," 4. It is likely that this was a more recent developing influence from the west (e.g., Gitksan). While this does not undermine the validity of the *bah'lhats*, it does explain some of the variation of information on this topic provided in the interviews. See, e.g., Rick Krehbiel, "Lheidli T'enneh Land Management under the *Framework Agreement on First Nation Land Management*" (paper presented at the "Aboriginal Self-Government: What Does It Mean in Practice?" Canadian Bar Association Aboriginal Law Conference, Victoria, BC, 2002), 5. For a description of similar Gitksan intercultural influences on the Sekani, see also Guy Lanoue, *Brothers: The Politics of Violence among the Sekani of Northern British Columbia* (New York: Berg, 1992).
122 Lheidli T'enneh Band, "Historic Summary," 2–3.
123 Lheidli T'enneh Band, "Historic Summary," 2–3.
124 See Krehbiel, "Lheidli T'enneh Land Management," 4. Lheidli T'enneh was formerly called the Shelly Band. A specific claim has been filed, but according a report by Chuck Strahl, the former minister of AANDC, that claim is no longer active. See Canada, Indian Specific Claims Commission, *Report on Plans and Priorities, 2008–2009* by the Minister of Indian Affairs and Northern Development and Federal Interlocutor for Métis and Non-Status Indians (Ottawa: IANC, 2009).

2. LHEIDLI T'ENNEH TODAY

Lheidli T'enneh has about 300 members, with equal numbers living on two reserves, and there are a number of members in the nearby mid-sized city of Prince George, B.C. At the time of the field work, Lheidli T'enneh was unaffiliated – that is, not a part of the Carrier Sekani Tribal Council. The band is governed by a chief and council in accordance with section 74 of the *Indian Act*.

Lheidli T'enneh is at Stage 5 in its negotiations for a treaty under the B.C. Treaty Commission regime.[125] The Community Treaty Council comprises representatives from fourteen families, in addition to formal designated seats for elders, youth, and the band council.[126] The treaty negotiations are based on what is described as a "pragmatic five-tier land and natural resources model involving preservation of the existing reserve land base, acquisition of additional treaty settlement lands, and varying forms of access to special management areas."[127] Lheidli T'enneh is claiming Aboriginal title to about 4.6 million hectares of provincial Crown lands that extend west to the Alberta border.

E. *What the Communities Said*

A number of themes emerge from the community interviews. While there are many similarities among the four communities, there are also marked distinctions in how each community approaches real property issues on reserve. In this part, we will first discuss the common themes that came to light in the interviews done by Napoleon, and we will then examine the key differences among the communities. Finally, we consider what lessons might be distilled from the interviews, to inform a broader level of abstraction with possible application for other Indigenous peoples.

Before turning to the interviews, it is helpful to note the shifting understanding of *culture* in the Indigenous discourse, which ranges "from a 'reified notion of a fixed and stable set of beliefs, values and institutions' to a 'flexible repertoire of practices and discourses created through historical processes of contestation over signs and meanings,'"[128] According to Rebecca Tsosie, "Contemporary scholars

---

125 See Rick Krehbiel, "BC Treaty Negotiations and the Framework Agreement on First Nation Land Management" (unpublished, 2004).

126 Krehbiel, "Lheidli T'enneh Land Management," 5.

127 Krehbiel, "Lheidli T'enneh Land Management," 4.

128 Rebecca Tsosie, "Reclaiming Native Stories: An Essay on Cultural Appropriation and Cultural Rights," *Arizona State Law Journal* 24 (2002): 300.

acknowledge that culture is fundamentally tied to systems of power. The maintenance of relations of power may depend upon the dominant group's ability to exercise control over specific cultural meanings. Similarly, a group's resistance to coercive power (e.g., colonialism) may depend upon adherence to another set of cultural meanings."[129]

Given Tsosie's observations, it is not surprising that the most significant theme is contestation about the relevance, function, and definitions of *tradition* and *culture* in "modern" times. It is our preference to avoid creating or perpetuating the unproductive dichotomy between what is authentic or traditional from what is modern. Tsimshian and Dakelh peoples have their own forms of modernity deriving from their historic and current experiences. It is our preference to avoid, wherever possible, using the language of "culture" in a wholesale and indiscriminate way that flattens and obscures societies complete with economic, social, political, and legal orders. However, interviewees from all communities described general internal discord about what *tradition* and *culture* mean and how they are applied to contemporary issues and decisions. Community members also disagreed about their own Indigenous legal orders and law and with historic practices, roles, and responsibilities. Most often these differences were about individual and collective responsibilities, economic development, governance, and conflict management.

A note of caution is warranted. Discord over the modern interpretation of societal and legal norms illustrate just how alive and important they are in everyday life. Internal tensions and disputes remain unexamined too often and are interpreted as indicators of societal erosion or disintegration. In contrast, we believe that these case studies reveal the extent to which people are attempting to reconcile historic legal practices with current demands and problems. The community reality is far more complex and nuanced than descriptors such as "loss of culture" reflect or capture. A more accurate and politically useful perspective is to consider that the discord indicates how deeply people care about political, legal, social, and economic matters. Seen from this angle, such discord is essential for understanding and creating meaning today – and is an integral part of citizenry engagement. We will come back to this point a little later.

The clearest examples of internal political discord revealed in the interviews are housing and issues with potentially serious financial implications for the communities. Given the small size of these

---

129 Tsosie, "Reclaiming Native Stories," 311.

communities, the extended families, and close connections, these disputes are deeply felt. No one has any distance from the disputes, and a conflict can last for generations if left unresolved or managed.

As explained earlier, the basic situation is that the band obtains loans from INAC and Canada Mortgage and Housing Corporation (CMHC) in order to build houses on reserve. Each band member must repay the band for the cost of building her or his house. As with a mortgage held by a bank, the band holds the CP or interest in the house until the debt is paid. These individual housing loans are usually called mortgages, but they are, in fact, part of a larger loan owed by the band to the lender. The four communities respond in different ways when band members fail to make their monthly payments, which we explain below.

1. SIMILARITIES AMONG THE COMMUNITIES

Obviously, the bands' property and housing decisions derive from a mix of social values regarding relationships and responsibilities. The interim band manager for Kitsumkalum, Laura Miller, explained that when band members fail to make their payments, there is a collective response in which the extended family and community meet with the non-paying band member to investigate the problem.[130] Kitsumkalum also employs other strategies, such as deliberately hiring band members who are in arrears and deducting payments from their paycheques. Kitsumkalum's housing debt is negligible, because while only a few band members are in arrears, the majority make their payments regularly. So far, the band has had to buy back only two houses for non-payment and only because CMHC threatened legal action. The members involved with these two buybacks must reimburse the band before they are eligible to apply for new housing. Miller admits that despite the band's efforts, some families are homeless. She strongly believes that the community is responsible to provide housing so that the children will have better lives.[131]

Miller also sees that housing problems may be exacerbated in the future because of an increasing on-reserve population. Apparently, in previous years, there were over seventy people on the Kitsumkalum's housing waiting list,[132] which increased to hundreds, many of whom are new band members as a result of the 1985 C-31 amendment to the *Indian Act*.[133] The Kitsumkalum Band expects to build forty houses per

---

130   Interview with Miller (Kitsumkalum uses CPs for all real property transactions on reserve at 4).
131   Interview with Miller.
132   Interview with Miller.
133   *An Act to Amend the Indian Act*, RSC 1985, c 27.

year, but it will take years and many millions of dollars to catch up to the waiting lists.

Miller is concerned that the continuing influx of new members will be paralleled by a decreased sense of collective responsibility in the community. She explains that many new members move from the city where they felt left out and suffered a lot, and now they bring "bad" attitudes to Kitsumkalum. She wonders whether this is perhaps because the new members did not experience the earlier hard times in Kitsumkalum, when people survived by sharing everything – moose, fish, and other seafood – and explains that the new (C-31) members advocate excluding newer members along with non-members who are married in. According to Miller, "Those that were excluded, are now the excluders."[134]

Alex Bolton explains that strong families at Kitsumkalum have worked out property, marital, and inheritance issues, so there are fewer internal conflicts over housing, or residential and commercial land use.[135] According to Bolton, the historic Kitsumkalum community ethic is that of the "common bowl," with collective management of land and resource use. However, he explains that the younger people do not know the Tsimshian system, because they were brought up under the DIA[136] system, and this causes local problems. As a result, Bolton observes that people are not very interested in changing the governance structure, because they are comfortable and familiar with the "DIA mentality."[137]

In contrast, the elected (now former) chief of Kitsumkalum Steve Roberts suggests that it is the Tsimshian hereditary system that is problematic, because it is about promoting cultural purity, which he sees as destroying the community. As he explains, "People are judged according to whether they can speak the language; the purist tries to exclude non-*smalgyex* speakers."[138] According to Roberts, historic Tsimshian values are too difficult to apply to modern lives, because people are "all over the map" – literally and metaphorically.[139] He sees the oral histories and laws as exclusive, and while recognition of the Tsimshian system will be important in the future, "we don't want to paint ourselves into a corner about who we will accept."[140]

---

134 Interview with Miller, 3.
135 Interview with Bolton, 2.
136 Many people still refer to AANDC as DIA or INAC. Where people refer to DIA or INAC, we will include those acronyms.
137 Interview with Bolton, 3.
138 Interview with Roberts (*Smalgyex* is the Tsimshian language, 2).
139 Interview with Roberts.
140 Interview with Roberts.

In Metlakatla the housing debt caused by members' failure to pay the band for housing is about $300,000.[141] On two previous occasions, the Metlakatla Band used its own economic revenues to pay off band housing debts,[142] and housing is described by one Metlakatla member as "a big headache."[143] The Metlakatla Band Council has established a housing committee that is responsible for dealing with housing matters and delinquent members who do not maintain their monthly payments.[144] According to Harold Leighton, the housing committee is supposed to deal with non-payments, but they do not want to evict anyone. From his perspective, kinship relationships get in the way of collecting payments, and consequently housing has become a band liability.[145] Leighton explains that members have become dependent on the band and do not think of the houses as their own. Instead, they complain to the band about every housing problem – windows, carpets, and repairs, etc. – and because the band responds, these dependencies are perpetuated.[146]

While many Metlakatla members make their payments and have paid off their housing debts completely, this is a contested area that generates internal tension and conflict. Band Manager Francis Reece explained that of the sixteen rental units Metlakatla owns, five tenants refuse to pay rent, and rent collection is a nightmare.[147] Some housing committee members think that evictions are the answer, but because of the personal repercussions and potential conflicts they are unwilling to proceed.[148] According to Sharon Morven, "The housing

---

141 Metlakatla uses the CP system for all real property transactions on reserve. There are two types of CPs for Metlakatla – residential and garden. People have CPs for small garden lots (50' × 100') on some of the islands and along Metlakatla Channel. It is too expensive to build on the garden sites because of access (by water) and lack of village infrastructure (e.g., sewage, water, transportation, and power). See interview of Harold Leighton by Val Napoleon, 26 August 2004, Metlakatla Development Corporation Office, Metlakatla, BC, 2.

142 Interview of Terri Spencer by Val Napoleon, 26 August 2004, Metlakatla Band Office, Metlakatla, BC, 2.

143 Interview of Spencer.

144 Metlakatla Band, "Metlakatla Housing Policies: Working Draft Seven," 14 June 2004, Metlakatla Band Office, Metlakatla, BC, 2. This document has provisions for evictions in the event non-payment for housing at 10).

145 Interview of Leighton, 2004, 2.

146 Interview of Leighton, 2004, 5.

147 Interview of Francis Reece by Val Napoleon, 26 August 2004, Metlakatla Band Office, Metlakatla, BC.

148 Interview of Reece, 2; interview of Sharon Morven by Val Napoleon, 26 August 2004, Metlakatla Band Office, Metlakatla, BC, 1–2.

committee members are held personally responsible by the families that are affected by the [housing committee's] decisions, and there are lots of personal issues because everybody is related to everybody."[149] Morven suggests that there is a need to build "more homes to resolve the conflict; the lack of houses is the main contributor to the conflict."[150] Morven's overriding concern is about the children: "Where will people go when there are kids involved?"[151]

At Kitselas, Wilfred McKenzie explains that the band housing debt reached about $100,000 during the late 1980s.[152] Then the band evicted three people and the debt was drastically reduced. Since then a few people have still been slow to make payments, but eviction warnings are given by the housing committee and this resolves the problems. McKenzie is concerned that band members depend on the band and it will take at least a generation to change this ethic. He explains, "New people are moving into houses, and they are used to renting in town [Terrace], so they are used to evictions and used to landlords fixing things, but it doesn't take long for the new people to get dependent when they move onto reserve."[153] According to him, there is no room for Tsimshian law in managing property, because the Tsimshian system is not in order. Mel Bevan also holds this view: "There is no customary law. Customary law creates problems for people.... Customary law has nothing to do with lots on reserve and you can't mix the *Indian Act* law up with customary law.... People are opportunistic about which laws they will recognize: one day they only recognize customary law and the next day they will only recognize Western law – it all depends on which will benefit them.... Customary law is romanticized. It is easy to say it is there, but they can't deal with it. People have to choose one system of laws or another."[154]

While housing debt was not explicitly identified as a problem of Lheidli T'enneh, this was more of an absence in the conversations – instead, people discussed other tensions and issues that they found more pressing. Lheidli T'enneh Lands Manager Regina Toth explained that there have been many disputes over real property on reserve in

---

149 Interview of Morven, 1.
150 Interview of Morven, 1.
151 Interview of Morven, 2.
152 Interview of Wilfred McKenzie by Val Napoleon, 30 August 2004, Kitselas Band Office, Kitselas, BC. Only four CPs have been issued for Kitselas members, and there has been much local conflict over these. As a result, Kitselas does not use the CP system for its land transfers, 5.
153 Interview of McKenzie, 5.
154 Interview of Bevan, 2.

recent times.[155] Historically, an informal dispute resolution was managed by the elders, and with the new land management code a community dispute resolution system has been developed. Toth believes that close proximity to Prince George and the residential school have caused the people of Lheidli T'enneh to "lose their culture."[156] Similarly, Ron Seymour believes the internal conflicts over property were created by DIA policies, and he explained that in earlier years, "Band meetings were held to decide use of the non-CP land. Generally, people used the land adjacent to their houses, usually behind their houses, and they had access to the community field. There were no conflicts when it came to land [on reserve]."[157] According to Seymour, there were only five CPs issued for Lheidli T'enneh, but the band bought them up because they were contributing to the local conflict. From Seymour's perspective, the conflict was caused by the individual nature of the CPs, which clashed with the former traditional collective ownership of lands.[158]

Lheidli T'enneh legal counsel (former), Rick Krehbiel, attributes some of the conflicts over descent of property to a breakdown of people's cultural knowledge: "Descent of property is always confusing; people think they are doing it, but the traditional systems have broken down."[159] According to Krehbiel, the dispute resolution processes no longer exist, so people had to create new processes as part of the land code. He states that there are "no community processes anymore; now there is the band council, lawyer, and petitions ... a huge problem. A generation ago, this [conflict] was not a problem."[160]

Turning to matrimonial real property, most of the people interviewed had the opinion that in marital dispute the house should go with the parent who had the children. At Lheidli T'enneh Toth explains, "Upon the separation of a couple, the house will follow the kids. This is a historic cultural practice that was in place long before the current land code was drafted."[161] According to Krehbiel, "Lheidli T'enneh has very

---

155 Interview of Regina Toth by Val Napoleon, 24 August 2004, Earl's Restaurant, Prince George, BC.
156 Interview of Toth, 1.
157 Interview of Ron Seymour by Val Napoleon, 24 August 2004, Lheidli Tenneh Lands and Resource Office, Prince George, BC, 2.
158 Interview of Seymour, 2.
159 Interview of Rick Krehbiel by Val Napoleon, 3 September 2004, Krehbiel residence, Prince George, BC, 3.
160 Interview of Krehbiel, 4.
161 Interview of Toth, 1. The Lheidli T'enneh Band Land Code, Annex 1, *Lheidli T'enneh First Nation Matrimonial Real Property Law (Provisional)*, [1 December 2000], 1, sets out the general principle that "the children of the Spouses, if any, should have a

strong women involved; no one would mess with them. Division is not the issue; the issue is the kids and the custodial parent."[162]

Violet Bozoki echoes the sentiments of Toth and Krehbiel: "If a couple separates, the house will always go to the parent with the children – usually the woman. This was the case with my brother who separated from his wife. She got the house because she had the kids. In another case, the husband kept the kids when the mother left, so he got the house."[163] Bozoki explains that there has been a historic practice of strongly encouraging male spouses from other communities to move to the Lheidli T'enneh villages. According to her, "People don't like to see women leave the community. Why? Maybe there were low numbers of women, so there are lots of men from other areas – McLeod Lake, Crees, Stoney Creek, Quesnel."[164] Bozoki observes that this intermarriage has influenced societal changes for Lheidli T'enneh: "Lots of people from Sekani are married into the Shelley group. The Sekani don't have clans, and this has caused the loss of clans in Shelley."[165]

In Metlakatla Sharon Morven explained that inf a marital dispute, the matrimonial home goes to the spouse who is a band member. Where both spouses are Metlakatla band members, the house goes to the parent who has the children.[166] According to Harold Leighton, the house will always go to the parent with the kids, but only band members can hold CPs.[167]

Laura Miller explains that, in Kitsumkalum, whoever "has the kids gets the house, but this is left up to the families. The band can't

---

right to remain undisturbed in the matrimonial home." Section 63 reads, "A court, in considering whether to direct that one Spouse have exclusive possession of an Interest in Lheidli T'enneh First Nation Land that is a Matrimonial Home, shall be guided by the principle that the custodial parent of a child should have exclusive possession of the family residence for a period sufficient to ensure that the child, or the youngest child if there is more than one child, reaches the age of majority and has the opportunity to complete their education, provided that observance of this principle is consistent with the best interests of the child."

Section 64 deals with joint custody, in which case the requirement is that the house will follow the principle residence of the child or children. If the child or children spend equal time with both parents, the principle is neutral between the spouses. Section 8 provides for the creation of a life estate if the custodial parent is not a Lheidli T'enneh member.

162 Interview of Krehbiel, 3.
163 Interview of Violet Bozoki by Val Napoleon, 24 August 2004, Bozoki residence, Northside Shelley Reserve, BC, 2.
164 Interview of Bozoki.
165 Interview of Bozoki, 2.
166 Interview of Morven, 1.
167 Interview of Leighton, 3–4.

dictate."[168] However, the band tries to be inclusive with non-band member spouses, so the "CP could not go to a non-band member, but we did not want non-native spouses to be kicked out. In this situation, the CP could go to the oldest status child of the non-member so that person could live in the house."[169]

In Kitselas, Mel Bevan's concern is with the men who lose their homes in marital disputes. According to Bevan, "People perceive things according to the *Indian Act* and they only know the wife's side. I know a lot of homeless men. If the male spouse is not a band member, he gets thrown out. It is mainly a man's problem, but men accept it."[170] Nonetheless, there is still uncertainty at Kitselas about matrimonial property. Francis Bennett gave an example of a non-Aboriginal spouse who was afraid of losing the family home on reserve when her husband died. Because of these fears, the family moved off reserve, even though the band assured her that she would not be evicted. In another example, which demonstrates Kitselas's inclusive practices, when a non-band member's husband died and his children from his first marriage evicted his widow (the second wife) from the family home, the band responded by providing the widowed second wife with a house, even though she was not a band member (she was from another band).[171]

2. DIFFERENCES AMONG THE COMMUNITIES

The most obvious difference between the four communities is in their varying responses to the *FNLMA*. Kitselas and Lheidli T'enneh have chosen to adopt land codes. While Kitsumkalum has no intention of adopting a land code, former chief councillor Steve Roberts was frustrated because band members could not use their homes as equity for economic development, nor could they get back their housing investment through private resale. He reasoned, "People in Terrace buy land as speculators, but this won't work here if people try to be pure and

---

168   Interview of Miller, 2.

169   Interview of Miller, 1.

170   Interview of Bevan, 3. *Kitselas Reserve Lands Management Act*, s 30, provides for the enactment of a spousal property law within twelve months of 19 June 2005. The spousal property law is to recognize the right of the children to reside in the matrimonial home until they reach the age of majority or other arrangements are made in the best interests of the children. Also, each spouse is to have an equal right to possession of the matrimonial home, but only Kitselas band members may hold a permanent interest in Kitselas land.

171   Interview of Francis Bennett by Val Napoleon, 30 August 2004, Bennett residence, Kitselas, BC, 1–2.

not sell to non-native interests."[172] In Metlakatla, Harold Leighton expressed frustration about his dealings with INAC over the band's commercial property developments and leases. Because of the ongoing bureaucratic obstacles created by INAC, he was considering the development of a land code, because "anything to do with DIA is a nightmare."[173]

Another difference is in how connected and comfortable people in the different communities are about their own histories and societies. Several representatives from Kitsumkalum feel very strongly about maintaining their Tsimshian institutions and practices. In Kitselas the responses about Tsimshian society were more divided, with some members clearly advocating the position that on-reserve management had nothing to do with Tsimshian culture or law. In Lheidli T'enneh the responses were mixed, because some people felt a loss of historic societal knowledge, while others were much more comfortable with their Dakelh practices and knowledge. Interestingly, in Metlakatla, while the question about Tsimshian culture was not dealt with explicitly, historic practices and norms were implicitly conflicted in the discussions about possible evictions.

Regarding action for non-payment for housing, Metlakatla is loath to evict, and of the four communities it had the biggest housing debt.[174] In contrast, Kitselas carried through with evictions when it first began to accumulate a housing debt, and this is no longer a problem. Kitsumkalum, which deliberately acts on Tsimshian collective kinship and legal responsibilities, bought back two houses from non-paying members and has very little debt. Despite the differing responses to the housing debt and non-payment, all communities struggle to be inclusive and responsible for their members.

3. REFLECTIONS ON THE CASE STUDIES
We draw five main reflections out from the community case studies, as these particular issues evoke important lessons, which will be addressed in the final section of the chapter: (1) the need for serious engagement with Indigenous law and the restatement of its potential intellectual

---

172 Interview of Roberts, 2. Val Napoleon spoke with Steve Roberts in June 2014, at which time he explained that he is now the housing coordinator and no longer so supportive of the *FNLMA*.
173 Interview of Leighton, 2004, 1.
174 According to anecdotal evidence, a number of bands had housing deficits of $5 million to $15 million (from author's work experience in the northwest 1973–2000).

resources, (2) the need for a larger property theory for each Indigenous legal order to provide a larger conceptual framework to reason through Indigenous law, and (3) the need for those property theories to make visible the issues and dynamics around gender, power, wealth, norms, and the practices and sources of law.

Reflection One: Housing Debt Responses

The two communities that had the least debt and housing problems were Kitsumkalum and Kitselas. Interestingly, the responses of both communities to non-payment by members were opposite one another, and this forces us to ask deeper questions about the future role of Tsimshian law in everyday society. What is the role of kinship and historic legal obligations in today's housing situation? Perhaps a lesson might be drawn from the experiences of Kitsumkalum, where it appears that if a community's historic kinship system is intact and people are able to act directly on their responsibilities to one another, then housing and the potential debt do not become major problems. The underlying philosophy that emerges from the Kitsumkalum interviews recognizes that each person is part of a relational network that creates a collective responsibility to intervene when one person gets into difficulty. Here the philosophical approach contains an understanding that everyone's personal circumstances are not just the result of hard work and virtue; rather, anyone could experience difficulties, financial or otherwise, at some point in their lives.

This is not to suggest that Kitsumkalum does not have problems. Despite the extended kinship network of support, the Kitsumkalum Band has had to buy out two houses because of non-payment by members. Furthermore, Miller expressed serious concern about the potential loss of the collective responsibility ethic because of increasing numbers of band members moving to Kitsumkalum from outside the community. She also wonders whether this erosion of Tsimshian collective responsibility will result in the increase of other social problems relating to crime and violence.[175] However, it appears that when compared to issues from other communities, Kitsumkalum has a real strength or social capital in its collectivity and kinship network that enable it to deal more effectively with contemporary problems such as housing.

The contradiction to this analysis, though, is Kitselas, which has deliberately chosen to opt for a Western approach to housing through the *FNLMA* and its land management code. As with Kitsumkalum, Kitselas does not have a housing debt, but in contrast it has a strict housing policy, and it enforces evictions of Kitselas members when they do not keep

---

175   Laura Miller, *supra* note 116 at 2.

up their housing payments. So perhaps the question of debt is too simple as a measure of a communities' success. Certainly there are people in Kitselas who act on their historic legal obligations to one another in other areas of their lives, as exemplified by several of the band's decisions to provide housing for non-band members. Has the Kitselas housing policy eroded Tsimshian kinship and responsibility? It is not clear to us that such a judgment can be made, since Kitselas, despite the denial of Tsimshian law by some members of leadership, still appears to be taking responsibility for its members according to Tsimshian legal norms. Perhaps it is the non-paying Kitselas members who are breaking Tsimshian law – and a determination of this question and responses to it require Tsimshian legal reasoning specific to this legal problem. We will come back to this thorny issue in the discussion of Tsimshian law below.

In Metlakatla, a number of people are considering enforcement of a more stringent housing policy that includes evictions specifically to deal with chronic non-payment for housing by some members. On one hand, people's reluctance to enforce evictions may well derive from a collective Tsimshian ethic similar to Kitsumkalum's, as well as from a well-founded fear of the local social repercussions that would follow. On the other hand, this collective ethic does not appear to be channelled in a way that is constructive or preventative, and consequently the problems continue unabated, compounding into serious financial liability for the band. As Leighton points out, the only result is a continued, destructive dependency on the band.[176] However, might one consider Metlakatla's payouts of the housing debt as responding to social responsibilities and obligations under Tsimshian law? If so, it still seems problematic, as the band council actions are not explicitly recognized as fulfilling Tsimshian legal obligations. Tsimshian legal reasoning would have to be applied to assess this question. There are also the "free riders" whose actions would have to be considered under Tsimshian law as well. Basically, it would appear that the band's payment of the debt does not effectively prevent future non-payment by Metlakatla members, and instead the debt cycle continues.

There are many dilemmas. Should Metlakatla continue with community-wide bailouts to release non-paying community members from their housing debts? It is important to note that, compared to many Indigenous communities, Metlakatla is in the unique position of generating revenues through its successful economic ventures, and this is the reason it has been able to take this course of action. Should Metlakatla begin to enforce evictions as the ultimate way to deal with members' chronic

---

176 Interview of Leighton, 152.

non-payment? Does eviction cause an inevitable slide into an atomistic and depoliticized philosophy? Or might Metlakatla develop an alternative housing policy that builds on and strengthens Tsimshian law, the collective responsibility ethic, which recognizes the larger political and gendered context around each individual? Whatever course of action these communities decide upon, the assumptions that inhere in such policies and their potential internal consequences should have careful and reflective deliberation by those who will live with their results.

Turning to Lheidli T'enneh, it has chosen to adopt a land code and is committed to interpreting and applying it according to Dakelh relationships and practices. As described earlier, Lheidli T'enneh was hard hit by the events in colonial history and also by the fact that it was located first in Prince George, then forcibly moved to two separate locations (on opposite sides of the river) outside of Prince George.[177] Despite this history and while Lheidli T'enneh members speak of a loss of cultural knowledge and ongoing low-level internal conflicts, it appears that there are still strong social and legal norms that guide community members and decision-making. Notable here is that Lheidli T'enneh women are encouraged to remain in the community upon marriage and their male spouses are encouraged to relocate to Lheidli T'enneh.

Reflection Two: Conflict
Conflict and conflict management for property on reserve that would enable leadership and members to constructively and positively deal with arising disputes need to be considered. For many Indigenous peoples in Canada, the current experience of colonialism includes pervasive internal conflict that too often spans generations. Such conflict finds many forms, including gendered violence, lateral violence, divisive and confrontational political behaviours, power struggles, ongoing feuds, and more recently, seemingly endless litigation.[178] Interviewees from all the communities describe ongoing internal conflict, and while they continue with the business of life, conflict is a constant drain.

This is not to suggest that there was a conflict-free golden age prior to contact, as no society is conflict-free, and such idealization is not supported by any of the oral histories.[179] In fact, the oral records of many Indigenous peoples evidence recurrent conflict and sometimes war – and

---

177 Interview with Toth, 1.
178 See Paul Barnsley, "White Paper Revisited? Assault on Rights," *Windspeaker* 20, no. 11 (2003): 14, 25. See also Shin Imai, *The 2004 Annotated Indian Act and Constitutional Provisions* (Toronto: Thomson Carswell, 2004).
179 Napoleon and Friedland, "From Roots to Renaissance."

crucially, they also include legal responses.[180] Historically, Indigenous peoples managed conflict through their legal orders and political systems,[181] and the undermining of these conflict management systems has created the deeply sedimented conflict found in many communities today.

Such internalized conflict experienced in the local community may be viewed as a microcosm of the larger combined forces of colonialism, hetero-patriarchy, neoliberalism, capitalism, Indigenous self-determination measures, and continual Indigenous resistance.[182] Arguably, contemporary efforts to resolve these conflicts are ineffective precisely because of consistent failure to frame them in their political and historical complexities. Many conflict resolution efforts decontextualize the conflict from its surrounding political, economic, and historical roots – effectively depoliticizing it, at least explicitly. Implicitly, it is reframed within the neoliberal framework as deriving from personal shortcomings and collective failure to forget being Indigenous. Conflict resolution initiatives that fail to take the power relations of the participants into account, or consider the wider context can congeal into yet another layer of oppression. In part, these failures persist because conflict resolution theories are drawn principally from dominant Western traditions without consideration or analysis of Indigenous legal orders,[183] histories, or experiences.

---

180 See, e.g., Martindale and Marsden, "Defining the Middle Period." See also Garfield, *Tsimshian Clan and Society*.

181 For example, according to Anderson and Halpin, crest management is an important aspect of the chiefs' responsibilities in order to prevent internal strife because there is always competition for the valued crests. These crest-management practices include carefully arranged marriages, adoptions, public proclamations of successors, and also strategic crest retirement. Anderson and Halpin question whether management of the crests can successfully happen outside the institution of the feast because of the critical need for active and knowledgeable elders to deal with the complexities of the adaawk, crests, and privileges. This raises serious considerations for future Aboriginal conflict management strategies. See Anderson and Halpin, *Potlatch at Gitsegukla*, 35, 49–50. "Houses that become depleted in numbers, or that do not take care of their crests, risk having others disregard or even usurp their rights," Anderson and Halpin, *Potlatch at Gitsegukla*, 17.

182 James Tully, "The Persistence of Empire: A Legacy of Colonialism and Decolonization" (paper presented to the Annual Conference for the Study of Political Thought: The Conference on Colonialism and Its Legacies, After Colonialism Panel, University of Chicago, April 2004), 27, 32, 44.

183 We use the term *legal order* to describe legal rules and procedures that are undifferentiated from social life and from political and religious institutions. *Legal systems*, on the other hand, may be described as distinct, integrated bodies of law, consciously systematized by professionals with specialized institutions, legislation, and the "science of law." See Harold Berman, *Law and Revolution* (Cambridge, MA: Harvard University Press, 1983), 49–50.

Reflection Three: Fragmented Legal Orders

This brings us to a third reflection. When considering conflict management and the potential application of Indigenous legal orders, it is important to ask whom the Indigenous legal order includes and over what
territory it extends. Arguably, an effective legal order requires recognizing
larger Indigenous societies that are beyond band structures in order to
incorporate matters of scale, concepts of the public good, distance and
disinterest,[184] accountability, and the full extent of the relationships and
responsibilities integral to the maintenance and governance of that society.
When the colonial cookie cutter, the *Indian Act*, divided nations into small
groups, reoriented them as bands, and then pinned them onto small fixed
geographical spaces, it cut across Indigenous legal orders and weakened
the efficacy and application of Indigenous laws. From this perspective,
law-making within a band is not viable. If the band system is to remain,
co-operative arrangements or alliances must be established that will enable bands to draw upon broader-based relationships of accountability at
the Indigenous nation level so that their laws might be effectively rebuilt
and implemented.[185]

Reflection Four: Ground-Up Citizenry Engagement

Turning to a fourth reflection, Krehbiel describes the process of drafting
and adopting the land management code as capacity building: "It took six
to eight months to develop a land code. When this was passed, it created a
sense of empowerment. Early on there were big disputes; now 40–60 people can debate complex issues."[186] Krehbiel explains that while the time it
takes communities to put a land code in place varies from six months to
several years, there is "always a magic moment at about six months."[187]
Communities that adopt the land code approach are forced to deal with
long-standing internal conflicts before they can successfully undertake
and complete the challenging work a land code requires. Alternatively,

---

184 John Ralston Saul, *The Unconscious Civilization* (Concord: Anansi, 1995), 167, argued
     that some distance creates a level of personal disinterest that is necessary in order
     for people to effectively maintain and protect the larger public good.
185 For example, Hedda Schuurman suggests that the current conception of "com-
     munity" does not derive from Innu language or culture, and the experience of
     living within a fixed settlement is entirely foreign – settlement has resulted in an
     anti-community consciousness that raises particular difficulties for leadership and
     the implementation of self-government. See Hedda Schuurman, "The Concept
     of Community and the Challenge for Self-Government," in *Aboriginal Autonomy
     and Development in Northern Quebec and Labrador*, ed. Colin Scott (Vancouver: UBC
     Press, 2001), 379.
186 Interview of Krehbiel, 4.
187 Interview of Krehbiel, 5.

communities could perpetuate ongoing social conflicts through land codes and other institutional development, and maintain constraints on citizenry engagement, exclusion, and marginalization. Krehbiel views the land code process as a positive capacity-building experience for communities, despite the setbacks created by the chronic lack of resources that would enable communities to actually manage their lands.[188] Diversity, local variation, and experience also determine how long it takes communities to make decisions, manage disputes, and develop long-term strategies.[189]

How and by what form Indigenous peoples act on their historic legal and political responsibilities changes over time, so the constant challenge is to discover, recognize, and support contemporary adherence to contemporary expressions of Indigenous legal norms.[190] Lheidli T'enneh is still able to act on elements of Dakelh norms and kinship responsibilities, despite its recent devastating history, and arguably can still act on them through present-day instruments such as the land code. Arguably, this is also the case for Kitselas, Kitsumkalum, and Metlakatla. The question is whether, over time the forms of decision making and authority in the land code will strengthen Lheidli T'enneh members' sense of Dakelh responsibilities and norms or weaken them. This question requires deliberation and reflection as it is impossible to "guess" the future of human relationships. And certainly, Indigenous communities and Indigenous legal orders are not isolated from ongoing external economic, political, social, and state legal influences, and the reality of constant change itself.

Reflection Five: Matrimonial Property

The interview reveals that local people are concerned with and responding to issues of marital property on reserve, primarily in a way that focuses on ensuring homes for children.[191] According to Garfield, in Tsimshian society, the children are understood as belonging to the clan. She explains, "Since a child had a home and relatives so long as any members of its own matrilineal lineage were alive, adoption to provide for the economic welfare of children was of much less importance than in our [i.e., non-Indigenous] society. Children raised by their own close clan relatives were not formally adopted, since they belonged to the lineage anyway."[192]

---

188 *Ibid* at 2.
189 *Ibid.*
190 See generally Napoleon et al., "Where Is the Law."
191 A note here about the research: the fieldwork conducted was qualitative rather than quantitative, so there is no statistical analysis on this issue.
192 Garfield, *Tsimshian Clan and Society*, 226–7.

Bevan's comments about the problem of homeless men in Kitselas seems to be a backhanded way of saying that it is usually the women who keep the children, so they usually keep the house.[193] Interviewees from the other communities confirm the usual practice of women keeping the children and the house, even when they are not band members, as in the example from Metlakatla[194] and Kitsumkalum.[195] However, Bozoki provided one example from Lheidli T'enneh, where the man was able to keep the house because he had custody of the children.[196] It would seem from the interviewees' perspectives, at least insofar as fulfilling historic legal obligations concerning children, that housing decisions in all the communities are made so as to ensure housing for children. Interestingly, it appears that this is the case even with the male interviewees from Kitselas who eschewed the application of Tsimshian law.

What is not readily apparent from the interviews is the extent to which single or separated women without children are considered in the housing decisions. Perhaps, given the extreme demand for housing described by Miller, that there has not yet been an opportunity to consider the housing needs of adults without children.[197] It is also not apparent that gender is explicitly or implicitly considered in housing decisions other than it is the women who usually have custody of the children. In other words, questions of gender are subsumed in the heteronormatively framed issue of marriage and marital property. The experience of transgender, gay, or lesbian couples or singles is absent, as are the experiences of single straight women.

Fiske has observed, "The process of colonization has not been kind to Tsimshian women."[198] More recently, when responding to the new B.C. government's pledge to end violence against Indigenous women and girls, Jodi Wilson-Raybould said, "Poverty, inequality, and marginalization [are] symptomatic of a far greater social malaise that can only be addressed through true reconciliation and dealing with the underlying reality of the devastating colonial legacy."[199] So we know that Indigenous women experience violence and marginalization in communities, yet their experiences remain below the surface in the management of property on

---

193 Interview of Morven, 3.
194 Interview of Morven, 1.
195 Interview of Miller, 2.
196 Interview of Bozoki.
197 Interview of Miller, 3.
198 Fiske, "Colonization and the Decline of Women's Status," 530.
199 Canadian Press, "B.C. Pledges to End Violence against Aboriginal Women and Girls," CBC News, 13 June 2014, www.cbc.ca/news/canada/british-columbia/b-c-pledges-to-end-violence-against-aboriginal-women-and-girls-1.2674985.

reserve. How does violence and marginalization play out in the lives of Indigenous women and in the decisions and policies of reserve property? How might gender be accounted for and dealt with at the community level? Gender issues will remain invisible unless attention is directed specifically at discussing gender in research interviews and case studies such as the ones focused on here (which admittedly fell short in the inclusion of gender). Consequently, there are gaps, which we aim to address below by returning to the tools that a critical Indigenous feminist property theory can provide when taken up during the work of articulating and developing Indigenous property theories.

IV. Critical Theory and Reflection

According to Kevin Gray, "'Property' remains ultimately an emotive phrase in search of a meaning. The value-laden mystique generated by appeals to 'property' exerts a powerful and yet wholly spurious moral leverage."[200] Gray goes farther to argue that "the ultimate fact about property is that it does not really exist: it is mere illusion."[201] Its particular ethnocentric conception within the common law remains unexamined and is being transplanted into Indigenous communities as if it were as real as what it is supposed to represent.[202] Carol Rose argues that too often dominant notions of property are treated as natural – questions are asked about those who deviate from the norm (for example, by imagining property in different ways) and why they do so, but the norm itself remains unexplained.[203] The challenge in deconstructing dominant discourses about property is to treat them as social constructions that are illusory, but to also recognize the ideological and material impacts and constraints created and sustained by dominant property discourses. As Blomley explains, "Access to property, including land, is an important predictor of one's position within a social hierarchy, affecting class, race, and gender relations."[204]

While many theorists have engaged with the concept of property, there has been little critical theory around the transformation of collectively managed reserve lands into individually managed parcels.[205] Andre Van

---

200 Kevin Gray, "Property in Thin Air," *Cambridge Law Journal* 50, no. 2 (1991): 305.
201 Gray, "Property in Thin Air," 252.
202 *Yanner v Eaton*, [1999] HCA 53 at para 17, (1999) 201 CLR 35 (High Court of Australia).
203 Rose, "Property as Storytelling."
204 Blomley, "Law, Property, and the Geography of Violence," 121.
205 But see Egan and Place, "Minding the Gaps," for a preliminary discussion on this topic.

Der Walt presents a very useful discussion about transformative property theories that attempt to explain "the legitimacy of political reforms of the institutions and systems that constitute property law."[206] According to Van Der Walt, property law is being transformed around the world, but a sound theoretical explanation of these reforms is yet to be developed.[207]

As mentioned above, Indigenous peoples have shown interest in the creation of the *FNLMA* (along with other statutes, such as pertaining to taxation and marital real property) with the hopes of being able to deal with the practical realities of economic disparity and poverty. Arguably though, such policy directives and legislation have uncritically incorporated a classic liberal property construct that is premised entirely on Western assumptions about human beings, relationships, and responsibilities.[208] It is important to consider the ways that people might be using Western property constructs strategically to gain power within a constraining system, or for advocating for change within a system. Yet this strategy is limited in many ways and risks embracing the very constructs that exclude and marginalize Indigenous people. Western property relations are very much about exclusion.[209] While it seems obvious that broader power dynamics concerning class, race, gender, and sexuality hierarchies would not cease to operate in those property relationships, property law is often treated as apolitical. Turning reserve land into individually managed private parcels, for example, does little to challenge the reserve system itself, the imposition of state laws, colonial oppression, and hetero-patriarchal racialized oppression, as it operates through property, poverty, and beyond. The suggestion that Indigenous peoples' best option is to work within the Western private property regime rather than reject that very system implicitly suggests that Indigenous societies have a serious societal and intellectual deficit that can be dealt with only by importing constructs from another society. Also implicit is the idea that Western property constructs are universal and culture-free and so are harmlessly and easily transportable across societal and cultural bounds without consequence.[210]

---

206 Andre Van Der Walt, "Property Theory and the Transformation of Property Law," in *Modern Studies in Property Law*, ed. Elizabeth Cook (Oxford, OR: Hart Publishing, 2005), 361.

207 Van Der Walt, "Property Theory."

208 Egan and Place, "Minding the Gaps," 130.

209 Davies, *Property*, 18, reflecting on Cohen's work, explains that property "is not just about power over an object; it is fundamentally about our ability to exclude others from a resource."

210 Celestine Nyamu-Musembi, "Breathing Life into Dead Theories about Property Rights: de Soto and Land Relations in Rural Africa," *Third World Quarterly* 28, no. 8 (2006): 1457.

It is evident that Western property constructs are firmly entrenched in, and the product of, very particular legal (here, state common law), political (neoliberal state governments), cultural (Western), gendered (male), and economic (capitalist) contexts. Writing in the 1950s, legal theorists such as Felix Cohen raise important questions about how property structures relationships. He asks, "Can we all agree at this point that essentially this institution of private property that we are trying to identify in outline is not a collection of physical objects, but rather a set of relationships – like our conversation or our differences of opinion? If we can agree on this, at least tentatively, perhaps we can go on to the narrower question, what sort of relationship exactly is this property? Is it a relationship of a man to a thing, or is it a relationship among men?"[211]

Cohen compels us to ask who the assumed legal subject is at the heart of discussions about property. The typical approach to property assumes that people will be/are/ought to be "self-interested rational utility maximizer[s]"[212] who are "bounded, discrete, self-determining units."[213] Notions of property contain within them norms regarding who and what is "proper," and what sort of behaviour and characteristics are acceptable.[214]

Indigenous legal scholars, feminist legal scholars, and other theorists have amply shown that white, middle- to upper-class heterosexual males stand in as the model liberal subject and ideal citizen, and their subject position is made both universal and invisible in the ways that it is normalized and naturalized. Feminist legal scholars have shown the ways that characteristics such as rationality are used in law to differentiate men from women and to empower male subjectivity and that women are treated more like objects than subjects – as "*unbounded*: as relational selves, carers, and physically penetrable."[215] An intersectional analysis is vital here, as the ways that women are objectified varies along axes of race, class, and sexuality. Further, racist and colonial ideologies also work to deny subject status to "racialized others." Colonial oppression utilizes and sustains other forms of systemic violence (and vice versa), including patriarchal and heteronormative violence.[216]

---

211 Felix S. Cohen, "Dialogue on Private Property," *Rutgers Law Journal* 9, no. 2 (1954): 361.
212 Rose, "Property as Storytelling," 37.
213 Davies, *Property*, 29.
214 Davies, *Property*, 25–7.
215 Davies, *Property*, 45.
216 See, e.g., Kiera Ladner, "Gendering Decolonisation, Decolonising Gender," *Australian Indigenous Law Review* 13 (2009): 62.

Our articulation of critical Indigenous feminist property theory at the outset of this chapter began from the vital starting point of understanding that class, race, gender, and sexuality matter when theorizing property, and that this is not just the case with state laws, but a crucial starting point with Indigenous laws as well.

While embracing private property on reserve might offer immediate temporary relief to some problems – keeping in mind that Indigenous women on average have less financial resources than Indigenous men[217] – overall this approach will merely solidify, if not worsen, current social problems under the guise of empowerment. The *Family Homes on Reserves and Matrimonial Interests or Rights Act,*[218] for example, could offer temporary relief to Indigenous women on reserve, though it does little to address the root problem of systemic sexism exemplified by the *Indian Act*'s explicit historic reliance on the male legal subject, which arguably remains implicitly through ongoing contestations over membership.[219] There is a need to turn to Indigenous laws and new theories to consider other ways for examining questions pertaining to property, law, and power.

A. Drawing on Indigenous Laws

In considering how a property theory might work for the Tsimshian, Napoleon's Gitksan legal theory[220] provides a helpful starting place, since the Gitksan are closely related to the Tsimshian and belong to the same linguistic group. While much of the Tsimshian law in the case studies actually closely reflects the Gitksan examples, the following Tsimshian property theory is only an extrapolation at this point, and further development is necessary to make this model applicable and workable. The intent of this exercise is to demonstrate the possibility and importance of creating a property law theory to frame and inform the actual operation of law in specific societies, rather than taking a more general approach that would fail to provide the internal perspective necessary to apply the law. The following elements are adapted from Napoleon's Gitksan legal theory:[221]

---

217 Canada, Aboriginal Affairs and Northern Development Canada, "Aboriginal Women in the Canadian Economy: The Links between Education, Employment and Income," Fact Sheet (Ottawa: AANDC, 2012), 1.

218 *Family Homes on Reserves and Matrimonial Interests or Rights Act,* SC 2013 c 20.

219 See generally Sharon McIvor, "Sharon McIvor's Response to the August 2009 Proposal of Indian and Northern Affairs Canada to Amend the 1985 Indian Act" (6 October 2009), http://www.socialrightscura.ca/documents/legal/mcivor/ McIvorResponse.pdf.

220 See Napoleon, "Ayook," 178–9.

221 Napoleon, "Ayook."

Element One: Coherent Picture of Tsimshian Property Law

The scope of the institutional structure of Tsimshian property law includes its forms, operations, processes, expressions, shared understandings, and implicit and explicit legal norms. The Tsimshian legal order is non-state, with legal and political authority distributed and acted upon through a highly structured and closely maintained decentralized governance system. Political and legal authority is dispersed through a closely interwoven, reciprocal, and matrilineal kinship network of house[222] groups and clans, and larger alliances of tribes that corresponded to village areas.

Since there was no separate group of legal professionals or a central bureaucracy, Tsimshian people had legal capacities according to rank, and corresponding levels of authority and responsibility in the kinship system. Tsimshian individuals have agency and legal capacity in the house group, but outside the house, the house holds the legal capacity and is the legal actor in relation to other house groups. This kinship system creates a legal order that is bound together and stabilized by a series of tensions created by parallel and mutually dependant behaviours that are at once highly competitive and collaborative. In other words, the Tsimshian legal order is founded on extensive family relationships and, as evidenced in the oral histories, the relationships extend to include other life forms and the land.

Legal decisions were recorded and formally archived as witnessed precedent and are drawn upon in legal practices that comprise public reasoning, legal problem solving, and dispute management. Forms of public legal record include crests, songs, poles, and types of oral histories (cognitive units that organize information and intellectual processes). Accountability in the legal order extends through the entire Tsimshian kinship system, across the entire territory (i.e., not in a present-day band).

Tsimshian houses owned individual territories that in aggregate form the overall Tsimshian territories, with the outermost boundaries forming the farthest reaches that could be defended physically, legally, and politically. This geographic space had and has more than one legal order within it as a result of marriage with other peoples, trade, access agreements, and international agreements (and now this includes Canadian law).

Element Two: General Concepts

Recorded legal cases demonstrate that Tsimshian law is applied, enforced, deliberated on, amended and changed, publicly pronounced, and archived

---

222 The Tsimshian word for this matrilineal kinship group is *walp*, plural *huwalp*. The English term *house* derives from the historic living arrangements in longhouses.

and recorded. Tsimshian law may be categorized into three types:[223] (1) primary rules containing reciprocal obligations with humans, non-human life forms, and the land, (2) secondary rules[224] that enable people to recognize and interpret the primary laws, change laws, and adjudicate when the primary laws are broken, and (3) strict laws, which are constitutional in nature and are concerned with establishing and maintaining the legal framework of the society and its ability to maintain its obligations to the land.[225]

Element Three: Normative Principles

The key normative principles that guided operation of the Tsimshian legal order were the maintenance and recognition of the chiefs' authority, ongoing public performance and confirmation of the oral histories, maintaining the honour of the names by avoiding shame or dishonour, resistance to hierarchy and centralization, and reincarnation.

Element Four: General Working Principles

The general working principles include compensation versus determination of guilt, collective compensation and liability, precedent knowledge of lineage, history, and kinship relationships, and strict liability for some accidents.

With this basic outline of a Tsimshian legal theory, one can begin to imagine how it underpins the operation of law and see how it might shape a preliminary body of Tsimshian property law with the proviso of: (1) the need to factor in the contemporary institutions and new Tsimshian law, which in turn needs to be reconciled with historical legal institutions and law; and (2) the need to engage with gender in that process. Failure to do the former would likely result in a fragmented and incoherent representation and understanding of Tsimshian property law, as noted in the reflections in the previous section. Failure to engage with gender will lead to an incomplete analysis.

---

223 The primary and secondary laws are drawn from Hart, the category of strict laws was developed by Richard Overstall. See H.L.A. Hart, *The Concept of Law* (Oxford: Clarendon, 1961); Richard Overstall, "Encountering the Spirit in the Land: 'Property' in a Kinship-Based Legal Order," in *Despotic Dominion: Property Rights in British Settler Societies*, ed. John McLaren, A.R. Buck, and Nancy E. Wright (Vancouver: UBC Press, 2004), 44.

224 Examples of secondary laws include those governing the feast hall where the houses, through their chiefs, validate and recreate the original relationships of the host house group, the succession of individuals within the host house to chiefly names, and the allocation of use rights to lands and resources.

225 Examples of strict laws include (1) the law against marrying within one's own clan, (2) the inalienability of territory, and (3) a lineage's absolute liability for human actions on its territory.

Critical Indigenous feminist property theory can work alongside and expand this basic outline of a Tsimshian legal theory. What follows are some examples of research questions that could be asked, based on the above elements and the case studies:

- Are ideas about property and land gendered in Tsimshian law, historically and today? In what ways?
- Do current housing policies (state and/or Tsimshian) affect members of the community differently, on the basis of gender?
  - What are the specific impacts? How might they be addressed by drawing on and engaging with Tsimshian law?
  - How do the current policies work (or not) with Tsimshian governance, legal authority, and a matrilineal kinship network?
- What are the Tsimshian legal principles concerning gender, and how are they intertwined with principles that involve property?
  - Do gendered power dynamics shape Tsimshian legal interpretation?
  - What norms exist in the laws (state and Tsimshian) about sexuality, relationships, family?
  - How do these norms inform (or not) understandings of property and gender in Tsimshian law?
  - Are these norms working to include or exclude citizens? Are these inclusions or exclusions justified? According to whom?
  - Do women with children have access to safe housing? Do women without children have access to safe housing? Do 2LGBTQI[226] citizens have access to safe housing?
    - What principles, legal reasoning, and processes can be drawn on in Tsimshian law for understanding the need for safety and shelter? What legal sources (e.g., stories, members of the community, etc.) can be engaged for discussion about these issues?
- What processes exist or can be imagined within Tsimshian law for appealing housing and land decisions?

As the case studies illustrate, there is substantial Indigenous legal knowledge as well as many legal processes contained in present practices and social interactions at the community level, and, as we cautioned earlier, there are also gaps and distortions. Nonetheless, this is a valid starting place and, in combination with broader inquiries into stories and precedent, and community engagement, this approach could create a substantive research process, a coherent and accessible body of Indigenous law, and a restatement of Indigenous law today. Thinking about how to deal with questions about real property on reserve with

---

226 Two-spirit, lesbian, gay, bisexual, trans, queer, intersex.

Indigenous laws is not to suggest that Indigenous laws are perfect or that power dynamics cannot also operate in and through Indigenous laws. The conceptualizations of property might be different from Western law, but this does not mean that questions regarding power, for example, should not be asked.

Generally, binaries can generate only a shallow space for dialogue and debate, if any, so it is critical that Indigenous law not be placed in opposition to state law – as incommensurable. Rather, we suggest an approach to broaden the way law is conceived so that the intellectual and reasoning resources in Indigenous law may be applied today as law – a way to solve problems and deal with the universal contestation of human beings living together. Given the destructiveness of colonialism, past and present, serious engagement with Indigenous law as imagined here will require Indigenous communities to rebuild law where necessary and to figure out the relationship with state law. This raises the question of the standards and measures by which to evaluate the rebuilding process for Indigenous law.

How might one assess success, given the contradictory findings between Kitsumkalum and Kitselas in the foregoing case studies? Neither has a housing debt and both would be considered successful if only a lack of debt was the measure. We suggest that the questions to ask are about the extent to which new Indigenous law (as per the *FNLMA* or through other governing arrangements with the state) and their contemporary governing institutions maintain or undermine the historic Indigenous legal order insofar as legal decision making, authorities, legal obligations, procedural and substantive rights, and outcomes are concerned. This is not to suggest that Indigenous law cannot or should not change, but that change and adaptation occur through deliberations and critical considerations rather than just ignoring (and breaking) Indigenous law which can only further its erasure and destabilization.

V. Conclusion

We conclude mindful of Paul Babie's counsel that when we focus on relationship as being central to private property and political-regulatory contexts, we begin to see that the externalities of private property create many other types of relationships in which the lives of many are controlled by the choices of a few.[227] Property in its various forms is not

---

227   Paul Babie, "Private Property: The Solution or the Source of the Problem?" *Amsterdam Law Forum* 2, no. 2 (2010): 20.

going anywhere for Indigenous peoples, but it is not a cure-all for the consequences of colonialism either. We have made the case for a much more complex treatment of property on reserve that engages seriously with the rebuilding of Indigenous law. We have also proposed that Indigenous property theories be developed to enable a deeper understanding of Indigenous law and its operation. And finally, we have proposed the development of a critical Indigenous feminist property theory that puts gender at the centre in order to create tools to evaluate power and wealth.

2 Market Citizenship and Indigeneity

SHALENE JOBIN[1]

Indigenous peoples rank first in marginalization, unemployment, and lack of education, so government responses focus on economic development as if it were the ultimate solution to these problems. Nonetheless, this type of economic development is mainly intended to open Indigenous lands to the market rather than to provide Indigenous peoples with the means for their social reproduction.[2]

There is a gap in the research on the implications of negotiating for state-defined institutions of governance and the movement towards neoliberal economies for Indigenous communities. Like other contributions to this book, this chapter examines the impacts of adopting pre-formed institutions and legal frameworks for land ownership on Indigenous peoples. However, this chapter examines Indigenous[3] identity, as defined through the institution of citizenship, and the extent to which these understandings of identity are conditioned by market

1 I would like to thank Metis Elder Elmer Ghostkeeper (Buffalo Lake Metis Settlement) and Melody Lepine (director at Government and Industry Relations, Mikisew Cree First Nation) for their helpful comments on this chapter. I would also like to acknowledge the instructive feedback from Robert Nichols, Val Napoleon, Rod McDonald, and Veronique Fortin.
2 Juliàn Castro-Rea and Isabel Altamirano-Jiménez, "North American First Peoples: Self-Determination or Economic Development," in *Politics in North America: Redefining Continental Relations*, ed. Yasmeen AbuLaban, Radha Jhappan, and François Rocher (Peterborough, ON: Broadview, 2008), 246.
3 *Constitution Act, 1982*, being Schedule B to the *Canada Act, 1982* (UK), 1982, c 11. In this chapter I use the term *Indigenous* to refer to Metis peoples, Inuit peoples, and First Nations peoples, and the term *Aboriginal* to refer to the identities and relationships entrenched in section 35 of the *Constitution Act, 1982*, defining "aboriginal peoples of Canada" as "Indian, Inuit and Métis," s 35.

liberalism. While Napoleon and Snyder or Morales and Thom use theoretical frameworks that seek to identify how diverse conceptions of Indigeneity operate within Indigenous and non-Indigenous institutions, this chapter is a cautionary tale of potential implications. Moreover, it ultimately questions the value of developing state-sanctioned mechanisms that promote Indigenous empowerment through land, as discussed by Graben and Morey in their rethinking of Aboriginal title, or by Morin in his identification of Indigenous traditions within *Indian Act* regimes.

Historically, colonial governing systems, and currently, neo-colonial economic forces have reconstituted Indigeneity, altering social relations, governing practices, and economic patterns in negative ways. The protection of Aboriginal rights pursuant to the *Constitution Act, 1982*, would seemingly protect Indigeneity, as the inherent right to self-government for Aboriginal peoples is found *within* the Constitution.[4] However, it is because the right to self-government is located in the Constitution, rather than within Indigenous laws and legal orders, that Indigeneity continues to be reconstituted in relation to majoritarian cultural practices. The constitutional framework has pushed many Indigenous peoples to pursue self-determination in ways that comply with the constitutional order and Western models of self-sufficiency, including economic self-sufficiency often embedded in extractive capitalism. In order to determine the constitutive effects of negotiating within the state's defined boundaries, these choices need to be examined more closely.

Colonial domination of Indigenous peoples in settler societies has taken a two-pronged approach: state domination (e.g., bureaucratic control) and economic exploitation (e.g., resource extraction, "development" programs, etc).[5] If we focus only on the state domination aspect of settler society, we miss how attempts to resist this may further entrench the second colonial logic. Indigenous resistance to state governance can support colonial forms of economic exploitation because attempts to gain "economic prosperity" require Indigenous collectivities to internalize neoliberal terms. In order to free themselves from state dominance through (*Indian Act*) governance, Indigenous peoples must often make choices that support a neoliberal economic agenda, compromising their Indigenous identities.[6]

---

4 *Constitution Act, 1982*, c 11.
5 Castro-Rea and Altamirano-Jiménez, "North American First Peoples."
6 Maria Bargh, *Resistance: An Indigenous Response to Neoliberalism* (Wellington: Huia Publishers, 2007), 2.

In this chapter I examine ideas of identity and citizenship through an analysis of Metis[7] and Cree peoples' conceptions of citizenship and its comparison with Western market notions of citizenship. I examine two societies, the Metis Settlements of Alberta and the Mikisew Cree First Nation in Alberta.[8] These two peoples provide an interesting cross-section of different self-determination aspirations, conceptions of identity, economic ambitions, and relationships with provincial and federal governments. The Metis Settlements and the Mikisew Cree First Nation illustrate how overarching federal and provincial involvement, especially through negotiated settlements[9] like the Treaty Land Entitlement (TLE) and Alberta-Metis Settlements Accord, affect communities, and can challenge Indigenous world views and relationships to the land. These cases represent different cultural groups, distinct histories with the Canadian state, and different Indigenous visions of self-determination and citizenship.

I. Indigeneity

Indigeneity is a contested concept steeped in colonial history with very real political implications. As a conceptual tool, it is fundamentally defined by inclusion and exclusion. Indigeneity is based on (1) the definition of who is Indigenous and (2) the politics surrounding Indigenous identity.[10] Depending on who is naming and when the naming was done, Indigeneity in Canada can be inclusive of the following identities: Aboriginal, First Nation, Métis, Inuit, Native, Indian, Status Indian, Non-Status Indian, Treaty Indian, and non-Treaty Status Indian. Each of these names take on a specific political connotation, which is framed by the corresponding constitutional rights it avails. These political "identities" do not specify the naming of the forty to

---

7 In this chapter I use the spelling of *Metis*, as opposed to *Métis*, to reflect how it is used by the Metis Settlement General Council, Metis Settlement legislation, and advice by Elmer Ghostkeeper (Metis Settlement Elder).

8 I would like to thank Metis Elder Elmer Ghostkeeper (Buffalo Lake Metis Settlement) and Melody Lepine (director at Government and Industry Relations, Mikisew Cree First Nation) for their helpful comments on this chapter.

9 Gabrielle A. Slowey, *Navigating Neoliberalism: The Mikisew Cree First Nation* (Vancouver: UBC Press, 2008). Slowey states that the "TLE was necessary to protect the integrity of the Alberta economy" and that "the neoliberal ideal for First Nations is self-determination, because self-determination re-establishes the proper balance between First Nations and the marketplace" (17, 34).

10 Mark Bennett, "'Indigeneity' as Self-Determination," *Indigenous Law Journal* 4 (2005): 72.

sixty Indigenous nations[11] that are distinct, "meaning peoples in the usually accepted international sense of a group with a common cultural and historical antecedence."[12]

The term *Indigeneity*, derived from, although different from, the term *Indigenous*, relates to the ways that the dominant state chooses to accommodate the cultural, social, and political distinctiveness of Indigenous peoples.[13] Indigeneity is not conceived outside of the "politicized context of contemporary colonialism."[14] Indigeneity comes into being only when constituted as distinct from "non-Indigenous." For Bennett, the "principle of 'self-determination' is the best liberal justification for the significance of Indigeneity, and best fits how Indigenous peoples view their claims and rights."[15] Furthermore, he states that his appeal to self-determination is based on the "historical fact of Indigenous self-determination – the fact that Indigenous peoples lived by their own laws, traditions and customs before they encountered colonizing powers – [and that this can be used] as a crucial basis for a return to that status in the present."[16] Turner and Simpson argue that although Indigeneity characterizes distinctiveness that occurs in part from the "unique political and historical experiences with European settlers," Indigenous relationships to their homelands "constitute the main moral and political force of their legal and political distinctiveness."[17]

Another way to understand Indigeneity is through Indigenous conceptions. *Nehiyawak* means "Cree people" and it is derived from the word *newo*, which means "four." The number four has special significance related to obligations and relationships to other living beings. It also can relate to the natural law teachings of physical, spiritual, mental, and emotional well-being. In the work of the Cree scholar Leona Makokis, she asks a Cree elder about this particular world view. The elder states that *Nehiyaw* "is the four directions, *newoyak*. There are four

---

11 Francis Abele, "Small Nations and Democracy's Prospects," *Inroads: A Journal of Opinion* 10 (2001): 141.
12 Paul Chartrand, "Aboriginal Peoples in Canada: Aspirations for Distributive Justice as Distinct Peoples: An Interview with Paul Chartrand," in *Indigenous Peoples' Rights in Australia, Canada and New Zealand*, ed. Paul Havemann (Auckland: Oxford University Press, 1999), 104.
13 Bennett, "'Indigeneity' as Self-Determination," 73.
14 Taiaiake Alfred and Jeff Corntassel, "Being Indigenous: Resurgences against Contemporary Colonialism," *Government and Opposition* 40 (2005): 597.
15 Bennett, "'Indigeneity' as Self-Determination," 73.
16 Bennett, "'Indigeneity' as Self-Determination," 74.
17 Dale Turner and Audra Simpson, *Indigenous Leadership in a Flat World* (West Vancouver, BC: National Centre for First Nations Governance, 2008), 18.

parts and those are our four directions and that is in our language."[18] The elder goes on to explain, "We are called *Iyiniwak*. That is the foundation of who we are, our identity. We are supposed to heal ourselves and others and *iyiniwaskamkaw*, that is, our relationship to our land, our connection here."[19] *Nehiyawewin*, the Cree language, provides a framework to understand the world based on the four directions teachings, which are considered central teachings that guide the Cree in daily living. The language itself demonstrates relationships and is based on the animacy of the world around us. Through this perspective, our relationship to land is constitutive. Therefore our economic relationships are constitutive; by this I mean that the relationships we have to the land, people, and other beings creates and co-creates who we are as individuals and as peoples.

II. Citizenship

In one of the dominant versions of the Western liberal framework, citizenship delineates procedural participation in the state through voting, paying taxes, joining organizations, or standing for office. "Citizenship refers to the status of being a citizen, usually enshrined in law. Citizenship may entail rights and responsibilities or result as a consequence of being part of a polity or a community. Participation entails a legal membership of a polity premised upon universal suffrage. Citizenship is a relationship between the state and the individual that comprises a series of rights and responsibilities. It may be defined objectively, as a legal status, or subjectively, as comprising a sense of belonging and identity."[20]

Citizenship is also said to establish a regime of inclusion and exclusion, defining both national and internal (to the nation) boundaries, where there is a separation within, to those citizens with complete rights, and those with limited forms of citizenship, conceptually "second-class citizens."[21] Indigenous peoples have historically been excluded from many rights associated with Canadian citizenship.[22]

---

18 Leona Makokis, "Teachings from Cree Elders: A Grounded Study of Indigenous Elders" (DEd diss. University of San Diego, 2010), 90.
19 Makokis, "Teachings from Cree Elders," 90.
20 Heather Savigny, "Citizenship," in *Encyclopedia of Governance*, ed. Mark Bevir (Thousand Oaks, CA: Sage Publications, 2007), 1:81.
21 Jane Jenson and Susan D. Philips, "Regime Shift: New Citizenship Practices in Canada," *International Journal of Canadian Studies* 14 (1996): 114.
22 *An Act to Amend the Canada Elections Act*, SC 1960, c 7. For example, Status Indians did not have the right to vote until 1960 at s 1.

Institutional instruments like constitutions can shape notions of citizenship in ways that differ from Indigenous beliefs about reciprocal roles and responsibilities.[23] The conceptions of Western liberal democracy and Indigenous beliefs on reciprocity point to different roles for the "citizen."

Through an Indigenous ontology, citizenship[24] has not historically related to rights and responsibilities to a nation state, but to a way of being in the world, to being a human being. This view of citizenship, or *pimâtisiwin* ("the act of living," in Cree), is related not only to roles and responsibilities to other humans but also to other living and inanimate things. Similarly, I once asked a Cree Elder the meaning of self-determination in the Cree language; after thinking a while, he said it is *Nehiyaw-askiy*. The suffix *askiy* is the Cree word for land. Therefore, he explained, *Nehiyaw-askiy* are the four spirited people of the land. This means that we have responsibilities and reciprocal relationships with the air, water, earth, and other living creatures. Therefore, through one reading of a Cree ontology, citizenship entails specific roles and responsibilities to all other living beings. Mikisew Cree First Nation knowledge-holders explain how *kitaskino* translates to "our land" in the English language with a more accurate translation being "the land that is ours to take care of" or "the land that we belong to and are related to." Furthermore, *kitaskino* as a Cree concept "describes a kinship-like relationship of interdependence, respect, and stewardship existing between a group of people and the living-being-that-is-land-and-water that the group relies upon for its existence."[25]

In this Indigenous view of citizenship there is a reciprocal relationship between economic interactions (relations to land) and modes of subjectivity (relations with land). How we relate to the land affects who

---

23 Margaret Kovach, *Indigenous Methodologies: Characteristics, Conversations and Contexts* (Toronto: University of Toronto Press, 2009). Kovach explains the importance of reciprocity and a relational way of being through the concept of *miyo-wîcêhtowin* (good relations) referred to as the "heartbeat of Plains Cree culture," including "sharing and generosity, respecting the earth and all inhabitants, working hard, and caring for other people" (63).

24 I am conceptualizing Indigenous citizenship very broadly. *Citizenship* might not be the proper term to use in Indigenous languages. For example, *îyinewiwin* means "being human" in Cree and can be related to certain responsibilities like that of developing good relations.

25 Craig Candler, Ginger Gibson, Molly Malone, and the Firelight Group Research Cooperative with Mikisew Cree First Nation, "Wîyôw'tan'kitaskino (Our Land Is Rich): A Mikisew Cree Culture and Rights Assessment for the Proposed Teck Frontier Project Update," September 2015, 14.

we are and the types of rights and responsibilities we can lay claim to. Stated differently and speaking as an Indigenous person, our relationships and normative practices to human and non-human relations are co-constitutive to who we are and who we will become. In contrast, the fungible character of land in a liberal economic model seems to presume that a fundamental alteration of a relationship to the land will not significantly alter the character of Indigenous peoples and the structures of their communities. Consequently, not only is extractive capitalism constitutive, it also constricts. With extractive capitalism there are negative impacts to the land, the water, the animals, and humans. These impacts limit (or constrict) the ability of people to live off the land so as to exercise self-determination through economic self-sufficiency. Through its negative impacts, extractive capitalism constricts options for achieving economic self-sufficiency – thereby restricting economic options to only those embedded in capitalist markets. This chapter identifies the ways that Canadian self-government limits Indigenous self-determination by requiring it to prioritize the individual who is self-sufficient and attempts to assimilate Indigenous collectives into individualized identities characterized by market citizenship. In conversation with the discussion by Morales and Thom in this volume on how state and Indigenous systems do co-exist as a matter of practice, this chapter cautions against the colonial logic that is embedded in the state system.[26]

III. Market Citizenship

In contrast to citizenship, market citizenship shifts the responsibility of government away from ensuring the social welfare of its citizens and towards responsibility for a political and social order in which citizens can pay to help themselves. As Judy Fudge has put it, the market citizen recognizes and takes responsibility for her own risks and that of her family.[27] Where the principles of market citizenship are enacted, neoliberalism can be understood as both a policy paradigm and as a practice:[28] it can be seen as encompassing a set of policies, as an ideology,

---

26 Sarah Morales and Brian Thom, "The Principles of Sharing and the Shadow of Canadian Property Law," in this volume.

27 Judy Fudge, "After Industrial Citizenship: Market Citizenship or Citizenship at Work," *Industrial Relations* 60, no. 4 (2005): 645; Amanda Root, *Market Citizenship: Experiments in Democracy and Globalization* (London: Sage Publishing, 2007).

28 Nicola Smith, "Neoliberalism," in *Encyclopedia of Governance*, ed. Mark Bevir (Thousand Oaks, CA: Sage Publications, 2007), 1:598.

and through the notion of governmentality.[29] As a policy, neoliberalism has been marked by the shift from a Keynesian economic model to a state favouring a comparatively "unfettered operation of markets" linked with the globalization of capital.[30] Three basic tenets of neoliberalism are free trade, the free mobility of capital, and a reduction "in the ambit role of the state."[31] As an ideology, neoliberalism is the belief that sustained economic growth is "the means to achieve human progress"[32] and that "human well-being can best be advanced by liberating individual entrepreneurial freedoms and skills."[33] Neoliberalism examined in this way goes beyond the state and explores other institutions, organizations, and processes.[34] Arguably, this has moved the market into all areas of social life,[35] changing the notion of freedom to market freedom and the "commodification of everything" assisted through privatization.[36] Market citizenship is a liberal version of citizenship based on market values. However, market citizenship and extractive capitalism are often inextricably linked for Indigenous peoples.[37] This type of citizenship model challenges Indigenous identity and connection to the land, creating an environment where Indigenous rights are settled through state negotiations and land is therefore free to be exploited by market interests.

Indigenous peoples striving for meaningful self-determination are being pushed into a settler-colonial version of citizenship based on the values of the market. Indigenous peoples' goal of self-government has often been constructed along a neoliberal trajectory, directly affecting communal ideologies and relationships with the land in negative ways. Zapotec scholar, Isabel Altamirano-Jiménez states that Western government responses to Indigenous demands are based in a neoliberal

---

29 Wendy Larner, "Neo-liberalism: Policy, Ideology, Governmentality," *Studies in Political Economy* 63 (2000): 6.
30 Larner, "Neo-liberalism."
31 Bargh, *Resistance*, 1.
32 Bargh, *Resistance*.
33 David Harvey, *A Brief History of Neoliberalism* (New York: Oxford University Press, 2005), 2.
34 Larner, "Neo-liberalism," 9.
35 Helga Leitner, Jamie Peck, and Eric S. Sheppard, *Contesting Neoliberalism: Urban Frontiers* (New York: Guilford, 2006), 28.
36 Bargh, *Resistance*, 80.
37 Isabel Altamirano-Jiménez, "Neo-liberal and Social Investment Re-constructions of Women and Indigeneity," in *Women & Public Policy in Canada: Neo-liberalism and After?* ed. Alexandra Dobrowolsky (Don Mills, ON: Oxford University Press Canada, 2009), 132.

ideology, disconnecting self-government from Indigenous territory.[38] Indigenous scholars Maria Bargh and Rauna Koukkanen have named neoliberalism as a new form of colonization affecting Indigenous peoples.[39] The marketization of Indigenous citizenship is "the fulfillment of Indigenous demands through market integration and the rhetoric of cultural recognition."[40]

One clear example of the Canada's neoliberal agenda for Indigenous peoples can be found in federal policy. In 2009 the Canadian government initiated a $200 million Federal Framework for Aboriginal Economic Development;[41] although this sort of investment is impressive, the plan has been criticized for failing to address important connections between Indigenous aspirations to citizenship and self-determination. The framework highlights resource development as a major "win" for Aboriginal peoples. "Over $315 billion in major resource developments have been identified in or near Aboriginal communities. In the North, the mining and oil and gas sectors have proposed developments in the range of $24 billion that will impact Aboriginal communities in the next decade."[42] The report goes on to suggest that the government will work with those "opportunity-ready Aboriginal communities that have stable, efficient and predictable investment climates attractive to business and investors."[43]

This caveat of "opportunity-ready" refers to communities that have adopted Western liberal institutional forms and are federally determined as a good "fit" for market citizenship. The framework then focuses on four strategies that are a good fit: (1) strengthening Aboriginal entrepreneurship; (2) developing Aboriginal human capital; (3) enhancing the value of Aboriginal assets; and (4) forging new and effective partnerships.[44]

---

38 Isabel Altamirano-Jiménez, "North American First Peoples: Slipping Up into Market Citizenship?" *Citizenship Studies* 8, no. 4 (2004): 349.

39 Bargh, *Resistance*, 2; Rauna Kuokkanen, "Sámi Women, Autonomy, and Decolonization in the Age of Globalization" (paper delivered at "Rethinking Nordic Colonialism," Rovaniemi, 9 July 2006); Kuokkanen, "Globalization as Racialized, Sexualized Violence," *International Feminist Journal of Politics* 10 (2008): 216.

40 Altamirano-Jiménez, "North American First Peoples," 350.

41 Canada, Minister of Indian Affairs and Northern Development & Federal Interlocutor for Métis and Non-Status Indians, *Federal Framework for Aboriginal Economic Development* (Ottawa: Minister of Public Works and Government Services Canada, 2009).

42 Canada, *Federal Framework*, 9.

43 Canada, *Federal Framework*, 20.

44 Canada, *Federal Framework*, 22.

These strategies are to make Indigenous communities "ready" for economic development and corporate partnerships, especially resource development on their lands. Through policies such as these, the government changes the idea of citizens receiving public goods, to one where individualized subjects are held responsible for their choices, thereby being conceived and constituted as market citizens.[45]

IV. Metis Settlements of Alberta

The eastern sky at sunrise is usually a brilliant yellow in my region. When I arise in the morning I face the east and say a prayer asking for a strong mind and giving thanks for my source of fire, heat, light, and energy.
                                                    – Elmer Ghostkeeper, Metis elder[46]

The Metis Settlements in Alberta are currently the only negotiated Metis land base in Canada and exercise specific self-government jurisdiction within the province of Alberta. In this chapter I follow the Settlements spelling of *Metis*. Following the 1934 Ewing Commission, the 1938 *Metis Population Betterment Act*[47] created twelve Metis Settlements (now eight). In 1989 the *Metis Settlements Accord* was finalized between the Federation of Metis Settlements and the Alberta government.[48] This self-governance agreement included "the foundational principles and framework for transfer and allocation of Metis settlement lands and resources; protection of settlement lands; and executive, legislative, and judicial branches of government."[49] A unique two-tier governance structure includes a local government and a larger governance structure including all communities, called the Metis Settlements General

45 Veronica Schild, "Neo-liberalism's New Gendered Market Citizens: The Civilizing Dimension of Social Programmes in Chile," *Citizenship Studies* 4 (2000): 305.

46 Elmer Ghostkeeper, "WECHE Teaching: A Partnership of Aboriginal Wisdom and Western Scientific Knowledge Applied to the Diabetes Mellitus Puzzle" (unpublished, 2000). 1.

47 *Metis Population Betterment Act*, SA 1938, c 6 (2nd Sess).

48 *Constitution of Alberta Amendment Act, 1990*, RSA 2000, c C-24. When the Alberta Constitution was amended in 1990, the amendment act states, "WHEREAS it is desired that the Metis should continue to have a land base to provide for the preservation and enhancement of Metis culture and identity and to enable the Metis to attain self-governance under the laws of Alberta." Metis Settlements Accord (1989).

49 Catherine Bell and Harold Robinson, "Government on the Métis Settlements: Foundations and Future Directions," in *Aboriginal Self-Government in Canada: Current Trends and Issues*, ed. Yale D. Belanger, 3rd ed. (Saskatoon, SK: Purich Publishing, 2008), 260.

Council (MSGC) or "the Federation." Each settlement has five members elected to local council who also sit on the MSGC, in addition to four seats chosen through the general federation election.[50] There is also a judicial arm through the Metis Settlements Appeal Tribunal. This judicial tribunal also incorporates a non-judicial settlement process through an ombudsman.

The Accord agreement provided settlement funding for seventeen years, ending in 2007. Alternative funding sources became necessary and were to be supplied by economic development efforts of the Metis Settlements. The MSGC now uses the Settlement Investment Corporation, an arm's-length corporation of the Metis Settlements, to stimulate economic development through agricultural and commercial loans. For example, in 2006 the MSGC spent $7 million investing in oil and gas projects.[51] These relationships with external corporations have governing logics of their own that are often facilitated by the state. These governing rationalities have exerted disciplinary pressures that can attempt to reconstitute Indigenous peoples as market citizens who can fund their own communal needs through intensive resource extraction. While financial independence is beneficial for the Metis Settlements, they are not in complete control of the method or pace by which it will be obtained. As Castro-Rea and Altamirano-Jiménez have explained, it is instead governmental policies that affect change. Government policies in Canada focus on (1) minimizing transfer payments to First Nations, (2) diminishing self-government to self-administration of services, (3) prioritizing and encouraging economic development, and (4) promoting relations between Indigenous peoples and corporations to respond to global market pressures.[52] The authors state that this is especially targeted to Indigenous peoples who have lands with oil and gas resources on them.[53]

Within this evolving relationship with the land, how are Metis values in reciprocal relationships with the physical and metaphysical affected? How does the value of being in reciprocal relationships with physical and metaphysical beings shape citizenship and challenge the values surrounding market citizenship?

Despite market citizenship forces, a Metis worldview of sustenance continues to exist and be referenced by communities. This type of Metis worldview is described by Elder Elmer Ghostkeeper as follows:

---

50 John Graham, *Advancing Governance of the Metis Settlements of Alberta: Selected Working Papers* (Ottawa: Institute on Governance, 2007), 2–5.
51 Graham, *Advancing Governance*, 4.
52 Castro-Rea and Altamirano-Jiménez, "North American First Peoples."
53 Castro-Rea and Altamirano-Jiménez, "North American First Peoples," 241.

Food to sustain life is created by The Great Spirit. It comes in the form of a gift (*mekiwin*), or something that is freely exchanged and shared between a donor and recipient through the relations of giving and receiving.... It is the gathering and harvesting of plants and animals in order to make a living with the land. In this livelihood, a ritual is considered to be a decision made through the recital of a prayer by a gatherer or harvester. The person requests permission from the Great Spirit, Mother Earth, and the aspects of the spirit, mind, and emotion of a plant or animal to sacrifice its body for human sustenance. The spirits of the donor and recipient are thought to be equal. This request is in exchange for an offering in the form of a gift of a pinch of tobacco or food, and it signals spiritual equality.[54]

Ghostkeeper sees this type of subsistence-based philosophy as a sacred relationship; living *with* the land. Through changes in subsistence patterns of the Metis Settlement of Paddle Prairie a shift occurred to one that Ghostkeeper described as a secular world view: living *off* the land.

Ghostkeeper documents his own shift from living *with* the land to living *off* the land. He describes moving from the patterns of subsistence-based living in the Paddle Prairie Metis Settlement to the wage economy, encompassing the construction of a natural gas field and the beginning of grain farming on Settlement land.[55]

In analysing these changes, Ghostkeeper examines the technical and social relationships involved; where the "land, equipment, and labour, or forces of production are more or less under the control of individuals from the community; the relationships, or means of production are under the control of forces outside the community."[56] Ghostkeeper explains that Metis traditionally see themselves as part of the land with all other living beings, and that one process in these relationships includes the exchanging of "aspects"; these include aspects of the mind, body, and spirit thought to "provide life for the body through the activities of ceremony, ritual, and sacrifice."[57] He explains this as spirit gifting, "when one makes a living with the land, using the gifts of plants and animals for food and medicinal purposes."[58]

---

54 Elmer Ghostkeeper, *Spirit Gifting: The Concept of Spiritual Exchange*, 2nd ed. (Duncan, BC: Writing on Stone, 2007), 11–12.
55 Ghostkeeper, *Spirit Gifting*, 6–43.
56 Ghostkeeper, *Spirit Gifting*, 4–5.
57 Ghostkeeper, *Spirit Gifting*, 4.
58 Ghostkeeper, *Spirit Gifting*.

Figure 2.1. Metis Settlements (MSGC website)

Normative principles of gifting and sharing are common in both Cree and Metis societies. In Cree culture the Give Away Ceremony, still practised today, is a way to express thankfulness for the gifts of sustenance throughout the year. During this ceremony people bring gifts to share with others. Part of the purpose of this ceremony is to provide the "necessities to live a prosperous life, with enough food to carry families through each winter."[59] Ghostkeeper writes that when the Metis lived

59 Leona Makokis, "Teachings from Cree Elders: A Grounded Study of Indigenous Elders" (DEd diss., University of San Diego, 2001), 107.

in relationship with the land, the norm of sharing was principal: "The harvesters would distribute and share a large portion of moose meat with other Metis, beginning with the elders, the next of kin, the most in need, and finally others that had shared with them in the past."[60] Moving to living *off* the land, Ghostkeeper viewed the land as a commodity instead of a gift; the shift from seeing the land as a gift changes Indigenous perceptions of sharing these gifts with others.[61] He explains that this Metis relationship with the land changed when he was awarded an oil field contract from the company in Calgary that was completing the natural gas development on Paddle Prairie land and that others were affected by mechanical grain farming.[62]

In the change to these two modes of production, land was viewed as a commodity and treated as an inanimate object as opposed to a gift and being part of a reciprocal relationship; this new view resulted in emotional and spiritual detachment.[63] Through this new economic and social system, Metis contractors did not have time to "gather and harvest wild plants and animals for food and did not have the time to enter into a relationship with the land."[64] The result, for Ghostkeeper, was dissatisfaction so intense that it motivated him to, in his own words, revitalize his repressed Metis world view.

The "group revitalization" model developed by Anthony Wallace[65] was instructive to Ghostkeeper to understand his own trajectory. He begins by noting that there is a "period of increased individual stress" where the Indigenous sociocultural system is increasingly pushed out of balance through disease, conquest, or internal decay, resulting in a "period of cultural distortion," where community members try to restore individual equilibrium through self-medicating strategies such as gambling and alcoholism to such an extent that these coping mechanisms become institutionalized in the "system."[66] Wallace explains that at this point the population will die off, separate into "splinter" groups, or be assimilated into another more stable society, unless the culture is revitalized.[67]

---

60 Ghostkeeper, *Spirit Gifting*, 44.
61 Ghostkeeper, *Spirit Gifting*.
62 Ghostkeeper, *Spirit Gifting*.
63 Ghostkeeper, *Spirit Gifting*, 68–9.
64 Ghostkeeper, *Spirit Gifting*, 74.
65 Anthony Wallace, *Culture and Personality*, 2nd ed. (New York: Random House, 1970), 188.
66 Ghostkeeper, *Spirit Gifting*, 76.
67 Wallace, *Culture and Personality*.

The Metis Settlements are in this transition of revitalization right now: Metis people are hopeful that the expanded self-governing powers and partnership agreements providing new economic resources will revitalize their people. However, an unknown number of people, like Ghostkeeper, have pinpointed their growing dissatisfaction with the negative impacts that these new market "relationships" bring. Ghostkeeper found a way to revitalize his Metis world view and sustain it within the current global neoliberal economic system; it is important to also examine how the community as a whole has responded.

Metis Settlements have taken steps to understand the impacts of resource development on their lands and move towards incorporating their values within their community planning and in relation to external market pressures. The Metis Settlements Traditional Land Use Mapping and Oral History Project began in 2004 as a proactive method to articulate the importance of their land, including traditional uses. The outcome is a set of traditional use atlases, which include traditional use occupancy, sacred sites, maps, and historical information gathered from Metis oral histories. This project will assist the Settlements in resource management and land use planning in its traditional territory.[68]

In another initiative, four settlements worked with EcoPlan International (EPI) to develop an Alberta Métis Non-Market Valuation Analysis to understand the impacts of resource development on settlement lands. Specifically, the Gift Lake Metis Settlement (GLMS) presented their report as evidence in a dispute with Devon Canada Corporation (Devon) before the Metis Settlements Appeal Tribunal, the judicial arm of the Metis Settlements.[69] Devon operates forty-three well sites and access roads within GLMS. Within the proceedings, GLMS provided information from community members and elders on the impacts of oil and gas development in Sandy Bay, an area of cultural and traditional economic importance within GLMS:

> GLMS submitted that, prior to oil and gas activity, the Sandy Bay area was the community's primary site for important traditional and cultural activities, including hunting, fishing, trapping and gathering of plants. The game and plants were used for purposes including: food, medicine, clothing, and crafts. GLMS explained these activities were no

---

68 "Alberta Metis Settlements Oral History & Traditional Land Use Project," EcoPlan International (EPI), https://ecoplan.ca/featured-projects/alberta-metis-oral-history/.

69 *Gift Lake Metis Settlement v Devon Canada Corp*, [2007] AMSATD no 2, para 3.

longer possible due to degradation of the wildlife and vegetation in the Sandy Bay area. GLMS submitted that these changes have also affected their ability to teach their children traditional ways and the Elders spoke of their concerns for future generations. GLMS submitted that these changes in the Sandy Bay area are attributable to oil and gas activity. Some of the specific examples GLMS gave of changes in the Sandy Bay area are:

• Reduced vegetation;
• Berries that do grow are less plentiful and are not good to eat;
• "Keep out" signs discouraging hunting;
• Wildlife being scared away from the area. For instance, noise from pump-jacks scare away deer and moose;
• The songbirds are gone and the population of other species of birds have been reduced;
• Difficulty calling moose because of noise from oil and gas activity;
• Traditional medicine from plants must be gathered in other areas;
• The roads give strangers greater access and there is a loss of privacy;
• Odour of petroleum and natural gas;
• Species such as grouse, rabbit and moose have disappeared from area;
• Members fear using game from the area because of fear of contamination;
• Métis sadness/mourning over the loss of these activities/way of life.[70]

Similarly, the EPI report describes the Metis values that were affected by oil and gas development. The eight listed values were "Bush Environmental Values, Community Improvement Values, Community Revenue Values, Employment Values, Social Values and Traditional Values.... All workshop participants marked loss of bush environment as the most important or second most important value. Loss to traditional values was also marked as having high importance."[71]

These changes demonstrate how extractive capitalism alters the ability of Indigenous peoples to live with the land in *miyo wichetowin* (good relationships) or to be able to have *miyo pimatsowin* (a good life or healthy livelihood) through hunting, fishing, or harvesting. The case of MSGC illuminates the tensions and inevitable links between self-government and extractive capitalism, and how the logics embedded in both self-government and extractive capitalism discipline market citizenship in a way that eventually limits other options of economic relationality with human and non-humans on the

---

70 *Gift Lake Metis Settlement v Devon Canada Corp*, [2007] AMSATD no 2, para 54.
71 *Gift Lake Metis Settlement*, paras 66–7.

land. This disciplinary power both constitutes identity and constricts economic self-determination (by limiting it to only capitalist market options). Nonetheless, these changes also illustrate how Metis Settlements increasingly chronicle the effects of market principles affecting Metis identity and Indigenous citizenship. Metis citizens are not only becoming aware of these negative impacts but also demanding recognition and restitution. Similarly, Metis Settlement Elders, like Elmer Ghostkeeper, are sharing their teachings of being in relationship *with* the land.

V. Mikisew Cree First Nation (MCFN)

The Mikisew Cree are located in northeastern Alberta; they signed Treaty 8 in 1899; and in 1986 a treaty land entitlement (TLE) was negotiated and settled with the federal government.[72] The TLE included 12,280 acres of land, including land for reserve sites, and a cash settlement. In 2009 a TLE cash settlement was ratified by MCFN membership related to the unaccounted Bill C-31 membership that was initially left off the band lists for the purpose of the first settlement.[73] In *Mikisew Cree First Nation v Canada*, the Supreme Court of Canada found that the Crown breached the duty to consult on a proposed road on traditional MCFN territory.[74] Regarding governance, the TLE provision of land to MCFN "facilitated government off-loading of control over band-related political and economic matters, proving once and for all that neoliberalism, government control, and resolved land claims are interconnected."[75] As the TLE was required to ensure Alberta's resource economy proceeded unencumbered,[76] these state negotiations have further entrenched the capitalist-exploitation logic of settler colonialism, exerting burdens of market citizenship logic on the Mikisew Cree. As the relationship to the land affects Indigenous identities and bodies, these pressures are intimately connected to all aspects of Mikisew Cree society.

---

72 Mikisew Cree First Nation Treaty Land Entitlement Agreement, 1986.
73 Mikisew Cree First Nation and Dalhousie University Cities and Environment Unit, *Mikisew Cree First Nation Comprehensive Plan* (Halifax, NS: Cities and Environment Unit, Faculty of Architecture & Planning, Dalhousie University, 2011), 8.
74 *Mikisew Cree First Nation v Canada (Minister of Canadian Heritage)*, [2005] 3 SCR 388, 2005 SCC 69.
75 Gabrielle A. Slowey, *Navigating Neoliberalism: The Mikisew Cree First Nation* (Vancouver: UBC Press, 2008), 10.
76 Slowey, *Navigating Neoliberalism*, 34.

The relationship to the land continues to be important to the community. Mikisew Cree's vision statement directly establishes the connection between the land and identity: "Our traditional culture and connection to the Land are essential to our future well-being. On this foundation, we will work together to build a strong, healthy and independent First Nation."[77] One MCFN value statement, identified within their most recent Community Plan, states that the "well-being of our people depends on the health of the Land and our traditional food from hunting, fishing and gathering. We have a right to safe food and water."[78] The MCFN explains that most members rely on wild game for a substantial portion of their diet, with time on the land also being important.[79]

Furthermore, the Elders Council of Treaty 8 adopted a Treaty Principles document to acknowledge the main tenets as told to them by their ancestors.[80] In this document they state, "As landowners of the land, we must find a balance between economic development and protecting the environment for generations to come."[81] For the Mikisew Cree, even within their economic development plans their goal is to protect their citizens' ability to continue to have traditional livelihoods.[82]

Many scholars advocate for neoliberal conceptions of capital accumulation and corresponding institutions of governance for Indigenous peoples.[83] Slowey writes that economic development is an instrument for Indigenous peoples to achieve self-government by copying neoliberal principles that constitute the "ideal citizen."[84] This "ideal citizen" is an individualized person who "competes in the market-place, is self-reliant, and does not act as a drain on the state.... And from a Canadian neoliberal perspective, an ideal First Nation would be one that does not impede resource development activity."[85] Specifically examining

---

77 Mikisew Cree First Nation, *Mikisew Cree First Nation Comprehensive Plan*, 73.
78 Mikisew Cree First Nation, *Mikisew Cree First Nation Comprehensive Plan*, 72.
79 Mikisew Cree First Nation, "Who We Are," http://mikisewcree.ca/.
80 Treaty Eight First Nations of Alberta, "Treaty Principles," http://treaty8.ca.dev-live.net/.
81 Treaty Eight First Nations of Alberta, "Treaty Principles."
82 Mikisew Cree First Nation, *Mikisew Cree First Nation Comprehensive Plan*, 123.
83 Slowey, *Navigating Neoliberalism*, 10; Terry Anderson, Bruce Benson, and Thomas Flanagan, *Self-Determination: The Other Path for Native Americans* (Stanford, CA: Stanford University Press, 2006).
84 Slowey, *Navigating Neoliberalism*.
85 Gabrielle A. Slowey, "The Political Economy of Aboriginal Self-Determination: The Case of the Mikisew Cree First Nation" (PhD diss., University of Alberta, 2003), xiv–xv.

MCFN, Slowey writes that neoliberal globalization "may be a reason of hope" and it can be considered a "remedy to First Nation dispossession, marginalization, and desperation because it opens up space for First Nations self-determination."[86]

Analysing MCFN in both her dissertation (2003)[87] and book (2008)[88], Slowey explores integration into market globalism and examines whether neoliberal globalization is the solution for First Nation self-determination. The argument is that Indigenous people thereby gain increased autonomy from the state. However, it is crucial to examine the power that multinational corporations can exert on Indigenous peoples. The shift to market-governing forces can also be hegemonic and not necessarily governed by the interests of MCFN citizens. Seemingly paradoxical to her later works, in 2001, Slowey argued "that self-government negotiated within the parameters of globalization, under the auspices of corporate dominance, does not represent decolonization but neocolonialism."[89]

Related to MCFN, Slowey notes that the majority of work-benefit partnerships with multinational resource development companies have focused on manual labour. One MCFN member emphatically stated, "When you think of these companies, they always try to get you in there to do labour work. They never offer to give you a percentage of the company, like we are only good enough to do labour. And we don't like that. We want to be part of that company which means we want a percentage of it so we can buy into what they are starting."[90] Slowey attributes the lack of meaningful participation in the economy by MCFN citizens to a deficiency in capital. The solution, for Slowey (2008), is to increase global economic development to be able to attain a more powerful position within the system. Market integration increases market citizenship pressures that often try to reproduce citizens in ways that benefit the neoliberal economy. In settler-colonialism economic exploitation includes both exploitation of lands and bodies, as well as unfair economic compensation to Indigenous peoples. Economic colonialism for Indigenous peoples includes both economic exploitation in terms of the inequitable sharing of power and profit but also in terms

86 Slowey, "Political Economy of Aboriginal Self-Determination," xiv.
87 Slowey, "Political Economy of Aboriginal Self-Determination."
88 Slowey, Navigating Neoliberalism.
89 Gabrielle A. Slowey, "Globalization and Self-Government: Impacts and Implications for First Nations in Canada," American Review of Canadian Studies 31, no. 1–2 (2001): 265.
90 Slowey, Navigating Neoliberalism, 69.

of the larger question of this chapter, how changing relationships with land co-constitutes identities. For many, providing increased financial benefits is the solution; however, this does not alleviate the negative impacts to lands and bodies – bodies of water, humans, and animals.

One Syncrude employee interviewed perceived a dramatic shift as a result of the global marketization of Indigenous citizenship:

> I have watched for 22 years how the community has gotten better and better. I mean, I can tell you when I first went up there it was not unlike a typical Aboriginal community – broken down cars in the front yard, the place looked like a mess. Now, you go up there today and people have their houses painted, they have fences, there is a new 4x4 in the driveway, there is a skidoo in the back of it and the kids have designer clothes on – all this stuff that has all come from getting out there and having an opportunity.[91]

At what cost? It is imperative to discuss the significant health-related illnesses affecting MCFN citizens due to oil sands extraction from multinational corporations.

On 17 February 2009, MCFN and the Athabascan Chipewyan First Nation (in partnership with the Forest Ethics environmental group) placed a full-page ad in *USA Today*, timing the ad to correspond to then U.S. President Obama's visit to Canada.

"The Mikisew Cree and Athabasca Chipewyan First Nations are both based in Fort Chipewyan, Alta. which is downstream from the oil sands developments in northern Alberta. Both bands have long waged a public campaign against the developments because they believe they are causing diseases such as cancer among their people."[92]

On 12 May 2009, MCFN and other First Nations appeared before the House of Commons Standing Committee on Environment and Sustainable Development, asking for a moratorium on development projects until health-related studies can be completed.[93] "In February, an Alberta Cancer Board report showed Fort Chipewyan residents had higher rates of certain types of cancer than they should have."[94]

---

91 Jobin, "Cree Economic Relationships Governance," 197.
92 CBC News, "Alberta First Nations Place Anti-Oilsands Ad in Major U.S. Paper," 17 February 2009, https://www.cbc.ca/news/canada/edmonton/alberta-first-nations-place-anti-oilsands-ad-in-major-u-s-paper-1.852412.
93 Submission of Mr George Poitras, Mikisew Cree First Nation, 40th Parliament, 2nd Session (12 May 2009, Oil Sands and Canada's Water Resources).
94 Hanneke Brooymans, "Protect Water from Oilsands or Risk Lawsuits: First Nations," *Calgary Herald*, 19 May 2009.

**President Obama,
You'll never guess who's standing between
us and our new energy economy...**

Canada's Tar Sands: the dirtiest oil on earth.

Figure 2.2. Anti-oilsands ad (CBC News, "Alberta First Nations Place Anti-Oilsands Ad in Major U.S. Paper," 17 February 2009, https://www.cbc.ca/news/canada/edmonton/alberta-first-nations-place-anti-oilsands-ad-in-major-u-s-paper-1.852412)

The marketization of Indigenous citizenship commodifies Indigeneity, where economic growth is positioned as paramount over other interests such as the health of community members.

The Mikisew Cree are increasingly aware that the changes to their land are based on principles of the market and maximization of profit for multinational corporations. In response to these pressures the *Mikisew Cree First Nation Comprehensive Plan* (2011) was developed, providing a vision for the community.[95] The plan has six action areas: education; land, water, and culture; recreation; community building; economic development; and health. Throughout the document, the connection to and importance of the land and environment to Cree culture, identity,

---

95   Mikisew Cree First Nation, *Mikisew Cree First Nation Comprehensive Plan.*

and livelihood remains clear. The extreme distress of community members over impacts of oil sands development is apparent:

> One of the greatest concerns for MCFN is the quality and quantity of water in the region. The resource extraction process in the Lower Athabasca Region has impacted the water supply in a number of ways. Oil sands development is licensed to divert 445 million cubic meters of freshwater, resulting in low-flow periods in the winter that are as much as ten times as low as the high season. Recently the long-standing commercial fishing season was cut as a result of low levels of fish in the region (Grant 2009). The lower water levels in the Athabasca River have limited the ability of Band members to travel to traditional hunting areas and spiritual gathering sites.... After the water is used to extract the oil from the bitumen, it is stored in end pit lakes or tailing lakes that seep toxic chemicals into the groundwater (Grant, 2009; Timmoney, 2007). This seepage threatens the long-term quality of both ground and surface water of the region.[96]

The impact on the quality of freshwater touches on all aspects of Mikisew life.

Elders teach that the Mikisew Cree are "keepers" of the land,[97] having specific roles and responsibilities. "The Mikisew Cree used the Cree word *Askiy* to describe the entire web of life supported by the Land and water – they do not refer to the natural environment as separate components."[98] Within the *Comprehensive Plan*, the land, water, and culture action area outlines specific priorities and plans:

A Protect the Land and Water
   o Enhance Mikisew Cree First Nation's position as a role model of environmental protection and stewardship.
   o Reduce pollution and waste. Advocate for and implement innovative technologies and best available technologies.
   o Keep pressure on industry and government to minimize pollution.
   o Position Fort Chipewyan/MCFN as a model for community-based monitoring and research.
   o Use the Plan to ensure a united front for MCFN, and all of Fort Chipewyan.

---

96 Mikisew Cree First Nation, *Mikisew Cree First Nation Comprehensive Plan*, 13.
97 Mikisew Cree First Nation, *Mikisew Cree First Nation Comprehensive Plan*, 101.
98 Mikisew Cree First Nation, *Mikisew Cree First Nation Comprehensive Plan*, 101.

B   Develop a Knowledge Base to Inform Protection of the
    Land and Water
    o Create a database of human impacts on the land and water.
    o Identify areas to protect, and areas where development will go.
       Define what protection means.
    o Anticipate possible future initiatives related to oil sands devel-
       opment and determine how best to respond to them, i.e., carbon
       capture, land reclamation. Take a position before something be-
       comes an issue.
C   Preserve Our Way of Life
    o Continue to establish a presence on the land.
    o Encourage members to continue traditional land uses.
    o Actively exercise our rights to use the land.[99]

MCFN has articulated a plan to move forward, providing a unified
response to external market pressures. They also have specific project
ideas based on the value they place on protecting the land. A few of
these ideas include solar energy, a land conservatory for traditional
medicines, health and environment monitoring, developing a Traditional Land Use (TLU) comprehensive study, raising external awareness of oil sands impacts, developing community gardens, creating
small sized farms, eco-tourism, and organizing Elder harvesting trips
for foods and medicines.[100]

Negotiating the Treaty Land Entitlement with the federal government provided land and financial compensation to the Mikisew
Cree. In settler-colonial logics it also provided an environment where
the capitalist-exploitation logic of settler colonialism can be further
ingrained through seemingly unfettered resource development on
traditional Mikisew Cree lands, with little economic benefit flowing to the Mikisew. The changing traditional lands of the Mikisew
Cree impacts Mikisew bodies, identity, and citizenship. Moving forward with a *Comprehensive Plan* is one way that the Mikisew Cree can
present their own voice and attempt to go ahead to create their own
future. The Mikisew Cree case study explores the tensions of how the
state and the market, especially extractive capitalism, exert disciplinary power to constitute a market citizenship and constrict the ability for the Mikisew to *live with the land* and to have *miyo-pimatsiwin*
(a good life).

---

99   Mikisew Cree First Nation, *Mikisew Cree First Nation Comprehensive Plan*, 101.
100 Mikisew Cree First Nation, *Mikisew Cree First Nation Comprehensive Plan*, 101–3, 124.

VI. Conclusion

This chapter has critiqued the application of neoliberal instruments of extractive capitalism and governance to Indigenous communities. Within a market citizenship system there is a widening gap between rich and poor. Historically, Indigenous communities had norms preventing this sort of stratification from occurring. However, these norms and the ceremonies that institute them, such as the Give Away Ceremony described above must navigate the shift from living *off* the land. If citizens view the land as a commodity instead of as a spiritual gift, this changes Indigenous perceptions and principles around normative practices.

For Ghostkeeper, his disconnect with the land translated to an unbearable dissatisfaction in life. It motivated him to reflect on the traditional knowledge he had been repressing, and to develop a "revitalization model" (see figure 2.3) to explain his own revitalization.[101] This model is informed by Anthony Wallace's group revitalization theory[102] and adapted to fit a Metis context. Within this rediscovery, Ghostkeeper reflected on the normative and behavioural ideals in a Metis world view, acknowledging the diversity within. For Ghostkeeper, "During the process of self-appraisal, using the concept of the ideal self (what I really wanted to be), I rediscovered a repressed code from my traditional knowledge, the concept of spiritual exchange, which I now refer to as 'Spirit Gifting.' I revitalized this concept as a part of my way of knowing to form a new code which blends both traditional and Western scientific knowledge in a way that had been impossible for me before."[103]

Elmer Ghostkeeper decided to once again live *with* the land. However, for him this did not mean a complete rejection of Western scientific knowledge or practices. The ethic does require a continual critical approach, thoroughly examining how decisions and actions will affect the roles and responsibilities that Indigenous peoples hold as central to their identities.

For Ghostkeeper and other Indigenous leaders, the intent is not necessarily to protect themselves and their communities from outside influences at all costs. It is, however, to critically examine detrimental governmental and market governing forces. It is crucial to fully understand the two-pronged approach of settler colonialism: state domination and economic exploitation. Self-determination is not achieved by

---

101 Ghostkeeper, *Spirit Gifting*, 81.
102 Mikisew Cree First Nation, *Mikisew Cree First Nation Comprehensive Plan*.
103 Ghostkeeper, *Spirit Gifting*, 80.

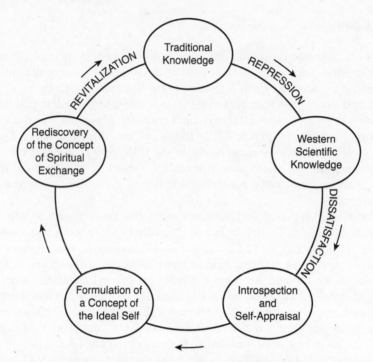

Figure 2.3. Revitalization Model (Ghostkeeper, *Spirit Gifting*, 81)

replacing one colonial logic with the other. Ghostkeeper's personal narrative shows how market citizenship can be incompatible with Indigenous world views of reciprocal relationships, especially extractive resource development. Relations with the land shape Indigenous identity. Without continual individual and collective reflexivity, perpetual discontent might settle in, making capital accumulation and self-determination a hollow achievement.

With settler-colonialism and economic exploitation, most scholars and the general populace tend to see only the tip of the iceberg: Indigenous economic relationships that fall within the view of the neoliberal lens. Indigenous practices that fall principally outside of capitalism are seen as non-economic, such as ceremonial practices fitting only within the spiritual realm. While Indigenous peoples can see Indigenous governance and economic relationships as embedded in the ceremonial cycle, settler-colonialism makes silos of these different practices. By removing the blinders to recognize Indigenous economic relationships in everyday practices and in the sublime practices, we witness acts of resistance as strong antidotes to "colonial dissonance."[104] In this paradigm, Giveaways are not only seen as ceremony. They can be seen as a Cree institution with spiritual, social, and economic functions. This Cree institution, as one of many examples, provides key insights into the collective world view and a foundation for understanding Cree economic principles and practices.

The work of the future is to go beyond a critique of colonialism and draw on Indigenous intellectual resources to provide a more situated understanding of the critique and intellectual norms, as well as applied practices embedded within our epistemologies that shed new light on economic relationships. Indigenous and non-Indigenous scholars in this text have increasingly recognized the pitfalls and gaps of neoliberalism. Indigenous societies who continue to draw on place-based knowledges situated within the historical and continuous relationships in their territories provide alternatives.

---

104 Shalene Jobin, "Cree Economic Relationships Governance and Critical Indigenous Political Economy in Resistance to Settler-Colonial Logics" (PhD diss., University of Alberta, 2014). Here I provide the concept of colonial dissonance to explore the breaking of *Wahkohtowin* (the governance of relationships), which affects the spiritual, physical, emotional, and mental aspects of Indigenous personhood, and peoplehood. It is also the breaking of relationships between Indigenous people, Indigenous-Cree people, non-human beings, and spirit beings (199–210).

3 The Principle of Sharing and the Shadow of Canadian Property Law

SARAH MORALES AND BRIAN THOM

I. Introduction

"Laws arise whenever inter-personal interactions create expectations and obligations about proper conduct."[1] They may be enumerated in many different ways, from declarations, to adjudicatory decisions, to agreements, and in some instances even implied agreements or customary norms. In most situations the expectations and obligations themselves will represent a common denominator of shared values and practices. However, this is not the case for legally pluralistic states like Canada, where the common law, civil law, and Indigenous legal traditions organize dispute resolution, and create legal expectations and obligations in our country in different ways.[2]

Long before Europeans arrived in their territories, the social, political, and spiritual customs of the Island Hul'qumi'num[3] peoples guided their interactions and relations. These customs and traditions

---

1 John Borrows, *Canada's Indigenous Constitution* (Toronto: University of Toronto Press, 2010), 7.
2 Borrows, *Canada's Indigenous Constitution*, 8.
3 The Island Hul'qumi'num peoples are an Indigenous community of approximately 7,500 people living in and around the southeast coast of Vancouver Island, British Columbia. Culturally and linguistically, they are Coast Salish peoples who have lived in this area since time immemorial, with archaeological sites in the area showing continuous occupation for at least 5,000 years. See Donald Mitchell, "Archaeology of the Gulf of Georgia Area, a Natural Region and Its Culture Types," *Syesis* 4, no. 1 (1971): 1; R.L. Carlson and P.M. Hobler, "The Pender Canal Excavations and the Development of Coast Salish Culture," *BC Studies* 99 (1993): 25; R.L. Carlson, "Excavations at Helen Point on Mayne Island," *BC Studies* 6 (1970): 113; Dave Johnstone, "The Function(s) of a Shellmidden Site from the Southern Strait of

are best understood in the context of an Indigenous system of law. With European colonization came the introduction of another legal system that sought to transform and subordinate Hul'qumi'num legal orders. The laws of the Island Hul'qumi'num peoples, including the laws relating to Indigenous land tenure, were generally not observed or respected by colonial authorities because of their "perceived incompatibility with, or supposed inferiority within, the legal hierarchy."[4] One might argue that there was a misunderstanding by the colonizers about the nature of Island Hul'qumi'num peoples' laws – that they were nothing more than protocol or tradition. However, a more critical view suggests that Hul'qumi'num legal traditions were denigrated because they conflicted with the exercise of colonial power.

Georgia" (MA thesis, Simon Fraser University, 1991); British Columbia, Ministry of Tourism, Sport and the Arts, *Archaeological Excavations and Monitoring DfRw 1, Silverstrand Road, Chemainus IR 13, Ladysmith* (Victoria: IR Wilson Consultants, 2004).

The Island Hul'qumi'num peoples we profile in this case study include the member First Nations of the Hul'qumi'num Treaty Group (HTG), a political organization formed in 1993 to engage in comprehensive negotiations with the federal and provincial governments for recognition of Hul'qumi'num peoples' rights, title, and governance. The five First Nations members of this organization include Cowichan Tribes, Penelakut Tribe, Lyackson First Nation, Halalt First Nation, and Lake Cowichan First Nation. While not every Island Hul'qumi'num community are members of the HTG (Stz'uminus First Nation has withdrawn from the table, Snuneymuxw First Nation is involved in independent negotiations, and Snaw-naw-as First Nation is negotiating as a part of the Te'mexw Treaty Association), these are the communities with whom we have worked closely over an extended period of time and have together articulated a clear vision for the recognition of their Aboriginal title, rights, and governance. See Hul'qumi'num Treaty Group, *Getting to 100%* (Ladysmith, BC: Hul'qumi'num Treaty Group, 2005); Brian Evans, Julia Gardner, Brian Thom, and Lee Joe, *Shxunutun's Tu Suleluxstst, in the Footsteps of Our Ancestors: Interim Strategic Land Plan for the Hul'qumi'num Core Traditional Territory* (Ladysmith, BC: Hul'qumi'num Treaty Group, 2005).

Their asserted core territory, which we will refer to here as Hul'qumi'num Territory, forms a geographically contiguous unit from the Nanaimo River in the north, the headwaters of Cowichan Lake in the west, the lands to the west of Saanich Inlet in the south, many of the Gulf Islands in the Salish Sea, as well as a portion of the lower Fraser River. This area has never been formally acknowledged or recognized by either the federal or British Columbia provincial governments. Indeed, at the Inter-American Commission, Canada denied this area as title lands. See Brian Thom, "Reframing Indigenous Territories: Private Property, Human Rights and Overlapping Claims," *American Indian Culture and Research Journal* 34, no. 4 (2014): 3.

4 Borrows, *Canada's Indigenous Constitution*, 8.

Although many examples could be drawn upon to illustrate this under-mining of Island Hul'qumi'num peoples' law, this chapter presents an analysis of Hul'qumi'num property law, and in particular highlighting its governing principle of sharing. We argue that though Indigenous property law continues to inform Island Hul'qumi'num peoples legal orders, conventional Canadian property law casts a strong shadow on the legal landscape and makes it difficult for these principles to be seen and exercised. We make the case that while operating in the shadow, Hul'qumi'num peoples legal orders are not entirely subordinated (con-tra Jobin, this volume), and indeed deeply inform their exercise of prop-erty relations – whether state-based or Indigenous – to this day. The idiom of sharing is one of the inherent legal principles that emanates from the concept of *snuw'uyulh*.[5] *Snuw'uyulh* is a Hul'qumi'num word that has many glosses in English, from "the teachings" to "our way of life" or "our way of being on Mother Earth."[6] Accordingly, it touches on all aspects of life and is inseparable from Island Hul'qumi'num peo-ples' relations to each other, the natural world, and the spiritual world.[7] It is also legal in nature. Through the principles that emanate from *snuw'uyulh*, Island Hul'qumi'num peoples can determine standards and practices for judgment and decision-making that help to regulate relationships and resolve disputes. One important area the principle of sharing works is in the way it significantly influences laws associated with land and resource ownership and access. This is reflected through practices that provide norms and standards for the access rights of kin to family- or community-owned locales, and the development of pro-tocols that allow for non-kin to access community and family-owned resources sites in certain circumstances.[8]

Despite the presence of this well-established legal tradition, over the past 160 years Western property law has cast a long shadow over the Island Hul'qumi'num peoples' legal orders. Under these condi-tions, it can be difficult to see the Hul'qumi'num law operating, and Island Hul'qumi'num peoples are challenged in having the light of their legal norms and practices recognized or distinguished. None-theless, they persist. This chapter attempts to examine this process of shadowing by (1) examining the principle of sharing within Island

---

5 See Sarah Morales, "Snuw'uyulh: Fostering an Understanding of the Hul'qumi'num Legal Tradition" (PhD diss., University of Victoria, 2014).

6 Morales, "Snuw'uyulh," 6.

7 Morales, "Snuw'uyulh," 17.

8 See Brian Thom, "Coast Salish Sense of Place: Dwelling, Meaning, Power, Property and Territory in the Coast Salish World" (PhD diss., McGill University, 2005).

Hul'qumi'num peoples' property law; (2) illustrating how Western concepts of property have overshadowed, and at times incorporated into, Island Hul'qumi'num peoples' property laws and practices; and (3) concluding with a few observations that demonstrate why a respect for the legal principle of sharing is required for Hul'qumi'num property law to emerge from the shadow of colonial law. We do not intend to definitively set out or codify this legal system — something only Island Hul'qumi'num peoples can do through their own accountable governance institutions and practices. Rather, as situated observers of these legal orders, we wish to reflect on their resilience and continuing importance in social relations today. Customary practice is largely undocumented, often as a result of conscious efforts to keep it that way. Yet legal principles still emerge from community members, framed in ways that incorporate contemporary and traditional legal methods.

II. The Principle of Sharing

Property can be understood as "relational sets of rights distributed among individuals and groups in ways that make existing property regimes and claims specific, limited and, frequently, shared."[9] This understanding of property as a distribution of relational rights arguably captures Island Hul'qumi'num peoples' understandings of property. However, issues arise when "our conceptions of property are premised on the drawing of bright lines,"[10] because the creation of those boundaries "entails the conversion of social relations into a set of discrete bounded things."[11] Some scholars have argued that Western property law is just like Indigenous land tenure systems, simply defining discrete territories by the use of place names, boundary points, and family and community histories.[12] Yet such an analogy over-simplifies the principles on which Island Hul'qumi'num property relations are grounded. Specifically, such an analysis ignores Island Hul'qumi'num peoples' recognition that the land is one of numerous subjects, along with ancestors, kin, and non-human agents like rocks, trees, or pools.

---

9 Scott Prudham and William Coleman, "Introduction: Property, Autonomy, Territory, and Globalization," in *Property, Territory, Globalization: Struggles over Autonomy*, ed. William Coleman (Vancouver: UBC Press, 2011), 8.

10 Nicholas Blomely, "Cuts, Flows, and the Culture of Geography," *Law, Culture, and the Humanities* 7, no. 2 (2011): 205.

11 Blomely, "Cuts, Flows, and the Culture of Geography."

12 See Tom Flanagan, Christopher Alcantara, and André Le Dressay, *Beyond the Indian Act: Restoring Aboriginal Property Rights* (Montreal and Kingston: McGill-Queen's University Press, 2010).

These subjects are all bound by reciprocal relations of sharing and respect, a fundamental principle of Island Hul'qumi'num peoples' property laws.

Island Hul'qumi'num oral traditions about the First Ancestors demonstrate some of the basic legal principles that people use to express their relationship to the land and each other.[13] Through these stories, ancestors are associated *with* and embodied *in* the land. The telling of these stories along with the experiences of these beings at these places brings these legendary people to life.[14] In essence, these places *are* the Ancestors; they are "living" legal scholars. They are places where the Island Hul'qumi'num legal tradition can be "applied, studied, perfected and taught."[15]

As one travels throughout the entire Coast Salish world to which the Island Hul'qumi'num peoples belong, the places where these First Ancestors fell are marked by contemporary village sites and stone landmarks.[16] For example, in the Cowichan Valley, Syalutsa' was the first Ancestor to fall from the sky. He fell to the warm ground of Quw'utsun' near present-day Koksilah Ridge.[17] His younger brother Stuts'un was the second ancestor who dropped from the sky. He and his legendary dog Wuq'us landed at Swuq'us (Mt Prevost). If one looks carefully at Swuq'us, one can see the face of Stuts'un in the profile of the mountain. His very being is indelibly inscribed in the land, while his descendants and namesakes continue to share a special connection to the area.[18]

The sites where these First Ancestors dropped serve as a reminder to the Island Hul'qumi'num peoples of their historic and continuing relationships to one another and the land. Just as the First Ancestors of the original communities were interrelated through kin, so too are their living descendants. As Cowichan Elder Angus Smith said, "Where you dropped is where you belong.... Particular areas were peculiar to certain groups or families, where our ancestors were dropped on earth. They

---

13 See Thom, "Coast Salish Sense of Place"; Morales, "Snuw'uyulh."
14 Tim Ingold, "A Circumpolar Night's Dream," in *The Perception of the Environment: Essays in Livelihood, Dwelling and Skill*, ed. Tim Ingold (London: Routledge, 2000), 92.
15 J.H. Merryman, *The Civil Law Tradition: An Introduction to the Legal Systems of Western Europe and Latin America*, 3rd ed. (Stanford, CA: Stanford University Press, 2007).
16 See Daniel Marshall, *Those Who Fell from the Sky: A History of the Cowichan Peoples* (Duncan, BC: Cowichan Tribes, 1999). However, note that the actual locations that First Ancestor stories are associated with are complicated and contested. See generally Thom, "Coast Salish Sense of Place."
17 Thom, "Coast Salish Sense of Place," 88–9.
18 Thom, "Coast Salish Sense of Place," 100.

were carrying cultural teachings.... The cultural teachings were shown them, instructing them what was good for their life. It was showing the First People what they could use.... That's the way it was with our ancestors; that's why the Cowichan people carry this tradition."[19]

The First Ancestors stories highlight the places with which these Ancestors are associated and provide a linking narrative for the residence groups – the named ancestral village and settlement sites people live in. In an early piece describing government and laws of the communities on the Northwest Coast, the famous anthropologist Franz Boas observed, "The Coast Salish derive their claims to certain tracts of land in the same way [as the Kwakwaka'wakw] from the fact that the ancestor of each gens [Boas's term for the group descended from a common ancestor] came down to a certain place, or that he settled there after the great flood."[20] The oral traditions detailing the First Ancestors buttress the ideological underpinnings of these property-owning groups' formation. The Ancestors' use of resources, skills, and technologies provided guidance for how those properties should be cared for and respected. Through establishing relationships between people, places, and cultural practices, the First Ancestor stories offer Island Hul'qumi'num peoples an important foundation of property law, which is reinforced through story, song, ceremony, and customary and other deliberative practices.

The property-owning family group, descended bilaterally from these legendary Ancestors, is called *hwunutsaluwum* in the Hul'q'umi'num' language.[21] It is not a lineage group, moiety, or clan, distinguishing Island Hul'qumi'num (and Coast Salish) social organization from that of northern Northwest Coast peoples. Rather, membership in a *hwunutsaluwum* tends to be flexible over time, emerging less from rigid social ordering, and more from the *actual practice* of ordered kin relations. Hence, Island Hul'qumi'num peoples can affiliate with a broad range of people who live in different areas throughout the Coast Salish world. Personal choice and life circumstance link others beyond the "core" descent group of individuals within the *hwunutsaluwum*. Through practised affiliation, a group can include in-laws or even visitors who claim membership through distant ancestors. Following principles of

19 *Hul'qumi'num Treaty Group Newsletter* 1, no. 10 (May 1998): 2.
20 Franz Boas, "First General Report on the Indians of British Columbia," in *Report of the Fifty-Ninth Meeting of the British Association for the Advancement of Science* (London: British Association for the Advancement of Science, 1890), 833.
21 Sarah Robinson, "Spirit Dancing among the Salish Indians" (PhD diss., University of Chicago, 1963), 27.

cognatic descent, an individual can often trace one's lineage through multiple ancestors. Merely claiming affiliation is not sufficient. Rather, to validate property claims within a potentially extensive network of kin, people have traditionally feasted and potlatched, and continue to bestow Indigenous names or ritual privileges and prerogatives, from which essential social and ceremonial practices are associated with property.

Following principles of bilateral kinship and post-marital residence exogamy, Island Hul'qumi'num peoples have enormous flexibility to choose the residence group they live within and the kin-group they associate with. Late Cowichan Elder Simon Charlie emphasized how a person can choose residence group affiliation and exercise associated property rights through connecting to kin:

> This was the old way. My grandfather's uncle in Lummi met him some-where in the States, and they told him his house site is still there. If he wanted to move there, he can move there. The same with Musqueam. The Points were closely related to my grandfather. Simon Point was my cousin. He was fishing in Fraser. And they met his uncle over there and they told him the house site was still open for him. So we didn't just belong to one area. It is the new thing that the Indian Affairs brainwashed our young people that we only come from one place. Any place where our family came from, it was open if we wanted to move there. It was opened.[22]

This is an important first principle. In the contemporary landscape of *Indian Act* rules that define band membership and constrain possibili-ties of multi-nation affiliation, "the old way" as Simon shared, of exer-cising property rights is shadowed.

Beyond where a person chooses to live, what group kin one associates with is even less well recognized in legal forms today, though they con-tinue to have important expressions in everyday life. In our experience, the Hul'qumi'num term *hwunutsaluwum*, which generally refers to the cognatic descent group, is not commonly used. However, the concept remains an important legal principle. In his dissertation on Musqueam, anthropologist Michael Kew articulated the contemporary expression of identity and association with this traditional family group.

> Villagers today refer to large divisions of themselves which more or less con-form to that of the bilateral kindred [the *hwunutsaluwum*]. The boundaries

---

22   Interview of Simon Charlie by Brian Thom, 18 July 2001.

of these units are not at all precise and to a large degree they are designated by current English surnames. For example, one hears such a unit referred to as "the Millers" or "the Blanchets." It might include several married siblings and their offspring and grandchildren plus others less directly linked, all resident in the village. The basis of these alignments is the consanguineal kin group and its immediate affines, and the closer the link the more likelihood that it will be meaningful.... Not all persons in the village are clearly members of such a "family," although all have sufficiently close ties to be claimed as members or to align themselves with a large group.[23]

Kew's description holds true in Island Hul'qumi'num communities where large families are significant and influential in local social, political, and ceremonial life. Through connecting to a descendant group of the First Ancestors, a person has opportunities to access the rights and cultural teachings associated with that group. So it is both through where one lives and who one's extended family is that property rights may be activated. This is illustrated in the sections below on sharing between kin relations; sharing with non-kin relations; shared resources areas; and sharing and the law of exclusion.

A. Sharing between Kin Relations

Ethnographers have long argued that for Coast Salish peoples, relationships between extended networks of kin are critical for understanding the workings of local systems of land and resource tenure.[24] While common residence in a village or settlement does offer access to areas in the collective commons, where you live is not as important socially, economically, and politically as who your family is and what properties, both real and intangible, your family belongs to. In Island Hul'qumi'num ways of relating, relatives are recognized bilaterally through consanguineal kin, and key alliances are made through affinal ties, resulting in an extensive network of people who may be able to claim residence at or access to sites of importance economically and socially, either permanent or on a temporary visiting basis.

---

23 Michael Kew, "Coast Salish Ceremonial Life: Status and Identity in a Modern Village" (PhD diss., University of Washington, 1970), 74.

24 See Homer Barnett, *The Coast Salish of British Columbia* (Eugene: University of Oregon Press, 1955); Wayne Suttles, "The Persistence of Intervillage Ties among the Coast Salish," *Ethnology* 2 (1963): 512; Dorothy Kennedy, "Qualifying 'Two Sides of a Coin': A Statistical Examination of the Central Coast Salish Social Network," *BC Studies* 153 (2007): 3; Thom, "Coast Salish Sense of Place."

Marjorie Louie, a Stz'uminus elder, shared with us the importance of knowing who your relatives are for knowing what areas could be used for harvesting. Knowledge of your family, and the dutiful engaging in relationships of respect and reciprocity with them, is key to unlocking the critical places that a person could travel to and harvest at.

> They [the old people] didn't say, "We owned this place." As they travelled they went to visit relatives, and they'd stop at places where they knew they could gather food. Generation after generation you know, travelling to these places that somebody says now, "I own this" [like Indian reserves]. Generation after generation, they knew where to go to gather food.
>
> It was just passed on. As you were growing up you knew where to go. I didn't realize this until I got into Indian names [ancestral family names bestowed upon people during their life] when my mother-in-law and grandmother-in-law started telling me to write down Indian names. And it showed how everybody was interrelated then, just through the Indian names.
>
> My grandmother-in-law went back seven generations and her name came from, what you call that place, Musqueam. That's where her Indian name originated....
>
> So you can see why these people now think we own that territory. But it was relationships, everybody was related. Certain time of the year like when the ducks are here, my in-laws knew that a relative in Cowichan would like some ducks. They'd shoot ducks and then travel down to Cowichan. Because the relatives came from there.[25]

Elder Louie makes a fundamental point in drawing the connection between Indigenous names, knowing who family are, and access to both residence group commons and family owned lands. It is through this knowledge of one's kin and the prerogatives associated with kin that the tenure system operates. Indigenous names are strategically given to children, linking them to ancestors who have lived in different parts of the Coast Salish world. An individual may have rights to access resource locations through the acknowledgment of these ancestral connections, in addition to the more direct consanguineal or affinal relations, which may also be claimed. However, merely carrying an ancestral name does not give complete access to resource harvesting areas. Activating those rights includes following expectations of sharing the benefits of the harvest, such as Elder Louie's example of sharing

---

25 Interview of Elder Marjorie Louie by Brian Thom, 19 January 2001.

ducks, and respecting local knowledge and ritual protocol with respect to those areas. In essence, one must be a law-abiding citizen to gain the benefits associated with the laws; with rights also come responsibilities.

Arvid Charlie, a Cowichan elder who has shared generously with us, also spoke to the importance of family connections, and the strategies that people took to maximize their ability to obtain resources in areas that were outside their immediate village-site areas:

> In the old days we went to many areas where there were material things we needed for our use. Some of it was not in our, I guess what you'd call our "core area" today. They were beyond – some of them way beyond.
>
> So how I was told was to keep peace and be able to harvest those materials, we married off or left a man over there. Married off the girls there, or that particular man over there. So we could have a – I don't know if you can call it family rights or community rights – to be allowed to come in there.[26]

Island Hul'qumi'num people generally recognize that marriage into a community brings with it rights for the incoming spouse and her or his children to take part in the common ownership of community territories. A prominent Stz'uminus family leader explained this principle with his own family, recalling that his wife originally came from Halalt, that her father was from Cowichan, but since their marriage she is "100 per cent Stz'uminus." The marriage gives her rights to use lands and resources associated with her family at Stz'uminus. However, this does not necessarily give the family from Stz'uminus rights to land and resources of the families in Halalt: "I have come from a position of respect for a people, basically, and that respect has to be that they are a people and a nation with their own core territory and a land. That's why I keep saying things like if a person married me, like my wife, she comes from Halalt. Just because my wife is from Halalt doesn't mean Stz'uminus owns Halalt, in terms of a core territory. I have it clear in my mind in terms of how I approach them."[27]

Rights to use certain productive land and resource locales come to the person who is marrying into a community, but rights originating in their home community must be negotiated through relationships with in-laws. This system works equally for women and men marrying into their partner's community. For instance, Roy Edwards was originally from Lamalchi Bay on Kuper Island and married into his wife's

---

26 Interview of Elder Arvid Charlie by Brian Thom, 3 April 2001.
27 Interview of Stz'uminus Family Leader by Brian Thom, 13 July 2001.

community at Stz'uminus, living there his entire adult life. Rights of that community were extended to him through his wife and her family. By contrast, Chief Peter Seymour emphasized that he would have to "butter up" his in-laws for access to their areas at sites away from his home at St'zuminus, but he could access areas of his own consanguineal family sites with less trouble. Within this system, there are many possibilities to activate and emphasize one's particular family connections in relation to land and resource rights. Hence, it is often key for one to actually reside on the land and pay respect to and share with the families associated with these places.

These examples point to the legal principle that areas held in common by local residence groups (like the named village communities) are open to their residents, and under normal circumstances there is an expectation of sharing with a resident's kin, unless they are explicitly closed. Particular locales held by corporate kin groups are more restricted, with technical and ritual knowledge, as well as physical access being more limited to in the case of distant kin. The right of access to these areas is negotiated through making one's residence or kin affiliation clearly known, though names, stories, genealogical knowledge, or ritual practice, and maintained through engaging with good relations of respect and reciprocity. These circumstances do not imply that most productive locations sites are simply open to all because of the potentially expansive kin network any individual could activity. As will be illustrated later on, these sites are closed unless open to non-kin or non-residents, with serious consequences for those who do not recognize and respect local protocols and laws.

B. Sharing with Non-Kin Relations

In an economy that thrives on reciprocal use of owned resource locations, the idiom and practice of sharing are important to maintain opportunity and future access beyond one's own residence group's area.

Several Hul'qumi'num elders shared with us their view about how some watersheds around Lake Cowichan were the property of certain families, while others were open to the whole Island Hul'qumi'num community. The following discussion with Cowichan Elders Dennis Alphonse and Angus Smith illustrates the way family hunting systems continue to be understood today.

AS: The hunting territory was originally ... Each family has their own hunting territories in Cowichan. Nobody can go in there. That's the

same way with Lake Cowichan. There was only four of them: one
from Cowichan, Qwam'utsun [Quamichan] and Lhumlhumuluts
[Clemclemaluts] and Qw'umi'iqun [Comiaken] can go up there and
hunt. They're strict on their hunting. If anybody went ... anyone can ask
them if they can go up there. You've got to get permission from them to
go up there. These people used to go up there on a canoe. So that was his
own hunting territory. This old man from Cowichan ...

BT: Were the other mountains in other places also family hunting territories?

AS: Well, in that area? I don't know if there's any other place in that area.
But over across, on this side is a place they call ... Xwaaqw'um [place
name for area east of Youbou on the north side of Cowichan Lake
meaning "place of mallard ducks"]. Yeah, right there. That's the creek
next to Honeymoon Bay. Not Honeymoon Bay but Youbou, the mill. Just
past that. There's a creek there, just past Youbou.

DA: A lot of Cowichan hunting?

AS: That's another hunting, everybody goes in there, it's open for them to
hunt.

BT: So some of the places were open to everybody and some of the places
were restricted?

AS: Some of them were really strict on their hunting.[28]

Privately owned family ungulate hunting areas are not common in
the literature, but the area around Cowichan Lake was recorded by an
early observer, Robert Brown, who said, "One or two Samena families
hunt on Cowichan Lake in the autumn ... [and that the Somenos] are
the only tribe to frequent the upper waters of the Cowichan River."[29]
This observation is further recognized by an intriguing short story told
by Abner Thorne about the defence of these family hunting grounds:
"There is a story of, I guess even with the arrival of firearms or rifles or
whatever it was that they used. I don't know which mountain it was,
but these two Cowichan met, and I guess this guy knew that was this
guy's hunting ground. They each put their gun on them, you know.
They stood there for I don't know how long, you know. I was thinking they were better that they didn't fire at each other. So they, I guess
they were particular. Yeah, they were particular about who was on the
territory."[30] These rules around hunting grounds are understood in the
broader context of sharing among networks of kin within the particular
territories of local residence groups.

28 Interview of Angus Smith and Dennis Alphonse by Brian Thom, 9 July 2001.
29 Robert Brown, *Vancouver Island Exploration* (Victoria, BC: Harries, 1864), 188.
30 Interview of Abner Thorne by Brian Thom, 21 November 2000.

Peter Pierre, a Katzie elder, stated that there was "no feeling of boundaries. Salt-water people came up here [to the Pitt River area] to hunt. All my friends came. My country is like a great table: everyone comes here to eat. Old people [are] good-hearted, glad to see everyone. People from here never went down to get clams, people who visited brought them up and traded them."[31] While this is a gratuitous statement of generosity and friendship, it does reveal the relationship of host and guest, which people are presumed to understand and respect. Use of the productive hunting and berry areas around Pitt Lake could be reciprocated by providing some acceptable value in return. Suttles, who worked with Pierre's son Simon, reflected that "when outsiders came, they had to get permission from the owners [of cranberry bogs] before they could gather the berries."[32] As long as the berries were ripe, "the bog 'owners' would not refuse anyone permission to pick them, nor did they exact any tribute from the outsiders."[33] From this, Suttles concluded that part of what made ownership of places like cranberry bogs important was that it enabled "the owners to play the role of hosts. A host at any one time and place is potentially a guest at another"[34] and thus an important part of the potlatch economy.

Indeed, there is abundant ethnographic evidence that sharing of use-rights to these areas with non-kin or extra-local visitors does not create an unrestricted commons resource. Boas, for example, noted that access to these sites was controlled, as "each gens has its proper hunting and fishing grounds, upon which neither members of other tribes nor of other gentes must intrude except by special permission."[35] He went on to describe the principle that ownership of these locations is inalienable and indestructible: "The right of a gens to the place where it originated cannot be destroyed. It may acquire by war or by other events territory belonging to foreign tribes, and leave its home to be taken up by others; the right of fishing, hunting, and gathering berries in their old home is rigidly maintained."[36]

Hill-Tout, another anthropologist working in the 1890s, likewise observed that Chehalis people were paid by visitors to allow access

---

31   Marion Smith, "Collected Manuscripts and Field Notes Ms No 268" (London: Museum of Mankind and the Royal Anthropological Institute, 1947), 3.
32   Wayne Suttles, *Katzie Ethnographic Notes* (Victoria: British Columbia Provincial Museum, 1955), 26.
33   Suttles, *Katzie Ethnographic Notes*.
34   Suttles, *Katzie Ethnographic Notes*.
35   Boas, "First General Report," 833.
36   Boas, "First General Report."

to the popular and distinctive spring salmon on the Harrison River, which have a fatty, golden flesh, unlike many other runs of Fraser River salmon: "Tribes from long distances used to come every salmon season and pay the [Chehalis] a kind of tribute or royalty to be permitted to fish in their waters. Bands from Interior Salish tribes and from far up and down the coast would congregate there in the fishing season. Sometimes disturbances and fights would occur, but the [Chehalis] were a strong and populous tribe and seem to have been able to more than hold their own with their visitors."[37]

Nooksack people, to provide a final example, "rigidly excluded some outsiders from hunting mountain goats within their territory,"[38] a resource associated with hereditary wealth and privilege, with the wool used to make blankets, and the horn to make bracelets and rattles. These examples come from a time in the nineteenth and early twentieth centuries before Coast Salish property law was largely overshadowed by government regulation, along with the wholesale transformation of Indigenous territories to private, fee-simple lands. Despite the Coast Salish peoples' numerous possibilities of sharing access to resource areas through networks of kin and non-kin, subject to terms and conditions including the explicit granting of permission and the payment for use, they upheld their laws, vigorously defending against uninvited or unauthorized access and use.

Island Hul'qumi'num peoples' strategies of redistribution emphasize the legal principle of sharing among kin. These strategies are practised by controlling specific technical and ritual knowledge about particular locales, including knowledge of their actual location, in areas held in common by a village community. "People also shared food with neighbours and relatives from other communities by sharing access to their techniques and/or resources. One conjugal family working alone had the instruments for and equal access to most types of resources within the territory of its community. But some of the most productive techniques required the cooperation of several persons. Moreover, access to some of the most productive sites was restricted by property rights."[39]

---

37 Charles Hill-Tout, "Ethnological Report on the Stseélis and Sk·aulits Tribes of the Halokmélem Division of the Salish of British Columbia," *Journal of the Anthropological Institute of Great Britain and Ireland* 34 (1904): 316.

38 Allan Richardson, "The Control of Productive Resources on the Northwest Coast of North America," in *Resource Managers: North American and Australian Hunter-Gatherers*, ed. Nancy Williams and Eugene Hunn (Boulder, CO: Westview, 1982), 101.

39 Wayne Suttles, "Affinal Ties, Subsistence, and Prestige among the Coast Salish," *American Anthropologist* 62, no. 2 (1960): 300.

Note, not every location within a territory is held in common. Many of the particularly important locales had more restrictive property relations associated with it, such as being owned by a particular family. However, even in these places, people developed relationships of sharing. For instance, in the reef-net fishery, sometimes characterized as being practised only by Straits Salish peoples, the principle of sharing offered opportunities for reciprocating in sharing access to a productive locale: "Some Cowichans fished in the summer on reef nets belonging to Saanich and some of the Saanich, who had no important stream in their territory, went to the Cowichan River for the fall runs of fish caught at weirs."[40] Suttles further observed that while owners were in charge of the fishery at these locations, the crews who fished them could be, and often were, hired from any of the surrounding communities.[41] Hence, the Island Hul'qumi'num peoples and their neighbours would share through hiring wage labourers, who would get a portion of the catch, rather than granting access of free use. As this example demonstrates, the legal principle of sharing diversely regulates and manifests the Island Hul'qumi'num system of land tenure.

These statements and ethnographic records exemplify how important the principle of sharing is to property law of the Island Hul'qumi'num peoples. Although access to territories or particular locales are controlled by residence groups or individual families, not mean all others are excluded from accessing these areas or the resources associated with them. Rather, the principle of sharing entails that residence groups or families open access to these areas, although with control mechanisms, to ensure reciprocal access to other important areas and the guarding against misuse or unwelcome exploitation. This is an important observation, because in Western land tenure systems, a primary benefit of ownership is the ability to exclude access.

C. Shared Resource Areas

As Thom has argued elsewhere,[42] an important principle of Coast Salish land tenure is that two or more residence groups may jointly own certain productive resource locales or portions of a territory. Such shared territories can be located at some distance from permanent

---

40   Suttles, "Affinal Ties."
41   Wayne Suttles, "The Economic Life of the Coast Salish of Haro and Rosario Straits" (PhD diss., University of Washington, 1951), 219.
42   Brian Thom, "The Paradox of Boundaries in Coast Salish Territories," *Cultural Geographies* 16 (2009): 179.

winter villages, where people have long-established amicable use and occupation of an area. Cowichan Elder Arvid Charlie described it in the following way:

> Here is a good example of a difference between overlapped and shared. I'm not sure the name of this bay, but on Mayne Island there's a point called Graveyard's Point and a bay, it might be called Miner's Bay, but I'm not certain. In my travels with the elders I was trying to map where the houses were at that bay – not big longhouses, but smaller individual houses. They were pointing out, "This is Big Joe's house, from Stz'uminus, this is So-and-so's house from Cowichan." I forgot the other ones. Those houses, older-time dwellings, were right next to each other. So those three were at that place in the bay, but within that spot they each had their own little spot. And there are teachings that come with that. Like, if Big Joe wasn't there, then those others could use his spot until he arrived. That's shared.[43]

Arvid's example is particularly instructive. Despite this location being near Helen Point Indian Reserve 6, which is held by Tsartlip First Nation under the *Indian Act*, from the perspective of Island Hul'qumi'num law, the locale is not exclusively for families from that Indian band. Rather, Island Hul'qumi'num people see this as an area held jointly and amicably by families from neighbouring residence groups who are today separate *Indian Act*–constituted First Nations. The waters around Active Pass are strategic and productive harvesting locales, and these families jointly and amicably share them.

While ritual knowledge and physical control over these areas may often be held collectively by the residents of these communities, the stewardship and management of these areas are limited to certain members. Barbara Lane recorded the novel solution that Penelakut and Lyackson hunters worked out for managing the jointly held sea lion hunting area in Porlier Pass. First, only members of these two communities knew the "secret and inherited ritual songs necessary to bring the animal under control."[44] The Lyackson hunters camped on their "permanent lookout" on the south tip of Valdes Island, while the Penelakut hunters resided at theirs on the north end of Galiano Island. The following description of the hunt shows an underlying principle of respect for another individual's ritual power and acknowledged rules for sharing jointly held resources, in the face of serious competition for an important resource:

---

43 Interview of Arvid Charlie by Sarah Morales, 29 December 2015.
44 Barbara Lane, "A Comparative and Analytical Study of Some Aspects of Northwest Coast Religion" (PhD diss., University of Washington, 1953), 76.

When the lookouts sighted a sea lion, they called to their camps and canoes were immediately dispatched.... As the canoes approached, the sea lion returned to the water and the chase began. If the first man who speared the animal were a T'eet'qe' [Lyackson] man, all the Penelakut canoes would have to abandon the chase and return home. If a Penelakut man struck it first, the T'eet'qe' were out of the running.

As soon as the first man had placed his spear, he laid his paddle across the canoe in front of him, took a little stick, and beat on the paddle while he "sang" (siuín si'win') to the sea lion to calm it and to make it surface again close to the canoes so that his co-villagers could also spear it.

Meanwhile, the "losing" party paddled off some distance, and then laying their paddles across their canoes they took up sticks and sang to make the sea-lion wild, so that he would break away or at least be difficult to subdue....

After several more of the victorious groups speared the sea lion, they put their paddles across their canoes, beat on them with sticks, and sang to "intercept" the song of the opposing group so that the sea lion would not be "rough."[45]

It is useful to know that the origin story of the sea lion connects these two communities by providing a charter myth for commonly held sea lion property rights.[46] These symbolic references highlight the tight interlinkage of residence, descent, and importance of the idiom of kin in the recognition of joint ownership.

These examples illustrate the legal mechanisms for the joint holding of commons property between residence group communities within the Island Hul'qumi'num tradition. Although the previous sections have demonstrated that sometimes the principle of sharing requires granting controlled access to certain ownership areas, this section illustrates that not all resource areas are owned exclusively. Island Hul'qumi'num property law recognizes joint ownership, a principle reinforced through shared histories or stories, which generate a source of such rights.

D. Sharing and the Law of Exclusion

The previous sections' emphasis on sharing represent only one aspect of Island Hul'qumi'num property law. Kinship is also a fundamental aspect of the legal tradition creating obligations and rights. While the Island Hul'qumi'num web of kin affiliation is wide, not

45 Lane, "Comparative and Analytical Study," 76–7.
46 Thom, "Coast Salish Sense of Place," 98.

everyone in the world is related. Accordingly, unfettered access to these resource areas for "different people" or "foreigners" (*nuts'uwmuhw* in Hul'q'num'num), such as non-Salish people with whom there are very few, if any, kin relations, is unlikely. Unless explicit understandings are reached between *nuts'uwmuhw* and local people, the residence group members will respond to and defend against such trespass. As Ts'ules (William Charles Seymour) explained, "There are traditional hunting boundaries in our territory. In the past, if someone wanted to hunt in our traditional territory, they had to seek permission to make it up the river. Even then, if they didn't have the knowledge to get up the river, they would have to have someone guide them. If we go into another nation's hunting territory, the mainland in particular, we will contact the other bands or tribes and ask permission to hunt mule deer and other game."[47]

To the south, for Coast Salish peoples in Puget Sound, anthropologist Sally Snyder recorded oral histories of Skagit peoples' defence of hunting and fishing areas against "trespass by uninvited strangers," which they thought of "the same as theft."[48] She used the Skagit term *ch'ech'it-sul* [*č'ač'izel*, as she writes it] to describe a system of laws that were understood throughout the region under which "any trespasser was expected to be killed and buried on the spot by the first armed Native who saw him."[49] Death was not the only historic solution. In one Skagit story, a boy who became lost at night was construed as a trespasser. The parties – the family of the boy and the owners of land – resolved the "dispute" by having the boy's family present gifts to the offended landowners. The story "underlines the insistence upon exclusive property rights and clannish suspiciousness about any and all strangers."[50]

Snyder's research also pointed out the distinction Skagit people made between neighbouring Coast Salish peoples and "outsiders" who did not have any rights to land or resources in the area: "Neighbours were humans *a'citibixw'* [us living here], because their lives were regulated in the same way, according to the same rules. They understood the subtleties of the feud, the snub, the verbal innuendo. But never, for most Skagits, could *sti'tlalh* [foreigners] be one of the *a'citibixw'*. They were capable only of physical not social destruction; in other words, they could not humiliate. And so Skagits dealt accordingly with *sti'tlalh*.

---

47 Interview of William Charles Seymour by Sarah Morales, 21 January 2010.
48 Sally Snyder, "Skagit Society and Its Existential Basis: An Ethnofolkloristic Reconstruction" (PhD diss., University of Washington, 1964), 432.
49 Snyder, "Skagit Society."
50 Snyder, "Skagit Society," 433.

Reprisals could be swift and brutal, consequences never were social but as impersonal as any in the world of Skagits."[51]

As Snyder's research demonstrates, "outsiders" whose behaviour towards resource management could not be controlled through social pressures, such as embarrassment and ostracizing, were often not permitted to use these resource areas. In fact, sometimes they were summarily killed if found encroaching on the territory.[52] Hence, access to resource areas and lands is limited to people who understand the law. These rules include both the legal rules applicable to resource extraction, such as respect, sharing, kinship, and the standards of conflict resolution. While sharing is a guiding principle within the legal tradition, exceptions are made to preserve the system itself.

III. The Colonial Transformation of Property

Although Island Hul'qumi'num property law relies heavily on sharing, property relations have been transformed in enormously powerful ways by colonialism. In *The Translation of Land into Property* Paul Patton examines the disappointing results that occur for Indigenous peoples when the law tries to interpret Indigenous property rights.[53] He argues that the resulting "weak and relatively restricted form of property right" is due to the stark differences between Indigenous systems of land tenure and kinship and non-Indigenous systems.[54] In Canadian contexts, this disconnect is demonstrated through the imposition of the land system of the *Indian Act*[55] and related legislation,[56] or through recent attempts by the court to define Aboriginal title.[57] In spite of significant socio-political transformations by the state, Island Hul'qumi'num ways of relating to the land, the values and norms of territoriality, and property relations among social groups persist. These resilient social institutions form the basis of how Island Hul'qumi'num peoples are grounding their twenty-first-century efforts towards recognition of

---

51 Snyder, "Skagit Society,"435.
52 Snyder, "Skagit Society," 432–3.
53 Paul Patton, "The Translation of Indigenous Land into Property: The Mere Analogy of English Jurisprudence," *Parallax* 6, no. 1 (2000): 28.
54 Patton, "The Translation of Indigenous Land."
55 RSC 1985, c I-5.
56 *First Nations Land Management Act*, SC 1999, c 24; *First Nations Certain of Land Title Act*, SC 2010, c 6.
57 *Williams v R*, [1992] 1 SCR 877, 90 DLR (4th) 129; *Delgamuukw v British Columbia*, [1997] 3 SCR 1010, 153 DLR (4th) 193; *R v Marshall*, 2005 SCC 43, [2005] 2 SCR 220; *Tsilhqot'in v British Columbia*, 2014 SCC 44, [2014] 2 SCR 257.

land rights and inter-community relations. These confound the state practices and aspirations to "normalize" property rights and gain economic certainly over the land. This section discusses the transformation and resilience of Island Hul'qumi'num property law by examining the history of land alienation; the resistance to land alienation; property in and on Indian reserves; and the continuation of aboriginal property.

A. The History of Land Alienation

One overwhelmingly important event in the history the Island Hul'qumi'num peoples was the massive transfer of land by the federal government to coal baron James Dunsmuir in 1884, known as the E&N Railway Grant, which overnight turned nearly all of Hul'qumi'num peoples' lands on Vancouver Island into private land owned in fee simple by a non-Indigenous landowner.[58] In addition to the E&N Railway Grant, the state promoted pre-emption on Vancouver Island and the Gulf Islands so that nearly the entire Island Hul'qumi'num traditional territory, other than a few small parcels of forest land that reverted to the Crown in the 1930s, is currently privately owned. This situation is in stark contrast to much of the rest of British Columbia where Indigenous territories are primarily Crown land.

The history of this large state alienation of Indigenous lands began in the late 1850s, when James Douglas, the colonial governor of Vancouver Island, ordered a formal survey of the Cowichan Valley and Saltspring Island for agricultural land settlement.[59] In 1862 Douglas further facilitated the taking up of land titles for agricultural settlement by having a Royal Navy gunboat accompany and regularly visit settlers in the Cowichan Valley.[60] Through the 1860s and 1870s about 60,000 hectares of Island Hul'qumi'num territory on Vancouver Island and the Gulf Islands, including extensive valuable ocean and river-front lands and good farming lands in the Cowichan and Chemainus valleys and

---

58 Brian Egan, "Sharing the Colonial Burden: Treaty-Making and Reconciliation in Hul'qumi'num Territory," *Canadian Geographer* 56, no. 4 (2012): 398; Egan, "Towards Shared Ownership: Property, Geography, and Treaty Making in British Columbia," *Geografiska Annaler: Series B* 95, no. 1 (2013): 33; Thom, "Reframing Indigenous Territories"; Robert Morales, Brian Egan, and Brian Thom, *The Great Land Grab: Colonialism and the Esquimalt & Nanaimo Railway Land Grant in Hul'qumi'num Territory* (Ladysmith BC: Hul'qumi'num Treaty Group, 2007).

59 Brian Egan, "From Dispossession to Decolonization: Towards a Critical Indigenous Geography of Hul'qumi'num Territory" (PhD diss., Carleton University, 2008).

60 Egan, "From Dispossession to Decolonization."

the Gulf Islands, were provided to settlers through Crown land grants. Island Hul'qumi'num peoples protested this intensified settlement – a protest met by gunboat violence[61] and coercive colonial law.[62]

Although these state seizures are significant, the single largest appropriation of Island Hul'qumi'num territory occurred in 1884 when nearly the entire east coast of Vancouver Island was granted in fee simple to coal baron Robert Dunsmuir in exchange for building a rail line from Victoria to Comox. The E&N Railway Grant included title to over 800,000 hectares of land, and timber and subsurface rights, including over 280,000 hectares in Hul'qumi'num Territory on Vancouver Island. Shortly after the land grant, Dunsmuir started to sell off properties to forestry companies and other interests while retaining coal and mineral rights. This in turn created a demand for a labour market and fuelled the expansion of towns like Ladysmith and Duncan. Agricultural lands within the E&N Railway Grant were advertised and sold off for farming. None of the governments of the day consulted, accommodated, or compensated First Nations for the E&N Land Grant or subsequent land sales.[63] Even the railway line itself, where it passed through Hul'qumiúmn Reserves, was acquired through expropriation with no consultation with the Hul'qumi'num leadership of the day.

Today the member First Nations of the HTG live in and around 5,790 hectares of reserve lands, on over twenty-three individual Indian reserves held in trust by the federal government and under the jurisdiction of the Department of Indigenous Affairs and Northern Development Canada. While many of these reserves are located at the ancestral village sites of the Hul'qumi'num peoples (though not all ancestral sites were made into reserves), and are striking places that people call home, these tiny areas – only 2 per cent of Hul'qumi'num Territory – have been a profoundly inadequate land base for communities to prosper.

The politics of place in Island Hul'qumi'num territories are now wrapped up in processes of and resistance to globalization, coloniality, and the flow of capital, all stemming from these historic land grants. The settling and recent population explosion on Vancouver Island and the mainland, for instance, has seen the state encourage the flow of

---

61 Chris Arnett, *The Terror of the Coast: The 1863 Colonial War on the East Coast of Vancouver Island & the Gulf Islands* (Vancouver: Talonbooks, 1999).

62 Bruce Stadfeld, "Manifestations of Power: Native Resistance to the Resettlement of British Columbia," in *Beyond the City Limits: Rural History in British Columbia*, ed. R.W. Sandwell (Vancouver: UBC Press, 1999), 33; Egan, "From Dispossession to Decolonization."

63 Egan, "Sharing the Colonial Burden."

capital through provision of "secure" fee-simple titles, irrespective of the continuation of Hul'qumi'num property relations and rights. These land grants create confrontational and largely incompatible spaces in which Hul'qumi'num and Western property relations must coexist.

Though the rights of the private land owner, enforced by the state, permeate strongly throughout the territory, distinctive Coast Salish relations of property, which at times show up as overlapping claims or the exclusive exercise of ritual prerogatives, nevertheless persist in these places. Island Hul'qumi'num property relations are currently being worked out to provide simultaneously for recognition of the collective nature of title in land, while seeking the financial security of state-defined individual or exclusive property rights, with instruments such as certificates of possession, treaty fee-simple title, or pursuing new forms of title under opt-in federal legislative regimes. While these kinds of state-recognized freehold enclosures increase the efficiency of exchange, they have material and semiotic consequences, deepening capitalist social relations and transforming the social nature of the Island Hul'qumi'num land tenure system.[64]

B. Resistance to Land Alienation

The alienation of Island Hul'qumi'num land, and the subsequent imposition of colonial property law within the territory, has not gone unresisted. By the early twentieth century direct resistance to colonial settlement had given way to methods of political protest that white politicians would recognize. Though recognition of the broader principles of Hul'qumi'num land tenure throughout their territories continued as a backdrop to these dialogues, many of the specific efforts focused upon the frustrating creation and subsequent incursions by non-native settlers into Indian reserve lands. Island Hul'qumi'num peoples pressured colonial officials by petitioning governments and sending official delegations to meet with provincial, federal, and royal representatives. In 1901 Island Hul'qumi'num leaders began to operationalize a plan to bypass the provincial and federal governments to resolve the land question within their territories by petitioning King Edward VII. As this action demonstrates, though the Island Hul'qumi'num legal tradition was expanding and adapting to best meet its citizens' needs, the principles of Hul'qumi'num land tenure continued to be articulated, with Island Hul'qumi'num leaders seeking that colonial society recognize and accept its principles.

---

64 Prudham and Coleman, "Introduction," 18.

A visit from Prince Arthur, the Duke of Connaught and the King's nephew, to Victoria in 1906 provided the impetus for increased political organization in the Coast Salish world. Chiefs Suhiltun (Quamichan), Tsulpi'multw (Khenipsen), Kakiel (Comiaken), Queoqult (Clem-clemeluts), and Ta-kat-sahlt (Koksilah) took the opportunity to prepare and sign an address that pledged their allegiance to the Crown.[65] This was the first in a series of events that reshaped the political map of the Coast Salish Nations and was a catalyst for province-wide organization that resulted in three chiefs travelling to Buckingham Palace.

During a conference of Indigenous leaders from many parts of BC, it was decided that a delegation would travel to England to petition the monarchy to resolve the land issue. Fearing any attempts by government to thwart their plan, preparations were conducted in secrecy and revealed only at the time of departure. Three chiefs were chosen to make the journey on behalf of all the Indigenous peoples in the province: Chief Joseph Kayapalánexw (Capilano) of the Squamish Tribe, Chief Charlie Tsulpi'multw of the Cowichan Tribes, and Chief Basil David of the Bonaparte Tribe.[66] Their strategy was a success in having obtained a personal audience with the highest constitutional authority in the land. Upon returning to BC, the three chiefs spoke of the outstanding issues of traditional land and resources claims with renewed vigour and confidence. They asserted that they had the personal guarantee of the king that action would be taken to resolve this issue.[67]

If earlier colonial promises regarding land were not resolved, as noted in the petition, now the Coast Salish people believed that they had something better, the king's promise, which they expected would

---

65   Marshall, *Those Who Fell*, 146–7.
66   Marshall, *Those Who Fell*, 149; Harry Hawthorn, Cyril Belshaw, and Stuart Jamie-son, *The Indians of British Columbia: A Study of Contemporary Social Adjustment* (Toronto: University of Toronto Press, 1958), 54; George E. Shankel, "The Development of Indian Policy in British Columbia" (PhD diss., University of Washington, 1945), 193; Paul Tennant, *Aboriginal Peoples and Politics: The Indian Land Question in British Columbia, 1849–1989* (Vancouver: UBC Press, 1990), 85.
67   The evidence is mixed with regard to the 1906 delegation, and it now seems highly unlikely that King Edward VII made such a promise. Before meeting with the king, the delegates were instructed that no petitions could be laid before the king, and that if they did have grievances, he had no control over British Columbia lands. However, in studying the history of this delegation, Keith Carlson has argued that the delegates may have assumed such promises had been made because communications and promises did not have to be in the same form in Salish society as they did in Edwardian England to be considered legitimate and valid. See generally Keith Carlson, "Rethinking Dialogue and History: The King's Promise and the 1906 Aboriginal Delegation to London," *Native Studies Review* 16, no. 2 (2005): 1.

supersede all others. For example, some Cowichan peoples, who were subsequently arrested for placing nets illegally in the Cowichan River, refused to acknowledge a summons that requested their appearance before the court, arguing that their chief, presumably Tsulpi'multw, "had it from the King himself that the white people had nothing to do with the Indians."[68] In essence, they were making a strong statement about the validity of colonial laws within their territory and making it known that they were governed by their own legal principles and practices. Furthermore, Island Hul'qumi'num leaders began to reassert their grievances more strenuously, and in essence, reclaim the land in the many letters, petitions, and addresses prepared for white audiences.

In 1909 legal counsel for the Cowichan sent a petition to take their complaints about loss of lands to King Edward, requesting a declaration in favour of their continued possession and occupancy of their territory, including Cowichan Valley, containing a large area, or for a reference to the Judicial Committee of the Privy. While these early efforts did not resolve the disputes over the continued alienation of the territory, they did set the stage for further discussions.

We spoke with Fred Modeste, a respected Cowichan elder, about his great-grandfather who was one of the representatives who petitioned in Ottawa in the early twentieth century against the alienation of Cowichan lands. Fred told part of his story:

> My great grandfather [Modeste Sahilton, Ts'ustseemulthw] was invited to go to Ottawa with all the rest of the Chiefs...
>
> They reached Ottawa and they came to his turn to speak up and he couldn't speak English so he spoke Chinook. And the government, federal government wouldn't accept Chinook. They wouldn't listen to him.
>
> And he came back and he told my grandmother what happened and he was crying ... because it was important for him to speak up over the lands, all the timber that they were taking.
>
> Because when the white man approached him they only came to get logs for their sail, for their ship and he told them they could take some logs, "But don't take the land. The land is ours." That was his words...
>
> They're all there for lands, because Sir Douglas promised to pay for all these lands. And that was his purpose to go there. And when he got back he says, "I guess we're not ready. I guess some day our young people are

---

68 *Victoria Daily Colonist*, "The King and the Indians," 20 October 1906, 4, https://ia601001.us.archive.org/22/items/dailycolonist19061020uvic/19061020.pdf.

going to learn how to read and write and speak English. Maybe they're the ones that's going to settle these lands."[69]

Elder Modeste's story is compelling. Though these leaders worked at the time to articulate the principles of Hul'qumi'num law, including the tenets of sharing of resources like timber, or the occupation of lands owned by Island Hul'qumi'num peoples, in this period it was nearly impossible for them to be heard.

These voices did provide an impetus for a Royal Commission on Indian Affairs in the Province of British Columbia between 1913 and 1916. Though the federal government requested that broad territorial land claims issues be addressed as part of the joint provincial-federal commission's mandate, the B.C. Premier Richard McBride vetoed this. When the Royal Commission finally made its appearance in Island Hul'qumi'num territory, the leadership had the opportunity again to have an adequate land base for their changing social and economic circumstances recognized as being owned by them. The Island Hul'qumi'num peoples needed adequate space to exercise Hul'qumi'num law and land tenure principles without undue incursion by colonial law. On 27 May 1913, Fred's great grandfather Ts'ustseemulthw made a submission to the Royal Commission, which was recorded in the official record, and accompanied by remarkable photographs that reveal the passion and determination of the leaders involved:

Charley Selpaymult (Qw'umi'iqun, Cowichan): I am very glad to see you gentlemen today, and I thank you for speaking very favourably towards us. I went to the King [Edward] a few years ago, to try and get some settlement from the King, and when I got there, the King gave me this photograph. His Majesty promised to do something for us, and said he would send somebody out to look into the matter. The King told me that I need not feel very sorry about these things, as, if there was anything that he [the King] could do anything for me, he would do it. His Majesty promised to give each male Indian on the reserves, 160 acres of land, as the land belonged to us Indians. I hope you will take what I say into consideration, and do what you can for us.[70]

---

69 Interview of Elder Fred Modeste by Brian Thom, 24 July 2001.
70 "Evidence of the Royal Commission on Indian Affairs for the Province of British Columbia," Library and Archives Canada (LAC), DIA, RG 10, vol. 11024, file AH3. Photos published in Marshall, *Those Who Fell from the Sky*, 159; Douglas Harris, *Fish, Law, and Colonialism: The Legal Capture of Salmon in British Columbia* (Toronto: University of Toronto Press, 2001), 169.

That same 160 acres per family head was argued by other Island Hul'qumi'num leaders, including Acting Stz'uminus Chief Sherman Lewis and Stz'uminus Chief Joe Seymour. Qwam'utsun Chief Charlie Seehaillton argued that the land that his people had was too small, with himself having only "3 ½ acres, and yet the white man says I have got too much." Penelakut Chief Edward Hulburtston argued that at Tsussie, he had a small amount of land to farm, but that "it seems to me that I have no place that belongs to me, in which to be buried." He went on to request also that for Kuper Island "we want to have a reserve by the water one mile all round" in order to resolve conflicts with encroaching non-Native fishermen.[71] The Penelakut demands for delineating spaces of exclusive marine tenure around Kuper Island reinforce the idea that Island Hul'qumi'num law does not make the same assumptions as the common law about where the "commons" starts and ends, rather, recognizing in this case a zone where it should be under Penelakut jurisdiction to determine how the marine resources are shared, not an open area commons, as under the common law.

In spite of these efforts, the results were clearly disappointing, as Fred Modeste shared above. The King's promises were not fulfilled by the Royal Commission, in any court, or by a subsequent Parliament. Indeed, while it has been over 150 years since settlers first arrived in the territories of the Island Hul'qumi'num people, there is still not a satisfactory settlement of the Aboriginal title and rights of the Hul'qumi'num people. If the promises that Island Hul'qumi'num leaders understood the King to have made were fulfilled today, it would require the Crown to allot at least 480,000 acres of land among the Island Hul'qumi'num communities – a significant area measuring two-thirds the size of the entire traditional territory. However, what has remained consistent throughout this time period is the efforts of the Island Hul'qumi'num to ensure the continuance and recognition of their own systems of land tenure.

C. Property in and on Indian Reserves

The establishment of Indian reserves complicates how land tenure is experienced today. On one hand, a kind of parallel is established by which reserves were established (often at named villages sites or important resource areas), or at individual house sites where certain families have registered certificates of possession, encoding exclusive rights at certain portions of land. On the other hand, Indian reserves

---

71 "Evidence of the Royal Commission."

transformed Island Hul'qumi'num peoples' property relations, massively narrowing the geographic scope of lands involved by restricting both residence group and kin group property relations to areas on reserves.

In a group discussion about the nature of Island Hul'qumi'num land tenure, Cowichan Elders Abner Thorne, Angus Smith, and Dennis Alphonse all agreed that principles of kin-based sharing are evidenced through lands held by family groups, communal lands held by members living in particular villages, and territorial regions held by co-resident groups. However, they also underlined that the *Indian Act* system of membership in Indian band communities has created problems for people trying to claim legitimate kin-based rights to resource areas. These claims are not recognized when unaccompanied by membership or residence in the Indian band whose lands are in question. Abner Thorne from Cowichan provided an excellent example:

> We can go to Kuper and dig clams now, but sometime in the future our young people are going to get confused. They are losing sight of our relationship with each other, the young people. And they're becoming strangers to each other. So there has to be agreements like that on paper [that, he mentioned earlier, this is our sole jurisdiction] for that purpose. Even though we're all interrelated.
>
> We hear that now at meetings that even though somebody's part Saanich, half Pun'e'luxutth' [Penelakut Village, Kuper Island] Penelakut, says, "No rights here." So it's changing. So we have to have something in place to keep that tradition going.[72]

In Thorne's example, the young people, who are often the ones making decisions about rights to clam, fail to appreciate the resource rights one has based on kin-relations.

In another conversation, Cowichan Elder Wes Modeste explained how "ownership" under the *Indian Act* has imposed another system of property that frustrates the Island Hul'qumi'num people's exercise of their legal principles in land tenure. When questioned how conflicts over land get resolved, Elder Modeste stated that conflicts arising from lands managed under the *Indian Act* manifest and are resolved in relatively new ways.

---

72   Elder Abner Thorn from group interview of Elders Abner Thorne, Angus Smith, and Dennis Alphonse by Brian Thom, 13 July 2001.

WM: Ownership of land [under the rules of the Indian Act] is a new concept. It's a little different [than under Island Hul'qumi'num legal orders]. I'll stick with the land. For example, this is a ten-acre block that my father bought.... Then me and Diane built this house.... I can do whatever I want with this property. I've prepared a will.... Legally, that house is on my property, it is in my name. So it can be to others in my family through a will.... Modeste family has a lot of land. Simlult came from Quamichan, and started tilling the land for farming, potatoes and grain. So they were among the first in British Columbia to obtain certificate of possession [a type of limited legal title under the Indian Act] of their property. In most communities land is considered communal, so no one individual owned land. But that was not so in Cowichan [where there are many certificates of possession]. So some people fail to prepare wills and they say if it's not clear how they obtained the land.... If the person does not prepare a will, and it's not clear how they obtained the land, it needs to be through a committee how the acquisition of the land took place, and make recommendations about ownership....

SM: Like a tribes committee or something? That's how it gets settled now? What about when you say Sahiliton and Simlult were the first to start doing CPs. During that time, would anyone have challenged anything?

WM: It was more a local agent placed that ownership. Ownership of land should be one of the first things of the people. Ownership of land by developing the land. People from Quamichan, quite a few, set out to start farming the communities. There were individuals that raised pigs, others raised grain, and potatoes. There were high demand for grain and potatoes.[73]

Here Elder Modeste reveals how Hul'qumi'num property law is overshadowed by the system created under the *Indian Act*. Land titles registered as certificates of possession under the *Indian Act* force people to employ mechanics of colonial law. One must receive the support of the local Indian agent, practise European-style agriculture, use a will to transfer property, and register property improvements in the federal land title system, to have ownership interests recognized by the Canadian state on reserve.

The creation of Indian reserves and the threat of pre-emption of lands that were not "cultivated" by Island Hul'qumi'num people created ripples in the customary tenure system. Individual band members had to settle and ideally (in the eyes of the Indian agents) farm community

---

73 Interview with Elder Wes Modeste by Sarah Morales, 23 June 2010.

commons areas so colonial administrators would not further reduce the size of Indian reserves. For some individuals, this created new opportunities to increase descent group–owned properties. For others in the community, it divided up common lands, enclosing them in a new social order.

In this example, Elder Marjorie Louie, who married into the Stz'uminus community from Saanich, explained how people were forced to move from Kulleet Bay down to the area around the Coffin Point–*Hwkwumlehwuthun* area to "cultivate" land to keep it from the settlers.

> When I first got here Madeline [Louie's] mother used to tell me that the old people said the water is our line. They didn't say, "This is our land here, this is our land there." The whole of this point [gesturing to the area around Coffin Point and Sharpe Point] into Ladysmith Harbour, they thought they owned it all, the older people.
>
> When the white man got here they told them [the old people], "You have to have your own land. You have to get a cow, you have to get horses, whatever, to show that you're using that land. If you don't use that land the white man is going to take it away from you."
>
> Aleck Louie's father originally from Chemainus Bay ... and because her grandparents had no son ... they told Aleck, "You stay here and help my daughter with her cows"
>
> So that's why they had this big property up here. They had it all fenced. Right up to where the gym is [near Shell Beach]. Their old fence was there.
>
> So that was only recent when the Indian Affairs started telling Indians, "You got to claim land, you got to use it, otherwise you're going to lose it."[74]

In another conversation, Elder Louie further elaborated this last point:

> That's the reason why we're living here now. There was a big fight ... after the white man came and they started getting liquor, so they started fighting amongst each other. They had a big fight, so my husband's grandfather's father moved out here.
>
> So the Indian Affairs got in then and they started telling Indians, "You have to have a farm so you can claim this land," because there's so many white people coming in, you have to own something. That's where ownership came in. They were told, "You have to fence your land," which was a concept our people didn't know.

---

74 Elder Marjorie Louie in group interview of Elders Mabel Aleck, Marjorie Louie, and Madeline Louie by Brian Thom, 19 January 2001.

After the big fight he moved over here, he put a little house up here. And then he started clearing this land here. It was all cleared when I first got here. They used to grow hay there and had real lots of cows, these people.

So her father gave her a share ... when she got married he told her husband to stay.... That's why the Louie's [Marjorie's family by marriage] are here, otherwise it would have been just her family.

... He cleared this part over and then another brother came and said he wanted to move out of Shell Beach, too much fighting there. "OK, put your house over here, already got the land cleared." ...

That's when people started fighting.... Because Alfred's grandfather moved here after the big fight in Shell Beach, he moved here and then somebody would come and say they'd need a place to stay. "OK, stay here, you're my nephew, you can stay here."[75]

In Elder Louie's example, the area in question was common property of the community. It then became family land through the creation of an *Indian Act* land holding certificate of possession (which we will refer to as a CP) administered under section 20 of the *Indian Act*.[76] Today, this area is one of only two CPs in the Stz'uminus community. Even these two CPs in the Stz'uminus have continued to be controversial and divisive. We have heard other stories challenging their legitimacy, claiming that the Louie family exploited warm relations with the Indian agents to claim this piece of property while other members of the community were away fishing, displacing other potentially legitimate claims to and uses of the area. Because of these events, Stz'uminus has been a community that, unlike the Cowichan and Penelakut, has been reluctant to create more such individual property interests on their common Indian reserve lands.

The final example comes from Abraham C. Joe who, like Abner Thorne above, lamented that younger people do not recognize the importance of family relations in granting use rights to community lands. Abraham recalled how old man Francis James told him that Cowichan people had a camping ground on the north end of Tent Island, a tiny island in an important resource harvesting area. Today, however, Joe finds that the young people say that this land, which is one of the Penelakut Indian reserves, is the exclusive property of the Penelakut.

---

75 Interview of Elder Marjorie Louie by Brian Thom, 18 December 2000.

76 See, generally, Claudia Lewis, *Indian Families of the Northwest Coast: The Impact of Change* (Chicago: University of Chicago Press, 1970).

Those young guys say, "All those men from Cowichan always want to claim everything. Claim, claim, claim everything. That's why you guys [the Cowichan] are getting ganged up on: you guys are claiming much too much."...
     Those young people never sat down to realize that their *stsa'lum'uqw* [great-grandparents] were agreeable because they were in-laws. Cowichan married an Indian woman and Indian woman married a Penelakut man. They got along together. That was the purpose for doing that.[77]

Common property tenures are enshrined in laws of Island Hul'qumi'num peoples, guided by the nuances of complex kin networks and strategic residence choices. Joe held that some of the younger people who do not understand these things well are wielding blunt instruments by trying to "claim, claim, claim everything" as open property to all First Nations communities. While such actions may be understandable in a context of resistance to colonial alienation of land, there is little room for them in the minds of the elders and others who recognize the more subtle issues of relationships and residence. This becomes acutely evident when such actions threaten to divide community opinion and further spread the limited opportunities Island Hul'qumi'num people have to derive wealth from their lands and resources. Any young leader who tries to "claim, claim, claim everything" in a court-centred Aboriginal title argument will quickly find that such tactics have little place and efficacy in that arena as well. To have legitimacy in the Canadian legal system, as well as the Island Hul'qumi'num land tenure system, claims must be embedded in the customary laws and traditions that elders have tried to teach their children, grandchildren, and indeed several generations of anthropologists and legal scholars.

D. The Continuation of Aboriginal Title

1. ABORIGINAL TITLE

Proving Aboriginal title in Canadian common law has proven to be an elusive task for Indigenous peoples in Canada. In fact, until the 2014 *Tsilhqot'in v British Columbia* decision, no definitive Aboriginal title claim had been successful in a Canadian court. This is particularly significant to the Island Hul'qumi'num First Nations, who, as previously stated, did not enter into a historical treaty with Canada and whose land rights were largely ignored by BC's early colonial government.

---

77 Interview of Abraham C. Joe by Brian Thom, 16 October 2001.

As a result, the so-called land question for the traditional territory of these nations – where precisely Aboriginal title exists and whose title it is – remains unresolved.

Although the Island Hul'qumi'num communities are not pursuing many Aboriginal title claims in the common law system (writs were filed by all Hul'qumi'num communities in 2007, but are in abeyance, and Cowichan has an active Aboriginal title case[78] regarding an ancient village site on the lower Fraser River), we ask if the finding of Aboriginal title would sufficiently recognize and protect the land tenure system of the Island Hul'qumi'num people. To this end, we will first consider the meaning of Aboriginal title. In *Tsilhqot'in* the Supreme Court of Canada confirmed that Aboriginal title is a unique and beneficial interest in the land that cannot be equated to other forms of property ownership.[79] As such, it confers ownership rights *similar* to fee simple, including the right of enjoyment and occupancy of the land; the right to decide how the land will be used; to possess the land; to reap the economic benefits of the land; and to proactively use and manage the land.[80] The only limitation is that Aboriginal title is not absolute and must be held collectively for the present and future generations, meaning it cannot be alienated to anyone except the Crown, nor encumbered in a way that would prevent future generations of the group from using and enjoying it.[81]

On its face, Aboriginal title appears to protect the types of interests recognized by the Island Hul'qumi'num land tenure system. The right to decide how the land will be used purports to recognize jurisdiction over the land.[82] As such, there seems to be space for Island Hul'qumi'num laws to operate within and upon Aboriginal title lands. Also the recognition of the collective nature of the land is in accordance with the principle of sharing recognized by the Island Hul'qumi'num land tenure system. However, it remains to be seen if there is space in Canadian law for the legal persons to whom property relations are owed can conform to Island Hul'qumi'num social orders. Would the term *collective*, for instance, refer only to First Nations represented today by Indian bands, or is there space for some recognition of other legal person to constitute the body of collective ownership. Examples of configuration of collective property ownership that come to mind might include, for example,

---

78 *Cowichan Tribes v Canada (AG)*, 2016 BCSC 420, [2016] BCWLD 2651.
79 *Tsilhqot'in*, para 72.
80 *Tsilhqot'in*, para 73.
81 *Tsilhqot'in*, para 74.
82 For a detailed discussion of this question, see Gordon Christie, "Who Makes Decisions over Aboriginal Title Lands?" *UBC Law Review* 48, no. 3 (2015): 743.

the property-owning family group described above, or property-owning residence groups in configurations that do not precisely match modern-day Indian bands, or even aggregations of families and residence groups across the region where collective title is demarcated to the entire diversity of Hul'qumi'num land holdings across territories.[83]

It is also necessary to consider the Supreme Court's test for Aboriginal title. In *Delgamuukw v British Columbia*, the Supreme Court of Canada stated that the test for Aboriginal title requires exclusive occupation and control of the land.[84] In *Tsilhqot'in*, the question was whether semi-nomadic Indigenous groups could satisfy this test in claims over broad territories, or if exclusive occupation was limited to definite tracts of land or settlement sites occupied by Aboriginal groups at the time of Crown sovereignty. Although initially the test is put in the context of "a semi-nomadic Indigenous group," the test does apply to claims for Aboriginal title by all Aboriginal groups. The Court reiterates the three-part test for Aboriginal title that was first set out in *Delgamuukw*.[85] Essentially, (1) the lands must have been occupied prior to sovereignty; (2) if present occupation is relied on as proof of occupation pre-sovereignty, there must be a continuity between present and pre-sovereignty occupation; and (3) at sovereignty, that occupation must have been exclusive.[86]

In a key passage, the chief justice spells out the standard for sufficient occupation:

> The Aboriginal group in question must show that it has historically acted in a way that would communicate to third parties that it held the land for its own purposes. This standard does not demand notorious or visible use akin to proving a claim for adverse possession, but neither can the occupation be purely subjective or internal. There must be evidence of a strong presence on or over the land claimed, manifesting itself in acts of occupation that could reasonably be interpreted as demonstrating that the land in question belonged to, was controlled by, or was under the exclusive stewardship of the claimant group.[87]

Considering the Island Hul'qumi'num land tenure system within this definition of "sufficient occupation" raises important questions

---

83 For a detailed discussion of this question, see Kent McNeil, "Aboriginal Title and Indigenous Governance: Identifying the Holders of Rights and Authority," 31 May 2016, http://digitalcommons.osgoode.yorku.ca/all_papers/264/.
84 *Delgamuukw*, para 156.
85 *Delgamuukw*, para 26.
86 *Delgamuukw*, para 143.
87 *Tsilhqot'in*, para 38.

about the sufficiency of Aboriginal title to recognize and protect the types of land tenure holdings described in the first part of this chapter. Who are third parties? What does it mean that the occupation cannot be purely subjective or internal, especially when dealing with overlapping or shared territories? What constitutes evidence of a "strong presence"? What is meant by control in a legal system that is deeply structured around the principle of sharing?

The Supreme Court also expands on the element of exclusivity in its decision in *Tsilhqot'in*. *Delgamuukw* required that the Aboriginal group (or groups under the notion of shared exclusivity) had to have the intent and capacity to retain exclusive control over the land. The Court in *Tsilhqot'in* expands on this notion with examples similar to those set out in *Delgamuukw*,[88] but it adds an emphasis on context and the need to use both the common law and the Aboriginal perspective.[89] This seems to suggest that while on its face, the requirement of "exclusivity" may not seem to accord with the Island Hul'qumi'num land tenure system, this requirement must be interpreted through the idiom of sharing described in this chapter. This means that the Island Hul'qumi'num people's protocols for sharing with kin and non-kin must be considered and taken into account when determining both the intent and the capacity to retain exclusive control over the land. For example, in a situation of a shared resource site, practices of hiring wage labourers, who would get a portion of the catch as payment, could be looked at to determine intent to retain exclusive control over that shared resource site. Suttles provides examples of shared use of owned resource sites such duck netting areas, fish weirs, tidal pounds, and reef nets locales.[90] Where owned resource locales take group labour and effort to utilize, or may be used when the owner is not present to manage and make decisions, there continue to be clear expectations and norms around sharing the harvest and accountability to the owners for land use.

2. MODERN TREATIES

In 1973 the Supreme Court in *Calder v Attorney-General of British Columbia* acknowledged the existence of Aboriginal title to land and that such title existed outside of, and was not simply derived from, colonial law.[91]

---

88 *Tsilhqot'in*, para 48.
89 *Tsilhqot'in*, para 49.
90 Wayne Suttles, "Central Coast Salish Subsistence," *Northwest Anthropological Research Notes* 24, no. 2 (1990): 147–52.
91 [1973] SCR 313, 34 DLR (3d) 145. The court held that Aboriginal title is an inherent right insofar as it is not dependent on legislative or executive recognition. That

Following this decision, the government of Canada issued the 1973 Statement on the Claims of Indian and Inuit People, its federal policy on specific and comprehensive claims. As a result, the Island Hul'qumi'num people returned to actively organizing around their land claims. In 1975 Abraham C. Joe, Abel Joe, and Joe Elliott formed the first Island Salish land claims committee, with Abraham as the chair. They were able to get the initial involvement of First Nations from Saanich to Nanaimo, and the group held meetings over several years. Though they did not successfully launch a comprehensive claim, the organization planted the seeds for what was to become the Hul'qumi'num Treaty Group.

On 16 December 1993, the then Cowichan Chief Philomena Alphonse submitted, on behalf of the Hul'qumi'num Treaty Group, its statement of intent to the British Columbia Treaty Commission. The statement of intent to negotiate the required formal first stage in the six-part process was initiated with a simple letter, accompanied by a map. The letter read in part as follows:

Who are the Aboriginal people represented by the First Nation?
(a) The Cowichan tribes (comprising Qwam'utsun, So'mena, Clem-clem-aluts, Comiaken, Khenipsen, Kilpahlas, and Koksilah sub-bands), (b) the Chemainus Band, (c) the Lyackson Band, (d) the Penelakut Band, (e) the Halalt Band, (f) the Malahat Band, and (g) the Lake Cowichan Band.

Are there other Aboriginal people represented by another/other First Nations within the traditional territory?
The First Nations that comprised the membership of the above bands intend to resolve any overlapping claims that may arise among them and any claims of other First Nations among themselves, or among themselves and other First Nations....

What is the First Nation's traditional territory in BC?
The Cowichan and Chemainus Valleys of southern Vancouver Island. The territory runs from Dodds Narrows in the north, south to and including Goldstream Park, west to and including the surrounding area of Cowichan Lake, and east to Georgia Straits including the Gulf Islands, and fishing station on Orcas Island.[92]

---

being said, it is still dependent on judicial recognition: see Michael Asch and Patrick Macklem, "Aboriginal Rights and Canadian Sovereignty: An Essay on *R v Sparrow*," *Alberta Law Review* 29 (1991): 498.
92 Statement of Intent, Cowichan Chief Philomena Alphonse to the British Columbia Treaty Commission, 16 December 1993.

Island Hul'qumi'num peoples have been involved (with varying degrees of activity and engagement since submitting their statement of intent in 1993) in this modern treaty process as an alternative to pursuing their title claims through the courts. While the particulars of the negotiations are ongoing, we want to highlight the approach these Island Hul'qumi'num peoples took in representing their communities within this process. The leadership of the day chose to highlight the residence groups (or in some cases aggregated residence groups) as the bodies representing the collective title holders, not particular family groups within those collectives. Collectively, they say, these First Nations have territorial rights by virtue of their property laws. They also explicitly envision a process of drawing on their own property laws to work through any *overlapping* claims between them, and to resolve their overall territorial claims working together – *nuts'umaat* in the Hul'q'umi'num' language. This was an important statement of confidence in the Island Hul'qumi'num peoples laws and practices as being well equipped to elaborate these property rights and resolve the particularities of property between the social groups that have overall territorial title. In this vision, the leadership of the day did not accept that governments could demand a cadastral division of properties between communities, but rather will rely on their laws to structure the future of property relations within their territories.

Unfortunately Indigenous laws have not played a prominent role within the modern-day treaty process. As a result, these statement of intent maps and the drafting of boundaries has produced extensive overlapping claims.[93] Alternative models for mapping territoriality that draws on Indigenous conceptions of land tenure have been rejected by governments.[94] As a result, the modern-day treaty process is creating new conflicts over land in the process of resolving the title question in BC. The state, however, has pushed on with First Nations who want to see immediate economic benefits of "settling" outstanding title questions with the state, such as Tsawwassen and Yale. In these cases, the First Nations entering into final agreement with Canada and BC have had a new "treaty right" to land titles and shared use rights recognized where neighbouring First Nations (Island Hul'qumi'num/W̲SÁNEĆ, Stó:lō) felt they had no history of exclusive property or access without following laws of sharing. Protocols entered into for temporary resolution, where they exist, are unsatisfying and have created ongoing problems.

---

93 Thom, "Reframing Indigenous Territories"; Brian Thom, "Confusion sur les territoires autochtones au Canada," in *Terres, territoires, ressources: Politiques, pratiques et droits des peuples autochtones*, ed. Irène Bellier (Paris: L'Harmattan, 2014), 89.
94 Thom, "Paradox."

The modern-day Tsawwassen Treaty is an example of such a conflict for the Island Hul'qumi'num communities. The issue was not limited to their treaty territory, but also stemmed from their refusal to acknowledge the rights of the Island Hul'qumi'num to those areas within their statement of intent. Wes Modeste noted,

What Tsawwassen did was take advantage of the treaty process because it allowed them to create their boundaries [referring to the Tsawwassen Territory and Tsawwassen Intertidal Bivalve Fishing Area defined in the final agreement][95] within our territory. We have attempted to meet with them to remove the boundary line but they wouldn't. They chose not to remove the boundary line back. But they didn't come from those islands. The Cowichan people had rights to those islands – from South Pender, Maine, and Galiano Island – that was known as the Cowichan archipelago....

This is what I don't understand about the process and law in general. How can it allow such a small community to encompass such a large land base that traditionally was held by the Cowichan? So in effect, they would have more rights to this through treaty than the Cowichan, and that is not acceptable.

So we went to court [referring to the petition filed by Chief Alphonse on behalf of the Cowichan Tribes in Action Vancouver S076136 but which did not go to trial].... We went to Washington, DC [referring to *HTG v Canada*[96]] and pulled the early records of the commission to establish the 49th parallel through the Gulf Islands in the mid 1800s.... The [Canada/U.S.] boundary line was supposed to come straight across the Georgia Strait and the U.K. said, "The Cowichan are here. There is no reason why their land should be in your waters" [referring to how the U.S. boundary diverts from the 49th parallel to not encompass the Gulf Islands]. So they went to those islands and there is substantial evidence of occupation of those islands by the Cowichan. So those islands remained in Canada. So it is because of our presence there that their location is in Canada. But we don't enjoy ownership of it.

With that evidence Tsawwassen said, "Oh, we can see that it's yours." And then they had the gall to come to our meeting and tell us how they would manage the resources in our islands.[97]

---

95 *Tsawwassen First Nation Final Agreement*, 6 December 2007, Indigenous and Northern Affairs Canada, https://www.aadnc-aandc.gc.ca/eng/1100100022706/1100100 022717.

96 *Hul'qumi'num Treaty Group v Canada* (2011), Inter-Am Comm HR, AMR 20/001/ 2011, Amnesty International, August 2011.

97 Interview of Wes Modeste by Sarah Morales, 23 June 2010.

Wes Modeste was clearly agitated by the elements of the talks that followed the initialling of the Tsawwassen Final Agreement, where Tsawwassen and their government partners explained to Cowichan the mechanisms the Tsawwassen Final Agreement provides for Tsawwassen to participate in the management of a wide range of lands and resources in Hul'qumi'num territory – including (among many others) archaeological sites, parks and protected areas, fisheries, and environmental protection. The BC treaty process thus creates new property relations that purport to transcend and supersede Indigenous legal orders. It is easy to see Wes's frustration with the unwillingness of the partners in the Tsawwassen final agreement to acknowledge and respect the rights and presence of the Island Hul'qumi'num peoples within their treaty area. Although the treaty process was established to help resolve Indigenous land rights in BC, this example illustrates how it has not been done in a manner that reflects and respects traditional Indigenous land tenure systems and processes.[98] As a result, it creates more conflicts than resolutions. As Stumin'uz Elder Willie Seymour explained,

You just look at the Tsawwassen Treaty – how it overlaps us. You know, they had no respect for us, to come over and explain their knowledge of the islands. They didn't do that....

How can we right that wrong? The treaty commissioners didn't do their job. They were supposed to help everybody and remain neutral. The government's supposed to allow First Nation–First Nation negotiations, but they stepped in and said, "No, we aren't going to change this boundary." They aren't supposed to say that. They are supposed to allow HTG and Tsawwassen to sit down and have a productive discussion on that.

But yes, I do say that today's modern thinking has changed us. What Tsawwassen don't have is affecting their decision-making. It's always up here – snuw'uyulh.[99]

---

98 See also Christopher Turner and Gail Fondahl, "'Overlapping Claims' to Territory Confronting Treaty-Making in British Columbia: Causes and Implications," *Canadian Geographer* 59, no. 4 (2015): 474; Mark East, "Addressing Overlapping Claims in the BC Treaty Process: A Federal Perspective," in *Overlapping Territorial Claims: Models for Dispute Resolution, Proceedings of the 2009 National Aboriginal Law Conference, 12–13 June 2009, Victoria* (Ottawa: Canadian Bar Association, 2009), 23; Robert Galois and Neil Sterritt, *Tribal Boundaries in the Nass Watershed* (Vancouver: UBC Press, 1998); Neil Sterritt, "The Nisga'a Treaty: Competing Claims Ignored!" *BC Studies* 120 (1999): 73.
99 Interview of Elder Willie Seymour by Sarah Morales, 16 June 2010.

In the kin-oriented social world of the Island Hul'qumi'num peoples over-simplified boundaries, whether treaty settlement areas or Indian reserves, create hard feelings between groups that otherwise were able to predictably and reliably look to Indigenous law to order relations and resolve conflicts. They "offend the kin- and ancestor-centred senses of place, and have the potential, if empowered with the institutions of the state, of limiting many of the other kinds of associations with land in the Coast Salish world."[100] As Elder Seymour's statement suggests, the failure to recognize and account for Indigenous systems of conflict resolution with the modern-day treaty process is overshadowing the legal traditions of the Island Hul'qumi'num people, not reconciling their position within Canada.

IV. Conclusion: Consideration for Reconciliation

Indigenous peoples themselves must be recognized as having the power and jurisdiction to determine the future expression of the legal principles inherent in their land tenure systems. The law must not somehow "lock in" the specificity of the practices over time, or posit their extinguishment as a price of the coexistence of settler and Indigenous nations. Instead, everyone must fairly share the wealth of the land, while decisions must be made together on equal footing. Indigenous legal principles must guide them, along with other important principles of justice that can help ameliorate social and economic differences. The "cost" of this ongoing coexistence in the short term may be destabilized investor certainty, unencumbered bureaucratic process, and so on. However, recognition and acknowledgment of principles of Indigenous land tenure also provide fair and non-violent processes for the resolution of conflict that are well grounded in Indigenous law. Reconciliation in this light is reframed from the language employed by current treaty negotiations where history (including Indigenous forms of property and Indigenous peoples marginalization by the state) is traded off for economic and government opportunities in the future,[101] to a language of ongoing relationality between persons, where "full and final settlement" (the language of modern-day treaty arrangements) is

---

100   Thom, "Coast Salish Sense of Place," 402.
101   See Paul Nadasdy, "'Property' and Aboriginal Land Claims in the Canadian Subarctic: Some Theoretical Considerations," *American Anthropologist* 104, no. 1 (2002): 247; Nadasdy, "The Antithesis of Restitution? A Note on the Dynamics of Land Negotiations in the Yukon, Canada," in *The Rights and Wrongs of Land Restitution: Restoring What Was Ours*, ed. D. Fay and D. James (London: Routledge, 2008), 85.

not the end. Rather the goal is to enable ongoing respect and reciprocity. Such a view of reconciliation through coexistence without subversion is not novel and is commonly the outcome of writers grappling with Indigenous legal orders,[102] ontologies[103] and property claims within contemporary cultural practice.[104]

We conclude by arguing that in exercising self-determination, Indigenous peoples must not be strictly limited to a precise that mirrors the Canadian state forms of property relations. They must be able to determine which legal persons are constitutive of property relations. This may be Indian bands, for example, or it may be other groups as sensibly constituted within the framework of the society. They must be able to determine what objects receive the attention of property relations, anything from land and resources to intangible cultural expressions, knowledge, and traditions.[105] They must be able to determine the rights, duties, obligations, and remedies that are involved in these property relations, from the consequence of trespass or over-exploitation, to the duties associated with carrying an inherited Indigenous name. Reconciliation will occur only through this kind of respectful recognition.

The practice of property relations internal to Island Hul'qumi'num communities is tightly woven into the fabric of their social, economic, and political system and that of their neighbours. This system continues to have the same weight and importance in peoples' lives and economies today in areas where few or no other incompatible forms of property rights have been created, such as (but not limited to) on-reserve and in fishing spots where "the commons" of Canadian fisheries law has left marine areas largely unallocated as private property. The expressions of property today that have the most wide-ranging power and effect are those made vis-à-vis non-Indigenous settler society who have taken their own powerful legal form of ownership and superimposed it on the Island Hul'qumi'num land tenure system. The Island Hul'qumi'num land tenure system has not been not supplanted. Rather, it struggles for

---

102 Richard Overstall, "Encountering the Spirit in the Land: 'Property' in a Kinship-Based Legal Order," in *Despotic Dominion: Property Right in British Settler Societies*, ed. John McLaren, A.R. Buc, and Nancy E. Wright (Vancouver: UBC Press, 2005), 22.

103 Bradley Bryan, "Property as Ontology: On Aboriginal and English Understandings of Ownership," *Canadian Journal of Law and Jurisprudence* 13, no. 1 (2000): 3.

104 Nadasdy, "'Property,'" 255.

105 Brian Thom, "Dis-agreement in Principle: Negotiating the Right to Practice Coast Salish Culture in Treaty Talks on Vancouver Island, BC," *New Proposals: Journal of Marxism and Interdisciplinary Inquiry* 2, no. 1 (2008): 23.

practical expression against these powerful, even dominant, systems. The institutions of local descent group and residence group land tenure are evoked in contexts of government and industry consultation over resource harvesting, treaty negotiations, and land claims–related litigation. They are realms in which these old institutions of land tenure take on new aspects of social power. They provide a major challenge for Canadian legal pluralism to embrace and recognize in a new era of incorporating Hul'qumi'num legal principles into Canadian law.

PART TWO

Political Issues

4 Property Rights on Reserves: "New" Ideas from the Nineteenth Century

SARAH CARTER AND NATHALIE KERMOAL

In *Beyond the Indian Act: Restoring Aboriginal Property Rights* Thomas Flanagan, with co-authors Christopher Alcantara and André Le Dressay, contends that individual ownership of reserve land will enhance First Nations economic activity, create jobs and business opportunities, and improve housing. They argue that First Nations had institutions of private property before European contact, and that a proposed First Nations Property Ownership Act would restore their property rights. Owning land in fee simple would implant pride and produce profits.[1]

Echoing Flanagan's call for individual ownership of reserve land are organizations such as the Centre for Aboriginal Policy Change of the Canadian Taxpayers Federation (CTF) and the Fraser Institute. They claim, "Property rights are critical to economic growth and social well-being" and call for "a frank discussion about providing First Nations people the same property rights as their fellow Canadians, for the betterment of aboriginal communities and the country as a whole."[2] Dividing up reserve land into fee-simple property would push "people [to] use the value of their homes as collateral to engage in other economic activities, helping increase the economic prosperity of First Nation communities."[3] "Fee simple" lands would then become available for sale to non-Aboriginal people and corporations. Overall, it is claimed, these measures would help alleviate the economic ills and burdens of reserve life, allowing "Indians" to enter the mainstream of Canada's economy.

---

1 See Tom Flanagan, Christopher Alcantara, and André Le Dressay, *Beyond the Indian Act: Restoring Aboriginal Prosperity Rights* (Montreal and Kingston: McGill-Queen's University Press, 2010).
2 Fraser Institute, "Individual Property Rights Key to Social, Economic Well-being for First Nations," news release, 30 June 2013.
3 Fraser Institute, "Individual Property Rights."

Presented as advocating a "new system," Flanagan and associates are in fact regurgitating old arguments that have been at the centre of projects aimed at assimilating Indigenous peoples since the nineteenth century.[4] They are now being dusted off and pressed into service once again to advance a neoliberal agenda. If the expansion of private property rights on reserves is framed as "a necessary ... precondition to attaining widespread prosperity,"[5] it also "furthers colonial practices of whitening."[6]

In this chapter we will analyse some of the arguments presented in *Beyond the Indian Act* by first establishing the philosophical influence on Flanagan's thinking of Friedrich Hayek, the father of neoliberalism. This analysis will help dissect the neoliberal logic behind the push towards private property as the path to prosperity. We will then turn to history to show that the "new" discourse is rooted in the same rhetoric government officials were using in the nineteenth century. As Dempsey et al. have pointed out, those who proclaim that private property on reserves is the path to prosperity "avoid any discussion of colonialism and the colonial legacy, while simultaneously calling forth dichotomies rooted in the colonial era such as backward/modern to describe property system on reserves."[7] The central rationale for promoting private property has remained the same, although it is usually obscured behind the predictions of a brilliant economic future. Generally they are schemes to divest First Nations of their land and make it available for sale. The objective is assimilation and the erosion of leadership through the dissolution of the communities they serve. Privatization projects are also generally predicated on stereotypes of First Nation people as indolent, thriftless and shiftless, unable to properly put their land to good use. Using the St Peter's reserve in Manitoba as an example, we will pay close attention to how the presence of private property on a reserve led directly to the alienation of the entire reserve in 1907. The complex issues of land ownership on the reserve, which was an agricultural community occupying valuable land, combined with the cupidity

---

4 See the description of *Beyond the Indian Act* at https://books.google.ca/books
   /about/Beyond_the_Indian_Act.html?id=zQ2_N1BPPngC.
5 Tom Flanagan and Christopher Alcantara, "Individual Property Rights on Canadian
   Indian Reserves," *Queen's Law Journal* 29, no. 2 (2005): 489.
6 Jessica Dempsey, Kevin Gould, and Juanita Sundberg, "Changing Land Tenure,
   Defining Subjects: Neoliberalism and Property Regimes on Native reserves," in
   *Rethinking the Great White North: Race, Nature and the Historical Geographies of White-
   ness in Canada*, ed. Andrew Baldwin, Laura Cameron, and Audrey Kobayashi
   (Vancouver: UBC Press, 2011), 241.
7 Dempsey, Gould, and Sundberg, "Changing Land Tenure," 252.

of their non-Indigenous neighbours, generated unrelenting pressure to eradicate the reserve and make the land available for sale.[8]

I. Hayek, Flanagan, and the Rethinking of the Reserve

In the introduction to *First Nations? Second Thoughts* (2000) as well as in his *Harper's Team* (2007) Flanagan explicitly recognizes the intellectual debt he owes to Friedrich Hayek. He writes, "I thought of myself as a conservative, liberal, and social democrat at different times in my twenties and thirties, until I encountered the works of Friedrich Hayek in 1977."[9] He adds in *First Nations? Second Thoughts* that his views "on politics and society owe a great debt to Friedrich Hayek, now widely recognized as one of the most influential thinkers of the late twentieth century."[10] He reiterates Hayek's influence in *Beyond the Indian Act*.[11]

Born in Vienna in 1899, Friedrich von Hayek is probably one of the most influential thinkers of the twentieth century. He is known as the father of neoliberalism, and his work has greatly influenced politicians such as Margaret Thatcher and Ronald Reagan. Hayek fled to Austria after its annexation to Nazi Germany and became a British citizen in 1938. While Hayek made significant contributions in the fields of jurisprudence and cognitive science, he was first and foremost an economist and a political philosopher known for his defence of liberal democracy and free-market capitalism against socialist and collectivist thought in the mid-twentieth century. Hayek was a key player in the strategy to restore the primacy of classical liberalism, which led to the rise of what many called neoliberalism.[12] In 1974 he received the Nobel Prize in Economics.

---

8 See Cole Harris, *Making Native Space: Colonialism, Resistance, and Reserves in British Columbia* (Vancouver: UBC Press, 2002); Mary-Ellen Kelm, *Colonizing Bodies: Aboriginal Health and Healing in British Columbia* (Vancouver: UBC Press, 1998).

9 Tom Flanagan, *Harper's Team: Behind the Scenes in the Conservative Rise to Power* (Montreal and Kingston: McGill-Queen's University Press, 2007), 12.

10 Tom Flanagan, *First Nations? Second Thoughts* (Montreal and Kingston: McGill-Queen's University Press, 2000), 8.

11 Flanagan, Alcantara, and Le Dressary, *Beyond the Indian Act*, 16.

12 See Keith Dixon, *Les évangélistes du marché: Les intellectuels britanniques et le néolibéralisme* (Paris: Raisons d'agir, 1998); Perry Anderson, "Histoire et leçons du néolibéralisme," in *L'Autre-Davos: Mondialisation des résistances et des luttes*, ed. François Houtard and François Polet (Paris: L'Harmattan,1999), 19–26; and Charles André Udry, "Von Hayek: des postulats largement diffusés," *A l'encontre*, 5 November 1996, https://alencontre.org/economie/von-hayek-des-postulats-largement -diffuses.html. On Hayek's influence on neoliberalism, see Jean-Claude St-Onge, *L'imposture néolibérale* (Montreal: Les Éditions Ecosociété, 2000); and John Gray, *Hayek on Liberty* (Oxford: Routledge, 2002).

The central thesis of Hayek's most famous book, *The Road to Serfdom*, is that all forms of collectivism lead logically and inevitably to tyranny like in the Soviet Union and Nazi Germany. For Hayek, central planning with its dismantling of the free market system ends in the destruction of all individual economic and personal freedom. Hayek is not only warning against the perils of dictatorship and totalitarianism, he is also very critical of the economic interventionism of government in time of crisis proposed by John Maynard Keynes. Hayek believed that various democratic nations are being led down the same road as socialism: "It may well be true that our generation talks and thinks too much of democracy, and too little of the values which it serves.... Democracy is essentially a means, a utilitarian device for safe-guarding internal peace and individual freedom. As such it is by no means infallible or certain.... Democratic control *may* prevent power from becoming arbitrary, but it does not do so by its mere existence. If democracy resolves on a task which necessarily involves the use of power which cannot be guided by fixed rules, it must become arbitrary power."[13]

Hayek's ideas are at the forefront of the movement towards a society based on freedom of association and exchange according to the rule of law, and away from the control of society from the centre according to the whim of government. For Hayek, "The effect of the people's agreeing that there must be central planning, without agreeing on the ends, will be rather as if a group of people were to commit themselves to take a journey together without agreeing where they want to go; with the result that they may all have to make a journey which most of them do not want at all."[14] He rejects the idea of government intervention in markets, perceiving such intervention as a loss of freedom.[15] Furthermore, for the economist, the most important guarantee of freedom is to own private property: "It is only because the control of the means of production is divided among many people acting independently that nobody has complete power over us, that we as individuals can decide what to do with ourselves."[16] Every citizen should not only have a piece of land, one should have the certainty that the property to which one is entitled can be used as one sees fit.[17]

Hayek's critique of "constructed or organized order" (*taxis*) planned by states led the theorist to promote "spontaneous order" (*kosmos*) or

---

13 Friedrich A. Hayek, *The Road to Serfdom* (Chicago: University of Chicago Press, 1944), 70–1.
14 Hayek, *Road to Serfdom*, 46.
15 Hayek, *Road to Serfdom*, 42.
16 Hayek, *Road to Serfdom*, 103–4.
17 Hayek, *Road to Serfdom*, 103–4.

unplanned and self-organized order – order that emerges spontaneously in a group as a result of individual behaviour, without being forced by external factors. It arises from the interaction of a decentralized, heterogeneous group of self-seeking agents with limited knowledge. The market is the perfect example of a spontaneous order, since it "was not designed by anyone but evolved slowly as the result of human actions."[18]

Like Hayek, Flanagan believes in the virtues of individualism, minimum state intervention, and formal equality in front of the law: "Society is a spontaneous order that emerges from the choices of individual human beings. The indispensable role of government is to make and enforce rules of conduct that allow society to function. Individuals naturally congregate in families and other associations, but these must be voluntary if society is to be free and prosperous. When government sorts people into categories with different legal rights, especially when those categories are based on immutable characteristics such as race and sex, it interferes with social processes based on free association."[19]

Flanagan criticizes an emergent consensus on fundamental issues related to Indigenous peoples that he calls the "Aboriginal orthodoxy" as well as the interventionist Indigenous policy of the federal government. For Flanagan, the "Aboriginal orthodoxy" is "widely shared among aboriginal leaders, government officials, and academic experts. It weaves together threads from historical revisionism, critical legal studies, and the aboriginal political activism of the last thirty years."[20] Overall, he sees an Indigenous militancy manufactured by an Indigenous industry and denounces the negative role of activism or advocacy groups, who see in the government's (centralized) action a voice of progress. In his attack against this idea of the "Aboriginal orthodoxy" Flanagan directly incorporates some key elements of Hayek's definition of liberalism.

For instance, Hayek believed in the superiority of the modern liberal society over other societies. Likewise, in *First Nations? Second Thoughts* Flanagan asserts that "European civilization was several thousand years more advanced than the aboriginal cultures of North America, both in technology and in social organization. Owing to this tremendous gap in civilization, the European colonization of North America was inevitable and, if we accept the philosophical analysis of John Locke and Emer de Vattel, justifiable."[21] Flanagan rejects the idea of

---

18 John J. Sarno, *Perils of Prosperity: Realities, Risks and Rewards of the Global Knowledge Economy* (Bloomington, IN: AuthorHouse, 2009), 21.

19 Flanagan, *First Nations?* 9.

20 Flanagan, *First Nations?* 4.

21 Flanagan, *First Nations?* 6.

"a multinational state embracing an archipelago of aboriginal nations" and argues that "there can be only one political community at the highest level – one nation – in Canada. Subordinate communities, such as provinces, cities, and ethnic or religious groups, cannot be nations."[22]

As well, Hayek believed that equality before the law is the only form of equality that the state can legitimately recognize. In *The Constitution of Liberty*, he writes,

> Equality of the general rules of law and conduct, however, is the only kind of equality conducive to liberty and the only equality which we can secure without destroying liberty. Not only has liberty nothing to do with any other sort of equality, but it is even bound to produce inequality in many respects. This is the necessary result and part of the justification of individual liberty: if the result of individual liberty did not demonstrate that some manners of living are more successful than others, much of the case for it would vanish.
>
> It is neither because it assumes that people are in fact equal nor because it attempts to make them equal that the argument for liberty demands that government treat them equally. This argument not only recognizes that individuals are very different but in a great measure rests on that assumption. It insists that these individual differences provide no justification for government to treat them differently. And it objects to the differences in treatment by the state that would be necessary if persons who are in fact very different were to be assured equal positions in life.[23]

For Flanagan, while the representative government has many imperfections, "under the constitutional rule of law [it] is the only form of government yet discovered that promotes individual freedom while protecting the spontaneous order of society."[24] Only the rule of law and of market self-regulation can ensure the development of Indigenous societies: "The only economic system that has brought a high standard of living to a complex society is the free market. Like representative government, it has many imperfections, but it is the most effective method ever discovered for inducing self-interested individuals to serve the needs of others."[25]

Overall, for Flanagan, the lessons taught by *The Road to Serfdom* have not been learned and applied, as the economic future of Indigenous

---

22 Flanagan, *First Nations?* 7.
23 Friedrich A. Hayek, *The Constitution of Liberty* (Chicago: University of Chicago Press, 1960), 85–6.
24 Flanagan, *First Nations?* 9.
25 Flanagan, *First Nations?* 9.

people on reserves continues to be planned. In his eyes, Indigenous people are sacrificed at the altar of interventionism, since they have no fiscal obligations and they are being pulled towards choices that in the end are harmful. According to Flanagan, this "Aboriginal orthodoxy" needs to be deconstructed to do away with Indigenous people's dependency on the state, considering that such dependency prevents a full participation in the market economy: "As Friedrich Hayek explained, the market is a process for bringing together dispersed knowledge; it functions most effectively when control over resources is also dispersed. Government ownership is too sluggish and too much influenced by perverse political incentives to be effective in a market economy."[26]

Since spontaneous order is at the centre of Hayek's philosophy as well as the idea that freedom cannot be attained without access to property, private ownership of reserve land seems the logical move towards the participation of First Nations in the market economy. According to Flanagan, Indigenous people should have the right to sell their land, which would not only make better use of their title but also create jobs on the reserves. He argued, "I don't think Native people have much choice in the matter because they are maybe three per cent of the Canadian population, [and] they are surrounded by western capitalism everywhere."[27]

Inspired by Hayek but not by the historical and colonial realities of First Nations, Flanagan is ultimately questioning the land titles collectively managed by First Nations, thus questioning the integrity of Indigenous territories:

Sadly, Canada's aboriginal people seem as far as ever from attaining a workable system of property rights. The treaties and the Indian Act have conspired to imprison them within a regime of collective rights that fit badly with the needs of a market economy. Now the Supreme Court of Canada, while asserting and redefining aboriginal property rights, has carved their collective and inalienable character in judicial stone. If there is anything for which Canadians should feel guilty, it is that our government, laws, and courts have kept Indians outside the world of individual property rather than encouraging them to step inside.[28]

---

26 Tom Flanagan, "Property Rights on the Rez: Contrary to Popular Belief, There Are Ways to Own Land on Reserves," *National Post*, 1 December 2001.
27 CBC Radio, "Selling Reserve Land Could Help Solve Poverty," 16 November 2006, https://www.cbc.ca/news/canada/calgary/selling-reserve-land-could-help-solve-poverty-professor-1.598505.
28 Flanagan, *First Nations?* 133.

Since collective property is perceived as the path to poverty, while private property is the path to prosperity, any other alternative leading towards the integrity of the territory as well as Indigenous sovereignty and autonomy has no viability and is doomed.

The ideas Flanagan presented in *Beyond the Indian Act* were central to the Canadian Taxpayers Federation (CTF), founded in 1990, and their Centre for Aboriginal Policy Change, founded in 2002. Before the publication of Flanagan's book the CTF called on Canada to abolish reserves, by dividing up reserve land among the residents.[29] The CTF proclaimed, "Private property rights ... are the foundation for wealth creation the world over and communally held property that produces wealth is the very rare exception, not the rule."[30] According to the CTF, "The most imperative ingredient for native communities to have long-term economic viability is individual property rights."[31] Private property will "empower individual Indians and facilitate market transactions necessary to attain widespread prosperity on native reserves," and will permit "Indian communities to compete successfully within the Canadian economic mainstream." As in *Beyond the Indian Act*, the CTF recommended that it be "up to the natives themselves to decide" if they want communal or individually owned property. These recommendations are combined with critiques of new treaties, corrupt reserve governments, and Canada's policy of isolating Indians on reserves, limiting their ability to fully participate in the economy.

The core concern of the CTF however, was the creation of "urban" reserves. The CTF recommended, "As a step toward the elimination of the Indian Reserve system, no new reserves or 'urban' reserves should be established."[32] It is odd that the CTF objected to "urban" reserves, as here prosperous Indigenous businesses may be found. The existence of these businesses, however, contradicts and defies the claims of the CTF that such enterprise is impossible on reserves. CTF objections are also curious because these reserves are in or beside cities such as Saskatoon, Winnipeg, Edmonton, and Vancouver; they address the issue of the isolation of reserves that the CTF claimed was why they were not able to participate in the economy.[33] The real concern of the CTF was

---

29   Tanis Fiss, "Apartheid: Canada's Ugly Secret," Canadian Taxpayers Federation, 5 January 2004, https://www.taxpayer.com/commentaries/apartheid---canada-s-ugly-secret.

30   Fiss, "Apartheid," 19.

31   Fiss, "Apartheid," i.

32   Fiss, "Apartheid," ii.

33   For a better understanding of urban reserves, see Evelyn Peters, "Urban Reserves" (draft prepared for the National Centre for First Nations Governance, 2007).

what the organization called the "unfair economic advantage" of Indigenous businesses because they are exempt from taxation. This "distorts the economy by giving an advantage to individuals living on the reserve and reserve-based businesses."[34] The CTF cannot both argue that successful businesses are impossible on reserves, and that reserve businesses have an unfair advantage. Other contradictions abound, including that the CTF wants to promote prosperity on reserves, but they want the reserves to be abolished altogether. Like the earlier schemes to abolish reserves through private property assignments, those of the CTF are designed to serve the interests, needs, and objectives of non-Indigenous people. The sort of jealous and covetous eye that the CTF is now casting on "urban" reserves also has a long history in Canada, where there were objections to "unfair Indian competition" whenever reserves threatened to participate in the wider economy.[35]

In sum, a consistent refrain, from the late nineteenth century on, is that individual tenure on small plots is the route to prosperity for First Nations, and that owning land would implant individualism, self-reliance, ambition, and pride. These schemes have always been bundled together with larger objectives of abolishing reserves, assimilating the residents into the mainstream, while ensuring that they not be permitted to expand their land base, and "compete" with the new settlers. The scheme presented in *Beyond the Indian Act* is yet another version of this view. What is slightly new is the claim that First Nations had institutions of private property before European contact and that these should be restored. But *Beyond the Indian Act* provides only simplistic generalizations about Indigenous ideas of property and does not take into account the colonization and the dispossession of Indigenous people in Canada. By using the example of the St Peter's reserve in Manitoba, in the next section we will show how ownership of land was used as a colonial tool for dispossession.

II. Privatization Schemes of the Past

For his ideas about the virtues of individual ownership of reserve land Thomas Flanagan also owes a debt to Hayter Reed, Indian commissioner (1888–93) and later deputy superintendent general of Indian affairs (1893–7). In 1888 Reed announced that Indian reserves were to be subdivided into forty-acre farms, and the rationale he advanced was

---

34 Fiss, "Apartheid," 14.
35 Sarah Carter, *Lost Harvests: Prairie Indian Reserve Farmers and Government Policy* (Montreal and Kingston: McGill-Queen's University Press, 1990), 184–90.

that individual tenure was the best means of undermining the "tribal" or "communistic" system, as it would implant a spirit of individualism and self-reliance. A sense of possessory rights was proclaimed to be "essential to the formation of those self-interested motives which attach individuals to localities and render them unwilling to leave them for any light cause."[36] Individual ownership would implant a "wholesome spirit of emulation," impossible under a system of community ownership. The "tribal" relationship would be broken, recalcitrant chiefs would lose their authority, and "progressive" leaders would emerge. Central to Reed's views on the transformative power of private property were his profoundly negative opinions of Indigenous people as thriftless and shiftless. Superintendent General of Indian Affairs Edgar Dewdney agreed, and wrote in 1890 that it was only by "inculcating such ideas and fomenting such motives in him will the Indian be reclaimed from his condition of savagery and led to adopt a mode of life which will render him both self-supporting and self-respecting."[37]

While official rationales (back then and today) emphasized the advantages to reserve residents who were seen to be in need of the stimulus of private property, the plan actually served non-Indigenous interests. Individual tenure on small plots was intended to consolidate settlement on the reserves, in order to declare unsettled areas "vacant" and available for "surrender" and acquisition by non-Indigenous settlers or speculators. These initiatives nicely dovetailed with a "peasant" farming plan that Reed concocted for Indian reserve farmers that limited their enterprise to an acre or two and required them to grow root crops, use rudimentary implements they made themselves, and have a cow each rather than herds of cattle. Like the 1887 Dawes Act in the United States, the plan was intended to identify "surplus" land that could be thrown open for sale. Many who supported the Dawes Act were interested in securing Indian land. Hayter Reed in Canada, and advocates of the Dawes Act in the United States, saw allotment as a path to assimilation, condemning segregation and isolation on reserves/reservations as dangerous to the nation. In the United States the Dawes Act resulted in 60 million acres of reservation land being declared "surplus" and sold.[38] Of the allotted land, 27 million acres, or two-thirds, was sold.[39] While the Dawes Act does not have a direct parallel

---

36 Carter, *Lost Harvests*, 196.
37 Carter, *Lost Harvests*, 196.
38 Carter, *Lost Harvests*, 200. See also Susan Campbell, "On 'Modest Proposals' to Further Reduce the Aboriginal Land Base by Privatizing Reserve Land," *Canadian Journal of Native Studies* 27, no. 2 (2007): 219–46.
39 Carter, *Lost Harvests*, 200.

in Canada, there was a similar dramatic loss of reserve land in the early decades of the twentieth century, particularly where the land was fertile and close to markets and the mainline of the Canadian Pacific Railway. Under the *Indian Act*, the majority of male members of a band had to consent to the "surrender" of reserve land, and through unscrupulous tactics in most cases, Department of Indian Affairs officials declared that they obtained this consent. Reserve land across the West ended up in the hands of speculators, including some DIA employees.

Reed was not a voice in the wilderness. His views on the virtues of private property and his objective of the diminishment and in some cases entire disappearance of reserves were widely shared in his day and beyond. David Laird, who served two terms as Indian commissioner, was Lieutenant-Governor of the North-West Territories, a minister of the interior, and government negotiator of the 1877 Treaty 7, believed in the advantages of private property that would transform the "indolent and thriftless" into the "industrious and provident." Laird wrote in 1878 that he did not agree with reserves and favoured granting treaty people individual property:

> I may say I have serious doubts as to the wisdom of the Canadian policy in perpetuating the tribal system among the Indians, and likewise as to the practice of granting reservations in large blocks of land. The great aim of the Government should be to give each Indian his individual property as soon as possible.
>
> In most Bands there is a large proportion of indolent and thriftless members who may be said to pray [*sic*] upon their more industrious and provident neighbors to the great discouragement of the latter. The Indian who makes a laudable effort to provide for the support of his family, seeing that his stores often have to go to feed his starving brethren, then loses heart himself, and drops down to the level of the precarious hand-to-mouth system of the Band generally. I am of opinion that instead of large Reserves, each Indian head of a family should receive non-transferable script [*sic*], or the right to locate on a certain quantity of land in any tract open for settlement. They would thus be able to ... enjoy the fruits of their industry on their own holdings.[40]

After the Metis Resistance of 1885, there were strident calls for the reserves to be divided up and erased from the landscape. Reed believed individual ownership of land would prevent protest and revolution, as

---

40 Canada, *Sessional Papers*, Extract of a letter dated 11 November 1878 from His Honour Lieut.-Governor and Indian Superintendent, Battleford 7:6 (Session 1879) at 65.

"the lawless and revolutionary element is to be found among those who have nothing to lose but may perhaps gain by upsetting law and order."[41] To "avoid periodical Indian wars," the reserves needed to be carved up and assigned to individuals and families. In this way "wild and troublesome Indians" would "peaceably be induced to give up savagery," and also give up their "tribal relations to take to civilized ways."[42] Advocates of the dividing up and parcelling out of reserve land included educators and missionaries. Reverend Thomas Ferrier, superintendent of the Methodist Industrial School Brandon, wrote in 1902 that to remove the "Indian problem" the tribe must be broken, the "reservation thrown open to settlement, and the Indian absorbed in our civilization."[43] In Ferrier's view, individual property would mean the disappearance of an Indian identity and entity, but "a gift of rarer value is tendered instead. To be a free man in the enjoyment of life is vastly better than to be bound to an ignorant tribe. The Indian must cease to be an Indian. He must be made primarily a Canadian citizen. It must be with the Indian a secondary matter that he is an Indian." Ferrier wrote succinctly, "The Indian massed in tribes is a problem. The Indian with individual opportunity is no problem."[44] Ferrier, like Reed, cast Indians as idle, without "energy, push and independence."

Reverend John Laurence, also a Methodist missionary and teacher, advocated dividing up reserves among the male members of every band and giving each a deed in fee simple. His rationales were rather different from Ferrier's, however, as Laurence praised the homes, farms, and other possessions of the people on the reserves where he had worked for fourteen years, and noted that many white people did not have such comforts and amenities. Laurence wrote in 1902 that it was time to abolish reserves: "There are hundreds of white people in our Dominion without farms or homes of their own, while there are many Indians who have, on their reserves, beautiful houses, well cultivated farms ... harrows, cultivators, and seeders ... the best breeds of horses and cattle, and their houses supplied with costly organs and pianos."[45] It is hard to understand why, in Laurence's view, private property could improve this happy and prosperous situation, but he proclaimed that if each man on a reserve had a deed to his land in fee

---

41 Carter, *Lost Harvests*, 146–7.
42 Editorial, "The World," *Canada School Journal and Weekly Review* 10, no. 34 (24 September 1885), 1.
43 Thomas Ferrier, "The Indian Problem," *Missionary Outlook* (July 1904): 150.
44 Ferrier, "Indian Problem," 127. (The article was written in two issues of *Missionary Outlook*: June and July 1904.)
45 John Laurence, "The Indian Problem," *Methodist Magazine and Review* 56, no. 4 (1902): 328.

simple, he could "hold up his head among his white neighbors and feel that he is somebody for himself. This will also lead to a manly honesty, an uprightness of character."[46] Both Laurence and Ferrier felt that private property was equated with manliness. Laurence wrote, "Take off his fetters and make him a man. Give him the deed of his land."[47] Despite the prosperity and comfort Laurence observed on reserves, he still felt that the Indian needed to "rise to be a man" and to develop his "energy, push and independence" (the exact same words were used by Ferrier).[48] Laurence noted that the argument against breaking up the reserves was that "some Indians, given such liberty, would become subjects of poverty and want." His reply was, "Do not white men do the same?" Laurence predicted a brilliant future, however: "At no distant day they will be the equals, if not the superiors of many of their white neighbors in all the arts and improvements of civilized life."[49]

While the virtues of private property were being promoted as the solution to the "Indian Problem," and the route to liberty and prosperity, the DIA and other government authorities devoted great push and energy to ensuring that no one defined as "Indian" could obtain land to call their own off a reserve, despite the immense sweep of real estate that the government of Canada acquired through treaties, and the lavish grants made to the Canadian Pacific Railway and the Hudson's Bay Company. Newcomers had many options to acquire lands, including purchase and homesteading. One hundred and sixty acres were provided virtually free to an immigrant male, and he could expand his holdings through opportunities such as pre-emption and second homesteads. His sons could also file on land, and in that way large family farms were created on the prairies. The people confined to Indian reserves had no mechanisms or options to permit expansion of their land base; the *Indian Act* and the treaties anticipated and provided for the diminishment but not the growth of reserve land.

Many twists and turns were required to dispossess any treaty Indians from land that they occupied individually or as a family before the treaty.[50] There were a large number of cases in the West of treaty people

---

46 John Laurence, "The Future of the Indians of Canada," *Methodist Magazine and Review* 61, no. 5 (1905): 444.
47 Laurence, "Future of the Indians," 444.
48 Laurence, "Indian Problem," 329.
49 Laurence, "Future of the Indians," 445.
50 See Sarah Carter, "Erasing and Replacing: Property and Homestead Rights of First Nations Farmers of Manitoba and the Northwest, 1870s–1910s," in *Place and Replace: Essays on Western Canada*, ed. Adele Perry, Esyllt W. Jones, and Leah Morton (Winnipeg: University of Manitoba Press, 2013), 14.

who wanted title to land occupied and cultivated before the treaties, and according to Irene Spry and Bennett McCardle there were "a remarkable variety of Indian-white claims and counterclaims to particular parcels of land."[51] By the mid-1870s federal government officials resolved that no one defined as "Indian" could actually own property, either before or after the treaty. One rationale was that they were not "persons," like other settlers. Through an 1875 amendment to *An Act Respecting the Appropriation of Certain Dominion Lands in Manitoba* it was enacted that "persons" who were in "undisturbed occupancy of any lands within the Province prior to ... the 15th day of July, 1870, shall be entitled to receive Letters Patent therefor, granting the same absolutely to them respectively in fee simple."[52] In 1877 the deputy minister of justice decided that "an Indian does not come within the word 'persons' in the Act referred to," and this position was adopted by the government. It was decided that no Indian could "claim a Patent for land of which he was in occupation at the time of the transfer of the territory."[53] If an Indian (who was not a person) had sold his land to another Indian, the sale was invalid, but sale to a person was also invalid. The Proclamation of 1763 was another rationale for not recognizing the individual ownership of land by Indians prior to treaties.[54]

According to the DIA, then, no treaty Indians had any property rights to land they occupied either before or after treaty, despite all the rhetoric of the day about the transformative power of owning land. Under the *Indian Act*, no one defined as "Indian" in the West could apply to homestead the 160 acres of land available virtually free to (mostly male) newcomers.[55] Enfranchisement was the only way to acquire a plot of land, although this was land that was taken from reserve land.[56] Enfranchisement was the process through which an individual lost Indian status and (supposedly) gained the full rights of citizenship. It was complicated

---

51 Irene Spry and Bennett McCardle, *The Records of the Department of the Interior and Research Concerning Canada's Western Frontier of Settlement* (Regina: Canadian Plains Research Centre, 1993), 140–1.

52 "An Act to Amend an Act Respecting the Appropriation of Certain Dominion Lands in Manitoba," *Treaties between Her Majesty the Queen and Foreign Powers* (presented to the University by the Rhodes Trustees), 292.

53 Library and Archives Canada (LAC), RG 10, vol. 236, file 7052, memorandum, Minister of the Interior, 6 June 1877.

54 See the text of the Royal Proclamation of 1763, http://www.bloorstreet.com/200block/rp1763.htm.

55 Carter, "Erasing and Replacing," 27–35. The 1876 *Indian Act* stipulated that "no Indian, resident in the province of Manitoba, the North-West Territories or the territory of Keewatin, shall be held capable of having acquired or of acquiring a homestead or pre-emption right." *Indian Act 1876*, SC 1876, c 18 (39 Vict.).

56 Carter, "Erasing and Replacing," 27–35.

and protracted. Consent of the band had to be acquired before an applicant could begin the process.[57] The applicant was then assigned a "suitable allotment" of under fifty acres of reserve land. A "competent person" was required to "report whether the applicant ... [demonstrated] integrity, morality and sobriety ... [and] appears to be qualified to become a proprietor of land in fee simple." If a favourable report was received, a location ticket was issued. There was then a probationary period of three years (or longer in the event of unsatisfactory conduct), after which the applicant might be granted title to the land in fee simple. Later amendments made the process even more challenging.[58]

Every time a person or family became enfranchised, the reserve shrank in size. Not surprisingly band councils were seldom willing to grant permission to an applicant, as in each case the land base was further diminished.[59] Treaty people detected and protested plots to diminish their reserves that were small and confining to begin with. In 1889, Treaty Four Saulteaux leader Louis O'Soup, one of the most prosperous farmers on his reserve, would not permit the surveyors to subdivide land on his reserve, understanding that "it was the intention of the Government to restrain him and his people within the lines that the surveyors were running inside the reserve."[60] Hayter Reed was surprised that "a man of his intelligence" would thwart the efforts of the DIA to advance the real interests of the Indians, and he advised the Indian agent to point out the advantages of the plan, which would improve and elevate them.[61]

If an enfranchised Indian did manage to jump through all the hoops and acquire a plot of her or his former reserve, the land was not exactly his or hers; it could not be sold, leased, or otherwise alienated without the sanction of the governor-in-council.[62] But there were to be some

---

57 Carter, "Erasing and Replacing," 47–50. The rest of this paragraph also draws on and quotes from this.

58 Carter, "Erasing and Replacing," 98; *An Act further to amend "The Indian Act, 1880"* SC 1884 c 27 (47).

59 Carter, "Erasing and Replacing," 30. See also Robin Jarvis Brownlie, "A Persistent Antagonism: First Nations and the Liberal Order," in *Liberalism and Hegemony: Debating the Canadian Liberal Revolution*, ed. Jean-Francois Constant and Michel Ducharme (Toronto: University of Toronto Press, 2009), 314. Brownlie notes that amendments to the enfranchisement process in 1918 protected the reserve base from erosion through enfranchisements, and between 1918 and 1939 about 2,400 people became enfranchised. This, however, represented only 2 per cent of the status Indian population.

60 Quoted in Carter, *Lost Harvests,* 207.

61 Carter, *Lost Harvests,* 207.

62 Sharon Helen Venne, *Indian Acts and Amendments 1868–1975: An Indexed Collection* (Saskatoon: University of Saskatchewan Native Law Centre, 1981), 146.

advantages; if a treaty man was enfranchised, it was possible he could apply for 160 aces of homestead land. An 1895 opinion of the DIA was that upon enfranchisement a male could homestead.[63] Homesteading on the prairies by Indians, or former Indians who became enfranchised however, was officially discouraged by the DIA and Department of the Interior, in response to enquiries about the right of a First Nations man from Ontario to homestead in the West.[64] The rhetoric about the transformative power of private property was called upon only when it was reserve land to be carved up and parcelled out.

The promotion of private property on reserves as the route to prosperity for First Nation people has a long history. The central rationale advanced has remained virtually the same over more than 100 years; a brilliant economic future is in store. Individual initiative and opportunity will flourish, and poverty and dependence will be eliminated. But while promoters of such schemes over 100 years ago did not hide the fact that the ultimate objective was assimilation and the disappearance of reserves and the political entities that governed these communities, this is now hidden from view, although still present. Objections and protests of reserve residents who correctly concluded that these plots served the interests of non-Indigenous people, and meant the diminishment of their land, also have a long history. Flanagan asserts that what is new about his scheme is that it would be voluntary, that reserve communities could decide to opt in. The voluntary approach too has a long history, except for a brief period of compulsory enfranchisement, and reserve governments of the past were not inclined to opt in to plans that would fragment their communities.

III. Private Ownership on Reserves: The Case of St Peter's, Manitoba

There is also a history of private land ownership on one reserve in Western Canada that is overlooked in *Beyond the Indian Act*. Private property on the St Peter's reserve in Manitoba led directly to dispossession of the entire reserve in 1907. *Beyond the Indian Act*, however, passes over troubling histories and does not seriously engage with histories of dispossession and marginalization that illustrate the limitations and drawbacks of the proposed scheme. The story of St Peter's is complex and only a brief outline can be provided here. St Peter's,

---

63 Lynwoode Pereira to John McKenzie, 31 August 1898, RG 15, series D II 1, vol. 750, file 478, 863, Library and Archives Canada.
64 Carter, "Erasing and Replacing," 32–3.

surveyed as Indian Reserve One following the negotiation of Treaty One in 1871, was an agricultural settlement of Saulteaux (Ojibway or Anishinabe) Cree, and mixed-ancestry people long before the treaty. Also long before the treaty there was a system at St Peter's of individual ownership of land, often river lots, that were granted initially by Chief Peguis and later by his son, Chief Henry Prince. Land was owned by those who identified as "Indians," by mixed-ancestry people, and settlers from the British Isles.

When St Peter's was surveyed as a reserve these plots of individually owned land became part of the reserve, and there were long-term occupants of land who were non-treaty people but were now resident on a reserve, even though under the *Indian Act* they were now "trespassers." All seemed well on the surface; in the late nineteenth century the DIA celebrated St Peter's as the sterling example of the wisdom of Canada's Indigenous policy, as it was a flourishing agricultural settlement. There were over 2000 acres under cultivation. Comfortable, whitewashed log homes were surrounded by cultivated fields and vegetable gardens.[65] But there was constant turmoil on the St Peter's reserve over the incredibly complex issues of land ownership from the time of the survey, and tensions became acute between the band members and the non-treaty people. All were angry that they were informed that they did not actually own the land they lived on and farmed, as all was now reserve land.

The settlement was described by one DIA official in 1884 as "in a turbulent state, a seething cauldron of conflicting elements."[66] DIA officials in Ottawa, in particular Deputy Superintendent General Lawrence Vankoughnet, believed that acceptance of treaty deprived a man of private property rights, and converted all land then occupied into reserve land. Anyone defined as "Indian" had no right to any property cultivated or occupied prior to the treaty.[67] If any land on the St Peter's reserve was to be divided up and alienated, a surrender would have to be taken under the terms of the *Indian Act*, according to Vankoughnet. Consent was required from the majority of the male members of the band over the age of twenty-one to alienate any reserve land. The

---

65 Sarah Carter, "'They Would Not Give Up One Inch of It': The Rise and Demise of St Peter's Reserve in Manitoba," in *Indigenous Communities and Settler Colonialism*, ed. Zoe Laidlaw and Alan Lester (Basingstoke, UK: Palgrave Macmillan, 2015), 173.

66 Quoted in Tyler and Wright Research Consultants Limited, *The Alienation of Indian Reserve Land during the Administration of Sir Wilfrid Laurier, 1896–1911*, no. 4, "St Peter's Reserve," unpublished report prepared for the Manitoba Indian Brotherhood, 1978, 92.

67 Tyler and Wright, *Alienation of Indian Reserve Land*, 99.

leaders at St Peter's were not willing to part with any of their reserve, and they increasingly clamoured to have non-treaty people evicted. Chief William Prince declared in 1887 that "they would not give up one inch of it, 'that they would lay down their lives in the highway by the white-man, before they would give it up.'"[68]

The land question at St Peter's proved vexing, intricate, and varied. In 1879 it was decided to eject all of the non-treaty people or "intruders," but they refused to leave their farms and homes. It was then decided that all of the "trespassers" could present a claim under the *Manitoba Act*, and this proved to be a lengthy and complicated procedure. In 1884 a commission was appointed to investigate and settle disputes at St Peter's, and in an 1885 report it was decided to eject those who had taken Métis scrip. Some of the band members decided to withdraw from treaty status and took Métis scrip, but they did not as a result wish to vacate their property at St Peter's. In fact they hoped it could strengthen their claim to actual ownership of their property.

The existence of the St Peter's reserve was vexing to officials such as Hayter Reed, and not only because of the turmoil of the land question, but because St Peter's band members were outspoken and effective in protesting, challenging, remonstrating, and objecting to the DIA and *Indian Act* regime. Reed demanded rigid discipline and strict adherence to rules and regulations and did not tolerate insubordinate behaviour. The St Peter's people were the "lawless and revolutionary element" that Reed feared and deplored. They were also capable farmers, with a history of individual land ownership. Yet in his reports, letters, and speeches, Reed cast Indians as "ignorant savages," as having no concept of property, and as lazy and incompetent workers, incapable of farming.[69] The St Peter's people defied these representations.

Although in turmoil, and despite the challenge that band members posed to the DIA, the St Peter's reserve survived the Hayter Reed and Conservative era. The victory of the Wilfrid Laurier Liberals in the federal election of 1896, however, brought a set of politicians to power who were even more sympathetic to the settlers who clamoured for Indian reserve land to be thrown open for purchase, speculation, and settlement. Indigenous people were seen as impediments to the progress of rural and urban districts, and as having an overabundance of land. DIA officials became zealous and relentless in pursuing reserve land alienation, using questionable and often fraudulent tactics. Officials of the DIA also speculated in and profited from the sale of reserve land.

---

68 Tyler and Wright, *Alienation of Indian Reserve Land*, 103.
69 Tyler and Wright, *Alienation of Indian Reserve Land*, 143.

Rarely, however, was an entire reserve surrendered, as was the case with St Peter's.[70]

Under the Liberal federal regime, it was decided that the best approach was not a time-consuming investigation of the individual and conflicting claims at St Peter's but a comprehensive settlement. A "plan" to get the entire reserve surrendered was proposed in 1900.[71] The fact that the St Peter's people were utterly opposed to these plans mattered little.[72] Prominent people of Selkirk, a town that began to undergo an economic "boom" after the turn of the century, campaigned for the surrender of the reserve and the removal of the Indians far away from the town. By 1905 the DIA jobs of Indian agent and inspector of Indian agencies responsible for St Peter's were given to men in favour of opening the reserve to speculation and settlement. Plans were made to remove the St Peter's people to a remote location.[73]

The residents of St Peter's remained adamantly opposed to the surrender of their land; only fraudulent measures and unrelenting pressure achieved this outcome. A commission made up of Liberal friends of the government was appointed in 1907 to settle the complicated and competing claims to land at St Peter's. In April of that year Commissioner Hector Howell held a meeting at St Peter's to discuss the surrender of the entire reserve and found the people unanimously opposed. At a second meeting about a month later, the proposal was also rejected. The offer was enhanced, but at a June meeting it was soundly rejected. More incentives were added. At a September meeting it was announced that $5000 was on hand and would be distributed as an advance on the sale of the land if they agreed to surrender. Following two days of meetings in late September the DIA declared that they had secured a surrender of the reserve, although the vote was haphazard. There was confusion about what "line" to stand in (one "for" and one "against," with those "for" being told they would get $90 each). There was no written list of voters and no recounts. There was not enough room in the old schoolhouse where the meeting was held for all of the people present, and many stood outside. The vote was announced as 107 in favour and 98 against. There were 233 eligible voters on the reserve, so the vote did not carry with a majority of total voters.[74] The St Peter's people

---

70 See Tyler and Wright, *Alienation of Indian Reserve Land*; Peggy Martin-McGuire, *First Nation Land Surrenders on the Prairies, 1896–1911* (Ottawa: Indian Claims Commission, 1998); and Carter, *Lost Harvests*, 193–258.

71 Martin-McGuire *First Nation Land Surrenders*, 211.

72 Tyler and Wright, *Alienation of Indian Reserve Land*, 128–9.

73 Tyler and Wright, *Alienation of Indian Reserve Land*, 212.

74 Tyler and Wright, *Alienation of Indian Reserve Land*, 289.

had lost their reserve through these tactics that were controversial at the time and since, leading to the 1998 decision that the "surrender" of their reserve was fraudulent, unlawfully taken from them without their consent.[75] The vast majority of the St Peter's people were forcibly relocated to the Peguis reserve, in the Interlake district of Manitoba. The land was not as good, the reserve was remote from markets and other infrastructure, and the people had to start again from scratch. The Peguis people and Canada agreed to a settlement in 2010.[76] The case of St Peter's is unique in Western Canada in the presence of private ownership of land on a reserve, and in the obliteration of the entire reserve, but many thousands of acres of reserve land were alienated under the Liberal regime.

IV. Conclusion

In the case of St Peter's individual land tenure did not result in the enhanced prosperity of the reserve. A once flourishing community, a model agricultural reserve celebrated by the DIA, was erased from the map entirely, despite the protests and opposition of the residents. Disputes over ownership of land on the reserve were seized on as the rationale for its extinguishment. Settler supporters of the erasure of the reserve argued that the question of conflicting property rights could be settled only by the deletion of the settlement and removal of the residents. This was also the fate of vast tracts of reservation land in the United States following allotment under the Dawes Act. While economic development on reserves remains a thorny problem, the optimistic projections proposed by the authors of *Beyond the Indian Act* conveniently ignore a history of disastrous results of private land ownership of reserve land. Hayter Reed and his contemporaries proposed the same idea, and their agenda was to eliminate reserves from the landscape, or at the least the most valuable tracts of land on reserves. A similar agenda still seems to be at work, and it is couched in much the same rhetoric. The proposed solution ignores history and also distorts and misconstrues the complexity of First Nations concepts of property and attitudes to land ownership.

In "The Cumberland Cree Nehinuw Concept of Land" Cree historian Keith Goulet provides insight into the complex concepts and categories of land in his own community, and how they have changed over

---

75 Peguis First Nation, "Surrender Claim Trust," http://www.peguisfirstnation.ca /about/surrender-claim-trust/.

76 Peguis First Nation, "Surrender Claim Trust."

time.[77] *Kituskeenuw* (our land) is used in the same sense as "our country" and is the Cree national territory or country. It is the land under the common authority of the people. *Nicuskeeganis* is the individual's own "private property lot," and this concept, and the phrase "this is my land," owned individually, has taken hold only recently. *Uskee* refers to land in general, while *uskeegan* refers to land that has been divided up and parcelled off, and the term carries the connotation of "artificial land." The land held in common, *uskee*, is the real, genuine land. If the authors of *Beyond the Indian Act* were truly interested in restoring Indigenous property rights, they would need to restore to the Cree of Cumberland House the land held in common, their country, the real, genuine land.

In his drive to push the neoliberal agenda, Flanagan uses Hayek uncritically to deride the state planning that he sees as hampering reserve economic development. The alternative he proposes does not recognize Indigenous rights, since they would be reduced to property rights, therefore rejecting the notion of the existence of collective rights, and, as suggested in the introduction of the book, such a notion would "represent a threat to self-determination." Jobin further points out in her chapter that "the shift of viewing the land as commodity instead of a gift changes Indigenous perceptions of sharing these gifts with others."[78] Instead of turning to private property or a marketized option of land and to individual ownership to break away from the reserve system, the solutions ought to be found in the many different ways Indigenous people relate to the land and the laws that inform such relationships. Indeed, the solutions ought to be coming from the First Nations themselves, favouring collective community-based approaches, as well as applying a critical Indigenous feminist lens, as Napoleon and Snyder propose in their chapter, to render visible gendered power dynamics that surround property rights and Indigenous legal interpretations.[79] As Egan and Place note, the idea is not to "romanticize Indigenous peoples' connections to land and nature but rather to acknowledge that collective ownership of land may offer important social and political benefits that individual private property does not."[80] It remains to be seen if Canada can rise to the challenge.

---

77 Keith Goulet, "The Cumberland Cree Nehinuw Concept of Land" (paper delivered at the Indigenous Knowledge Systems: International Symposium, University of Saskatchewan, Saskatoon, 2004), 10–12.

78 In this book, see Jobin, "Market Citizenship and Indigeneity."

79 In this book see Napoleon and Snyder, "Housing on Reserve: Developing a Critical Indigenous Feminist Property Theory."

80 Brian Egan and Jessica Place, "Minding the Gaps: Property, Geography, and Indigenous People in Canada," *Geoforum* 44 (2013): 136.

5 Conceptualizing Aboriginal Taxpayers, Real Property, and Communities of Sharing

RICHARD DALY*

Introduction

During the 1980s and 1990s when I worked as an anthropological researcher for First Nations peoples in their preparation of constitutional test cases in British Columbia,[1] I was frequently witness to tirades by exasperated Aboriginal people who regarded themselves as "responsible taxpayers" who remained unacknowledged by the wider society. These interlocutors of Indigenous communities constituted a rather atypical form of irate taxpayer. Mostly, they were irate about the way their people were stereotyped whenever Aboriginal taxation became the subject of public discourse by government, courts, or the media. They opposed the public image of themselves as childlike creatures too simple-minded to succeed in the complex and competitive life of the nation state. However, they also opposed the public, often media-driven view that they lacked the self-assurance that accompanies first-class citizenry that is vested in proprietary holdings;[2] that is, those who signal their participation in the politics of the country

* The author is grateful for positive criticism and timely suggestions made by anonymous reviewers, all of which enriched the subject and caused the writer to look more closely at certain aspects of Aboriginal/First Nations taxation. I am not a scholar of Aboriginal law; therefore this chapter has benefited greatly as well from the editorial suggestions made by Sari Graben and her colleagues.
1 Richard H. Daly, *Our Box Was Full: An Ethnography for the Delgamuukw Plaintiffs* (Vancouver: UBC Press, 2005).
2 Gerald Sider has drawn attention to the common ownership roots of the English words *proper, property,* and *proprietorship.* Gerald Sider, "The Ties That Bind: Culture and Agriculture, Property and Propriety in the Newfoundland Village Fishery," *Social History* 5, no. 1 (1980): 1.

by making a financial contribution to the state of Canada by paying taxes on income and real property. In essence, they were irate because they saw themselves as responsible contributors to society who, unlike conventional taxpayers, were denied recognition of responsibility and respect based on their longstanding material contributions to society.

Instead of seeing themselves as exempt from taxation, these individuals pointed out that by virtue of their productivity on the land they had always "paid taxes" and thereby exercised legitimate ownership and control over real property. Through their hard work and reciprocal social interaction between families, they had acted as "proper" property-holding citizens in their respective societies. Moreover, they argued that the continuing relations of sharing in their communities today follow the teachings of predecessors who had been producing, exchanging, and "paying taxes" for generations before them. They argue that while Canada continues to profit from the export of raw materials taken from often unjustly acquired "Indian lands," it is only just that "status Indians" receive transfer payments, but they also add that it would be much more just to allow Aboriginal people to use, not only for subsistence but also for profit, at least some portion of their traditional lands and territories.

The idea that First Nations have always been taxpayers may seem odd in light of colloquial understandings of the issue. In law, Indians and the Inuit who are not the beneficiaries of contemporary treaties possess only certain residual rights to land (usually construed as usufruct rights in relation to lands not currently of interest to foreign investors or other Canadians) and, in certain circumstances and under certain conditions, may be exempt from some provincial or federal forms of taxation – to the extent that some Indigenous peoples do indeed now explain to outsiders their old forms of disbursing wealth as activities analogous to tax-paying. Some of my interlocutors have felt the need to explain their institutions as analogues of "the white world," which reinforces the hegemonic power of the nation-state system, its governance, fee simple ownership, and market development. Today the social life of the world's Indigenous peoples is woven into the fabric of encapsulating nation states and, increasingly, they are being washed by the transnational ebbs and flows of capital around the globe.

First Nation activists might do well not only to criticize – as they do – the factual and political nature of European colonial sovereignty, its social imaginary, its ideology and its mythology, but also they might deconstruct and rebuild this model, to see what empirical, historical, and factual basis it has for organizing twenty-first-century Aboriginal social life and jurisprudence according the traditions of First Nations,

Métis, and Inuit peoples. This requires documenting and contextualizing the social and cultural structures, rules, and discipline involved
in actual Aboriginal life – both of the past and of today.[3] Of course one
size does not fit all. Aboriginal communities in Canada subscribe to
many different forms of pre-European land-holding and redistributive
practices by which such land-holding is recognized and legitimized.
As Aboriginal peoples move away from land-based everyday life, it
is more, not less important politically and jurally to document, promote, and explain fundamental or pre-existing Aboriginal social institutions and practices that had made the bountiful Canadian landscape
what it was at the time of European arrival.[4] In this chapter I examine
these dynamics as they were practised in the previous two centuries,
and to some degree still are, among certain Aboriginal peoples on, and
adjacent to, the Pacific Coast. The Aboriginal law of these peoples, particularly the Wet'suwet'en and Gitxsan peoples, provides insights into
Indigenous practices that these people liken to tax-paying and might
provide a way for other Aboriginal peoples to reflect upon, in light of
their own traditions and practices.

Drawing on Indigenous practices of reciprocity and counter-giving
in the Northwest Coast ethnographic region, I argue that Indigenous
peoples in this part of Canada have long exercised traditions that are
analogous to taxation. At least the *internal* social and cultural procedures of Indigenous traditions provide evidence of social relations
that mirror some of the characteristics of taxation (see below). This

---

3 Val Napoleon, "Thinking about Indigenous Legal Orders" (paper delivered at the
   National Centre for First Nations Governance, 18 June 2007), http://fngovernance.
   org/ncfng_research/val_napoleon.pdf; Catherine Bell and Val Napoleon, eds, *First
   Nations Cultural Heritage and Law: Case Studies, Voices and Perspectives* (Vancouver:
   UBC Press, 2008).
4 Social relations to the land are now recognized as manifested in the nature of
   ecology that human intervention created all over the Americas prior to European
   arrival. See, for example, Charles C. Mann, *1491: New Revelations of America before
   Columbus* (New York: Alfred A. Knopf, 2006); Thomas W. Neumann, "The Role of
   Prehistoric Peoples in Shaping Ecosystems in the Eastern United States: Implications for Restoration Ecology and Wilderness Management," in *Wilderness and Political Ecology: Aboriginal Influences and the Original State of Nature*, ed. Charles E. Kay
   and Randy T. Simmons (Salt Lake City: University of Utah Press, 2002), 141; Darrell
   Posey, "A Preliminary Report on the Diversified Management of Tropical Forest
   by the Kayapó Indians of the Brazilian Amazon," in *Advances in Economic Botany*,
   ed. Ghillean T. Prace (New York: New York Botanical Garden, 1984), 1:112; Anna C.
   Roosevelt, "South America: Archeology," in *The Cambridge Encyclopedia of Hunters
   and Gatherers*, ed. Richard B. Lee and Richard H. Daly (Cambridge: Cambridge University Press, 1999), 86.

conceptualization of tax-paying assumes various modalities in different parts of Aboriginal Canada, but at its core there are various forms of reciprocal giving, sharing, and counter-giving that, in the eyes of many Indigenous communities, validate and sanction ownership, stewardship, and management of territories – by those who give, share, and "pay back." Prior to the arrival of Europeans, many Indigenous peoples effected control over lands in accordance with rules that were held and sanctioned collectively on the basis of reciprocal relations between kin, classificatory kin, and affinity (relations through marriage rather than descent).

In this chapter I draw on ethnographic evidence of Indigenous understandings of reciprocity to question the current discourse on the question of real property ownership and taxation, especially as it pertains to the Northwest Coast. I examine certain calls for greater taxation from the federal government, the media, and industry, as well as current expectations of Indigenous taxation. I then contrast these concerns against Indigenous perspectives as "irate taxpayers." This is undertaken by a response to calls for the application of standard taxation schemes to Indigenous peoples who, facing charges from society that they are beggars who demand handouts and pay no taxes, have shown me their exasperation. They have suggested that the hegemonic society and culture ought to recognize the social responsibilities they and their predecessors have carried out for generations, and that they were still carrying out in the management of lands and resources. Senior members of the Gitxsan and Wet'suwet'en peoples were adamant, as I worked on my opinion evidence for the Delgamuukw case between 1986 and 1988, that they had spent their lives giving, sharing, and paying from the fruits of their traditional lands, for the right to continue to hold the land, and manage it for the coming generations.[5] Land management was indeed central to their public identity.

In its broadest contours, this type of concern for land management prevails among many First Nations west of the Rocky Mountains. To understand its ramifications and seek commonalties over a wider area, it is important to sketch out some principles of sharing and reciprocity in these communities where the calculation of responsibility in paying certain amounts or undertaking certain tasks can be understood to have a sociological function not unlike that of taxpaying in the mainstream society. In undertaking this comparison, I hope to raise questions that, despite claims of proprietorship of traditional territories being treated

---

5 *Delgamuukw et al v British Columbia* [1997] 3 SCR 1010, 153 DLR (4th) 193.

as irrelevant to discussions of taxation by some Aboriginal leaders, and despite some on-reserve entrepreneurs now believing that privatization will solve socio-economic problems in communities, it is more than likely that business-oriented demands (that government convert allodial, inalienable, collective rights to the existing parcels of land into *fee simple* ownership) threaten Indigenous conceptions of taxation, and indeed Aboriginal rights.

I. Reserves and Taxation Revenue: The Ongoing Discourse

Taxation, that "pecuniary burden laid upon individuals or property owners to support the government,"[6] is a financial charge imposed by a state or other governing body on a taxpayer (an individual or legal entity). Payment is mandatory: failure to pay one's taxes is punishable by law. When taxes are not fully paid, civil penalties such as fines or forfeitures of property, or criminal penalties such as incarceration, may be imposed on the non-paying entity or individual. Definitions such as this presuppose the existence of the state as the authority for both imposing taxation and generating the laws behind it. Throughout history, pre-industrial states also commonly imposed taxes composed of foodstuffs, resources, and a labour levy (corvée) to support state projects. But it is important to ask what happens in non-state social formations, such as those that occupied the landmass of Canada prior to Confederation in 1867. Are we sure such societies lacked taxation?

Where there are no state instruments of enforcement, and where compliance is strictly through moral and social pressure, can a taxation system exist or be seen to have existed? Can, for example, non-payment of material contributions to the public good lead to punishment, loss of prosperity, and/or forfeiture of property? This chapter argues that there is indeed a case to be made for the existence of Indigenous non-state taxation in northern North America prior to the existence of Canada, and moreover, an awareness that at Confederation and thereafter, not only by British constitutional authorities but also certain First Nations leaders of the day understood the dangers of forfeiture that modern taxation could bring to Aboriginal communities. First Nation "taxpayers" who failed to make the requisite payments in their respective systems could suffer forfeitures of property.

Pursuant to section 87 of the *Indian Act*, First Nations people are exempted from paying provincial and federal taxes if and when they are

---

6 *Black's Law Dictionary*, 7th ed., s.v. "taxation."

deemed to have status as "Indians" and if and when they are resident on designated reserves. This does not apply to non-status Indians or Inuit, or to the more than 50 per cent of the First Nations population, which at any given time is not resident on reserve lands. Similarly, for all "status" people covered by section 87, the provisions have been interpreted by the courts according to specific features of the issue at hand; for example, some cases of unemployment insurance payments accruing from work expended off-reserve have been deemed by the courts to be taxable and such issues are considered by government and the courts to be far from simple. This is only one area where there are limitations to "status" Indian tax exemptions.[7] Tax exemptions, as limited as they are, have long been contentious in the public sphere but were devised before Confederation, from Canada's point of view, partially in light of the government's fiduciary responsibility towards First Nations and the preservation of reserves as self-sustaining homesteads. Part of the assumptions behind the *Indian Act* was that, given their limited economic possibilities in the reserve system, First Nations would not risk forfeiting their houses and their relatively small parcels of land when they could not afford to pay taxes, since they had already lost control of most of their revenue-generating territories to the immigrant-invaders from Europe. From the vantage point of many First Nations, however, resolving tax status is crucial to the social and economic well-being of Aboriginal communities, because tax exemptions help them rebuild their socio-economic life, especially with regard to the growing number of non-status and urban-based First Nations people. Aboriginal leaders argue that tax exemption is a more effective way of dealing with homelessness, unemployment, and poverty than the current system of minimal welfare payments and can lead the people into more productive lives in the home areas and back into Canada's workforce.[8]

---

7 Jane Allain, Law and Government Division, "Income Tax for Status Indians: Revenue Canada's New Policy," Parliamentary Research Branch MR-130E, 19 January 1995, 2: "Furthermore, as can be seen from our discussion of the test for the situs of unemployment insurance benefits, *the creation of a test for the location of intangible property under the Indian Act is a complex endeavour.* In the context of unemployment insurance we were able to focus on certain features of the scheme and its taxation implications in order to establish one factor as having particular importance. *It is not clear whether this would be possible in the context of employment income, or what features of employment income and its taxation should be examined to that end*" (emphasis added). For case law on this issue, see *Dubé v Canada*, 2011 SCC 39, [2011] 2 SCR 764; and *Bastien Estate v Canada*, 2011 SCC 38, [2011] 2 SCR 710.
8 "The Shilling Case and Protecting Aboriginal Tax Exemption," Turtle Island Native Network News, http://www.turtleisland.org/news/news-taxation-shilling.htm (site discontinued).

It has been estimated that fewer than 275,000 First Nations persons over the age of fourteen are eligible for such tax exemptions.[9] The infrastructure that supports today's global economy is underwritten by taxation, even in avowedly neoliberal economies. Providing services, roads, education, welfare, health, governance, and communications is based largely on taxes of one sort or another, and populists in politics and the media often point out that Aboriginal people are not "pulling their weight."

Accusations are often levied that reserve residence is little more than a tax haven for various entrepreneurial persons of First Nations background and, as such, constitutes special treatment and is less than equitable and "democratic."[10] There is seldom, if ever, any discussion of First Nations peoples as longstanding "taxpayers" within their own governance heritage, where usually payments were made in the public sphere, and these tended to sanction their legitimate participation in society. The mainstream image of First Nations is frequently composed of a sense of deficiency. Aboriginal societies are often portrayed as suffering a conceptual "lack of property," a "lack of market," and a "lack of sophisticated social organization." Since such societies are considered to have lacked most institutions of modernity, they are urged simply to accept modern Canadian institutions, such as calls for "Indians to pay taxes."

The Confederacy of Canadian Municipalities, the Indian Taxation Advisory Board, the National Aboriginal Land Management Association, the Lands Advisory Board, and Indian and Northern Affairs Canada have all supported a project to assess such joint tax ventures.[11] The First Nations Taxation Commission, led by Manny Jules, explains that FNTC supports First Nation taxation under the *First Nations Fiscal Management Act* and under section 83 of the *Indian Act* and provides a toolkit for the many First Nations with property tax powers, which, he argues, are responding to community needs and providing local services to thousands of property taxpayers.[12] The object of this project is to generate revenue by resorting to "municipal-like" taxation schemes.

---

9 Chelsea Vowel, *Indigenous Writes: A Guide to First Nations, Métis and Inuit Issues* (Winnipeg: HighWater, 2016), 135–42.

10 Tom Flanagan, *First Nations? Second Thoughts* (Montreal and Kingston: McGill-Queen's University Press, 2000).

11 Canada, Federation of Canadian Municipalities, *Building Capacity through Communication: Municipal-Aboriginal Partnerships in Land Management*, book 1–5 (2016), https://fcm.ca/Documents/reports/Building_Capacity_Through_Communication_EN.pdf.

12 First Nations Tax Commission, "s. 83 Toolkit," (2017), http://fntc.ca/s-83-toolkit/ (site discontinued).

Moreover, such initiatives have received support from a number of reserves, as well as from Indian and Northern Affairs Canada, the Lands Advisory Board, the National Aboriginal Land Managers Association, and the Indian Taxation Advisory Board.[13] The new openness of reserve communities to taxation arises from their own attempts to address the poverty and defeatism of their members with limited resources and limited options under the existing conditions of the *Indian Act*.[14] Avenues for financing economic development are few and far between, and revenue generation is limited. Consequently, the notion of levying taxes to supplement transfer payments for on-reserve services can look attractive, especially when paired with the advantages of Aboriginal tax benefits coming into reserve communities from section 87 of the *Indian Act*. Their publications document a number of Aboriginal taxation case studies in First Nations bands and communities in Alberta (Wood Buffalo), British Columbia (Westbank), Manitoba (The Pas/Opaskwayak), and Ontario (Temagami/Teme Augama Anishnabai). It is sometimes argued that if on-reserve members of First Nations pay all of the taxes levied on Canadian residents (and not just the current portion they pay), they will gain a degree of esteem in the eyes of the public.

However, those First Nations communities contemplating taxation tend to face a number of critiques aimed at the goals and aims of new tax arrangements. Communities face criticism that they are market entrepreneurs hiding their wealth in on-reserve "tax havens." Moreover, because modern class divisions exist even on reserves, there is debate, both internally and across the country, that some of the proposals coming from economic advisors within reserve communities

---

13 See Federation of Canadian Municipalities, *Building Capacity through Communication*, 3.
14 Negotiators for both First Nations and provincial and federal governments in Canada desire changes to the taxation systems in their specific jurisdictions. However, their interests are not identical, and the present topic of taxation is nurtured both by government initiatives and First Nations' demands and frustrations. Legal scholar Douglas Sanderson suggests adopting the concept of overlapping consensus (borrowed from philosopher John Rawls) as a basis for expanding cooperation by both sides, within the framework of the *Indian Act*, especially on membership integration and financial accountability and integration. Sanderson suggests that tax authorities allot First Nations' taxes to local First Nations communities, since this would provide an incentive to recruit non-status and urban Native persons into these communities (given that communities would receive increased funding for increased membership). Local First Nations would be more positive about taxation if they saw accountable tax funding coming regularly back to them and their social and economic needs. See Douglas Sanderson, "Overlapping Consensus, Legislative Reform and the *Indian Act*," *Queen's Law Journal* 39, no. 2 (2013–14): 511.

would be beneficial to the interests of a few and detrimental to the interests of the many. In other words, when many residents are poorly educated and unemployed, they cannot contribute meaningfully to the tax base. As such, employment of taxes generated from the surrounding non-reserve community using reserve resources will not generally represent the interests of the impoverished majority with much political rigour and transparency when it comes to public investment and accounting for such tax revenues. Most importantly, calls for taxation obscure the historical experience of First Nations who have engaged in political and economic exchange between one another for centuries and have conducted clear, kinship-based property holding within their nation community and between it and its neighbours.[15]

It is also not entirely certain that a shift to taxation would guarantee a better future or more protection against destitution and homelessness – not without the basis for an improved local economy. Such taxation initiatives are not really capable of solving problems of discrimination and endemic poverty, but rather they provide a creeping infrastructure for the termination of First Nations identity and rights under the *Indian Act* by melting First Nations into municipal status. The municipalization process, begun with the Sechelt Nation decades ago, remains the preferred solution to dealing with Indians who stand in the way of development.[16] Today in light of *Delgamuukw* (*Delgamuukw et al v British Columbia* [1997] SSC 23799), and more precisely, in light of *Haida Nation* (*Haida Nation v British Columbia [Ministry of Forests]*, 2004, 3 SCC 73), First Nations must now be consulted before their traditional lands (wherever proprietary rights to these lands are at least partially acknowledged by the judicial and legislative bodies of Canada) are leased out by Canada or otherwise tapped as part of the current intense rate of extraction of raw materials for the global market. With regard to the 40th and 41st Parliaments of Canada (2008–15), one First Nations blogger, Russell Diabo, warned of growing coercion by government, arguing that the federal government was threatening to end treaty negotiating tables, offering financial incentives to whichever negotiating tables agreed to terminate their Aboriginal sovereignty status in return for municipal status; and threatening that those who did not

---

15 For example, see Daly, *Our Box Was Full*; and Richard Overstall, "Encountering the Spirit in the Land: 'Property' in a Kin-Based Legal Order," in *Despotic Dominion: Property Rights in British Settler Societies*, ed. John McLaren, A.R. Buck, and Nancy E. Wright (Vancouver: UBC Press, 2005), 22.

16 Mario Blaser, Harvey A. Feit, and Glenn McRae, *In the Way of Development: Indigenous Peoples, Life Projects and Globalization* (London: Zed Books, 2004).

agree would lose the possibility for future negotiations. And he predicted that all current First Nations' band and tribal council funding[17] for advisory services would be terminated for all who did not concur with the government initiative.[18]

Lastly, First Nations concerns about implementing contemporary tax responsibilities relate partly to the ideological foundations of its advocates. Advocacy for Aboriginal taxation is often based on a political ideology that is ahistorical and dismisses the multinational and multicultural realities. Flanagan, for one,[19] is alarmed that if fully implemented, the recommendations of the Royal Commission on Aboriginal Peoples would create a Canada that is a "multinational archipelago of aboriginal nations that own a third of Canada's land mass, are immune from federal and provincial taxation, are supported by transfer payments from citizens who do pay taxes, are able to opt out of federal and provincial legislation, and engage in 'nation-to-nation' diplomacy with whatever is left of Canada."[20] In his discussion of Flanagan's point of view, Colin Scott has pointed out that the neoliberal view of governance according to the principle of "freedom of choice" cannot logically be applied to governance and taxation. Flanagan speaks rhetorically of the oppressive lack of freedom in instances of Aboriginal collective decision-making. Scott notes, however, "If society is to be based on free choice and voluntary association, how does the nation-state exempt its own constitutional order from this standard? Is the 'spontaneous order of society' not compromised when peoples are incorporated against their will, on terms without their consent?"[21] This, of course, is relevant to the theme of taxation everywhere.

The colonial mentality – still not completely exorcised from Canadian society – holds that European state systems of governance and economy are, at least in the eyes of the settler culture, truly magnanimous and intrinsically superior to the purported simplicity and emptiness of both the physical landscape and the social order they thought they

---

17 Russell Diablo, "Harper Launches Major First Nations Termination Plan: As Negotiating Tables Legitimize Canada's Colonialism," Intercontinental Cry, 9 November 2012, https://intercontinentalcry.org/harper-launches-major-first-nations-termination-plan-as-negotiating-tables-legitimize-canadas-colonialism/.
18 Diablo, "Harper Launches Major First Nations Termination Plan."
19 Flanagan, First Nations? 5.
20 Cited by Colin Scott, "Conflicting Discourses of Property, Governance and Development in the Indigenous North," in Blaser, Feit, and McRae, In the Way of Development, 302.
21 Scott, "Conflicting Discourses of Property," 304.

had encountered at contact.[22] First Nations peoples were removed from control of their lands and administratively defined as "Indians." But unlike real Aboriginal peoples living and producing on the land, "Indians" were now moved to "reserves" where they have been detained and administrated under the *Indian Act* in conditions that still have not transcended the colonialism that moved them from their territories to the "reserves." Life on reserve has been protected and sculpted by a form of administration that follows the government's model of local councils. This system has created both societal problems and protections that are currently the basis of negotiations between First Nations and government. The "bands" and "tribal councils" were devised to act as part of the bureaucratic, government-conceived infrastructure, and these "bands" function as basic administrative units of the Canadian state. This was part of state-building, of industrial modernity's project of social and administrative integration and progress. At the same time it was ideologically justified by the creation of the social imaginary of modernity, contrasted with the idea of socially free, pristine Indians nobly eating, sheltering, and clothing themselves directly from the wilderness until they were magnanimously protected from modernity (and market relations) by the Canadian state.

These deeply institutionalized, ethnocentric, ahistorical, and undemocratic points of view need to be "permanently provoked" by all who want a more democratic society. One way to do so is for First Nations and others to reveal the often subtle and sophisticated forms of proprietorship and governance that have long been obscured behind the fictive veil of *terra nullius* – an empty land populated by empty people.

II. Indigenous Traditions: Taxation and the Rights of Social Inclusion

Despite the recurring debates over taxation, the common law has upheld state-based tax exemptions as one of national integrity. In the recent decision of *Bastien Estate v Canada,* the Supreme Court of Canada rejected the "tax haven" view of reserves. The court reaffirmed the reasons for property tax exemptions to Canada's First Nations and affirmed that the exemption is integral to Canadian law without respect to traditional First Nations ways of life: "The purpose of the tax exemption is to preserve Indian property on a reserve. While the relationship

---

22 Michael Asch, "Governmentality, State Culture and Indigenous Rights," *Anthropologica* 49, no. 2 (2007): 281.

between the property and life on the reserve may in some cases be a factor tending to strengthen or weaken the connection between the property and the reserve, the availability of the exemption does not depend on whether the property is integral to the life of the reserve or to the preservation of the traditional Indian way of life."[23]

According to *Black's Law Dictionary*, a tax is not a voluntary payment or donation, but rather, an enforced contribution, exacted pursuant to legislative authority, that is, imposed by government.[24] While many Canadians would dispute that Indigenous communities have paid taxes (through the collection and redistribution of valued items within their communities), Indigenous traditions seem to indicate long-standing practices that might be construed as analogous to tax, in the sense that such expenditures of valued items by extended families have long been sanctioned socially and culturally in accordance with Indigenous legal traditions and upheld by senior members of the community. Thus families known locally as those who assiduously pay off their debts to the local society (often in the form of hospitality, gift-giving, and sharing of access to resources), and do so on the basis of their members' labour power and the fruits of their territories, tend to be socially sanctioned as good citizens, proprietors, and people of influence. Conversely, it is true that Indigenous peoples in Canada have not "since Time Immemorial" paid annual set amounts to the federal or provincial government for the material maintenance of Canada and the provinces. However, even prior to contact, they instituted what have been analogous to local taxation schemes. For example, Gitxsan elders have noted that a complex system of obligated payments are levied as debts. As one elder said, "A strict law commands us to honour the dead and mount our feasts. We must *xhla'um*, hold a funeral feast and pay our debts. We *an xhomstxw* – we send the young people to fetch things from our land so that we can pay our debts. Then and only then everybody knows we are 'have' people. We glow with the respect of our ancestors, the power of our land, and the energy of our young people."[25]

What people in this community regard as the public payment of their debts, especially following the death of a person and the installation or "robing" of a new incumbent into the traditional name of

---

23 *Bastien Estate*, 711–12.
24 *Black's Law Dictionary*, s.v. "taxation."
25 Interview of Pearl Trombley, Gwamoon, by Richard H. Daly (1986) in Richard H. Daly, "Notes and Interviews with the Plaintiffs for *Delgamuukw*" (author's collection).

the deceased[26] takes the form of an extremely complex and highly metaphoric set of gift-givings in public ceremonial settings, in "the feast hall."[27] Gifts collected for distribution in the feast hall – by the hosts (from their members by blood and from their affinal ties through marriage) in the course of the transfer of one of the family's ancient names to a new incumbent – are given to the guests who witness the host family's changes of personnel, rights, and duties. The gifts are indeed public payments that reinforce kin and in-law relationships down the generations. These relationships are solidified across the local society through public events sealed with payments made by a "taxpaying extended family and clan" to its publicly witnessing and ratifying opposite. Each extended family pays and receives in relation to others, thus upholding the unwritten laws of social relations. These inter-family payments are differentiated into as many types of "payment" as there are types of relationships.[28]

When one specific Gitxsan *wilp* (matrilineal "house" group whose core members once lived under a common roof) suffered severe population decrease a century ago, a relative from another clan assumed the chiefly names and duties of the decimated house. When this house began to prosper again, it "repopulated" its own names and came to the point where it considered retiring or "resting" the name by which the house had been identified for a century, so as to re-establish its old hierarchy of names. In the end, the interregnum name and the previous chiefly name continued to stand side-by-side as two separate but equal head chief names of that house. The reason given by matrons in the house to explain why they made this decision was that "too much money had been given out in the feast hall" on behalf of the interregnum name, and thus this name had stood for the legitimacy of the land, the fishing sites, and the history of the house through these payments to the local society – through feast hall witnesses over the course of many years. Since so much had been paid out this way to hold up the reputation of the house, as exemplified through this name, it would thus have been incorrect to retire the name abruptly from active service in the local community.

In relation to feasts or potlatches, this form of taxpaying exists in a culture encapsulated within a nation state, and as such pays out not

---

26 Doreen Jenson and Polly Sargent, *Robes of Power: Totem Poles on Cloth* (Vancouver: UBC Press, 1986).
27 Daly, *Our Box Was Full*, 57–106.
28 Daly, *Our Box Was Full*, 93–4.

directly to the nation state of Canada like other taxpayers, but rather to the local encapsulated community, and does so in order to legitimate land ownership within that culture. The taxpayer is not an individual, but rather a kinship collective, with heavy burdens placed on all members of the collective to participate at times of feasting, so as to contribute to the payment of dues that legitimate the group's ancient ownership of territories and fishing sites. The negative sanction is the awareness of possible forfeiture, that, through non-participation, the extended family group could lose its right to possess land. Among the matrilineal Gitxsan, if deceased family members are not sent off to the afterworld lavishly by the extended family, then the deceased's father's side – which pays the initial funeral costs – will, with time, become that house group's creditor and will begin to assume proprietary airs regarding the group that does not requite its indebtedness. The positive sanction is that these payments take the form of gifts and gift obligations that link families across the local community for yet another generation. Linkages occur according to the idiom of reciprocal inter-family relations (including periodic marriages between adjacent land-holding groups, or marriages with strategic neighbouring communities), according to the image of the traditional pre-contact "big house." In those earlier times, hosts and their "father's side" guests sat on opposite sides of the fire. Depending upon which family was undergoing a succession to names following the death of the previous incumbent, they alternated in the role of host and guest as they passed words, gifts, payments and prerogatives (often temporary usufruct to land and fishing sites) over the fire, from one side to the other. The ritual was always performed before an audience of peers, who were, and are, "paid" with gifts and food for having witnessed these transactions. The responsibility of reciprocation would be expected in the future. In the absence of free choice, this process of "paying back" to society was (and still is) considered to be the law. Anyone who did not engage in such contributions would lose the status of being an upstanding and responsible local citizen with legitimate roots in the land.

III. Traditions of Taxation as Shared Responsibility

Most social relations in small kinship societies are conducted face-to-face. Virtually all members of such societies are known to one another, personally or by family reputation. Such interpersonal forms of societal life in societies without state infrastructure place great store in personal responsibility for peacekeeping. Not possessing police or a standing army, social control takes the form of inter-group diplomacy and responsibility to sustain daily relations. Communities do so by ameliorating potential conflicts and avoiding hostilities that arise from social and economic inequalities. They seek to institute customary gifts or payments from one group or individual to others, and these public transactions embody the distribution of values from those with more to those with less. Anyone who pays or makes sacrifices of personal wealth can expect peaceful relations in return, at least for the time being; the person can also foresee receiving a return payment when his or her opposite in the community is, in turn, pressed to make payments, or, in the idiom of nation state, to "pay taxes to society."[29]

These public payments are not deposited in state coffers; they do not pay for education or roads, but they pass back and forth, from year to year, between family blocs and generations. They tend to diminish social and economic inequalities. Those who make such payments reaffirm their status as responsible and productive members of society, and thus their giving and sharing sanctions their proprietary rights in local society. Those who receive such payments feel the social pressure to reciprocate. If a group fails to make such gifts or payments, it is often reminded to do so by the less fortunate, in what anthropologists call "demand sharing."[30] For their part – where they are not economically reduced to the role of multi-generational state welfare recipients – the less fortunate also feel societal pressure to work with their fellows

---

29 Anthropologists who first encountered these public payments on the Northwest Coast, and whose ethnocentric "rational man" views have persisted, analysed these transactions not as payments to society but as "agonistic giving" or individual investments in personal status and power by entrepreneurs, which may sometimes have grown out of the tax-like payments in the public arena, especially during the era of sudden wealth that arose with the coastal sea otter trade in the eighteenth century. See Franz Boas, *The Social Organization and the Secret Societies of the Kwakiutl Indians: United States National Museum Annual Report for 1895* (Washington, DC, 1897), 311; Helen Codere, *The Kwakiutl Ethnography of Franz Boas* (Chicago: University of Chicago Press, 1966); Maurice Godelier, *The Enigma of the Gift* (Cambridge: Polity, 1999). First Nations of the region more generally refer to this process as "paying" in order to keep up the name of the kinship group, rather than viewing it as a status-building investment. So-called agonistic giving of the late fur trade period was not typical of the general phenomenon found in one form or another from Alaska to Washington State, either before that period or today: Daly, *Our Box Was Full*, 35–6.

30 Nicholas Peterson, "Demand Sharing: Reciprocity and the Pressure for Generosity among Foragers," *American Anthropologist* 95, no. 4 (1993): 860; Barbara Bodenhorn, "Sharing Costs: An Exploration of Personal and Individual Property, Equalities and Differentiation," in *Property and Equality*, vol. 1, *Ritualisation, Sharing, Egalitarianism*, ed. Thomas Widlok and Wolde Gossa Tadesse (New York: Berghahn Books, 2005), 77.

to produce goods and services so as to eventually requite their own status in terms of a reciprocal inter-family system of production and taxation that sanctions a traditional proprietorship of land and resources.[31]

The aim is always to minimize social discord and enmity between local groupings and keep the fabric of rights and duties vibrant. This entails maintaining the good name of the family by making payments to other units in society for the common good. These payments are proof of good management and production on the lands used and controlled by the family. Anthropologists have extensively recorded such transactions, particularly among foraging or hunter-gatherer peoples around the world.[32] It is my contention that such public distributions of personal and family holdings function as an analogue to social, legal, and economic aspects of taxation.[33]

Anthropologists working with Indigenous peoples around the world have argued that many of these communities operate with similar concepts of shared responsibility, although they seldom describe the phenomenon as taxation. Richard Lee, a specialist on foraging peoples of the Kalahari Desert, refers to the socio-economic relations of such local kin societies as constituting "moral economies of sharing."[34] He, like many others,[35] stresses the feature of reciprocal sharing that marks such societies, even when encapsulated within modern states. In response to those who argue that sharing is nothing more than a modern defence

31 In such societies, technological practices do not dominate the natural world and the relationship between people and land is fraternal, such that an aspect of proprietorship is the duty of sustainability and stewardship for coming generations.
32 Richard B. Lee, "Power and Property in Twenty-First Century Foragers: A Critical Examination," in *Property and Equality*, vol. 2, *Encapsulation, Commercialisation, Discrimination*, ed. Thomas Widlok and Wolde Gossa Tadesse (New York: Berghahn Books, 2005), 16; Richard B. Lee and Richard H. Daly, "Introduction," in *The Cambridge Encyclopedia of Hunters and Gatherers*, ed. Richard B. Lee, and Richard H. Daly (Cambridge: Cambridge University Press, 1999), 1–13; Tim Ingold, "On the Social Relations of the Hunter-Gatherer Band," in Lee and Daly, *Cambridge Encyclopedia of Hunters and Gatherers*, 399; Nicholas Peterson and Toshio Maysuyama, eds, *Cash, Commoditisation and Changing Foragers: Senri Ethnological Studies No. 3* (Osaka: National Museum of Ethnology, 1991); James Woodburn, "Egalitarian Societies," *Man* 17, no. 3 (1982): 431.
33 The importance of sharing and its complexity in relations with the state is also taken up in Morales and Thom, "The Principle of Sharing and the Shadow of Canadian Property Law," this volume.
34 Lee, "Power and Property," 20.
35 Ingold, "Social Relations of the Hunter-Gatherer Band"; Peterson and Maysuyama, *Cash, Commoditisation and Changing Foragers*; and Woodburn, "Egalitarian Societies."

mechanism of small disempowered peoples,[36] Lee argues, "Given the enormous emotional and spiritual power of its presence, it is hard to believe that the moral economy of sharing is a recent invention, existing solely as a defence mechanism against an encroaching dog-eat-dog world."[37]

Lee lists the persistence of generosity and sharing practices among encapsulated, market-oriented, post-foraging peoples from the Nayaka and Paliyan of south India, the Baka Pygmies of Congo Brazzaville, the Inupiat of Point Barrow, the Cree of James Bay, the Ju/'hoansi of the Kalahari, and the Aboriginal urban fringe dwellers outside Darwin, Australia.[38] And he suggests that, through their moral rules of sharing, these peoples erect social barriers – traditionally against outsiders, and more recently against the penetration of capitalist production. These relations of payments in the name of sharing weave the social relations of the community together. They usually have the positive effect of maintaining cultural boundaries and underpinning a longstanding system of local governance wherein ownership of real property is central.

Ingold has examined the sharing of foraging and post-foraging peoples in contradistinction to ideal type social relations in the modern state.[39] He points out that in the state there are institutionalized contractual relations between disparate individuals, where each is conceived as holding a contract with the central or regional administration. This contract has to do with taxpaying, the receipt or non-receipt of services, and infrastructure important to everyday life. In contrast to governance relations within the state, those of small-scale Aboriginal communities are marked by autonomy, trust, and sharing.[40] Ingold argues there is an intersubjective investment in relationships here that is missing in relations between citizens of the nation state.

In small-scale kin societies, a "person acts *with* others, not against them; the intentionality driving that action both originates from, and seeks fulfilment through the community of nurture to which they all belong."[41] The independence of the actor in such societies is *relational*; it is defined by her or his dependence on others. Autonomy thus relies

36 Thomas Gibson, "From Humility to Lordship in Island Southeast Asia," in *Property and Equality*, vol. 2, *Encapsulation, Commercialisation, Discrimination*, ed. Thomas Widlok and Wolde Gossa Tadesse (New York: Berghahn Books, 2005), 231.
37 Lee, "Power and Property," 26.
38 Lee, "Power and Property," 17, 25.
39 Ingold, "On the Social Relations of the Hunter-Gatherer Band."
40 Ingold, "On the Social Relations of the Hunter-Gatherer Band," 406.
41 Ingold, "On the Social Relations of the Hunter-Gatherer Band," 402.

on dependence, and dependence relies on a sense of trust that involves sharing one's self and one's identity with others. Thus Indigenous answers to taxation, in the idiom of sharing, involve more than disbursing resources; they entail being co-engaged in responsible participation in everyday life.

Among Canada's present-day First Nations, whose members have arisen from Indigenous pre-contact societies, there remains a local awareness of the rules of social reciprocity in the community that is consistent with Ingold's findings. Interlocutors refer to these rules of making public payment as "strict laws." With the benefit of their current knowledge of the Canadian nation state and its taxation, they regard their own contributions to responsible membership in Indigenous life as a venerable form of taxation that has always been necessary for sanctioning rights to local property and citizenship. Indeed, we can infer that in specific instances and regions of Canada, "traditional" real property has not been a question of inalienable or allodial rights, but rather a system that, not unlike the nation state, involves constant risk and incentive to produce value that must be circulated in the local society. Here a local or regional moral community fulfils functions that roughly parallel some of the duties of the state in exercising rights to real property. The established procedures, rationale, and moral values associated with landholding among encapsulated kinship societies today, as in pre-state times, revolve around the threat of being deprived of proprietorship if the owner/owning group of kin fails to make acceptable public disbursements in return for the right to continue to enjoy the possession of lands. In small kinship societies, lands tend to be conceptualized as sentient extensions of the proprietary family and symbolic of the identity and productive success of that same family. Thus the maintenance of vibrant inter-family relations through the responsible public payment of values to others is bound up with inter-family identification and interaction with specific lands, where their names, histories, and ancestors lie.[42]

IV. A Discursive Research Agenda

Prior to contact, First Nations and Inuit had respectful relations with the world around them. The level of technological sophistication did not allow for human domination over other species to the degree we

---

42 Tim Ingold, David Riches, James Woodburn, eds, *Hunters and Gatherers*, vol. 2, *Property, Power and Ideology* (Oxford: Berg, 1988).

see today. The land belonged to the people, and conversely the people belonged to the land. Public forms of taxation sanctioned proprietorship and signalled responsible management of people and the land. Successful land-based economic pursuits required dynamic relations with the territory, as well as keen observation, skill, and planning – initiatives that have been eroded by reserve incarceration, generations of welfare dependency, and the associated social problems. The more traditional and more dynamic relationship with the land was accompanied by conceptualizing the natural world not as sets of inanimate resources, but as a united nations of life forms surrounding and enabling human life. The ethic instilled in the young was to accord the natural world the same respect one accorded to human society. In kinship societies, people felt their survival demanded public expression of their appreciation of nature's bounty. They invested their labour in the lands and waterways, and they returned their bodies to the land, as the generations succeeded one another. They made public presentations of wealth derived from the lands they controlled (and that functioned much like an informal taxation regime). This ethic has been an integral part of social responsibility and is usually conducted in a spirit of reciprocity.

Such claims to proprietorship of traditional territories are today treated as irrelevant to discussions of taxation, even by some Aboriginal leaders who appear to be impatient to participate in the current market for energy and other resources required by today's centralization of industrial production in Asia. Some on-reserve entrepreneurs now believe that privatization will solve socio-economic problems in communities. For its part, the government of Canada generally encourages privatization and the cessation of Aboriginal rights. The government viewpoint permeates the municipal model of governance and the current proposals for initiating the generation of local revenue through taxation. This model does not necessarily encourage a dynamic relationship to traditional lands. It does not seem to address the protection of the disadvantaged who, if land were taxed, could be rapidly divested of their homes, even on reserves, and be forced to join other dispossessed on the streets of the large urban centres. This is a major problem still not addressed by those who demand that government convert allodial, inalienable, collective rights to the existing parcels of land into *fee simple* ownership. Nor does this approach tend to uphold consultation with the elder generation and the needs of sustainability in order to improve the quality of land and labour for future generations.

Taxation schemes predicated on municipal status do not provide extensive solutions to the poverty and powerlessness experienced under the current system. Unemployed and under-skilled First Nations people, both on reserve and off, need economic possibilities that build on their longstanding identities with the world around them. The municipal model is not based on collective or family action, such as in the past, but rather on possessive individualism – in which individuals rely on elected representation – which obviates their own influence and responsibility.[43]

Underlying most government initiatives in the modernization of First Nations life – including the increasing use of impact and benefit agreements, and memorandums of understanding between government or the private sector and First Nations entities – is the assumption that the First Nations who are party to such negotiations can be legally treated as a corporate entity acting as a "possessive individual." With regard to the heritage or tradition of non-government local taxation in such communities, the population does not totally share the same understanding of individualism as those who want to negotiate from outside the community. First Nations habitual individuality is relational. This means individuality is defined in relation to all those who have rights to share or compete with others, and this tends to form a complex web of relationships based on marriage, kinship, and local history. When government or private sector actors approach First Nations whose members adhere to traditional kinship organization, these actors continue to treat or negotiate with the traditional institution as though with an "entrepreneurial individual." In contrast, among their First Nations interlocutors, each specific collective entity, and each individual member of the local society, is defined by a network of relationships. Thus, when, a Gitxsan house group (*wilp*) or a Wet'suwet'en house group (*yex*) is approached regarding resource extraction, the rights of most people associated with that body, beyond those of the named chiefs, are not addressed, since each member has different ongoing and overlapping ties with several house groups—beyond direct maternal inheritance, including father's side, affinal-in-law relations, grandparental rights, and rights to land use that are temporary but may, be intergenerational nonetheless.[44]

---

43 From the seventeenth century onwards, "The individual is essentially the proprietor of his own person and capacities, for which he owes nothing to society." C.B. MacPherson, *The Political Theory of Possessive Individualism: Hobbes to Locke* (Oxford: Oxford University Press, 1962), 63.

44 Some of this complexity is discussed in this volume by Valerie Napoleon and Emily Snyder, "Housing on Reserve: Developing a Critical Indigenous Feminist Property Theory." See also Overstall, "Encountering the Spirit in the Land"; also Daly, *Our*

While the economic health of a community may indeed improve with municipal restructuring and taxation reform, the costs will probably be great. The distinct identity of First Nations in such arrangements is suffering, and will continue to suffer. Citizens without sufficient educational, social, and cultural capital[45] to make use of new entrepreneurial opportunities risk losing their housing and benefits, as well as their assumed rights by virtue of kinship and marriage or adoption. Also, the municipal model does not activate and engage – and thereby emancipate – the general population. Decisions are not often open and transparent. Moreover, the corporate and legal requirement placed on investors and developers to consult First Nations often leads to the enrichment of the few at the expense of the many.

Rather than endorsing the calls for municipal-like administration and linked rights to local taxation, interested parties could build, if not directly on past traditions of taxation and land-holding, then at least on a possible interweaving of rights and bases for cooperation between Canada, First Nations, and other local populations in order to reduce conflicts and inequalities. As the introduction to this volume points out, with reference to chapters by Brown as well as Napoleon and Snyder, "Communal land systems contain complex and interlocking rights, in which the rights of individuals are tied intimately to the collectively held land system. Not only do such systems emphasize community responsibility, but change in this context requires more than superimposing Western rights on top of Indigenous laws: it requires that Indigenous laws internalize bespoke critiques and that state law internalize Indigenous laws that contain those critiques." Now, in the twenty-first-century negotiations, representatives of state and Indigenous approaches to ownership and governance would do well to develop a positive reciprocity of respect for one another's interests and traditions.

Modernists of the West and the Aboriginal communities could benefit from understanding reciprocal relations that predate the modern state. The spirit of reciprocity in Aboriginal relations – among people and between people and the bounties of the land – was central to taxation-like practices in pre-colonial First Nations history. Indeed, despite urbanization and new ways of living, many Aboriginal

---

Box Was Full; and James A. McDonald, "Tsimshian Wil'naat'al and Society, Historicising Tsimshian Social Organization," *New Proposals: Journal of Marxism and Interdisciplinary Inquiry* 8, no. 1 (2016): 11.

45   Pierre Bourdieu, "The Forms of Capital," in *Handbook of Theory of Research for the Sociology of Education*, ed J.G. Richardson, 241–58 (New York: Greenwood, 1986).

communities in Canada adhere to and find strength and guidance from old forms and traditions among their peoples. Conceptually, these old forms have the power to inspire innovations in "Indian and Inuit" administration in Canada, and to reorganizing tax revenue relating to Aboriginal peoples. Actors from both sides would do well to go beyond adopting homogenized taxation practices that are centralized within governments and transnational firms; new alliances can be forged to meet new conditions, and even here, the assumptions that underlie traditional practices may have a fruitful role to play.

Whereas exclusivity is intrinsic to European property relations and individual taxation schemes, traditional or non-European property and taxation was conceptually and organizationally a collective responsibility of the local group of landowners or land-users towards like groupings. Relations could become adversarial, and because the societies were constituted without central instruments of coercion, they were by nature diplomatic. Members of the group contributed to the tax and collectively enjoyed the benefits of being "taxpayers in good standing," thereby validating their continuing production on, and long-term management of, the land and overcoming challenges to their specific activities on that land. Members of interacting families were inspired and pressured to share responsibility for making a prosperous and peaceful society by "paying back" to each other and to a nurturing and sustaining earth.

Leaders seeking to use their taxation authority would therefore do well to consult with the local populations, their constituents, and their non-Native neighbours (both in physical space and cyberspace), to generate new concepts and dreams about sharing the wealth of the land. Consultation could be followed by more meaningful negotiations over overlying rights and responsibilities of governments, First Nations, and non-Natives.

The approach taken by the plaintiffs in *Delgamuukw*, for whom I worked as a researcher between 1986 and 1989, illustrates this approach. The plaintiffs of that generation of Gitxsan and Wet'suwet'en people envisioned a different solution to their economic and political problems. They saw the possibility of recognizing an interplay or over-layering of proprietary rights, taking into account interests of the state but holding firm to the use and care for lands traditionally held and worked by groups of kinfolk. They argued that they could apply the energy of their people to the lands to generate value that would lead them away from government dependency. Traditionally, the Gitxsan and their Wet'suwet'en neighbours "paid," from their land-based wealth, to their own societies for the right to hold land and make decisions about its use, through the feasting or "potlatch" system. As some of the elders explained, it was their "form of taxation."

Neoliberalism would detach First Nations from land allotted them by government in the name of making them more socially capable individual citizens of the state – capable of buying and selling "Indian land" on the market by severing reliance on government, but also severing ties to the collective kinship group and the moral economy of sharing. People of Flanagan's thinking advocate such changes of policy putatively for the good of First Nations communities, in order to increase freedom of choice, democratic decision-making, and entrepreneurship. By contrast, the plaintiffs in *Delgamuukw* envisioned a different solution to their economic and political problems. They envisioned much more freedom and democracy that would arise from court recognition of their title – or degrees of over-layering title – to traditionally kinship-held lands. As one of the plaintiffs, Simoogit Tenimget, explained on the eve of the trial,

> The court may wonder how we will make our decisions in the future when this court recognizes our jurisdiction. As I have described, we are not chiefs alone. Decisions in the future will be made as they have in the past. Our *Wilksiwitxw* [houses in the same clan as the chief's father] will be involved in the decisions with us. So will the chiefs of the neighbouring territories. So will the chiefs [of other clans] who have privileges as *Amnigwootxw* [non-transferable rights through their respective fathers to use the lands of this chief]. In other words, the decisions of the chiefs and the authority of the chiefs will be done by consensus and by decisions of the head chiefs. I will not be able to make decisions alone involving my territory.[46]

These societies have a tradition of inviting strangers and members of other First Nations to adopt local Aboriginal customs and practices. Such persons are tolerated if they participate in good faith, but may also be adopted into the kinship system. Thus, Gitxsan peoples are not averse to cooperating with non-Aboriginals to improve local shared conditions. However, building on such a tradition requires a commitment to inclusivity. As Richard Overstall has pointed out in relation to the Gitxsan and their neighbours, sharing makes for a very contingent

---

46 Transcript of witness preparation, Delgamuukw plaintiff documents, Chief Tenimgyet, proof of evidence taken 16 February 1988, on file in the Delgamuukw archives of Grant Huberman, Barristers & Solicitors, 1620–1075 West Georgia Street, Vancouver, BC.

form of ownership of real property. The idea of "property" arises only out of reciprocal interaction. The thing possessed is created in the space between two legal entities. It relies on inclusivity. In contrast, the concept of property in Western legal systems appears to have at its core the monopolistic barring of others from the thing possessed. The thing possessed is owned by one legal entity. It relies on exclusivity.[47]

Sharing with relatives, other peoples, and with nature herself was integral to societal organization; it has been and continues to be integral to negotiations regarding future taxation.[48] Sharing is relational and involves sophistication and subtlety that is psychological, political, and diplomatic. It has to do with common or overlapping interests. Anthropologists have documented how First Nations can make "traditional" use of a state institution such as the band council election and adapt it to exercise awareness of the need for sharing and for achieving balance in local social intercourse daily.[49] Such balancing acts as presented by Sieciechowicz, in those band council elections that seek to balance interests between different extended families, like the taxation system described here, gain their strength from combining diplomatic decisions and "internalized laws," rather than from implementation of jurally constituted institutions. In other words, "a living taxation system" in a stateless society emerges from a variety of informal activities. Just as the Pacific Coast potlatch system illustrates that the actions and functions of taxation existed informally, they can be a model for local taxation negotiations based on peaceful coexistence and sharing, or at

---

47   Overstall, "Encountering the Spirit in the Land," 46. Indeed, in the Tsilhqot'in case, the Supreme Court determined that the plaintiffs had demonstrated the "exclusivity" of their ownership. *Tsilhqot'in Nation v British Columbia,* [2014] 2 SCR 56, 2014 SCC 44.

48   In this volume, Morales and Thom discuss other complexities that have arisen among the Hul'qumi'num when they strive to negotiate land overlap issues, where opponents are unwilling to discuss longstanding practices of Aboriginal sharing (*snuw'uyulh*). A similar issue, where colonial forms and boundaries of administration have come face-to-face with traditional reciprocity-based, kinship landholding is found in Richard Overstall, "One Common Brotherhood: Utopian Communities and Present Governance in the Nisga'a Final Agreement" (paper delivered at the BC Studies and BCPSA Conference, University of Northern British Columbia, Prince George, 2005). Overstall addresses the same issue in his contribution to Neil J. Sterritt, Susan Marsden, Robert Galois, Peter R. Grant, and Richard Overstall, *Tribal Boundaries in the Nass Watershed* (Vancouver: UBC Press, 1998), 15–58.

49   Krystyna Sieciechowicz, "Effective Politics: Band Elections and Decision Making in Northern Ontario Anishnaabek Community," in *Confronting Capital: Critique and Engagement in Anthropology,* ed. Pauline Gardiner Barber, Belinda Leach, and Winnie Lem (London: Routledge, 2012), 53.

least new ideas of generating local tax rights and duties between Aboriginals and non-Aboriginals. But this would be feasible only if local people began to accelerate the sharing of their plans for the future, including their own involvement in land use and control, and resource extraction, testing the laws of Aboriginal consultation and participation in resource use on traditional territories.

The proprietary question of including and excluding has much to do with relations with nature and society, not simply in the contrast between states and kinship societies, but also in relation to the dominant strata that make up modern society. The Aboriginal voice has been subjected to nation-state assumptions and viewpoints for at least a century. However, new initiatives stemming from the local regions can manifest in change. Aboriginal systems of real property ownership and local governance of the past should not be left like an ancient trilobite fossilized inside a piece of sedimentary rock. The power of the past is not always past. It can often be taken up afresh and, as the Iroquois say, "requickened" to be used in new and important ways.

6 Indigenous Land Rights and the Politics of Property

JAMIE BAXTER[1]

I. Introduction

Contemporary struggles to create space for Indigenous property regimes inevitably confront bedrock socio-legal questions about the dynamics of institutional change. How can this work be most effectively pursued? Which institutional and interpretive settings for law are relevant, and how do they interrelate? This chapter addresses these questions by exploring how popular democratic mobilizations and social movement politics contribute to reshaping public legal discourses around Indigenous land rights in Canada. As Sarah Morales and Brian Thom make clear in chapter 3, the politics of resistance has a long history in Indigenous property regimes, and as Ibironke Odumosu-Ayanu describes in chapter 9, Indigenous communities globally continue to use popular forms of resistance to reassert their interests and protect their resources rights. Drawing from a new generation of research on the connections between social movements and legal change, and using the recent Idle No More mobilization in Canada as an early case study, in this chapter I explore how modern politics of resistance also plays an interpretive role, serving both disruptive and constitutive functions in ongoing discursive contests over the privatization of Indigenous lands. As Morales and Thom argue, "In exercising self-determination, Indigenous peoples must not be strictly limited to a precise mirroring of the Canadian state forms of property relations." I take up the dynamics of this challenge from the standpoint of interpretation, demonstrating how social movement politics may work, in part, to disrupt stark

1 With many thanks to Dean McPhadden (JD Class of 2017, Schulich School of Law) for his invaluable insights and dedicated research assistance on this project. All errors are my own.

divisions between the public and private dimensions of property, causing certain legal principles to become "unstuck" from their regulatory moorings in received statutory and common law understandings about the relationship between market and state.[2] Simultaneously – but not without complications and sometimes contradictions – activists have sought to reconstitute public understandings about Indigenous land rights by navigating alliances, opponents, and diverse positions of disagreement and dissent.

One way to explore the interpretive work of social movements in relation to law is to begin with pervasive uncertainties in common law judges' own attempts to define Indigenous land rights. For example, in *Osoyoos Indian Band v Oliver (Town)* – a case about the nature of rights in reserve lands – Justice Iacobucci exposes an intriguing ambiguity in the Court's attempts to define Osoyoos lands as inalienable (i.e., non-transferable in the market):

> It is clear that an aboriginal interest in land is more than just a fungible commodity. The aboriginal interest in land will generally have an important cultural component that reflects the relationship between an aboriginal community and the land and the inherent and unique value in land itself which is enjoyed by the community. This view flows from the fact that the legal justification for the inalienability of aboriginal interests in land is partly a function of the common law principle that settlers in colonies must derive their title from Crown grant, and partly a function of the general policy "to ensure that Indians are not dispossessed of their entitlements."[3]

From one angle, the principle of inalienability here seems to find its source in the "relationship between an aboriginal community and the land," inviting questions about how the Court perceives that relationship in connection to the community's own legal order. From another angle, inalienability appears to "flow from the fact" of justifications offered in other institutional settings, including common law doctrine and British North American imperial policy[4] – settings that, from the Court's perspective, work to regulate markets for private rights in land and thereby safeguard against its commodification. These sources for

---

2 Jack M. Balkin and Reva B. Siegel, "Principles, Practices, and Social Movements," *University of Pennsylvania Law Review* 154, no. 4 (2006): 928.

3 *Osoyoos Band v Oliver (Town)*, [2001] 3 SCR 746, para 46.

4 See George R, Proclamation, 7 October 1763 (3 Geo III), reprinted in RSC 1985, App II, No 1 at 5.

the principle of inalienability appear at once plural and contradictory. Below I ask how new forms of contentious politics have begun to pry open such ambiguities, contributing to the several ways in which Indigenous land rights in Canada are now being constituted and made "real."[5]

Observers have offered competing answers to this question. From one view, Indigenous and allied activism has been credited with successfully working to unsettle the status quo, edging Canadian legal institutions and their constituencies away from a narrow construction of Indigenous rights as precarious personal entitlements and, gradually, closer to recognition of Indigenous peoples' political jurisdictions and rights to self-determination.[6] In the other view, this activism has been characterized as largely fragmented and disorganized, and its practical impact on law and politics has been cast as limited, or at least too episodic to pinpoint with any accuracy.[7] Below I suggest that neither view wholly captures the work of direct action politics in this context. Social movements are undoubtedly relevant to law, but not merely because they generate political pressures for legal reform. More compelling is the idea that social movements help to unmask, if not resolve, some of the deeper ambiguities and assumptions of legal interpretation framed in other settings. At the same time, as I describe below, these politics may themselves be forcefully shaped and constrained by the "gravitational pull" of received legal frames that have come to define Indigenous land rights in Canadian law.[8]

This chapter therefore attempts to explain some of the institutional dynamics to which Justice Iacobucci alludes in describing "an Aboriginal interest in land." Part I briefly outlines the history of the inalienability principle discussed in the passage from *Osoyoos* above, along with the "inherent limit" by which the Supreme Court has circumscribed

---

5 See Lisa Vanhala, *Making Rights a Reality? Disability Rights Activists and Legal Mobilization*, Cambridge Disability Law and Policy Series (Cambridge: Cambridge University Press, 2010), employing this phrasing to describe how rights activists have worked to make legal rights "real" in the disability rights context.

6 See Howard Ramos and Kathleen Rogers, "Conclusion: What We Can Say about the Promise of Social Movement Societies," in *Protest and Politics: The Promise of Social Movement Societies*, ed. H. Ramos and K. Rogers (Vancouver: UBC Press, 2015), 300, describing how Indigenous social movements in the late 1960s laid the groundwork for many influential Indigenous organizations that would come after.

7 See, e.g., Paul P.G. McHugh, *Aboriginal Title: The Modern Jurisprudence of Tribal Land Rights* (Oxford: Oxford University Press, 2011), 61, observing that protests are by nature "episodic zigzagging from one controversy to another."

8 Amy Kapczynski, "The Access to Knowledge Mobilization and the New Politics of Intellectual Property," *Yale Law Journal* 117 (2008): 859.

Aboriginal title and the uses of title lands. I read the common law and historical justifications offered for these principles as part of a contest over the conceptual framing of Indigenous land rights as either private or public rights, as *property* versus *territory* – framings that today remain largely unstable.[9] Part II describes the events surrounding the Idle No More counter-mobilization and illustrates how movement actors and their allies worked to shift the ground of public discourse about environments, economic development, and regulatory governance that lay behind preceding doctrinal ambiguities and discursive struggles. Finally, part III examines how both received legal frames and the structure of the Idle No More counter-mobilization influenced and constrained its public engagements, posing challenges for how its contributions may ultimately be translated back into law.

II. Part I

By the time the *Osoyoos* case was being decided early in the twenty-first century, the principle of inalienability that concerned Justice Iacobucci had become a hallmark of both common law Aboriginal title and of land rights on reserve under the federal *Indian Act*.[10] It had come to define, in part, "an Aboriginal interest in land," even as the principle's justifications – including that it properly served to protect the inherent value of land – remain deeply contested. At the heart of this contest are interpretive struggles over the "true" character of Indigenous land rights as either property rights or territorial rights – a debate that approaches these concepts as open-ended legal frames as much as formal legal categories.[11]

---

9 See Ghislain Otis, "Constitutional Recognition of Aboriginal and Treaty Rights: A New Framework for Managing Legal Pluralism in Canada?" *Journal of Legal Pluralism and Unofficial Law* 46, no. 3 (2014): 333, describing related common law tensions in terms of legal pluralism.

10 See *Osoyoos*, para 42.

11 I use the term *territory* here to reflect prominent legal frames deployed in the course of the Idle No More mobilization: see Part III below. Formally, *territory* might be understood to include concepts of "jurisdiction," "self-governance," and "public authority." For contrasting accounts of property and jurisdiction, see Kent McNeil, "Aboriginal Rights in Canada: From Title to Land to Territorial Sovereignty," *Tulsa Journal of Comparative and International Law* 5 (1997): 253; Gordon Christie, "Who Makes Decisions over Aboriginal Title Lands?" *University of British Columbia Law Review* 48, no. 3 (2015): 749–50. See also P.G. McHugh, "A Common Law Biography of Section 35," in *From Recognition to Reconciliation: Essays on the Constitutional Entrenchment of Aboriginal and Treaty Rights*, ed. Patrick Macklem and Douglas Sanderson (Toronto: University of Toronto Press, 2016), 145–6, 149–51, distinguishing concepts of *dominium* and *imperium*.

The Supreme Court's characterization of Aboriginal title as a "beneficial interest in land,"[12] that is, a form of property ownership and not merely a set of personal rights[13] during the "breakthrough era" of title adjudication in the 1970s and 1980s, had marked for many a signal victory for Indigenous rights activists against the assimilationist politics embodied in the case law and given prominent expression in Trudeau's 1969 White Paper.[14] Moreover, by casting Aboriginal title in the frame of common law property rights, the breakthrough-era courts softened the perceived impact of their rulings on and for some non-Indigenous publics, while simultaneously distancing themselves from the "incendiary language of separate and retained sovereignty."[15] But, as Paul McHugh notes in his recent history of common law Aboriginal title, the "propriety paradigm" that emerged in Canada during this era would, by later decades, itself become a barrier to judicial recognition of title claims and against a more expansive interpretation of Indigenous territorial authorities. What had supplied the undercurrents for recognition of Indigenous land rights in the Canadian courts and linked them to emerging norms of anti-discrimination would later form the very cement hardening title doctrine against more "radical," territorial-based interpretations that might afford greater space to Indigenous lawmaking over time.

Nevertheless, even if the early title cases helped to cast Indigenous land rights in a proprietary mould, the Supreme Court's characterization of sui generis title in *Guerin*[16] and its early elaboration in *Delgamuukw*[17] at least opened new possibilities for alternative or competing frames,

---

For judicial warnings against the usefulness of received legal categories, see *St Mary's Indian Band v Cranbrook*, [1997] 2 SCR 647, para 14: "Native land rights are in a category of their own, and as such, traditional real property rules do not aid the Court in resolving this case." See also *Blueberry River Indian Band v Canada (Department of Indian Affairs and Northern Development)*, [1995] 4 SCR 344, para 7: "When determining the legal effect of dealings between aboriginal peoples and the Crown relating to reserve lands, the *sui generis* nature of aboriginal title requires courts to go beyond the usual restrictions imposed by the common law"; *Delgamuukw v British Columbia*, [1997] 3 SCR 1010, para 190: "This *sui generis* interest is not equated with fee simple ownership; nor can it be described with reference to traditional property law concepts."

12 *Guerin v The Queen*, [1984] 2 SCR 335.
13 *St Catherine's Milling Co v The Queen* (1888), 14 AC 46 (PC), 54. See also *Smith v The Queen*, [1983] 1 SCR 554.
14 Canada, Department of Indian Affairs and Northern Development, "Statement of the Government of Canada on Indian Policy, 1969" (Ottawa: Indian Affairs and Northern Development, 1969).
15 McHugh, *Aboriginal Title*, 45–6.
16 *Guerin*, 382.
17 *Delgamuukw*, para 112.

sparking a flurry of activity by a group of influential writers who quickly perceived the downsides of too much property talk. Early critiques in the post-*Delgamuukw* era focused attention on the justificatory stories behind the inalienability of Indigenous lands and the inherent limit on land uses as emergent characteristics of Aboriginal title. Together these common law principles attempt to shape Indigenous land rights by imposing constraints on the present use of title lands and on their circulation in commercial land markets, but for cases where the Crown acts as a kind of transactional intermediary with third parties. Recently the Supreme Court wove these ideas together on the basis of their shared consequences for future generations, writing that title lands "cannot be alienated except to the Crown or encumbered in ways that would prevent future generations of the group from using and enjoying it. Nor can the land be developed or misused in a way that would substantially deprive future generations of the benefit of the land."[18] The inalienability principle, as Justice Iacobucci observed in *Osoyoos*, had long been defined by imperial policy and the common law,[19] and had been refracted back in the *Indian Act*'s definition of reserve lands to prevent the transfer of property interests to non-band members without prior designation or surrender to the Crown.[20] Inherently limited title has a more recent pedigree. It was defined for the first time in *Delgamuukw* as an internal constraint on sui generis Aboriginal title, such that "lands held pursuant to title cannot be used in a manner that is irreconcilable with the nature of the claimants' attachment to those lands."[21] Perhaps in part because of its relative novelty, the precise contours of that idea remain mostly uncertain, charted through a few hypotheticals sketched out by the Court.[22]

Delgamuukw's immediate critics cast both inalienability and the inherent limit as blunt, paternalistic constraints on the free use and governance of title lands by title-holding nations.[23] But they were also

---

18 *Tsilhqot'in Nation v British Columbia*, 2014 SCC 44, para 74.
19 See Proclamation, 5; *Calder v British Columbia (AG)*, [1973] SCR 313, 320–2, 377–9, 381–5; *Delgamuukw*; *Osoyoos Indian Band*, paras 42, 46.
20 *Indian Act*, RSC 1985, c I-5, ss 29, 81(1), ss 24, 29, 89(1). See also *Guerin*, 383, describing the purpose of the *Indian Act* surrender requirement as being "to interpose the Crown between the Indians and prospective purchasers or lessees of their land, so as to prevent the Indians from being exploited."
21 *Delgamuukw*, para 125.
22 *Delgamuukw*, para 128, speculating that uses such as strip mining or paving for a parking lot may be irreconcilable with generative practices such as hunting or ceremonial uses.
23 See, e.g., Kent McNeil, "Self-Government and the Inalienability of Aboriginal Title," *McGill Law Journal* 47 (2002): 478–81; William F. Flanagan, "Piercing the Veil of Real Property Law: *Delgamuukw v British Columbia*," *Queen's Law Journal* 24 (1998): 279.

concerned with the potential for Aboriginal title to open up constitutional space for Indigenous self-governance and worried that this path would be foreclosed if title was too heavily conceived from a private and proprietary standpoint that afforded courts an undefined discretion to construct the content of Indigenous land rights and subordinate those rights to provincial and federal regulatory power. The inalienability principle – steeped as it was in British North American colonial policy to protect against, as the Royal Proclamation put it, the "great Frauds and Abuses ... committed in purchasing Lands of the Indians,"[24] and thereby to safeguard Crown interests in the security of its colonies[25] – was undoubtedly, in part, the expression of a discredited paternalism and premised on discriminatory views about the governance systems and legal orders of Indigenous peoples. The inherent limit expressed a similar logic based on preserving the "special bond between the group and the land" as part of "the group's distinctive culture."[26] Not only was this logic targeted by critics because it severely constrained the use of title lands to those activities practised at the time of assumed Crown sovereignty,[27] it was also seen as an affront to the legitimacy and diversity of Indigenous legal orders, both in its generic application and in its failure to consider substantive limits that were derived from Indigenous laws.[28]

In spite of these problems, many of *Delgamuukw*'s critics also recognized the value of common law principles that might maintain focus upon the injustices of historical and contemporary land transactions and protect the unique value of title lands and their central place in culture and community. So rather than concede to the limiting consequences of "an Aboriginal interest in land" understood as a constrained property right, critics sought to situate Indigenous land rights in the frame of territorial self-governance by reworking the inalienability doctrine from its historical roots. Implicitly, this strategy lent credence to the evolving line of Aboriginal title cases and held out the hope of reconciliation from the earlier breakthrough era. Kent McNeil, for example, pointed out that courts had traditionally justified inalienable title based on the legal incapacity of settlers to acquire

---

24 Proclamation, 6.
25 McNeil, "Self-Government," 478.
26 *Delgamuukw*, para 128.
27 Kent McNeil, "The Post-*Delgamuukw* Nature and Content of Aboriginal Title," in *Emerging Justice? Essays on Indigenous Rights in Canada and Australia* (Saskatoon: University of Saskatchewan, Native Law Centre, 2001), 117.
28 McNeil, "Post-*Delgamuukw* Nature,' 117. See also Gordon Christie, "Delgamuukw and the Protection of Aboriginal Land Interests," *Ottawa Law Review* 32 (2000): 93.

land interests with a "governmental" dimension – interests that could be modified or exchanged only on a nation-to-nation basis.[29] Inalienability therefore ambiguously expressed a private dimension of Aboriginal title flowing from prior occupation, in which the property rights of title holders, and thus their access to the market, were limited under the colonial state's claimed authority to balance the competing interests of owners, both current and future. But title also expressed a public dimension that captured the territorial basis for a title-holding nation's lawmaking powers. In the latter frame, the inalienability of Indigenous lands flowed from the premise that Aboriginal title mapped a jurisdictional space that could only legitimately be vested in and exercised through public authority.[30] This move contested the judicial privatization of Indigenous land rights by, in effect, publicizing their inter-societal roots.

These prescient critiques and interpretive struggles would not, however, be confined only to the courts. Despite *Delgamuukw*'s exhortation that any ambiguities in the nature of Aboriginal title would best be resolved through "a process of negotiation and reconciliation that properly considers the complex and competing interests at stake,"[31] the ongoing contest over the legitimate frame for Indigenous land rights pervaded these other settings. Both negotiated land rights and legislative reform of reserve land regimes have largely reproduced the struggle between alternative framings, as participants work to give meaning to the "generative right" of sui generis title.[32] For example, Nicholas Blomley has documented how title is "performed" in negotiations that navigate between assertions of territorial authority on one side and the Crown's insistence on translating all negotiated land rights into the form of fee simple estate on the other.[33] Meanwhile, the "ambiguous

---

29 McNeil, "Self-Government," 478–81. See also Brian Donovan, "The Evolution and Present Status of Common Law Aboriginal Title in Canada," *UBC Law Review* 35 (2001): 4, para 52, arguing that the protection justification misreads the basic rationale behind the Proclamation, which was premised on the legal disability of settler-purchasers rather than the characteristics of Aboriginal title.

30 See Kent McNeil, "Aboriginal Title in Canada: Site-Specific or Territorial?" *Canadian Bar Review* 91 (2012): 749: "Indigenous land rights are not limited to property rights.... Instead, Indigenous peoples have governmental authority (that is, political jurisdiction) over the territories occupied by them at the time of Crown assertion of sovereignty, in addition to rights to the lands and resources within those territories."

31 *Delgamuukw*, para 207.

32 Brian Slattery, "The Metamorphosis of Aboriginal Title," *Canadian Bar Review* 85 (2006): 263, describing the nature of sui generis title as a generative right.

33 Nicholas Blomley, "Making Space for Property," *Annals of the Association of American Geographers* 104 (2014): 1291.

promise of reconciliation"[34] over competing visions has persisted well beyond the finalization of treaty texts, as signatories such as the Tsawwassen First Nation turn to more direct enactments of their jurisdictions to ground the legitimacy of territorial claims. As Blomley observes, "For now," the "truth" of Tsawwassen rights in land "is made by what one Tsawwassen representative termed 'the exercise of the tool'; that is, jurisdiction."[35] "For Tsawwassen," he notes, "jurisdiction and allodial title are coperformative: the enactment of law requires jurisdiction; jurisdiction flows from allodial title; and the exercise of allodial title advances jurisdiction."[36] Likewise, Brian Thom, a former Hul'qumi'num Treaty Group negotiator, argues, "Indigenous peoples have ... asserted their own categories of 'territory' and 'property' within these debates. At the same time as they mobilize these concepts in ways that make their own territorial relations familiar to state actors, they also work to retain their local character and to enfold the fabric of social, economic, and political orders in ways that make sense in indigenous terms."[37]

It would be an oversimplification, however, to suggest that such struggles have merely aligned state institutions against Indigenous communities and a progressive politics of territorial self-determination. By the late 2000s a group of Indigenous leaders, academics, and economists began to critique the inalienability of reserve land title from the perspective of market liberalization, emphasizing the impact of market constraints for private and community economic investment – both directly through incentives for development, and indirectly through land title collateralization and access to credit markets.[38] The foundations of this critique rooted in Hayek's neoliberalism and in the historical discourses of Canadian bureaucrats is traced by Sarah Carter and Nathalie Kermoal in chapter 4. This critique of inalienability has also traded heavily on arguments put forward more recently in land reform programs at the leading edge of a global development agenda, backed by the World Bank and other lenders, to "formalize" land titles in post-Soviet countries and the Global South.[39] The work of these

---

34 Blomley, "Making Space for Property," 1293.
35 Blomley, "Making Space for Property," 1302.
36 Blomley, "Making Space for Property," 1302.
37 Brian Thom, "Reframing Indigenous Territories: Private Property, Human Rights and Overlapping Claims," *American Indian Culture and Research Journal* 38 (2014): 22.
38 See Tom Flanagan, Christopher Alcantara, and André Le Dressay, *Beyond the Indian Act: Restoring Aboriginal Property Rights* (Montreal and Kingston: McGill-Queen's University Press, 2010).
39 See Jamie Baxter and Michael Trebilcock, "Formalizing Land Tenure in First Nations: Evaluating the Case for Reserve Tenure Reform," *Indigenous Law Journal*

actors in Canada gathered around the idea of a "First Nations Property Ownership Act" (FNPOA), which would provide a federal legislative option for First Nations to move outside land provisions of the *Indian Act* and create a form of transferable and registerable title to reserve lands. In early 2012 Prime Minister Stephen Harper announced that his Tory government was "focused on the unlocking of First Nations lands and the integration of First Nations into Canadian society for the 'maximized benefit' of all Canadians,"[40] followed by media reports that a draft of the FNPOA legislation was in active development.[41] But while the FNPOA ultimately failed to emerge as official legislation, perhaps the most significant impact of this work was to reorient public debates around Indigenous land rights in the conceptual space of private property. Its proponents' arguments were "discursively framed to acknowledge Indigenous land rights while the [FNPOA] simultaneously introduce[d] contentious measures to individualize and municipalize"[42] property rights on reserves. Trading on connections with prominent property scholars on the political right from the United States and South America, the FNPOA's proponents made the question of land reform perceptible mainly in the language of property, fee simple, and market liberalization. Likewise, the proposal cast the salient issues of governance in terms of market governance and the elimination of red-tape bureaucracy associated with lands allocation and management under the federal *Indian Act*.

Returning briefly to the common law context prior to the Supreme Court's ruling in *Tsilhqot'in* in 2014, it was becoming increasingly clear that invitations from *Delgamuukw*'s critics to recognize the public or territorial dimensions of Aboriginal title were not being readily accepted by the Supreme Court.[43] In fact, progressive advocacy may have

7 (2009): 45; Sari Graben, "Lessons for Indigenous Property Reform: From Membership to Ownership on Nisga'a Lands," *UBC Law Review* 47 (2014): 410.

40 The Kino-nda-niimi Collective, ed., *The Winter We Danced: Voices from the Past, the Future and the Idle No More Movement* (Winnipeg: ARP Books, 2014), 39.

41 See John Ibbitson, "Do Opponents of Native Property Rights Think Things Are Okay Now?" *Globe and Mail*, 8 August 2012, http://www.theglobeandmail.com /news/politics/do-opponents-of-native-property-rights-think-things-are-okay-now /article4468909/.

42 Shiri Pasternak, "How Capitalism Will Save Colonialism: The Privatization of Reserve Lands in Canada," *Antipode* 47, no. 1 (2014): 2.

43 See, e.g., Jeremy Webber, "The Public-Law Dimension of Indigenous Property Rights," in *The Proposed Nordic Saami Convention: National and International Dimensions of Indigenous Property Rights*, ed. Nigel Bankes and Timo Koivurova, 82–92 (Oxford: Hart Publishing, 2013).

reinforced title's proprietary qualities within the common law by driving the Court to outsource questions of Indigenous governance to the emerging duty to consult. In McHugh's view, "It was ... no surprise that the courts might try to take another route that did not stumble on the pitfalls of the proprietary paradigm so markedly,"[44] leading common law judges to "consultation" as a conduit for political action that "was not overtly depicted as an alternative to [A]boriginal title but which nonetheless has ... seemed increasingly like it."[45]

Questions about the nature of "an Aboriginal interest in land" thus remain as highly unstable, across several interpretive settings, as they did in *Osoyoos* and preceding cases. Next, I examine what the direct action politics of the Idle No More counter-mobilization may have contributed to these interpretive struggles by describing how its evolving public discourses drew new attention to background assumptions about the relationships between market and state, and to the changing scene of regulation in environmental and economic governance.

III. Part II

In the autumn and winter of 2012, Canada's federal Tory government moved quickly to enact Bill C-45 – a hefty compendium of legislative amendments that, no doubt unwittingly, opened the way for the contentious politics of the early twenty-first century to enter decisively into interpretive struggles about the nature of "an Aboriginal interest in land."[46] Over the main arc of the counter-mobilization that would eventually coalesce behind "Idle No More," Indigenous rights activists and their allies – many from a generation at ease in the rapidly changing ecologies of online social media networks – worked to articulate their aims and interests across a range of issues rooted in mounting frustrations over First Nations–Crown relations.[47] Like its modern contemporaries around the world, this counter-mobilization situated itself explicitly as a grassroots and decentralized movement, and its open-ended rallying cry under the banner of "We will be Idle No More" self-consciously defied capture by any narrow set

44 McHugh, *Aboriginal Title*, 148.
45 McHugh, *Aboriginal Title*, 148.
46 Bill C-45, 41st Parliament, 1st Session, 60–61 Elizabeth II, 2011–12, assented to 14 December 2012, ss 206–8 [Bill C-45]. This is now the *Jobs and Growth Act*, SC 2012, c 31.
47 Kenneth Jackson, "The Tweet That Sparked a Movement," APTN National News, 11 December 2012, http://aptn.ca/news/2012/12/11/the-tweet-that-sparked -a-movement/.

of issues or constituencies.[48] Nevertheless, much of the public discourse generated by the mobilization encompassed contests over how to understand and interpret Indigenous land rights, and was suffused with the frames of property and territory from the earlier legal developments traced above. In the next two sections, I describe the social field of contentious politics as a setting for contesting and interpreting the public understandings that contribute to structuring Indigenous land rights in Canada. Taking Idle No More as a selective case study, and drawing on the uniquely digital dimensions of the movement, I introduce some early empirical work to explore the role of direct political action in legal interpretation and, reciprocally, the influence of law and legal frames on the structure and discourses of social movements.

Scholarship on these topics has grown rapidly over the last decade by expanding its inquiries into "the dynamic equilibrium of power between lawmaking and social movements."[49] Developed mainly in the context of American constitutional law, this approach aims to track changes in legal norms against the shifting canvases of contentious action, dialogue, and practice. A central insight of this work is that social movements can, uniquely, cause longstanding legal principles to become "unstuck," "disrupt[ing] public understandings, contest[ing] received framings, and help[ing] to reshape and reform public opinion" in ways that "connect legal norms to the beliefs and practices of ordinary people."[50] Law-and-social-movements scholarship has thus afforded a prominent role to direct action politics in broader processes of legal interpretation, by motivating sometimes conservative legal institutions to action (as in the grassroots actions of the American civil rights movement) and by forging the interpretive communities that help to construct and carry forward changes in law. Likewise, this work has started to show how social movements can play a constitutive role

---

48 See W.L. Bennett and Alexandra Segerberg, "The Logic of Connective Action: Digital Media and the Personalization of Contentious Politics," *Information, Communication & Society* 15 (2012): 739. "Compared to many conventional social movement protests with identifiable membership organizations leading the way under common banners and collective identity frames, these more personalized, digitally mediated collective action formations have frequently been larger; have scaled up more quickly; and have been flexible in tracking moving political targets and bridging different issues."

49 Lani Guinier and Gerald Torres, "Changing the Wind: Notes toward a Demosprudence of Law and Social Movements," *Yale Law Journal* 123 (2013): 2749.

50 Balkin and Siegel, "Principles, Practices, and Social Movements," 946. See also Guinier and Torres, "Changing the Wind," 2743.

in shaping emergent legal principles, especially by giving voice to previously excluded or marginalized groups and "organized constituencies of non-expert participants ... [who] play an important role in the creation of authoritative interpretative communities."[51]

In line with this body of scholarship, I suggest that counter-mobilizations such as Idle No More deserve to be taken seriously as settings of legal interpretation by linking them to other forums for lawmaking.[52] In examining the earliest stages of the mobilization, it becomes clear that activists and their allies engaged in disruptive interpretive practices that opened the way for new foundations on which to shift public attitudes and perspectives about the meaning of Indigenous land rights. At the same time, the relatively optimistic outlook of the new law-and-social-movements scholarship should be approached with caution in this context. Even as Idle No More made new meanings available, its organizational structures and messages were determined by what Amy Kapczynski has called the "gravitational pull" of received law.[53] As Kapczynski has observed, legal discourses are "semantically permeable" – and thus open to interpretive moves by social movement actors that can realign public understandings – but also "semantically constrained" in ways that direct public arguments and cause them to conform in predictable ways.[54] Moreover, identifying certain movements as a unified or coherent set of interests and aims while ignoring the role of disagreement and dissent raises its own challenges, as I describe below. All of these dynamics were are work in Idle No More, and each helps partially to explain the complex relationships between this counter-mobilization and the legal frames that preceded it.

---

51 Guinier and Torres, "Changing the Wind," 2743, 2756. But see Jedediah S. Purdy, "The Politics of Nature: Climate Change, Environmental Law, and Democracy," *Yale Law Journal* 119 (2009): 1122, describing concepts of nature interpreted through social movements that, at times, were mainly the domain of elites.

52 Quoting from one of the earliest tweets of #IdleNoMore ("Tweeting up on Sunday, December 2, the #IdleNoMore event in Alberta. Lets get it trending! Here is the FB event"), participant and commentator Wab Kinew noted that it was "not necessarily 'I have a dream' type material, but significant in its own right," thereby drawing explicit reference to, and legitimating authority from, an earlier era of social mobilization in the American civil rights movement. See Wab Kinew, "From a Grassroots Hashtag to a Real Opportunity for Change," *Winnipeg Free Press*, 6 December 2012, http://www.winnipegfreepress.com/opinion/columnists/from-a-grassroots-hashtag-to-a-real--opportunity-for-change-kinewview-182324221.html.

53 Kapczynski, "Access to Knowledge Mobilization."

54 Kapczynski, "Access to Knowledge Mobilization," 860.

A. The Bill C-45 Amendments

Central to theories about the relationship between law and social movements is the premise that movements work to disrupt received legal principles by challenging public perceptions about the "imagined regulatory scene" in which those principles are read and enacted.[55] Social movements are thought to "construct the semantic normative climate in which people talk about the great constitutional issues of the day.... [They] apprehend and construe social, economic, and technological change" and thus work to "reinterpret the changing scene of regulation."[56] Movements address the background conditions against which the legitimacy of law is tested and transformed, thereby helping to "[re]construct interest, aims and norms."[57]

It was in this mode that Idle No More predominantly approached Indigenous land rights in the post-*Delgamuukw* era, leveraging the Tories' omnibus reforms in the fall and winter of 2012 to address public perceptions about the nature and scope of environmental regulation and economic governance in Canada. Bill C-45 introduced two key regulatory changes that would lay the groundwork for this counter-mobilization. First, the bill included changes to the *Indian Act* rules governing the long-term leasing of reserve lands to non-member leasees. While not going so far as to make reserve land title freely alienable, these changes attempted nonetheless to make certain statutory interests in those lands more fungible, promoting residential and commercial investment by third-party market actors. Prior to the Bill C-45 reforms, First Nations were required to designate reserve lands for lease at a meeting by a double majority of their members – that is, by a majority vote of the majority of eligible electors in the band.[58] Bill C-45 proposed to change this community decision rule by requiring only a single majority of voters actually present and voting to approve a land lease designation.[59] Additionally, the bill granted the minister of aboriginal Affairs, rather than the governor in council, power to approve the designation of the lease.[60]

---

55 Balkin and Siegel, "Principles, Practices, and Social Movements," 928. "A principle always comes with an imagined regulatory scene that makes the meaning of the principle coherent to us."
56 Balkin and Siegel, "Principles, Practices, and Social Movements," 948.
57 Balkin and Siegel, "Principles, Practices, and Social Movements," 948.
58 *Indian Act*, RSC 1985, c I-5, ss 37–9. Where a majority vote succeeded at a first meeting where quorum was not reached, the minister was empowered to call a second meeting or referendum at which a simple majority of those voting was required.
59 *Indian Act*, RSC 1985, c I-5, ss 37–9.1, as am. by *Jobs and Growth Act*, ss 206–8.
60 *Indian Act*, s 40.1, as am. by *Jobs and Growth Act*, s 208.

Given the inalienability of reserve land title, long-term leasing arrangements may play an important role in drawing outside investment for some First Nations economies. Proponents of these changes argued that the new voting rules would ultimately reduce the transactions costs of leasing reserve lands, thereby providing new possibilities for land-based investments and stimulating on-reserve economic growth.[61]

Second, Bill C-45 proposed significant changes to the federal regulatory oversight of natural resources across the country, including fisheries and fish habitats under the federal *Fisheries Act*[62] and natural waterways covered by the *Navigation Protection Act*.[63] Amendments to the *Fisheries Act* were in fact second-stage reforms following a prior omnibus budget implementation bill that signalled an important shift from regulating "harmful alternation, disruption or destruction of fish habitat" to preventing permanent "serious harm to fish" that falls within three protected classes of commercial, recreational, or Aboriginal fisheries.[64] This shift substantially narrowed the scope of fish habitats subject to the *Fisheries Act* regime, raised the threshold from temporary to permanent damage, streamlined the approvals process for projects affecting protected fish habitats, and reframed ministerial discretion in granting those approvals by requiring consideration of economic, as well as environmental, impacts. Bill C-45 further expanded the definition of "Aboriginal fisheries" introduced in the first-stage reforms to include fishing "for the purposes set out in a land claims agreement."[65] In replacing the *Navigable Waters Protection Act* with its new title, the *Navigation Protection Act*,[66] Bill C-45 also precipitated a parallel shift in waterways regulation, transforming the central role of federal oversight from protecting waterways as natural environments to regulating commercial navigation. In the course of this shift, Bill C-45 likewise reduced the scope of federal regulation from all navigable waters to a short list of waters listed in the regulations. Overall, these sweeping changes signalled a clear retreat by the federal government from its

---

61 Tom Flanagan, "Bill C-45 Simply Makes It Easier for First Nations to Lease Land," *Globe and Mail*, 29 December 2012, http://www.theglobeandmail.com/globe -debate/bill-c-45-simply-makes-it-easier-for-first-nations-to-lease-land /article6780103/.
62 *Fisheries Act*, RSC 1985, c F-14.
63 *Navigation Protection Act*, SC, 1985, c N-22.
64 *Fisheries Act*, s 35(1), as am. by *Jobs, Growth and Long-term Prosperity Act*, SC 2012, c 19, s 142(2).
65 *Fisheries Act*, s 2, as am. by *Jobs, Growth and Long-term Prosperity Act*, s 133(3).
66 *Navigation Protection Act*, s 1, as am. by *Jobs and Growth Act*, s 316.

pre-existing position in regulating broad categories of natural resources through comprehensive environmental governance.

But even while these changes significantly weakened formal environmental controls, equally important was the symbolic impact of eroding two pillars of Canada's environmental regulatory regime. As "one of the oldest and most widely-used pieces of legislation for environmental protection in Canada,"[67] the *Fisheries Act* had become a powerful marker for national environmental standards since it was first passed in 1868.[68] Its "gutting" by a little-debated pair of federal omnibus bills signified an off-handed rejection of long-standing public ideals of ecological integrity and environmental oversight and a ceding of regulatory ground to decentralized markets. Likewise, as a central piece of Canada's nation-building project that aimed to balance conservationist and commercial objectives, the regulation of waterways under the *Navigable Waters Protection Act* had long been a symbol of a federalist administration mediating between the demands of economy and environment.[69] By winnowing federal responsibilities to cover only a fraction of formerly protected waterways and refocusing oversight on the management of commercial navigation, the Tories left themselves vulnerable to claims that they had, with only marginal public debate, charted a new path that threatened to upset the crucial balance underwriting sustainable development.

This deep background to Bill C-45's reforms grounded the Idle No More as a counter-mobilization to the ongoing decline of Canada's modern regulatory state. The claims of movement participants were frequently couched in terms that appealed directly to "all Canadians"[70]

---

67 William K. McNaughton, "Bill C-38 Fisheries Act Changes: Jobs Growth and a Little Gutting of the Act," Borden Ladner Gervais LLP, 21 December 2012, http://www .lexology.com/library/detail.aspx?g=777ca6ae-141b-4fa7-a0cc-842383dfadc3.

68 *Fisheries Act*, 1868, 31 V, c 60.

69 See Frank Quinn, "The Evolution of Federal Water Policy," *Canadian Water Resources Journal* 10 (1985): 21.

70 See, e.g., Jenna Leah, "#billc45 doesn't just affect first nations people, it affects all canadians. Stand with us and tell Harper that you will be #idlenomore," Twitter, 12 December 2012, http://twitter.com/annejhael/statuses/278659801821626368; "I thought there were lots of Canadians who believe in protecting Canada's waters? Where r they? C-45 isn't opposed by only FN's. #IdleNoMore," Twitter, 12 December 2012, http://twitter.com/Sahra1Taylor18/statuses/278914540509483008, on file with author; Quentin, "Fighting for the rights of our people and canadian citizens everywhere, down with bill C45 it well only cause mayhem #idlenomore," Twitter, 12 December 2012, http://twitter.com/rez_ndn/statuses/278899303500627968; Cherish, "Its irritating that some ppl think bill C45 is affecting just first nations, while it is affecting everyone + future generations #idlenomore," Twitter, 12 December 2012, http://twitter.com/cAlexson/statuses/278986376773500928.

and to a pervasive failure of representative politics in the public interest. Moreover, within this space vacated by federal regulators, movement actors positioned the recognition and exercise of Indigenous land rights as sites of responsible governance that responded directly to a broader decline in environmental stewardship. As one activist put it, "Something that Canadians don't often realize is that First Nations are the last best hope that they have of protecting lands for food and clean water for the future, not just for our people, but for Canadians as well, because we have constitutionally protected aboriginal and treaty rights that they don't have."[71] This discourse was symbolically reinforced by the direct action strategies of the movement – organized across a burgeoning social media network – that led to a national day of action just days after Bill C-45 was passed in the House of Commons. The product of impressive coordination by groups of decentralized grassroots activists, this show of unity among Indigenous activists and their allies stood as a defiant counterpoint to the federal retreat from the public sphere.

The counter-mobilization's approach therefore built on preceding doctrinal critiques, described above, in that they emphasized the public qualities of Indigenous land rights and thereby sought to shift those rights in part from a proprietary to a territorial frame. But by addressing their claims to the regulatory vacuum in national economic and environmental matters, movement actors uniquely worked to disrupt the latent background assumptions of received law that prior critiques had largely overlooked. Idle No More made clear, for example, that the common law's inalienability principle was infused with certain – and sometimes competing – ideals about the nature of the marketplace and the role of the Crown in mediating market relations. One the one hand, inalienable rights presupposed a set of market relationships that were fundamentally hostile to the interests of Indigenous peoples. Set in the context of cases such as *Johnson v M'Intosh*,[72] the market for Indigenous lands was populated by predatory, unscrupulous buyers and land speculators, who in turn were enabled by weak state monitoring and failed enforcement measures. Meanwhile, imperial policy characterized the Crown as a willing intermediary in these "imperfect" market conditions. Thus the Royal Proclamation stood as an early "manifestation of government intervention in the free market"[73] – one that signalled

---

71 Nermeen Shaikh, "Idle No More: Indigenous-Led Protests Sweep Canada for Native Sovereignty and Environmental Justice," *Democracy Now*, 26 December 2012, http://www.democracynow.org/2012/12/26/idle_no_more_indigenous_led_protests, quoting Pam Palmater.
72 *Johnson v M'Intosh*, 21 US (8 Wheat.) 543 (1823).
73 McHugh, *Aboriginal Title*, 25–6.

imperial commitments to interpose "the Crown between the Indians and ... market forces,"[74] in "a key intermediary ... role dating from the earliest imperial era."[75] That position would later carry over into the statutory construction of reserve lands and ground the Crown's fiduciary obligations in this context.[76] The construction of Indigenous rights in land by courts therefore reflected fundamental assumptions about colonial state–market relations that presumptively normalized the regulation of those rights as if they were proprietary – but equally importantly, as if the colonial state were fundamentally committed to active regulatory oversight.

Similarly, though in a different historical and political context, inherently limited Aboriginal title rested on its own imagined regulatory scene upon concerns about resource management and environmental stewardship. Whereas inalienable title traded on the idea of a predatory land market, inherently limited Aboriginal title apprehended the threat of environmental degradation by "wanton or extravagant acts of destruction."[77] Although the *Delgamuukw* Court declined to identify exactly *who* it thought might pose such a threat, by implication it emanated from title holders themselves or by those acting under their authority – either of whom might be subject to pervasive market incentives for resource overuse. In this sense, the predatory and imperfect market also lurked behind inherently limited Aboriginal title as the source of corrosive intergenerational externalities threatening the long-term sustainability of lands and environments. Likewise, the inherent limit imported key assumptions about Crown intermediation between Indigenous peoples and their environments, implying that "most forms of economic development ... entailing conferral of licences – that is, the issuing of lesser rights of a non-proprietary sort – would have to be brokered through the Crown," a feature that gave Aboriginal title "the suspicious ring of a common law version of the *Indian Act*."[78]

Just as the regulatory scene of inalienable rights was rooted in the context of colonial land markets and administration, the concept of inherently limited title was also conceived against the background of growing federal and provincial participation in environmental regulation over the latter quarter of the twentieth century. Early in this era,

---

74 *Mitchell v Peguis Indian Band*, [1990] 2 SCR 85, para 85.
75 McHugh, *Aboriginal Title*, 27.
76 See *Guerin*, 383: "This policy with respect to the sale or transfer of the Indians' interest in land has been continuously maintained" by colonial and federal authorities.
77 *Delgamuukw*, 1090.
78 McHugh, *Aboriginal Title*, 148.

Canada's federal *Fisheries Act* had been substantially strengthened with the addition of provisions that directly protected fish habitats.[79] By the later 1980s and early 1990s, the federal government had introduced a suite of environmental legislation establishing key regulatory frameworks for natural resource developments, including the *Canadian Environmental Protection Act*[80] and the *Canadian Environmental Assessment Act*.[81] These initiatives ushered in a period of active federal oversight and management of Canada's natural resource sectors and saw federal regulators contributing to a new regulatory space – one that had already seen considerable provincial involvement throughout the 1970s and 1980s.[82] Against this activity, it was likely a short step for the *Delgamuukw* Court to formulate its inherent limit on Aboriginal title as the common law expression of Canada's growing commitments to regulate proprietary freedoms in pursuit of long-term sustainable development goals.[83] This conception of inherently limited title would also, of course, dovetail neatly with the justified infringement framework established in *Delgamuukw*, including the Court's broad view of federal or provincial regulatory objectives that would amount to legitimate infringement.[84]

By reading the Bill C-45 amendments into public debate as part of an encroaching program of neoliberal deregulation, Idle No More would help to unmask the inverted logics of a new set of state–market relationships that threatened to destabilize the political ground of inalienable and inherently limited Indigenous land rights as interpreted through common law and federal statute. Whereas these principles – whatever else they might assume – had been crafted against the backdrop of willing state intervention to protect private interests in economic and environmental spheres, that setting had largely crumbled in an era where public power was increasingly deployed in service of market institutions, market actors, and decentralized forms of economic organization.[85]

---

79 See Jeffrey A. Hutchings and John R. Post, "Gutting Canada's *Fisheries Act*: No Fishery, No Fish Habitat Protection," *Fisheries* 38 (2013): 497.

80 *Canadian Environmental Protection Act* RSC 1985, c 16 (4th Supp).

81 *Canadian Environmental Assessment Act* SC 1992, c 37.

82 See Melody Hessing, Michael Howlett, and Tracy Summerville, *Canadian Natural Resource and Environmental Policy* (Vancouver: UBC Press, 2005), 84.

83 It is also important to note that First Nations were actively involved in natural resources regulation during this period. See Hessing, Howlett, and Summerville, *Canadian Natural Resource and Environmental Policy*, 878.

84 *Delgamuukw,* para 202, listing "general economic development" through "agriculture, mining, forestry, and hydroelectric power, as well as the related building of infrastructure and settlement of foreign populations" as valid legislative objectives.

85 David Singh Grewal and Jedediah Purdy, "Introduction: Law and Neoliberalism," *Law & Contemporary Problems* 77, no. 1 (2014): 1.

As a result, the rationales offered for these principles no longer fit neatly with a broader story about the relationship between Indigenous peoples and their lands as a set of bounded practices constrained by colonial legislatures or by common law judges. Idle No More's contribution would thus be to draw a stark contrast between the breakdown of public and private precipitated through federal deregulation on one side, and the inadequacy of interpreting Indigenous land rights without substantial recognition for the public dimensions of Indigenous governance and lawmaking on the other.

IV. Part III

Earlier I described generally how the Idle No More movement shifted the frame of Indigenous land rights by uniquely disrupting the background regulatory scenes in which common law principles had come to be interpreted. However, that description approaches Idle No More as a unified collective action that comprised actors with common interests and aims, raising important questions about how diverse viewpoints and internal contestation shaped the counter-mobilization. Below I ask the critical question of how control over movement discourses and resources were distributed across particular individuals and groups, and how this distribution may have changed to influence interpretive outcomes. First, I observe how, as the counter-mobilization moved past early December 2012 and built momentum around the national day of action on 11 January, Idle No More participants increasingly made common cause with allied movements and issues, forging rhetorical and organizational alliances that may have pulled back towards exclusionary property frames to confront natural resource exploitation seen as an urgent threat to climate and the environment. Second, I describe how Idle No More participants came to position themselves as part of a counter-mobilization focused on resisting the commercialization and transfer of Indigenous lands. By responding to arguments about *Indian Act* reforms in the register of private property, movement actors were drawn into debates about land ownership and away from questions of Indigenous lawmaking and governance. Finally, I briefly address the difficult problem of how we are left to think about social movements as interpretive communities that not work only to create space for Indigenous laws, but might also attempt to reinterpret substantive legal norms as part the process of lawmaking itself. Critical attention to these aspects of social movement action underscore the indeterminacy of this new politics, as well as the powerful pull of received legal frames on movement discourses over time.

A. Movement Structure and Alliances

One increasingly well-studied feature of law's relationship with modern social movements – especially those with a digital identity – is the conditioning of public language and debate on the structures of collective action that produce them. Because these movements are self-consciously decentralized and non-hierarchical over large networks of diffuse individuals, organizations, and communities, their discourses are inherently open-ended and subject to competing frames inhabited by distinct subgroups. In other words, the interpretive work of social movements like Idle No More is likely to be shaped by their strategic linkages and alliances with activists in other domains. Likewise, mobilizations such as Idle No More share a dual existence between their embodied actions, such as round dances, drumming circles, protest marches, blockades, and land occupations, and their disembodied network of social media participants – with the latter often serving as an organizing schema for the former, as well as a forum for producing and shaping substantive discourses in its own right. These features, combined with the persistent digital footprints that characterize online interactions, provide a way to study mobilizations by "analyzing social technologies ... as organizing mechanisms in complex collective action ecologies."[86]

To explore the structure of Idle No More in more detail, I compiled a dataset of all messaging on the Twitter media platform that employed the hashtag identifier "#idlenomore" over the period 1 December 2012 to 31 January 2013. The dataset includes 729,121 data points or "tweets," comprising both the message text (a maximum 140 characters in length) and the message metadata (such as the date and time of posting, and user information where available). These data provide a window onto the early life of the Idle No More movement during its formative stages, prior to Bill C-45's passage through Parliament and for the duration of the movement's most active public and media attention. Figure 6.1 charts the total tweets per day during these two months. The bold vertical lines mark (1) 14 December 2012, the day on which Bill C-45 received royal assent, and (2) 11 January 2013, the global day of action coinciding with a Crown–First Nations meeting in Ottawa and the highest volume of Twitter messages per day over the study period.

---

86 Alexandra Segerberg and W. Lance Bennett, "Social Media and the Organization of Collective Action: Using Twitter to Explore the Ecologies of Two Climate Change Protests," *Communication Review* 14, no. 3 (2011): 198.

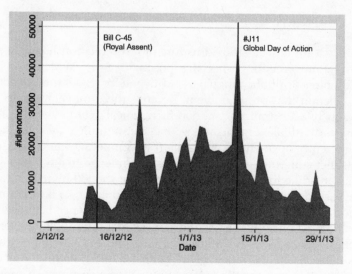

Figure 6.1. Aggregate Twitter activity in #idlenomore

Perhaps the most useful feature of these data for studying the structure of the Idle No More mobilization is the presence of Twitter "hashtags" as digital markers that are self-selected by participants to organize the ecology of the movement into digital "streams" or data flows. The co-occurrence of hashtag markers in any given user message indicates a convergence of these digital streams, and when combined, these data provide a good overall picture of interactions between different actor networks. From this perspective, the Twitter platform operates as a "network of networks" that stiches together different groups, issues, and movements by facilitating multiple points of confluence for share interests.[87] Table 6.1 lists the twenty most prevalent hashtag markers within the full study dataset, the right-most column representing hashtag co-occurrences with #idlenomore in December 2012 and January 2013.

Of particular interest in table 6.1 are intersecting data streams that carry the signature of mobilizations occurring at the same time as Idle No More – the anti-KeystoneXL pipeline mobilization (#nokxl), which focused on proposed pipeline developments from Alberta to the Gulf of Mexico, and the Occupy Wall Street mobilization (#ows and #occupy),

---

87 Alexandra Segerberg and W. Lance Bennett, *The Logic of Connective Action: Digital Media and the Personalization of Contentious Politics* (Cambridge: Cambridge University Press, 2013).

Table 6.1. Twitter hashtag co-occurrences in #idlenomore

Rank	Hashtag identifier	Co-occurrences with #idlenomore
1	cdnpoli	87,309
2	canada	13,892
3	firstnations	11,686
4	indigenous	10,803
5	chiefspence	8,953
6	nokxl	8,722
7	theresaspence	7,224
8	ottawapiskat	5,817
9	solidarity	5,493
10	attawapiskat	4,566
11	harper	4,397
12	cpc	4,168
13	ows	4,011
14	yeg	3,994
15	nativewinter	3,611
16	occupy	3,443
17	chieftheresaspence	3,365
18	toronto	3,270
19	vancouver	3,191
20	aboriginal	3,138

which began with occupations in New York City's financial district in 2011. These overlapping streams connect activism within Idle No More to other contemporary environmental, anti-poverty, and anti-capitalist movements organized around widespread public concern about environmental degradation and growing social and economic inequality. Figure 6.2 maps the distribution of the co-occurring No KeystoneXL and Occupy Wall Street streams against the total online activity of Idle No More (taking the logarithmic form of these data to better reveal comparative patterns).

Figure 6.2 uncovers some revealing information about mutual participation in both Idle No More and either the No KeystoneXL or Occupy Wall Street mobilizations. First, the two co-occurring streams (represented by the dashed lines in figure 6.2) follow substantially different trajectories over the study period, with simultaneous participation in Occupy Wall Street tracing a pattern of activity, similar in rough

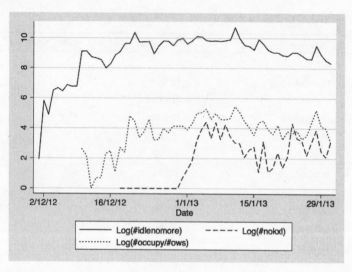

Figure 6.2. Two co-occurring Twitter streams in #idlenomore

terms to Idle No More overall – at least after the passage of Bill C-45 in mid-December. Second, and in contrast, the confluence of Idle No More and the No KeystoneXL mobilization lagged behind, with the two networks remaining almost entirely separate from each other until early January 2013 and prior to, but in close proximity with, the national day of action on 11 January. After this time, simultaneous participation with No KeystoneXL encompassed a significant proportion of the Idle No More activity online.

One important question for understanding the relationship between law and social movements is about the degree to which linkages or alliances between mobilizations might influence the interpretive struggles described in Part II, above. In theory, such structural linkages can have a dramatic impact on how movement actors understand, interpret, and convey public language – as well as their own aims and interests – leading to discernible changes in the relevant frames of the movement.[88] Although a full evaluation of that theory in the case of Idle No More requires further empirical study, we might make some initial observations about the discursive consequences of movement alliances based on the available data. Given the lag in intersections between #idlenomore and #nokxl during December 2012, as revealed in figure 6.2, we

---

88   Kapczynski, "Access to Knowledge Mobilization."

might expect the growing overlap between these two movements in January 2013 to produce a discernible change in shared discourses. Indeed, this idea was implicit in mainstream media reports: "The 'Idle No More' movement began as a series of protests against a controversial government budget bill but has since expanded into a nationwide movement for political transformation. Aboriginal and environmental activists are teaming up to resist what they say is the conservative Canadian government's attempts to appropriate resource-rich lands and to assimilate aboriginal nations. They are calling on Prime Minister Stephen Harper to honor treaties with aborigines [sic], open dialogue with environmentalists, and reject tar sands pipelines that would infiltrate First Nation territories."[89]

For example, as alliances and overlapping narratives between the two movements emerged, it appears that anti-pipeline activists began to inhabit, in part, the frame of Indigenous land rights seeded by earlier voices in Idle No More. But these allied actors also worked in part, to privilege their own framings of Indigenous land rights in ways that were presumably suited to separate aims. As journalist and Canadian environmentalist Martin Lukacs wrote, "Amidst a hugely popular national movement against tar sands tankers and pipelines that would cross aboriginal territories, Canadians are starting a different narrative: allying with First Nations that have strong legal rights, and a fierce attachment to their lands and waters, may, in fact, offer the surest chance of protecting the environment and climate. Get behind aboriginal communities that have vetoes over unwanted development, and everyone wins. First Nations aren't about to push anyone off the land; they simply want to steward it responsibly."[90]

Even as these arguments recognized the concept of stewardship, they also reinforced a largely singular focus on the exclusionary rights of Indigenous landowners to achieve the strategic end of vetoing "unwanted development." Here, Indigenous ownership and property rights were invoked pragmatically to garner support from publics concerned centrally about the pace, scale, and impact of extractive industries. Likewise, appeals to the exclusionary rights of Indigenous communities may link to a strong set of common law remedies, such as injunctive relief, to achieve these ends. But this language contributed little to a public

---

89 Shaikh, "Idle No More."
90 Martin Lukacs, "Canada's First Nations Protest Heralds a New Alliance," *Guardian*, 20 December 2012, http://www.theguardian.com/commentisfree/2012/dec/20/canada-first-nations-new-alliance.

interpretation of Indigenous land rights as territorial rights through which First Nations enact their own legal orders and decision-making authorities for environmental regulation. This proprietary frame may also have been reinforced by the very practices of some movement actors, especially those expressing the prominence of physical occupation and possession. For example, while blockades of pipeline routes proved to be an effective strategy that manifested Indigenous and allied resistance against the injustices of ongoing land rights infringements, these actions also foregrounded ideas of exclusion, possession, and proprietary boundaries. That is, while the language of exclusive occupation by no means precluded a territorial framing of Indigenous land rights, it is not clear that something other than a concept of private property was best suited to, or in fact pursued by, allied mobilizations focused most immediately on their opposition to pipeline developments.

Here we might suppose that, just as the private-proprietary model of Aboriginal title lent legitimacy to the judicial decisions of the breakthrough era of title litigation – at least in the eyes of some non-Indigenous publics – it continues to function as a technology of consensus that links coalitions of allied actors and movements. Whether or how this framing privileges some aims, interests, and values while disadvantaging others are largely questions I leave for future work, suggesting only at this stage that the language of private property continues to powerfully influence social movements and to ground large-scale collective action. This view underscores the power of received interpretations of law "to provide groups with frameworks to understand a particular field of regulation,"[91] as well as to constrain emerging understandings around which new mobilizations and publics might organize.

B. Counter-Mobilization

A second reason why proprietary frames may have continued to pervade and shape Idle No More was its posture as a counter-mobilization to preceding actions that sought to undermine the inalienability principle in pursuit of property freedoms, land market liberalization, and economic growth, which I described above. Social movements research has shown that the path dependency of movement discourses flow in large part from actors' attempts to frame their arguments in order to gain control over the "instrumental power of law"[92] and to respond

---

91 Kapczynski, "Access to Knowledge Mobilization," 864.
92 Kapczynski, "Access to Knowledge Mobilization," 874.

on terms that can leverage that power to persuade or discredit opponents. To the extent that Idle No More's participants understood themselves as engaged in a contest over justifications for the inalienability of Indigenous lands, they tended at key moments to modulate their arguments in the language of property rights. For example, in responding to concerns over Bill C-45's reforms to the *Indian Act*'s leasing provisions and the proposed FNPOA legislation, activists invoked the values protected by community ownership over private ownership, as well as the potential threats of absentee ownership to community cohesion and resilience.[93] These discursive moves traded, in part, on some of the long-standing rationales for the inalienability principle described by Justice Iacobucci in *Osoyoos*, though not necessarily in ways that endorsed its more problematic assumptions. Notably, movement actors did not tend to respond in terms of the economic development and investment rationales put forward by the FNPOA proponents – despite the growing availability of arguments based on successful traditional and commons-based forms of economic organization and production.

C. *Social Movements and Legal Change*

While attention to both allied and opposing mobilizations helps to clarify complex dynamics associated with these new politics, they may also mask the role of disagreement and dissent within Idle No More itself. If modern social movements "play an important role in the creation of authoritative interpretative communities,"[94] to what extent can these movements themselves be said to form interpretive communities that participate directly in generating or reinterpreting substantive legal norms as part of Indigenous lawmaking? As I have shown, Idle No More played a unique role in breaking down entrenched divisions between public regulation and private rights that emerged within the common law, helping to create new space for Indigenous lawmaking amid the instability of property and territory as conceptual legal categories. This disruptive function of social movement politics is distinct from – but certainly connected to – the forms of peaceful popular resistance to law described by Ibironke Odumosu-Ayanu in chapter 9. Social movements in this mode may have significant implications for Indigenous communities such as the Island Hul'qumi'num, discussed by Sarah Morales and Brian Thom in chapter 3, whose land tenure system "struggles for

---

93 See, e.g., Shannon Houle, "Idle No More – Alberta," YouTube, 2 December 2012,
    https://www.youtube.com/watch?v=1FNfrbFe0hs.
94 Gunier and Torres, "Changing the Wind."

practical expression against ... powerful, even dominant, systems [of law]." That function is distinct, however, from understanding social movements constructively, as a source of authoritative interpretation for Indigenous laws or legal norms by virtue of the participation or leadership of Indigenous peoples. Certainly social movements may be an effective conduit for the public expression of substantive legal norms from different Indigenous legal orders, but we might be more cautious about how to characterize the authority or authenticity of substantive interpretations of law produced by or within Idle No More as a community of interpretation in its own right. That caution is reinforced by attention to disagreement and dissent among participants within Idle No More – a task for which further study of the data above may be especially well suited.

There may be good opportunities to combine these insights towards the goal of understanding emerging relationships between contemporary social movement action and Indigenous laws. For example, Sylvia McAdam, one of four women who motivated and organized some of Idle No More's earliest actions, describes the role of *nêhiyaw* (Cree) law in "guiding and directing" the counter-mobilization as organizers turned to social media to reach broader audiences.[95] McAdams explains how, as the group planned initial teach-ins around the consequences of Bill C-45, they were advised by community elders to invoke *nâtamâwasowin*, a law meaning "to defend for all human children the world as well as future generations."[96] Noting the resonance of this concept with several of the movement discourses described above, future work might explore the interpretation of *nâtamâwasowin* and other Indigenous laws within Idle No More, including related challenges.

Ultimately this chapter leaves open questions about how the interpretive work of Idle No More may be connected to future changes in law, partly because these effects are likely still being played out. In addition to the dynamics just described, returning to the ambiguities unearthed by Justice Iacobucci in *Osoyoos*, we might also ask how the mobilization's attempts to navigate between the frames of property and territory are, or will be, reinscribed into common law, federal statute, or modern treaty negotiations and implementation by tracing the flow of actors, rhetoric, and ideas into these different settings. For example,

---

95 Sylvia McAdams (Saysewahum), *Nationhood Interrupted: Revitalizing nêhiyaw Legal Systems* (Saskatoon, SK: Purich Publishing, 2015), excerpted in "Indigenous Law and Idle No More," *Justice as Healing: A Newsletter on Concepts of Aboriginal Justice* 20, no. 1 (2015): 5.

96 McAdams (Saysewahum), *Nationhood Interrupted*.

during the early stages of Idle No More in mid-December 2012, the Mikisew Cree First Nation launched a challenge against Bill C-45 and other legislative reforms in the Federal Court, claiming that the responsible federal ministers breached their duty to the Mikisew Cree by failing to consult on changes in environmental regulation affecting Treaty 8 lands before tabling the legislation in Parliament.[97] While the Court rejected this claim in part, it agreed that the Crown owed the Mikisew Cree a duty to consult after Bill C-45 was introduced, but before it was passed into federal law. If we interpret this case as a claim and response about the role of First Nations in federal lawmaking, we might ask how the legal strategies and claims of the litigants were shaped by the discursive struggles that both preceded and were taken up by Idle No More, especially given the common participation of key actors in both settings.[98] Other linkages and examples will be available and provide fertile ground for future work. This chapter aimed to develop a framework and methodologies for thinking about these connections, along with their attendant challenges and opportunities.

---

97 *Mikisew Cree First Nation v Canada (Minister of Aboriginal Affairs and Northern Development)*, 2014 CarswellNat 5539, 2014 FC 1244.

98 April Eve, "Idle No More Speaker Chief Courtoreille Mikisew Cree First Nation," 22 December 2012, https://www.youtube.com/watch?v=Ck3Q8N_ccx0.

PART THREE

Common Law's Response

7 The New Law-Making Powers of First Nations over Family Homes on Indian Reserves

MICHEL MORIN[1]

I. Introduction

The historical absence of provisions governing the division of matrimonial real property on reserves has resulted in what is often referred to as a legislative gap that harms First Nation women after the breakdown of conjugal relationships.[2] Because lands reserved for the "Indians" fall under exclusive federal jurisdiction,[3] and because the *Indian Act*[4] contains a detailed scheme for the occupation of reserves, many (though not all) provincial rules dealing with the division of matrimonial property are constitutionally inapplicable after a divorce or the breakdown of the relationship.[5] Therefore an ex-spouse with dependent children cannot rely on a provincial law

---

1 Research for this chapter has been conducted under the auspices of the Aboriginal Peoples and Governance project, funded by the Major Collaborative Research Initiatives program of the Social and Humanities Research Council of Canada. The author is grateful to professors Jean Leclair and Noura Karazivan for their comments on a previous version of this chapter, as well as for the editorial assistance of Professor Sari Graben. As always, he is solely responsible for any shortcoming. Though updated, the initial version was written in 2013.
2 Richard H. Bartlett, "Indian Self-Government, the Equality of the Sexes and Application of Provincial Matrimonial Property Laws," *Canadian Journal of Family Law* 5, no. 1 (2006): 188–95. For certain critics, the real problem was the denial of First Nations' jurisdiction over their own affairs. Martha Montour, "Iroquois Women's Rights with Respect to Matrimonial Property on Indian Reserves," *Canadian Native Law Reporter* 4 (1987): 1–10; Mary Ellen Turpel, "Critical Perspectives on Family Law: Race, Gender, Class," *Canadian Journal of Family Law* 10 (1991): 17–40.
3 *Constitution Act, 1867* (UK), 30 & 31 Vict, c 3, s 91(24), reprinted in RSC 1985, Appendix II, No 5.
4 RSC 1985, c I-5.
5 *Derrickson v Derrickson*, [1986] 1 SCR 285, 26 DLR (4th) 175.

that would prevent her expulsion from a family home located outside a reserve.

In order to address this lacuna, Parliament passed the *Family Homes on Reserves and Matrimonial Interests or Rights Act* (hereafter the *Family Homes Act*) on 19 June 2013.[6] The *Family Homes Act* purports to provide spouses or common-law partners living on reserve with matrimonial real property protections and rights similar to those of Canadians not living on reserves. In deference to the widespread call by First Nations to assume jurisdiction over the governance of property, the Act authorizes First Nation communities to enact their own community-specific matrimonial real property law. However, for First Nations that do not opt to legislate or do not fall within other exempted categories, the federal law will govern "the use, occupation and possession of family homes and the division of the value of interests or rights held by spouses or common-law partners in or to structures and lands on its reserves."[7]

---

6 SC 2013, c 20. Since 16 December 2014, the Act is fully in force at s 56, SI/2013-28. See also Stacey L. MacTaggart, "Lessons from History: The Recent Applicability of Matrimonial Property and Human Rights Legislation on Reserve Lands in Canada," *University of Western Ontario Journal of Legal Studies* 6, no. 2 (2016): 1–23. *Bradfield v Brydges*, [2016] BCJ No 215, 2016 BCSC 189, paras 37–8. For a thorough discussion of the origins of the Act and its application to a non-Indian survivor, see *Toney v Toney Estate*, [2018] NSJ No 292, 2018 NSSC 179; in other cases, only passing reference has been made to it: *McMurter v McMurter*, [2016] OJ No 3798, 2016 ONSC 1225, para 249; *Poitras v Khan*, [2016] SJ No 609, 2016 SKQB 346, paras 30–2; *Droit de la famille – 162829*, 2016 QCCS 5685, paras 20–8; *Droit de la famille – 19338*, 2019 QCCS 754, paras 25–7.

7 Exempted categories include communities governed by the *First Nations Land Management Act*, SC 1999, c 24, who have the power to adopt a land code and must "establish general rules and procedures, in cases of breakdown of marriage, respecting the use, occupation and possession of first nation land and the division of interests in first nation land." De facto relationships are not mentioned (s 17(1)). If neither a land code nor First Nation laws adopted pursuant to the *Family Homes Act* is in force, the default regime of the latter legislation will apply (s 12(2)). For First Nations having land-management powers under a self-government agreement, the parties may recommend that the *Family Homes Act* be made applicable by a ministerial order. After this has been done, if a First Nation fails to adopt a law pursuant to the Act or to a self-government agreement, or if such a law is not in force, the default regime will apply (s 12(3)). See Scott Hitchings, "Real Property Security Interest on First Nations Reserved Lands," *Saskatchewan Law Review* 80 (2017): 125–56, for recent discussions of the *First Nations Land Management Act*; Malcom Lavoie and Moira Lavoie, "Land Regime Choice in Close-Knit Communities: The Case of the First Nations Land Management Act," *Osgoode Hall Law Journal* 54, no. 2 (2017): 559–607.

In theory, the *Family Homes Act* could move the rules applicable to reserve lands closer to the private ownership paradigm.[8] However, we will show in this chapter that there is no substantive mandatory content for First Nation laws adopted pursuant to the *Family Home Act*, although their ultimate meaning will be determined by superior courts. Thus, with few exceptions, First Nations can choose the model that best suits their needs. As for the default regime that applies in the absence of such laws, it is based on the monetary value of family homes and interests in reserve lands. It will replace provincial laws providing for compensatory payments that were also based on the value of these homes and interest.[9] Furthermore, only a spouse who is a member of the reserve where the relevant lands are situated can benefit from their increase in value. As well, only a spouse who satisfies this condition can benefit from an order transferring an interest in reserve lands, and then only in three exceptional cases. Thus the collective interest of First Nation lands is clearly acknowledged.[10] Courts can also make exclusive occupation orders of limited duration to protect vulnerable spouses.

In the typical scenario, under the default regime, only a sum of money will be awarded. If this occurs more frequently, family homes and interests in lands will be treated more like private property, and less like a community or family resource. But to repeat, a First Nation could adopt a law providing that no monetary order can be made by the courts, and prescribing rules determining which spouse must leave the family home after a family breakdown (for example). Furthermore, all members of a First Nation can vote on a proposed law. This will generally give women members a greater say in this matter than in band council deliberations or in the adoption of federal legislation. To that extent, it may contribute to redress gender imbalance in decision-making and more generally in law. Of course, this is not to deny that the remaining rules of the *Indian Act* reflect their colonialist and patriarchal origins, that the *Family Homes Act* does nothing to address the housing crisis in First Nations communities, that the issue of Aboriginal self-government remains unresolved,[11] and that Indigenous legal traditions are not recognized by this legislation.[12]

---

8   See Angela Cameron, Sari Graben, and Val Napoleon, "The Role of Indigenous Law in the Privatization of Lands," this volume.
9   See text corresponding to note 25.
10   Cameron, Graben, and Napoleon, "Role of Indigenous Law."
11   *Family Homes Act* (clearly recognized in the preamble).
12   See Val Napoleon and Emily Snyder, "Housing on Reserve," this volume; a recent law attempts to make far greater room for Indigenous Legal Traditions: *An Act respecting First nations, Inuit and Métis children, youth and families*, SC 2019, c 24.

Be that as it may, restoring Indigenous legal traditions will be gradual, and narrowly focused experiences could play a useful role. This chapter will therefore pay attention to the eventual recognition by the Canadian courts of Indigenous norms and decision-making processes. It will discuss the interaction between the *Family Homes Act* or First Nations laws and the pre-existing powers of bands over land allocation and transfer, inasmuch as this relationship affects matrimonial property.[13] So-called customary law and contractual leases enforced by the band provide a network of legal rights that effect the division of matrimonial property and exist in parallel with the statutory rights under the *Family Homes Act*. Put simply, rights that arise under the Act (including any new legislation regarding matrimonial property brought into force by a First Nation) must still be interpreted in light of the powers exercised by First Nations pursuant to the *Indian Act*.[14] Thus, while the Act is meant to introduce a certain degree of clarity about interests or rights in property when a conjugal relationship breaks down, there is a death, or an emergency occurs, there is still significant uncertainty as to how a spouse or partner's continuing interests will rank against rights that arise from contract, custom, and regulation forwarded under the *Indian Act*.

In an effort to understand the impact of the legislative provisions, part II of this chapter will introduce the default regime to be implemented under the *Family Homes Act*, which applies in the absence of a First Nations Law. This section will provide an overview of the wide-ranging nature of First Nation's law-making power in the use, occupation, or possession of a family home, as well as the division of the value of interests in buildings or lands in a reserve. It will also give the reader an understanding of what rights now automatically apply to

---

13 This chapter does *not* discuss Indigenous conceptions of property, except to the extent they are related to matrimonial property on reserves. My previous writings on the legal norms of Indigenous peoples observed during the French colonial regime generally agree with the conclusions of many contributors to this volume. See Shalene Jobin, "Market Citizenship and Indigeneity," this volume; Sarah Morales and Brian Thom, "The Principle of Sharing and the Shadow of Canadian Property Law," this volume; Richard Daly, "Conceptualizing Aboriginal Taxpayers, Real Property, and Communities of Sharing," this volume; Michel Morin, "Propriétés et territoires autochtones en Nouvelle-France I: Contrôle territorial et reconnaissance de territoires nationaux," *Recherches amérindiennes au Québec* 43, no. 2–3 (2013): 59–75; Morin, "Propriétés et territoires autochtones en Nouvelle-France II: La gestion des districts de chasse," *Recherches amérindiennes au Québec* 44, no. 1 (2014): 129–36; Morin, "Indigenous Peoples, Political Economists and the Tragedy of the Commons," *Theoretical Inquiries in Law* 19, no. 2 (2018): 559–86.
14 RSC 1985, c I-5.

individuals resident on reserve. We will then examine difficulties associated with this default regime.

Part III will examine how issues concerning matrimonial property play out on a reserve when different kinds of rights to occupy or possess lands are considered. We will examine ways in which First Nations might devise rules or policies that address the issue of matrimonial property situated on an Indian reserve. To this end, we will explore the distinction between customary and legislated possession of reserve lands. The latter form of possession is subject to a detailed scheme contained in the *Indian Act*. Nonetheless, courts have recognized the existence of "customary" possession and "customary law," as well as the wide discretion enjoyed by the band council when making decisions in this regard. To understand the potential usefulness of custom in the latter case, we will pay attention to customary rules governing the transfer of land between family members. Courts sometimes mention the alleged existence of a custom, without taking a position on this issue, or on the enforceability of its rules. Therefore, the extent to which their recognition is possible in Canadian law remains uncertain.

II. The Family Homes Act

A. The Expansive Jurisdiction of First Nations

Following extensive governmental review[15] and consultation[16] that began in 2002, the *Family Homes Act* received royal assent on 19 June 2013.[17] The purpose of the *Family Homes Act* is to provide for the adoption by all First Nations (whether or not subject to the *Indian Act*[18]) of laws that will apply during a conjugal relationship, upon its breakdown or the death of a spouse or common law partner, and that pertain to the "use, occupation and possession of family homes on First Nation reserves and the division of the value of any interest or rights held by

---

15 House of Commons, Standing Committee on Aboriginal Affairs and Northern Development, *Walking Arm-in-Arm to Resolve the Issue of On-Reserve Matrimonial Real Property*, June 2005, 47; see also Senate, Standing Senate Committee on Human Rights, *Seventeenth Report*, May 2005.

16 But see Assembly of First Nations, *Matrimonial Real Property on Reserves: Our Lands, Our Families, Our Solutions*, Dialogue Sessions Final Report (Ottawa: AFN, March 2007). For critique, see 11 and 37.

17 See Cameron, Graben, and Napoleon, "Role of Indigenous Law."

18 RSC 1985, c I-5. The word *reserve* includes the Kanesatake Mohawk interim land base, s 2 (6). This chapter will address only the case of communities subject to the *Indian Act*.

spouses or common law partners in or to structures and lands on those reserves" (section 4). Until such laws are adopted, the provisional federal rules contained in other part of the Act apply ("default regime").

Section 7 (1) declares that a First Nation "has the power to adopt" laws described in section 4 (hereafter First Nation laws). Such laws must include amending and repealing procedures and provisions for their administration as well. They must provide enforcement procedures, on a reserve of the First Nation, for any "order of a court," decision, or agreement based on their contents, "despite subsection 89 (1) of the *Indian Act*" (section 7 (2)). This raises the question of whether only a superior court may be given jurisdiction by the First Nation, since that is the meaning given to the word *court* in the *Family Homes Act* (see section 2 (1)).[19] The enforcement procedure must extend to any "decision" made under laws adopted pursuant to the *Family Homes Act* (section 7 (2)). Therefore, nothing prevents First Nations from creating tribunals, committees, and traditional or innovative institutions. Indeed, the parties may reach an agreement "through the use of traditional dispute resolution" (section 2 (3)). But these institutions cannot be given exclusive jurisdiction over the breakdown of a union or marriage, because the core jurisdiction of superior courts to review their operation is constitutionally protected, and because the Act concerns only interests in reserve lands.

Laws concerning family homes must be submitted by the band council for approval by all adult members of the First Nation concerned, whether they are considered residents or not (section 8). While the Act was strongly criticized for not recognizing an inherent or pre-existing lawmaking power for First Nations,[20] two things are striking about these sections. First, there is almost no constraint on the contents of the laws, except for the inclusion of amending and repealing procedures and of an enforcement procedure on a reserve of court orders, decisions, or agreements (section 7 (1)). After a successful vote with a participation rate of at least 25 per cent, the law will come into force (sections 9–11). The governor in council may make regulations that it

---

19 The court given jurisdiction is the one mentioned in the *Divorce Act*, RSC 1985, c 3 (2nd Supp), s 2 (1).

20 Assembly of First Nations, *Matrimonial Real Property on Reserves*, 14–17, appendix L; Native Women's Association of Canada, "Reclaiming Our Way of Being: Matrimonial Real Property Solutions Position Paper," in Canada, Office of the Ministerial Representative, *Report of the Ministerial Representative: Matrimonial Real Property Issues on Reserves*, ed. Wendy Grant-John (Gatineau, QC: Indian and Northern Affairs Canada, 9 March 2007), 39.

"considers necessary for carrying out the purposes and provisions" of the act (section 53 (1)), and these regulations will apply even if a First Nation has adopted its own laws (see section 12 (1)). However, no regulation currently applies to these laws. The requirement in section 7 (1) that an enforcement procedure be put in place "despite section 89 (1) of the *Indian Act*" could be seen by some to imply that a First Nation cannot derogate from other sections of that act concerning occupation or possession of lands (see also sections 15 (1), 31 (2) (a), and 36 (3) (a) of the *Family Homes Act*). But the very wide formulation of sections 4 (1) and 7 (1) shows that this is not the case: the "power to enact First Nation laws ... respecting the use, occupation and possession of family homes on its reserves" would be almost meaningless if the rights flowing from certificates of possession could not be restricted. Furthermore, in the preamble, Parliament declares that it "wishes to advance the exercise ... of First Nations law-making power over family homes on reserves and matrimonial interests or rights in or so structures or lands on reserves."

Assuming that First Nations have the power to specify in their laws which sections of the *Indian Act* will continue to apply to ex-spouses, the relative autonomy granted by *Family Homes Act* contrasts starkly with the total subordination of band councils under the *Indian Act*. While far from self-government, this legislation represents a clear recognition of the power of First Nations communities to have their members decide which rules will apply to the division of matrimonial property.

B. Federal Rules Applicable in the Absence of a First Nation Law

If a First Nation adopts no legislation, a default regime is put in place. However, it can be displaced at any time by a new First Nation law. In cases of domestic violence, the court may grant emergency and long-term occupation orders. Most importantly, the Act provides for the division of the interests of the spouses in reserve lands in cases of separation. It gives a seemingly exclusive jurisdiction to superior courts, allows the band council to play a role during hearings, and makes it responsible for the enforcement of court orders.

1. RESIDENCY RIGHTS AND PROTECTION OF THE FAMILY HOME
In the absence of a First Nation law, section 13 grants to a legally married or de facto spouse (hereafter referred to as a "spouse") the right to occupy the family home, "whether or not that person is a First Nation member or an Indian." In general, former spouses (married and de facto) enjoy the same right as spouses (section 2 (4)). Section 14 allows a survivor (whether a member or not) who does not hold

an interest in the family home, or a right to it, to occupy the premises for 180 days after the death of his or her spouse. The right of a former spouse to occupy the family home will presumably prevail over the by-laws on residence (see section 81 (1) (p. 1) of the *Indian Act*) that, in a few cases, have denied to certain non-member spouses the right to reside on a reserve. Such a by-law has been declared valid by one trial court.[21] However, First Nation laws can now address the issue at any time.

If the spouse who holds an interest in or a right to the family home disposes of it or encumbers it without the free and informed consent of the other, the latter may ask that the contract be set aside and that the court impose conditions on any future disposition or encumbrance in the future, unless the other contracting party acquired it for value and acted in good faith (section 15). However, this is "subject to the *Indian Act*." The effect of this restriction is not perfectly clear. It probably means that the *Indian Act* continues to apply, except to the extent that section 15 of the *Family Homes Act* provides differently. For instance, a certificate still cannot be transferred to a non-member. If this caveat is intended to give priority to the *Indian Act* in every case, one wonders if a court could set aside the transfer of a certificate of possession approved by the minister. Does compliance with the relevant rules of the latter Act preclude this? If so, this protection would be useless.

2. EMERGENCY AND EXCLUSIVE OCCUPATION ORDERS

The *Family Homes Act* regulates in detail the granting of emergency orders after family violence has occurred, to ensure the immediate protection of a person who is at risk of harm, or of property that is at risk of damage (sections 16–27). A provincial judge authorized to act in the matter by the lieutenant governor in council, including a justice of the peace, may grant a ninety-day order for the exclusive occupation of the family home or to insure that the violent spouse will vacate it (section 16). The superior court of the province must then review and, if need be, modify or revoke the order or extend its duration (sections 17–18). A superior court may also grant a spouse or survivor the exclusive occupation of the family home, if need be on an interim basis, "subject to any conditions and for the period that the court specifies" (sections 20–1). The jurisdiction conferred on a justice of the peace attempts to

---

21   *Grismer v Squamish Indian Band*, [2006] FCJ no 1374, 2006 FC 1088; see Sebastien Grammond, "Equality between Indigenous Groups" (2009) 45 SCLR (2nd) 91–121.

provide a more accessible forum, but this will hardly compensate for the lack of legal and human resources on many reserves.[22]

A long list of factors must be taken into consideration in such cases, mostly related to others who have relations with those subject to the order (i.e., children, collective interest of a First Nation, family, elderly etc. (section 20 (3)). Such orders do not deprive a person of a right to the family home or an interest in it, nor do they prevent administrators of estates or executors of wills from transferring such a right or interest (section 23). In other words, when the period of time specified in the latest order expires, the person benefitting from it must leave the house.

If the family home was leased and a spouse or survivor obtains an exclusive occupation order without having entered into the contract, he or she will be bound by its terms (section 26). Therefore, the *Family Homes Act* applies to all leases found on an Indian reserve. In effect, it transfers the rights and obligations of the initial lessee to the spouse or survivor for the duration of the order. To ascertain these obligations, it may be necessary to rely on provincial or territorial laws, since no federal rules exists for residential tenancies (we will return to this issue below). Although an argument could be made that this type of contract necessarily requires a rent to be paid, on Indian reserves, accommodations are often provided freely by the band. This militates against such a narrow interpretation, since the objective of this legislation is clearly to provide a minimal measure of protection to all spouses.

3. DIVISION OF THE VALUE OF MATRIMONIAL INTERESTS OR RIGHTS

The division of matrimonial interests is the most complex part of the *Family Homes Act*, as it requires alternating between the highly technical definitions of section 2(1) and sections 28–40. Furthermore, many subsections often contain different but similar wording, which tends to obscure the differences between them. For instance, various categories of rights are established in subsection 2 (1). The expression "family home" refers only to the structure where the spouses habitually reside but does not include the underlying land. "Interest or rights" includes, for the *Indian Act*, a right to lawful possession, a permit under section 28 (1) and leases under section 53 (for designated lands) or 58 (for reserve lands). Other interests in, or rights to, a family home must have been recognized either by the First Nation or by a court order pursuant to section 48 of *Family Homes Act*; this refers to what is usually called

---

22 MacTaggart, "Lessons from History," 6; see also *Emergency Protection Orders Regulations*, SOR/2014-266.

customary tenure.[23] Finally, section 2 (1) recognizes three kinds of "matrimonial interests or rights." First, they are rights acquired during the conjugal relationship (a) or in contemplation of it (b), which we will call *conjugal relationship rights*. The second category includes rights acquired before the beginning of the relationship and without contemplating its existence, as long as they have appreciated during the time it lasted (c), which we will label *pre-conjugal rights whose value has increased*. In all three cases, property received by gift, legacy, devise, or descent is excluded (see section 2 (1)).

Upon the breakdown of a conjugal relationship, each spouse is entitled to one half or the value of an interest in, or a right to, the family home (which, to repeat, does not include the land) (section 28 (1)). A spouse who is a member of the First Nation on the reserve where the family home or the lands are situated (hereafter called a "member spouse") is also entitled to half the value of *conjugal relationship rights* in respect of *structures or lands* held by the other spouse in that same reserve (section 28 (2) (a)). For *pre-conjugal rights whose value has increased* and which pertain to *structures and lands*, he or she may then add the greater of (i) half the increase in value between the date on which the conjugal relationship began and the valuation date determined for the separation according to subsection 28 (6) (sections (28 (2) (b) (i)), or (ii) for the same period, the difference between the payments he or she made towards improvements to those structures and lands, and the amount of outstanding debts or liabilities assumed for this purpose (section 28 (2) (b) (ii)). Essentially, the latter total takes into account the contributions of one spouse made out of personal funds to pay for improvements to structures and lands over which only the other held some right. Even if there has been no increase in value of the rights held prior to the conjugal relationship, these cash advances may still be recovered (section 28 (2) (c)).

A non-member spouse has also the right to half the value of the family home (section 28 (1)). To this may be added half the value of *conjugal relationship rights* to *structures* held by the other spouse (section 28 (3) (a)), exclusive of underlying lands. The rule for *pre-conjugal rights whose value has increased* is the same for member and for non-member spouses, except that for the latter, only structures are taken into consideration (section 28 (3) (b)). Moreover, the difference between payments and outstanding liabilities can be recovered for improvements to "lands that are the object of matrimonial rights or interests"

---

23 See *Family Homes Act*, s 2 (1) "interest or right" (c).

(section 28 (3) (c) (i)), and for structures over which the other spouse has *pre-conjugal rights*, even though their value has not increased (section 28 (3) (c) (ii).[24]

In effect, non-members are deprived of the right to claim any part of the increase in value of reserve lands and can recover only the net contribution they made to the acquisition of rights or interests in them. Presumably, this is because only members hold title to the lands of Indian reserves. Nonetheless, since we are talking of value and not of occupation and possession, it should be noted that currently, for the application of provincial laws, this amount is considered during the division of family assets.[25] Thus the Act deprives non-members of a financial benefit that they currently enjoy. One should also note that lands on reserve do have a value, although it is inferior to other types of land.[26] On the other hand, leases, permits under section 28 of the *Indian Act*, and customary rights are specifically included in the definition of "interest or right" (section 2 (1), (a) (ii), (a) (iii) and (c)).

The court has also a wide discretion to modify an amount owed to a former spouse that it considers unconscionable, by taking into consideration a long list of factors (section 29). It may determine the amount owed by each spouse and how it should be paid (section 30). It may also order that an agreement in writing shall be enforced, provided it was entered into after the spouses had ceased to cohabit, it was made freely

---

24 See, e.g., *L(M) v G(N)*, 2016 QCCS 5685, JE 2016–2082.

25 *Derrickson v Derrickson* 304; see *NIL/TU, O Child and Family Services Society v BC Government and Service Employees' Union*, [2010] 2 SCR 696, 2010 SCC 45, paras 70–3, McLachlin CJ, Binnie J, & Fish J, concurring; *Canadian Western Bank v Alberta*, 2007 SCC 22, [2007] 2 SCR 3 ("relationships within Indian families and reserve communities" is a "vital or essential federal interest," para 51); see Michel Morin, "La coexistence des systèmes de droit autochtones, de droit civil et de common law au Canada," in *Évolution des systèmes juridiques, bijuridisme et commerce international*, ed. L. Perret, A.-F. Bisson, and N. Mariani (Montreal: Wilson & Lafleur, 2003), 159 (for Quebec cases, 182 *ff*); *AG v GG*, [2002] JQ No 3351 (CS); *JL c KR*, [2006] JQ No 24216, 2006 QCCS 5356; *Droit de la famille – 071863*, [2007] JQ No 7965, 2007 QCCS 3630; see also Canada, Department of Indian Affairs and Northern Development, "Discussion Paper: Matrimonial Real Property on Reserve," by Wendy Cornet and Allison Lendor (Ottawa: IAND, 28 November 2002), 41–9; *Dunstan v Dunstan*, [2002] BCJ No 433, 2002 BCCS 335; *Oppenheimer v Oppenheimer*, [2004] BCJ No 1854, 2004 BCSC 1153; *Paul v Paul*, [2008] NSJ No 157, 2008 NSSC 124.

26 *Musqueam Indian Band v Glass*, [2000] 2 SCR 633; *Simard-Vincent v Conseil de la Nation-Huronne-Wendat*, [2010] JQ No 694, 2010 QCCA 178; *Musqueam Indian Band v Musqueam Indian Band (Board of Review)*, 2016 SCC 36; Tom Flanagan, Christopher Alcantara, and André Le Dressay, *Beyond the Indian Act: Restoring Aboriginal Property Rights* (Montreal and Kingston: McGill-Queen's University Press, 2010), 94.

and voluntarily, and is not unconscionable, having regard, among other things, to the factor listed in section 29 (section 33). All agreements may be "reached through the use of traditional dispute resolution" (section 2 (3)). Also noteworthy is the power to provide against improvident depletion (section 32).

The court may order the transfer, but only to a member spouse, of certain rights to, or interests in, structures and lands, namely a certificate of possession or of occupation under the *Indian Act*, as well as rights or interests in a reserve recognized by the First Nation or by a court order pursuant to section 48 (section 30 (1) (b) (iii)). However, such a transfer can be ordered only if one of the following conditions is met: there is a written agreement based on the free and informed consent of the parties and it is not unconscionable; the applicant held the relevant right prior to the cessation of cohabitation; the spouses hold more than one right to lands situated on the reserve (section 31 (1)). A transfer under these conditions will probably be rare, since few agreements will have been reached, and in most cases, the rights to only one house will be in dispute. These restrictions seem to reflect the view that as a general rule, transfers should remain exceptional and should not be imposed against the will of the spouse holding a specific right or interest in reserve lands.

Certificates of possession or occupation and lands held under customary tenure may also be transferred to settle the amount owed to the survivor who is a member of the First Nation where the lands in question are situated (section 36 (1) (iii)). A spouse or survivor who obtains a court order for a sum owed under section 30 or 36 may not take advantage of the will of the deceased or of the provisions of the *Indian Act* applicable to intestates (section 37). If there are two survivors, the common law partner will be paid before the spouse (sections 38 (3)). However, an agreement between the executor or administrator and the survivor will be respected by the court if it was entered into freely and voluntarily and was not unconscionable (section 43).

4. JURISDICTION OF COURTS AND THE ROLE OF BAND COUNCILS

A copy of an application made pursuant to the *Family Homes Act* must be sent to the band council (section 41 (1)), except for emergency protection orders (section 16) and related orders that impose in camera hearings or prohibit the publication of information that is likely to identify a person, or that is specified by the court (section 19). Band councils must also be notified of emergency protection orders (section 42). Upon request, the court must allow the council to make representations "with respect to the cultural, social and legal context" relevant to the application and to present its views on whether or not the order should be made (section 41 (2)). The court must also notify the minister of its orders, except for in camera hearings or restrictions on publication (section 50)).[27]

Finally, the non-member and non-Indian spouse or survivor who has obtained a judgment ordering the payment of a sum of money under section 30 (1), section 33, subsection 36 (1), or section 40 may request the band council to enforce it on the reserve "as if the order has been made in favour of the First Nation" (section 52 (1)). If the band refuses or neglects to act within a reasonable period, the court may order the initial defendant to pay into court the amount specified in the judgment if it is satisfied that this is "necessary for the enforcement" of the order (section 52 (2)). Although a First Nation law adopted by its voters must provide for an enforcement mechanism despite subsection 89 (1) of the *Indian Act*, under the default regime, nothing is said about that subsection for court orders. Presumably, in the latter case, the real and personal property of an Indian situated on a reserve is still protected, as against a non-Indian. Since failure to comply with an order to pay a sum of money is generally not a valid reason to hold someone in contempt of court, except in cases of wilful non-compliance, this sanction could turn out to be symbolic in a majority of cases.[28]

Under the default regime of the *Family Homes Act*, Courts have the power to grant emergency protection orders for the benefit of a spouse or children (sections 16–27).[29] As well, the regime provides for the division of the value of the matrimonial interests or rights upon the breakdown of the conjugal relationship or upon the death of a spouse or partner (sections 28–53). However, if First Nation laws deal only with some issues related to matrimonial interests, there is a possibility that different laws will regulate the others (for instance, leases, emergency orders, temporary rights of occupation for ex-spouses, etc.). We will now turn to these issues.

---

27 *Family Homes Act*. The only First Nations that must be notified are those that have adopted a land code under the *First Nations Lands Management Act*, those that have entered into a self-government agreement and whose request to be subject to sections 18–56 has been accepted by the minister, and the Mohawks of Kanesatake at section 50 (a)–(c).

28 See Gillian Calder and E. Llana Nakonechny, "Dickie v. Dickie: Smells Like Family Law," *Canadian Journal of Family Law* 23 (2007): 253; MacTaggart, "Lessons from History," 10.

29 *Family Homes Act*. Different rules apply to First Nations that are subject to the *First Nations Land Management Act* or have entered into a self-government agreement, s 12(2)–(3)).

III. Continuing Jurisdiction on Indian Reserves

How will the *Family Homes Act* coordinate with the laws and customs that have been developed or will be developed by First Nations governments? The Act expressly gives priority to First Nation laws promulgated after exercising their jurisdiction (section 7(1)). However, other powers could play a useful role if some laws omitted some issues and amending them turns out to be time-consuming and costly, or if the minimum participation rate is problematic. Such a gap could be filled by laws promulgated as a result of (A) continuing band council authority over possession, residency, membership, or contractual relations pursuant to the *Indian Act*, (B) incorporation of the customs and practices of First Nations as a matter of evidence in applications before the court,[30] and (C) contractual leasing. Actions undertaken pursuant to the *Indian Act*, custom, and contract can affect the disposition of lands on reserve. The following discussion therefore highlights the continuing relevance of band authority, especially in circumstances where there are multiple owners of these interests, where community needs dominate, or where the disposition would have a deleterious effect on property rights.

A. Regulating Possession

An Indian may have "lawful possession" of lands situated on a reserve. This requires an allotment by the band council and the approval of the minister (section 20).[31] This is normally evidenced by a certificate, although tacit recognition is also possible, for instance if both the band council and the minister approve a loan for the building of a house.[32] Indeed, under the *Family Homes Act*, "interest or right" includes "a right to possession, with or without a Certificate of Possession" (section 2 (1)). The *Indian Act* also allows the minister to grant a conditional certificate. Upon fulfilment of the conditions imposed, a certificate of possession

---

30 RSC 1985, c I-5. For instance, the court must consider, among other things, the collective interests of First Nation members in their reserve lands and the representations made by the council of the First Nation on whose reserve the family home is situated with respect to the cultural, social, and legal context that pertains to the application pursuant to s 20 (1).

31 *Indian Act*, RSC 1985, c I-5.

32 *George v George*, [1997] 2 CNLR 1019 (BCCA); Tom Flanagan and Christopher Alacantara, "Individual Property Rights on Canadian Indian Reserves: A Review of the Jurisprudence," *Alberta Law Review* 42, no. 4 (2005): 1023–4; see also Flanagan, Alacantara, and Le Dressay, *Beyond the Indian Act*, chapter 6, "A Review of the Jurisprudence."

will be issued; otherwise the land will be available for re-allotment by the council (sections 20 (4) to (6)). A register for both types of certificates and for "other transactions respecting lands in a reserve" is kept in the Department of Indian Affairs and Northern Development (section 21).[33]

Lawful possession may be transferred to the band or to another member, subject to the approval of the minister (section 24).[34] This may be done to guarantee loans; bands may obtain a transfer of the borrower's certificate of possession. When the loan has been paid off, the certificate is transferred back to the original holder. In the event of default, the band, as the nominal holder, may expel the borrower and re-allot the land, to compensate for the fact that it must repay the debt.[35] In passing, one may note that on the Six Nations Reserve, defaults or late payments under this scheme were significantly lower than for off-reserve loans.[36] Similarly, in Northern British Columbia, one community, who had evicted defaulting borrowers in the past, had a very low housing debt, as well as another where the kinship system was strong; but a third one, who was loath to proceed with evictions, had a much larger debt, although it could support it because of successful economic ventures.[37] The band council who holds the certificate of possession for the family house may force a spouse out of it after a separation, possibly according to its own policies, traditional values, or custom.[38]

---

33 Sarah Carter and Nathalie Kermoal, "Property Rights on Reserves, 'New Ideas' from the Nineteenth Century," this volume. See text accompanying notes 56–65. Lawful possession was historically conceived as a first step towards granting lands in fee simple to Indians after their enfranchisement. This would allow the gradual elimination of reserves.

34 *Jones Estate v Louis*, [1996] FCJ No 248, 108 FTR 81 (FCTD). If the conditions specified in the agreement to transfer the certificate are not fulfilled prior to the approval by the minister, the holder of the certificate may withdraw its consent (para 40).

35 Tom Flanagan and Christopher Alcantara, "Individual Property Rights on Canadian Indian Reserves," *Queen's Law Journal* 29, no. 2 (2004): 509–12; Christopher Alcantara, "Certificates of Possession and First Nations Housing: A Case Study of the Six Nations Housing Program," *Canadian Journal of Law and Society* 20 (2005): 183–205 at 191. A rent-to-own agreement on unallotted lands may provide for issuing a certificate of possession if all its terms have been complied with. See Napoleon and Snyder, "Housing on Reserve," note 50.

36 Alcantara, "Certificates of Possession," 195.

37 Napoleon and Emily Snyder, "Housing on Reserve," nn167–71; see also Thomas Flanagan and Christopher Alcantara, "Customary Land Rights on Canadian Indian Reserves," in *Self-Determination: The Other Paths for Native Americans*, ed. Terry L. Anderson, Bruce L. Benson, and Thomas E. Flanagan (Stanford: Stanford University Press, 2006), 153–4; Flanagan, Alcantara, and Le Dressay, *Beyond the Indian Act*, chap. 5.

38 *Membertou Band Council v Johnson*, 2003 NSSC 225.

Under section 25 (1), an Indian who ceases to be entitled to reside on a reserve is given six months, or a longer period determined by the minister, to transfer his or her right of lawful possession to the band or to another member. Failing that, possession reverts to the band, but the minister must determine the amount of compensation due for permanent improvements (section 25 (2)). Furthermore, if an Indian is lawfully removed from reserve lands, the minister may, in his or her discretion, order that the band or the person going into possession pay an amount to the initial occupier as compensation for permanent improvements that he or she made there (section 23). Thus the Act recognizes the possibility that an Indian might lose a right to occupy reserve lands, whether or not this qualifies as "lawful possession." In some cases, compensation may be ordered by the minister. However, it seems clear that the right to lawful possession cannot be withdrawn unless the *Indian Act* specifically authorizes such a measure.[39] Prior to the *Family Homes Act*, this posed a problem for ex-spouses who were not themselves in possession of the certificate of possession, since they would not be entitled under provincial or territorial law to request a transfer of family property, notably of the family home.[40] It was not possible to make such an order conditional on the approval of the minister, because this amounts to making provincial laws applicable to Indian lands.[41] In the leading case on the question, the Supreme Court mentioned that "Section 89 prohibits mortgages except to another Indian," completely overlooking the fact that "seizure, distress or execution" were allowed by that same section at the instance of "an Indian or a band."[42] Since the two ex-spouses were members of the Westbank Indian Band, this omission is hard to understand. In any case, the Supreme Court of Canada held that even though federal legislation could make provincial laws providing for the division of family assets applicable to Indian lands, this had not been done.[43] Now, under the default regime of the *Family Homes Act*, lawful possession of lands situated on a reserve set aside

---

39 See *Stoney Band v Poucette*, [1999] 3 CNLR 321 (AB QB), aff'd [1998] AJ No 842, 1998 ABCA 244, where the Court suggests that to obtain the title to lands in the lawful possession of an Indian, a band needs the consent of the minister under section 18 (2), which would trigger a right to compensation; at para 22.

40 *Derrickson v Derrickson; Paul v Paul*, [1986] 1 SCR 306.

41 *Derrickson v Derrickson*, 302.

42 *Derrickson v Derrickson*, 302.

43 Flanagan and Alcantara, "Individual Property Rights on Canadian Indian Reserves," *Alberta Law Review*, 1030; Christopher Alcantara, "Individual Property Rights on Canadian Indian Reserves: The Historical Emergence and Jurisprudence of Certificates of Possession," *Canadian Journal of Native Studies* 23 (2003): 413–14;

for a First Nation can be transferred only to a former spouse who is a member of that First Nation, and then only if the spouses have validly agreed to do this, if one spouse has lost his or her right after cohabitation stopped, or if they hold an interest in more than one location on the reserve (section 31 (1)).

It is unclear what effect lawful possession would have for a spouse when ownership is split among many individuals. For instance, often more than two persons hold certificates of possession to the same lot. Until 1997, the minister would not sever a joint tenancy of a certificate of possession (which, in the common law tradition, provides for reversion of the interest in the certificate to the surviving joint tenant) or partition a certificate held in common by both spouses.[44] It is now possible to transfer voluntarily the interest in a joint tenancy to another band member or to the band itself. The tenants will then hold in common instead of jointly, which means there will be no right of survivorship.[45] In circumstances where ownership in certificates is fractured, the transfer of possession in matrimonial disputes may not achieve the ameliorative effect for spouses that the law intended. Under the *Family Homes Act*, joint or common possession is considered an "interest or right," which can be transferred only when the conditions discussed above are met (section 31 (1)), so little progress has been made on this front.

Reserve lands are not "subject to seizure under legal process" (section 29). It has long been assumed that this rule applied to lands in the "lawful possession" of an Indian. Recently, a band was awarded damages against some members who had refused to vacate reserve lands after an aborted sale made pursuant to the *Indian Act*. A debate arose regarding the possibility of seizing a certificate of possession. The Ontario Court of Appeal decided that "reserve lands" refer only to the legal title held by the Crown, as opposed to possession.[46] Otherwise, the real and personal property of an Indian situated on a reserve is subject to a "charge,

---

Paul v Kingsclear Indian Band, 148 DLR (4th) 759, 132 FTR 145; *Darbyshire-Joseph v Darbishire-Joseph*, [1998] BCJ No 2765 (BCSC) at para 26; *Simpson v Ziprick*, [1995] BCJ No 1740 (BCCA) at para 24.

44 Flanagan and Alacantara, "Individual Property Rights on Canadian Indian Reserves," *Alberta Law Review* 42, no. 4 (2005): 1030; Alcantara, "Individual Property Rights on Canadian Indian Reserves," 413–14; *Kingsclear*; *Darbyshire*, para 26; *Simpson*, para 24.

45 See Canada, Department of Indian and Northern Affairs, "Indian Lands Registration Manual," section 9.1, https://www.aadnc-aandc.gc.ca/eng/1100100034806/1100100034808#a09-1.

46 *Mohawks of the Bay of Quinte v Brant*, [2014] OJ No 3605, paras 79–97.

pledge, mortgage, attachment, levy, seizure, distress or execution" at the instance of "an Indian or a band" (section 89 (1)).

More recently, in litigation between band members or between the band and some of its members, the holder of a certificate of possession has been ordered by the court to complete the documents required for a transfer and to submit them to the Indian land registrar; failing this, he or she would be deemed to have consented to this operation. The *Indian Act* still applies, including the requirement that the minister approve the proposed transaction.[47] The Court can retain its jurisdiction to deal with an eventual refusal of the minister.[48] These orders are possible because no provincial law is relied upon.[49] If this is allowed under the *Indian Act*, the *Family Homes Act*, whose objective is to give additional powers to First Nations, must authorize them to provide for the forced transfer of lands in the lawful possession of an Indian.

Finally, it should be noted that the movable or personal property of Indians is subject to provincial laws of general application that do not conflict with federal legislation, treaties, or band by-laws.[50] This allows the courts to divide the value of matrimonial interests for all types of property, whether or not they are situated on a reserve, and to order a compensatory payment; however, it is not possible to order the transfer of an interest in a home, or the expulsion of a spouse.[51] The *Family Homes Act* is clearly intended to replace these rules for lands and structures situated on the reserve, but not for personal property.

B. Regulating Residency

Although band council powers are often compared to those of a municipality, they have been slightly widened in the past decades, in particular for rules governing residency and residence. A purposive reading of the *Indian Act* shows that band councils can regulate occupation or possession of the family home, at least on a temporary basis.

The right to reside on an Indian reserve is regulated by the *Indian Act* in a manner that is often problematic for ex-spouses who are not band members, although a band council could decide to accommodate their particular situation. More importantly, the power to adopt

---

47 *Mohawks of the Bay of Quinte v Brant*, paras 28, 32–41.
48 *McMurtrer v McMurtrer*, [2016] OJ No 3798 (SC); security for spousal support payment awarded under the *Divorce Act*, paras 210–30.
49 *Mohawks of the Bay of Quinte v Brant*, paras 38–41.
50 RSC 1985, c I-5, s 88.
51 See note 25.

a regulation concerning the "residence of members and other persons on the reserve" (section 81 (1) (p.1)), as well as "the rights of spouses or common-law partners and children who reside with members of the band" (section 81 (1) (p. 2)), seems wide enough to regulate the transfer of a dwelling. This result seems more difficult to achieve for a non-member.[52]

1. RESIDENCY RIGHTS

A band member residing on the reserve is formally recognized the right to live there with his or her dependent children, or those under his or her custody (*Indian Act*, section 18.1), though this is assumed elsewhere for non-member spouses (section 81 (1) (p. 2)). Although theoretically, an "Indian" from a different band could be granted a right of lawful possession by the band council (see section 20 (1)), this does not guarantee a right to reside on a reserve. Indeed, losing the latter will result in the obligation to transfer a certificate of possession to a band member or to the band itself (section 25). Furthermore, section 28 (1) of the *Indian Act* voids any agreement purporting to authorize a non-member to reside on a reserve or to exercise any right upon it. Under section 28 (2), the minister may issue a permit granting such a right for a period not exceeding one year or, with the consent of the band council, for a longer period. A non-member ex-spouse may be forced to leave a reserve because of the combined effect of a separation and section 28, even if he or she belongs to another band. Of course, administrative law safeguards can still come into play. For instance, in one case, a non-member residency permit was revoked after hearings were held in accordance with a residency by-law. However, the council and the appeal board gave no reasons to support their conclusion that the respondent had breached unnamed band by-laws or that her actions were "detrimental to the best interests of the First Nation"; the band's application for an eviction order was therefore dismissed.[53] The *Canadian Human Rights Act* also protects First Nation members against discriminatory decisions.[54]

---

52 See, e.g., *Bradfield v Brydges*, order for trespass against surviving spouse.

53 *Mississaugas of the New Credit First Nations v Landry*, [2011] OJ No 1435, 2011 ONSC 1345. For recent cases holding that the duty to act fairly was breached, see *Hill v Oneida Nation of the Thames Band Council*, [2014] FCJ No 841; *Hengerer v Blood Indians First Nation*, [2014] FCJ No 259, 2014 FC 222.

54 SC 1977, c 33. Until its repeal in 2008, section 67 shielded from such challenges decisions based on the *Indian Act*; see *An Act to amend the Canadian Human Rights Act*, SC 2008, c 30, s 1. See MacTaggart, "Lessons from History," 15–17; *Beattie v Canada (Attorney General)*, [2017] FCJ No 1103, 207 FCA 214.

However, a band can adopt its own membership rules (sections 10–13); in such a case, all its members will be entitled to reside on the reserve (see section 4.1). This could include persons who would not have been considered members under the Act, such as spouses. Thus a widow made an application for membership of the Sakimay First Nations No. 74, promising to renounce her original membership in another First Nation if it was successful. This change needed to be approved by the council and by a majority of Sakimay First Nations members, but no action was taken. Instead, the First Nation sought to expel the widow from the housing unit where she had lived with her husband until his death, since its housing policy restricted the right to occupy such units to band members. The motion was dismissed, since there was an arguable issue to be tried, namely whether the membership application had been dealt with fairly and in a non-discriminatory manner.[55]

Another exception to the prohibition against the residency of non-members is found in section 48 (3) (b). In cases of intestacy, the minister may order that "the survivor shall have the right to occupy any lands in a reserve that were occupied by the deceased at the time of death" (section 48 (3) (b)). The survivor is defined as a "surviving spouse or common-law partner," which need not be a member of the band (section 2). The governor in council may also make regulations for the case where more than one person can be considered a survivor (art. 50.1), but it has not done so. Somewhat similarly, the minister has broad powers to void the will of an Indian ordinarily residing on a reserve and to assume this power over one who doesn't (see sections 4 (3) and 46). He or she can refer the case to the court which is normally competent for non-Indians (section 44 (1) and (2)) and consent in writing to the enforcement of "an order relating to real property on a reserve" (section 44 (3)) – a quite exceptional power.[56] Thus the minister has a wide discretion to void the devise of a certificate of possession and, in cases of intestacy, to authorize a survivor to occupy lands situated on a reserve, even if he or she is not a band member. Therefore, it cannot be said that the policy of the Act is incompatible with the recognition of a right of temporary residence or occupation by a non-member former spouse, since widows or widowers are granted such a right. This is an important point to remember when dealing with the power to regulate "residence."

---

55 *Sakimay First Nations No 74 v Bunnie*, [2008] SK No 103, 2008 SKCA 24.

56 See, generally, Jean Leclair, "Le droit des successions autochtones: entre liberté et contrainte," in *La liquidation des successions: Collection Blais 2009*, ed. Yvon Blais (Cowansville: Yvon Blais, 2009), 1:110–14.

2. RIGHTS OF MEMBER SPOUSES OVER THE MATRIMONIAL RESIDENCE

Pursuant to section 81 (1) and (2) of the *Indian Act*, band councils are empowered to adopt by-laws for the following "purposes":[57]

(p. 1)   the residence of band members and other persons on the reserve

(p. 2)   to provide for the rights of spouses or common-law partners and children who reside with members of the band on the reserve with respect to any matter in relation to which the council may make by-laws in respect of members of the band

The power to regulate the "residence" of band members (under section 81 (1) (p. 1)) extends to the rights of their spouses or common-law partners and children who reside with them over such "residence," since this is a "matter in relation to which the council may make by-laws in respect to members of the band" (under section 81 (1) (p. 2)). It is easily applied to lands that have not been allotted to a member, in which case a by-law would supplement the managerial power over reserve lands possessed by the band council.

If the family home is in the lawful possession of one spouse, one could argue that the power to make by-laws concerning "the residence" of members and their spouses (section 81 (1) (p. 1) and (p. 2)) is distinct from the power to regulate the transfer of lands lawfully possessed. But the word *residence* can also mean a house or a dwelling.[58] It can be easily distinguished from the right to "reside on" a reserve (sections 18 (1), 25, 28, 50), which is narrower than "the residence of band members and other persons" (section 81 (1) (p. 1)). For "purposes of voting, *residence* may be defined by regulations, which implies that the word has a wider or different meaning in other contexts (section 76 (1) (e)). If section 81 (1) (p. 1) covers only the right to decide who may live on a reserve, spouses or children "who reside with members of the band on the reserve" have few if any rights left to be regulated under section 81 (1) (p. 2). Thus, this subsection is wide enough to authorize a by-law that restricts the rights of an Indian who is legally in possession of reserve lands, in order to authorize an ex-spouse to continue to reside in the family home.

However, the minister of Indian affairs and northern development, pursuant to section 82 of the *Indian Act*, has disallowed two by-laws

---

57 *An Act to Amend the Indian Act*, RS 1985, c 32 (1st Supp), s 15.

58 See Denis Blanchette and Michel Morin, "La Loi sur les Indiens et la résidence familiale: l'émergence d'un pouvoir normatif?" *Cahiers de droit* 45 (2004): 693. For a more extensive discussion, see 708–19.

attempting to regulate possession of lands on a reserve following a separation.[59] According to Tom Vincent, a lawyer of the Department of Justice of Canada, the regulatory power under subsection 81 (1) (p. 1) and (p. 2) does not extend to such matters:

> The significant limitation to the Indian Act bylaw-making power is that there is no power to regulate relationships for property regimes between band members. As a mere bylaw power, all that a band council can do is create bylaw offences and these are punishable by fine or imprisonment, which you will see under 81 (1) (r), to a maximum of $1,000 or 30 days, or both. Therefore, a band bylaw cannot dictate who can use reserve lands. It can only make provision that if someone uses reserve lands in a certain way they may be punished by fine or imprisonment.[60]

This argument is premised on the view that "the bylaw making power is not a source of local autonomy for band councils" or that it is "mostly local in nature."[61] Admittedly, historically, band councils were never empowered to deal with family law issues. But they exercise considerable powers over lands situated in a reserve. Furthermore, subsections 81 (1) (p. 1) and (p. 2) were enacted in 1985 to enlarge the scope of their regulatory powers; the wording used is wider and of a different nature than the one found in the older subsections. Thus, a by-law dealing with the residence of members certainly has the potential to "dictate who can use reserve lands," contrary to what Mr Vincent states, if only for residences on non-allotted lands. As for the "authority to establish rights between individuals," it is true that provincial matrimonial property law applies to Indians' movable or personal property, as well as to immovable or real property situated outside a reserve.[62] To that extent, there is no power to enact a comprehensive matrimonial regime, which may explain why two by-laws of this kind have been disallowed in the past by the minister. But the issue is whether the word *residence* is large enough to encompass rules dealing with immovable or real property on reserves, not whether this affects individual rights. With the repeal

---

59   House of Commons, Standing Committee on Aboriginal Affairs and Northern Development, *Evidence*, 38th Parl, 1st Sess (19 April 2005), at 11:45 am (Tom Vincent), http://www.parl.gc.ca/infocomdoc/38/1/aano/meetings/evidence/aanoev30-e .htm#Int-1235771.
60   Standing Committee, *Evidence* (Tom Vincent).
61   Standing Committee, *Evidence* (Tom Vincent).
62   See note 25.

of the power to disallow by-laws, it will be up to the courts to decide the precise meaning of that term.[63]

As for enforcement, many powers of the band council would be almost useless if they always required the imposition of a fine to be exercised. Think, for instance, of "the health of residents" (81 (1) (a)), appointing pound-keepers and regulating their duties and fees (81 (1) (e), "the construction and maintenance of ... local works" (81 (1) (f)), " survey and allotment of reserve lands ... and the establishment of a register" (81 (1) (i)) and "the construction and regulation of the use of public wells, cisterns, reservoirs and other water supplies" (81 (1) (l)). In any case, subsections 81 (2) and (3) both speak of "any other remedy and ... any penalty imposed by the by-law," while the latter subsection authorizes a court to restrain a contravention of a by-law at the instance of the band council. Thus, it cannot be said that the band council "can only make provision that if someone uses reserve lands in a certain way they may be punished by fine or imprisonment," as stated by Mr Vincent, although this may be true of the majority of the powers enumerated in subsection 81 (1). Finally, it is hard to imagine a by-law under subsection 81 (1) (p. 2) whose violation would be sanctioned only by a fine or by a term of imprisonment.

Taking an expansive view of these regulatory powers, this type of by-law could allow a court of competent jurisdiction[64] or even the band council to order the transfer of a certificate of possession to an ex-spouse who is also a band member. This would not have the effect of creating an inconsistency with the relevant sections of the *Indian Act*, in which case the by-law would be void by virtue of the introductory clause of section 81 (1). Measures of this kind seem to be implied by section 23, which deals with the case of an Indian "who is lawfully removed from lands in a reserve on which he has made permanent improvements." Obviously, an order based on a valid by-law would constitute a lawful removal. This would be subject to the power of the minister, under this same section, to order the payment of compensation for permanent improvements.

This discussion provides the background to the *Family Homes Act*. Clearly, First Nations laws can regulate the transfer of lands in the lawful possession of an ex-spouse who is a member of the band where

---

63 *Indian Act Amendment and Replacement Act, SC 2014, c 38, repealing s 82; see* Naiomi Metallic, "Indian Act By-Laws: A Viable Means for First Nations to (Re)Assert Control over Local Matters Now and Not Later," *University of New Brunswick Law Journal* 67 (2016): 211.

64 RSC 1985, c I-5. There is no power under the *Indian Act* to create such a court.

these lands are situated. Failing this, a by-law concerning the residence of spouses can fill the gap. However, we have seen that under the default regime of the *Family Homes Act*, such a transfer can occur in only three cases (section 31 (1)). Therefore, it could not be supplemented by a band by-law.

3. RIGHTS OF NON-MEMBERS SPOUSES OVER THE MATRIMONIAL RESIDENCE

Subsection 81 (1) (p. 1) speaks of the "residence of band members and other persons on the reserve," so a band council by-law can definitely authorize the residence of non-members (or, of course, prohibit it). Admittedly, in the numerous reserves confronted with a housing shortage, a narrow land base, and recurring budgetary problems, the possibility of granting a right of residence to non-members is rather theoretical. Indeed, in *Six Nations of the Grand River Council v Henderson*,[65] a by-law provided that non-member spouses could not reside on the reserve with their spouse. Taking into account the historical policy of reserving Indian lands for First Nations, it concluded that there was a socio-economic, historical, and legal justification for the by-law.[66] A similar result was reached in *Grismer v Squamish Indian Band*, where the refusal to grant membership to an adopted child with only one Squamish parent was considered discriminatory, but justified under section 1. This was because the relevant membership rule was a means of preserving the collective culture and identity of the Squamish Nation.[67]

As we have seen, a regulation authorizing the forced transfer of a certificate of possession to the other spouse who is an Indian, or ideally a member of the band to which the reserve "belongs," does not contradict expressly any provision of the *Indian Act*. It seems therefore authorized by section 81 (1) (p. 1) and (p. 2), although the minister has rejected this view, for the reasons given by Tom Vincent. On the other hand, a non-member ex-spouse loses the right to reside on the reserve and cannot be allotted lands or hold a certificate of possession. At most, a band by-law could grant him or her a right to reside in

---

65 [1996] OJ No 1953, [1997] 1 CNLR 202 (OCJ).
66 See also *Canada (Human Rights Commission) v Gordon Band Council*, [2001] 1 FC 124 (FCA); recently the Quebec Superior Court found no convincing evidence justifying a Kahnawà:ke Membership Law demanding that members marrying or living with non-members leave the reserve: *Miller v Mohawk Council of Kahnawà:ke*, [2018] QJ No. 3526, 2018 QCCS 1784.
67 *Grismer v Squamish Indian Band*.

a home for a limited time.[68] The *Family Homes Act* will provide First Nations with the opportunity to make such choices. If the laws they adopt fail to do so, the band council could step in by recognizing customary possession.

C. *Customary Possession*

In addition to regulations, band councils can regulate possession and transfer through informal or unofficial possession, which is often found on Indian reserves. Generally, "customary possession" refers to the occupation of land with the tacit acquiescence of the band council or the community, rather than to a body of rules indicating precisely how land can be possessed. Because they developed within reserves that are a creation of the colonial state, rules on customary possession should not be confused with the laws that existed prior to the first contact with Europeans or before First Nations were divided into small bands.[69] Of course, more recent norms may correspond to older ones, but this cannot be taken for granted.

Using the classification of Étienne Le Roy, rules that developed within a reserve represent popular or people's law.[70] An express or tacit decision from the band council may give rise to a right of occupation in a reserve. Often the band builds and manages houses or buildings for the benefit of its members. In other cases, individuals have been authorized informally by the band or by the community to build a house on a specific piece of land. The door is therefore wide open for specific policies, peoples' laws, or "customs." In this regard, Baxter and Trebilcock's distinction between "non-formal tenures" and "Indigenous tenures" corresponds roughly to the traditional and modern elements of popular

---

68 Assembly of First Nations, *Matrimonial Real Property on Reserves*, 21; see also Teressa Nahanee, "Matrimonial Property on Reserves: Rights and Remedies by Law or Policy," in Grant-John, *Report of the Ministerial Representative* (which limits the reach of section 81 (1) (p. 2) to customary allotments, 16–17).

69 Cameron, Graben, and Napoleon, "Role of Indigenous Law," n129; Sarah Morales and Brian Thom, "Principle of Sharing," Part III C; Napoleon and Snyder, "Housing on Reserve"; Val Napoleon, "Thinking about Indigenous Legal Orders" (paper delivered at the National Centre for First Nations Governance, 18 June 2007), http://fngovernance.org/ncfng_research/val_napoleon.pdf.

70 Alain Bissonnette, "Un regard d'anthropologue sur le dialogue entre les traditions juridiques notamment en matière de rapports au territoire," in *La justice à l'épreuve de la diversité culturelle*, ed. Myriam Jézéquel (Cowansville, QC: Yvon Blais, 2007), 207–4; see also Étienne Leroy, *Le jeu des lois, une anthropologie dynamique du droit* (Paris: LGDJ, 1999), 190–7.

law in Le Roy's classification.[71] Ultimately, the *Indian Act* says very little about this type of tenure, leaving open the possibility that "custom" will regulate it. However, the *First Nations Land Management Act* specifically provides for the protection of "interests in first nation land held ... pursuant to the custom of the first nation."[72] It is self-evident that similar customs may exist in First Nations communities that have refused to be governed by this legislation. As a consequence, Indigenous legal traditions can play an important role in addressing the consequences of a separation. Indeed, the default regime of the *Family Homes Act* applies to an "interest or right in or to a structure ... recognized by the First Nation ... or by a court order" (section 2 (1)). Again, First Nation laws can address the issue; if they are silent about this, the regulatory power of the band could be resorted to.

The Royal Commission on Aboriginal Peoples has also discussed the existence of this customary system,[73] and a substantial number of court decisions have done the same.[74] In fact, much of the information about the legal effect of customary practices has come from judicial recognition in the context of litigation on the wide discretion enjoyed by the band council when taking a decision in this regard. In passing, they sometimes mention the alleged existence of a custom, which concerns family relations (1). Nonetheless, there are some references to customary rules indicating to whom such lands should be transferred, especially after the death of their possessor (2). Less frequently, the rights of former spouses have been discussed (3).

The precise way of proving the existence of these rules has not yet been determined, but this should require the appearance of witnesses from the First Nation community, if possible elders, and the documenting of precedents. The court could then ascertain which practices are generally acceptable to the members of the band and are the object of consensus.[75] In some cases, oral tradition may provide

---

71 Jami Baxter and Michael Trebilcok, "'Formalizing' Land Tenure in First Nations: Evaluating the Case for Reserve Tenure Reform," *Indigenous Law Journal* 7, no. 1 (2009): 75–7.

72 SC 1999, c 24 s 6(1)(b)(ii), 16(4).

73 Canada, Royal Commission on Aboriginal Peoples, *Gathering Strength*, vol. 3 (Ottawa: Communication Group, 2005), c 4, s 2.

74 Flanagan and Alcantara, "Individual Property Rights," *Queen's Law Journal*, 496–7; Flanagan and Alcantara, "Individual Property Rights," *Alberta Law Review*, 1026–30.

75 *Francis v Mohawk Council of Kanesatake*, [2003] 3 CNLR 86; proof of an electoral custom, para 23.

evidence of specific entitlements.[76] Band council resolutions may also be used, as well as registers.[77] Nonetheless, it is quite possible that, absent a conscious discussion of custom, only a case-by-case approach to housing issues will emerge, rather than customs or generic norms, especially when the issue has become extremely divisive within a community.[78]

1. JUDICIAL RECOGNITION OF CUSTOMARY POSSESSION

Lawful possession of reserve lands requires an allotment by the band council and the approval of the minister (section 20). Failing this, the band council has full authority over the management of lands within the reserve. Thus, in *Squamish Indian Band v Findlay*,[79] Mr Findlay's request for an allotment was denied. Therefore, he installed his mobile home on an unoccupied parcel of land. The band obtained a declaration that he was trespassing. In appeal, Carrothers J.A. held that lawful possession vests in a member "all the incidents of ownership in the allotted part with the exception of legal title to the land." In its absence, a member cannot exercise "through possession the right of use and benefit which is held in common for all Band members" (para. 9). Indeed, upon the expiration of a licence to occupy un-allotted reserve lands, any licensee, even a band member, will be considered a trespasser.[80] Similarly, private law principles, such as equitable estoppels, trust, or simulation cannot restrict the rights of the band over reserve lands.[81]

This may allow for the development of customary rules, although their enforcement in court would be very difficult. In *Lower Nicola Band v Trans-Canada Displays Ltd*, Mr Shuter, a member of the Lower Nicola Band, purported to allow the defendant company to display billboards on an eighty-acre parcel of land situated in a reserve over which he claimed a right of customary possession.[82] Smith J. held that "traditional or customary use of land" cannot contradict the provisions of the Indian Act" (para. 151); she declared that the company was trespassing.

---

76 Flanagan and Alcantara, "Customary Land Rights," 139.
77 Flanagan and Alcantara, "Customary Land Rights," 141–2.
78 Alcantara, "Certificates of Possession," 200–1; Napoleon and Snyder, "Housing on Reserve," this volume; Baxter and Trebilcok, "'Formalizing' Land Tenure," 65–6.
79 (1981) 122 DLR (3d) 377 (BCCA), [1981] BCJ No 366 (hereinafter quoted in BCJ).
80 *Squamish Indian Band v Capilano Mobile Park*, [2012] BCJ No 526, 2011 BCCA 126, para 74.
81 *Paul v Cooper*, [2009] BCJ No 763, 2009 BCSC 515; *Sault v Jacobs*, [2001] OJ No 1996, [2001] 4 CNLR 284 (OSCJ); *Bordeau Santoro (Estate of)*, [2011] QJ No 3824, 2011 QCCS 1736, paras 24–7, 56; *Paul v Paul*, [2008] NSJ No 157, 2008 NSSC 124, para 10.
82 [2000] 4 CNLR 185 (BCSC).

In any case, such customs or traditions "have generally been associated with residential or agricultural purposes," as opposed to commercial advertising (para. 152). If the band council decided to ratify the agreement by allotting the parcel, it would be bound by a duty of fairness (para 154). Because of its fiduciary obligations, it would be required to consider the interests of all band members and their residential or agricultural needs, as opposed to commercial ones (paras 155–7). However, in a later case, these duties were satisfied, because the band council made numerous attempts to allow the administrators of the Shuter estate to provide evidence in support of their position, which it ultimately rejected (para. 157). One wonders if the Court would have dismissed a customary claim that would have been substantiated and disregarded casually by the band council.[83]

The Courts may also grant a measure of protection to persons who do not have a right to lawful possession by relying on administrative law grounds. Indeed, the band itself may challenge the validity of a purported band council resolution allocating reserve lands. This will be the case, for instance, if the rules governing the convocation of a council meeting have not been followed, the grantee is a band council member who took part in the decision-making process with his father, the latter has an interest in the project, and the newly elected band council is about to take office in a few hours.[84]

When dealing with challenges of this kind, courts sometimes discussed customary possession. Thus, in *Campbell v Cowichan Band of Indians*[85] a lot situated on a reserve had been sold by one member to another and was inherited first by his wife, then by her second husband, the applicant. According to him, his interest was generally acknowledged by members of the band and the council. No certificate of possession or other official act confirmed these transactions. After the death of his wife, her sister and nephew had built homes on this lot. In 1987 the band council allocated parts of it to relatives of these persons who, it would seem, now occupied these houses. The applicant did not receive sufficient notice of the hastily convened meeting during which the allocation was made; he was not provided with a copy of the unfavourable recommendation of the Land Investigation Committee; and he was not given an adequate opportunity to respond to this document. In effect, he was denied a fair hearing. The Federal Court held that the band

---

83 *Kelly v Leq'a:mel First Nation*, [2010] BCJ No 2519, 2010 BCSC 1801.
84 *Kamloops Indian Band v Gottfriedson*, (1981) 21 BCLR 326 (BCSC), [1980] BCJ No 551 (hereinafter quoted at BCJ).
85 [1988] 4 CNLR 45 (FCTD).

council had breached its duty to act fairly. Thus, he was given another chance to argue that the band should formally recognize his customary possession of land or, at the very least, a right of occupation tacitly acknowledged by other band members.

In *Many Guns v Siksika Nation Tribal Administration*,[86] the Court emphasized strongly the continued existence of customary rules. The band was found to have been negligent in maintaining a community pasture. It replied that the Crown, as the entity holding legal title to the reserve, had the power to make decisions concerning legal dispositions of its lands and should have been made a defendant for this reason. But in reality, the pasture was used by livestock owners and band members on the basis of an informal agreement with the band administration. The issue was whether this could be done without a specific authorization under the *Indian Act*. Judge Mandamin started with the proposition that Aboriginal title includes the capacity of a First Nation to make decisions about the use of lands, whether through its chiefs and council or through other administrative structures it has chosen. In his view, the same is true for interests in reserve land, especially when they are occupied according to a custom of the First Nation (i.e., no certificates of possession have been granted), as was the case on this reserve. It followed that the Siksika Nation could create a community pasture but, on the other hand, that it would be liable for its negligence in operating it. Here again, the responsibility of the band council over unallocated reserve lands is reaffirmed.

The band council can also formulate its own policy, without necessarily adopting a by-law or a law under the *Family Homes Act*. In one case, it argued that banishment was a sanction recognized by custom, but no elders were called to testify, nor was evidence produced to support this assertion. Therefore, the Court held that only a by-law adopted pursuant to the *Indian Act* could authorize such punishment.[87] However, with appropriate evidence, it may have recognized it. There is also the possibility of writing down and revising the custom, which is regularly done for the customary selection of band councillors.[88] Such a

---

86 [2003] AJ No 1182, (Prov Ct), paras 80–6.
87 See *Gamblin v Norway House Cree Nation (Band Council)*, [2002] FCJ No 2132 (TD).
88 See especially Gordon Christie, "Culture, Self-Determination and Colonialism: Issues around the Revitalization of Indigenous Legal Traditions," *Indigenous Law Journal* 6 (2007): 13–29; Sébastien Grammond, "The Reception of Indigenous Legal Systems in Canada," in *Multijuralism: Manifestations, Causes, and Consequences*, ed. Albert Breton (Aldershot: Ashgate Publishing, 2009), 45; Ghislain Otis, "Elections, Traditional Governance and the Charter," in *Aboriginality and Governance: A Multidisciplinary Perspective*, ed. G. Christie (Penticton, BC: Theytus Books, 2006), 220.

"custom," of course, takes the form of provisions that are quite similar to mainstream legal norms. Nonetheless, their contents may reflect, at least in part, traditional values, such as by providing for a council of elders or of family representatives. In this regard, some cases provide interesting examples of customs concerning the occupation of lands by family members.

2. JUDICIAL RECOGNITION OF CUSTOMS CONCERNING THE TRANSFER
OF LANDS WITHIN FAMILIES

In addition to cases where courts have recognized customary possession, there are numerous cases where the application of customary rules are raised by one or both of the parties and the judgments provide detail their application in a community, though the judges do not give them express legal effect.

For instance, the judgment in *MacMillan v Augustine* illustrates both the extent of the discretion conferred on the band council and the difficulty posed by the recognition of customary rules.[89] In that case, the band council allocated the property of a deceased member to one of her grandsons, Mr MacMillan, who abandoned it after four years. A granddaughter, Mrs Larry, was then allowed to live in it. According to another grandson, Mr Augustine, she gave him permission to enter the premises. Subsequently, according to the affidavit of Chief Ginnish, the majority of her aunts and uncles agreed with her suggestion that the house be allocated to her cousin MacMillan. The band council adopted a resolution to this effect. It asked that Mr Augustine be ordered to vacate the property. No ministerial approval or certificate of possession was ever requested.

In an affidavit, Mr Augustine alleged that there had been no consultation of his brothers and children; furthermore, in his opinion, there was no "no customary practice or written housing policy that support[ed] the reallocation of a property of one family member over another at the whim of only a few distant family members." According to letters signed by the chief, the council had a policy of supporting "the wishes of the family in regards to disposition of family homes" (paras 8 and 28). This was perhaps considered a custom by some members. Riordon J. held that "technically the respondents are trespassers even though they have occupied the property in question with the apparent acquiescence of the Band or its Council" for five years. However, they would be entitled to compensation under section 23 of the *Indian Act* (para. 47).

---

89   [2004] 3 CNLR 170 (NBQB).

The Court thus gave effect to a band council resolution that seemed to follow a band custom, although this latter fact played no part in its reasoning.

In *Dale v Paul*,[90] the holder of a certificate of possession had allowed her brother to stay in her house. Later, the latter's wife separated from him. After his death, the widow moved back into the house, alleging that he had told her she would be entitled to do so. Her former sister-in-law, who still held the certificate of possession, asked that she deliver the property to her, but the widow relied on a "native custom that this type of oral bequest be honoured" (para. 2). However, there was absolutely no evidence that such a bequest was "recognized by either Indian custom or legislation" (para. 6); the question whether this was so in certain circumstances was left open (para. 3). Here again, the possibility that an Indian custom might apply was considered, but the issue did not arise on the facts of the case.

Somewhat similarly, in *Hepworth v Hepworth*, the ex-husband had never requested a certificate of possession for the lot on which he and his former wife had built a house and lived for over ten years, perhaps because of surveying fees. Since obtaining a certificate of possession appeared to be a mere formality and the band had expressed no concerns regarding the use or possession of the home, the Nova Scotia Court of Appeal considered this property interest a matrimonial asset whose value was subject to division between the parties.[91]

Though concerned with a lease, the case of *Vollant v Innu Takuaikan Uashat Mak Mani-Utenam*[92] offers an example of a conflict between traditional customs and Canadian law. Petitioner David Vollant, together with his father, entered into a written lease with the band council for a house in a reserve. After his father died, he was evicted and her sister moved in. She offered to let him live with her on condition that he stop drinking, a demand supported by other siblings, since he had regularly fallen asleep while smoking, thus running the risk of starting a fire. Nonetheless, he asked for an interlocutory injunction ordering his return into a house, as well as her expulsion from it.

According to the local housing agent, the band council always "respected the will of the family when the lessee of a house dies intestate and has no surviving spouse" (my translation). The general director of the band council also explained that there was a custom regarding the right to inhabit a rented house after the lessee dies. In such a case, the

---

90 [2000] AJ No 751 (AQB).
91 2012 NSCA 117 (CanLII).
92 *Vollant v Innu Takuaikan Uashat Mak Mani-Utenam*, JE 95-936 (QSC), 2.

band council would respect a family consensus or the will expressed by the lessee prior to his death. The respondent's affidavit was to the same effect.

The Court held that the petitioner appeared to be entitled to the order sought, since he was a co-lessee. It added that the Band Council must abide by the clauses contained in the lease and that it could not "act under the pretence of the [best] interest or the justification of the 'reasonable person' [bon père de famille]" and "do what it wants, as it wants, when it wants" (my translation). Nonetheless, the Court refused to order the return of the petitioner in the house, since "he could suffer serious and irreparable harm, because his current situation regarding alcohol leads one to fear that he will make some irresponsible gesture."[93] So, even though the Court proclaimed that the *Civil Code* was applicable to the lease, because of safety concerns, it declined to grant an injunction and reached a result analogous to what the Innu custom provided (i.e., the will of the family should be respected). Incidentally, the rule in question was quite similar to the one described in *Macmillan v Augustine*[94] and *Dale v Paul*.[95]

These cases recognize a very broad power to manage reserve lands that are not in the lawful possession of an Indian. They also allude to customary rules but make no pronouncement on the issue, in the absence of satisfactory evidence. This could allow a band council to implement a new policy, to act according to traditional values, or to enforce long-established customs.[96] Indeed, the adoption of a land use policy may mark the end of the era when "band members simply marked the land that they would occupy."[97] This document could include rules concerning the occupation of non-allotted reserve lands following a separation. However, the decision of a band council to deprive a member of lands he or she has possessed for a long time may be unimpeachable from an administrative point of view (although courts will no doubt scrutinize the proceedings very closely, to make sure that the duty to act fairly has been fulfilled).[98] Under the *Indian Act*, the only remedy, in such a case, appears to be a request that the minister, in his or her discretion, order compensation for permanent

---

93 *Vollant v Innu Takuaikan Uashat Mak Mani-Utenam*, 5–6 (translation by the authors).
94 [2004] 3 CNLR 170 (NBQB).
95 [2000] AJ No 751 (AQB).
96 Flanagan and Alcantara, "Customary Land Rights." (Indeed, lands held under customary possessions could be allocated through contracts, 155).
97 *Sayers v Batchewana First Nation*, [2013] FCJ No 878, 2013 FC 82, paras 7, 24.
98 See, e.g., *Johnstone v Mistawasis First Nation*, [2003] SJ No 366 (SKQB), (QL).

improvements to the property (section 23). This obviously is very problematic for ex-spouses. We have seen that the default regime of the *Family Homes Act* addresses the issue, but if First Nations laws are silent on the subject, the powers implicitly recognized by the *Indian Act* are still relevant.

3. CUSTOM AND POLICIES CONCERNING EX-SPOUSES

Overall, even though they have been eager to support the jurisdiction of band councils, courts have sometimes mentioned the existence of customary rules and rendered decisions that did not contradict them, more by accident than by design. In this regard, many First Nations have a tradition of letting family members reassign lands possessed customarily, and some, though by no means all, allow a parent with dependent children to remain in a house after a separation. This provides examples of the types of rules First Nations could adopt in their laws, policies or regulations.

In *Membertou Band Council v Johnson*, the Membertou Band entered into a renovation loan agreement with Simon Marshall Jr, which included a lease of the house to be renovated. Following repayment of the loan, a certificate of possession was to be issued. After the parties separated, Mrs Johnson, the common-law wife of Mr Marshall, continued to make the monthly payments. The three children remained in her custody until 19 December 2002, when Marshall was awarded sole custody of two of them and joint custody of the third. But, by the time of the hearing, Mrs Johnson was the custodial parent of the only dependent child, the others having come of age.

The band council claimed it had a policy dictating that, in cases of separation, the parent who exercised care and control of a majority of the children would be entitled to remain in the dwelling. In 2003 it requested that Mrs Johnson be ordered to vacate the premises. The Court noted that the band council had a duty to administer the *Indian Act* in a fair manner. Because Mrs Johnson was in charge of the sole dependent child, her eviction would seem to run afoul of the band's stated (but unwritten) policy. Furthermore, she had been making all the payments pursuant to the loan agreement since 1999, so the fairness or equity of expelling her seemed "to say the least, debatable."[99]

At this point, there was a serious issue to be tried, the band would not suffer irreparable harm if the respondent remained in the house. and the balance of inconvenience favoured the status quo. The band's

---

99 *Membertou Band Council v Johnson*, para 15.

application for an interlocutory injunction was therefore denied. Hence the Court used its discretion to thwart what appeared to be an attempt to favour a band member unduly, in direct contradiction to the official band policy. This comes close to recognizing the band policy, although the issue could not be resolved at this preliminary stage.

Many communities have grappled with the issues surrounding the separation of spouses. In British Columbia, Professor Val Napoleon has conducted interviews in Metlakatla, Kitselas, Kitsumkalum, which are Tsimshian communities, and in Lheidli T'enneh, a Carrier Nation.[100] Most interviewees felt that the custodial parent, often a woman, should stay in the family residence until all the children have come of age or have completed their education. In Metlakatla and Kitsela, however, a band member was given priority over a non-member for possession of the house. In Kitsumkalum, if the custodial parent was a non-member, the certificate of possession would apparently be transferred to the oldest status child. In Kitsela, in one case, a non-member widow belonging to another band was evicted from her home by the children of a first marriage; nonetheless, she was provided with a house by the band. Professor Napoleon points out that in some communities the informal dispute resolution provided by elders has disappeared. Nowadays, it may happen that elders have abused children and that the motivation behind traditional rules is no longer relevant.[101] Housing and land issues also have generated a lot of tension and conflicts.[102] In this context, customary norms might very well reflect the position of power and dominance traditionally occupied by men, although not in Lheidli T'enneh or Kitselas.[103]

After holding "regional discussions sessions" in 2006, the Assembly of First Nation (hereafter AFN) summarized the situation in some reserves for ex-spouses who did not have a certificate of possession for the family home. The housing policy of the Mistawasis states that in cases of separation, "the title of ownership ... shall be made to that spouse who shall have the greatest need for the said unit in the opinion of the Housing Authority."[104] The Squamish Nation has decided that non-member spouses who are primary caregivers of minor children or dependent adults will be allowed to remain on the reserve until these persons are able to care for themselves. Otherwise, the non-member

---

100 Napoleon and Snyder, "Housing on Reserve."
101 See Napoleon, "Thinking about Indigenous Legal Orders."
102 Napoleon and Snyder, "Housing on Reserve."
103 Napoleon and Snyder, "Housing on Reserve," 145, 147.
104 Assembly of First Nations, *Matrimonial Real Property on Reserves*, 14–17.

must vacate the residence within three months of the separation.[105] In Manitoba, custom councils, justice committees, and elders' councils "have been grappling with this issue through their own means," although band councils or housing authorities are also forced to deal with the problem.[106] In the Maritimes, traditional dispute resolution mechanisms, such as elders' councils, are used.[107] In Quebec, some housing policies give priority of residence and possession of the family home to the custodial parent; in some case, this ceases when all the children come of age.[108] This is evidence, if any was needed, that First Nations can establish and have established their own rules to deal with the consequences of a separation where lands are possessed under a customary tenure.

D. Lease of Dwellings, between Federal and Provincial Law

It is important to realize that the *Indian Act* explicitly allows Indians and band council to enter into leases, which run the gamut from large-scale development projects to seasonal rights on uncultivated lands (1). Although it is often stated that inter-jurisdictional immunity prevents the application of provincial laws (including protective measures for ex-spouses) to Indian lands, because they fall under federal jurisdiction, this assertion is debatable (2). In any event, Parliament may decide to adopt these rules, even implicitly, in which case they will apply if they are not in conflict with the provisions of the *Indian Act*. If this is the case, under provincial law, leases may incorporate band council policies and perhaps customs, opening the door for specific rules dealing with occupation of a dwelling after a separation (3).

1. TYPES OF LEASES UNDER THE *INDIAN ACT*
As a general rule, the creation of lease or another interest in reserve lands requires a formal designation by the band, assented to by a majority of electors voting at a referendum held for this purpose (sections 38 (2), and 39.1 and 40.1).[109] Designated lands may be leased or managed

---

105 Assembly of First Nations, *Matrimonial Real Property on Reserves*, 14–17.
106 Assembly of First Nations, *Matrimonial Real Property on Reserves*, 17.
107 Assembly of First Nations, *Matrimonial Real Property on Reserves*, 22.
108 Assembly of First Nations, *Matrimonial Real Property on Reserves*, 25.
109 From 2008 to 2012, this operation was known as a "surrender." See *St Mary's Indian Band v Cranbrook (City)*, [1997] 2 SCR 657 (prior to 1988, a designation was called a conditional surrender); *Re Park Mobile Homes Sales ltd and Le Greely*, (1978) 85 DLR (3d) 618 (BCCA) (in one case, provincial laws were held to apply). But see

by the minister or a delegate (see sections 53–6). Such leases, or other interests in the lands, can be assigned, with ministerial approval (section 54). Obviously, they are made for development purposes. Section 89 (1.1) provides that "a leasehold interest in designated lands is subject to charge, pledge, mortgage, attachment, levy, seizure, distress and execution."[110] Therefore, the *Family Relations Act* of British Columbia has been held to apply to such lands.[111] More generally, this seems a clear indication that provincial laws will generally apply to such lands, in the absence of conflict with the *Indian Act*.

However, on Indian reserves, dwellings are often leased or even occupied without any rent being paid. Section 28 (1) prohibits any contract or agreement entered into by a band or a member that purports to authorize the occupation or use of reserve lands by a non-member, unless the minister has authorized it in writing, with the consent of the band council if the term exceeds one year. This implies that leases between a band and its members, or between the latter, are not subject to the requirement that leases be preceded by a formal designation approved by a majority of band electors, a very cumbersome process (see sections 37 (2) and 38 (2)).[112] It is also conceivable that the lease of a dwelling could be entered between a non-member spouse and the band council, with the appropriate approvals (section 28 (2)). This raises the question of which rules would govern this agreement.

The issue arises under other sections of the *Indian Act*, such as 58 (3), which allows the minister to lease lands that are in the lawful

---

Sechelt Indian Band v British Columbia (Manufactures Home Park Tenancy Act), [2013] BCJ No 1168, 2013 BCCA 262 (in the case of leases in general), leave to appeal refused, [2013] SCCA No 353 (a case based on different legislation); Morin v Canada, [2000] FCJ No 1074 (FCTD), appeal quashed, [2003] FCJ No 1902; Millbrook Indian Band v Northern Counties Residential Tenancies, (1978) 84 DLR (3d) 174 (NSSC), aff'd on other grounds Attorney-General for Nova Scotia v Millbrook Indian Band, (1978) 93 DLR (3d) 230 (NSCA); Reference re Stony Plain Indian Reserve No 135, (1982) 130 DLR (3d) 636 (ABCA) (answer to question 2.1); Toussowasket Enterprises Ltd v Matthews, [1982] BCJ No 293 (discussing removal of unused vehicles and restoration of the water supply). See especially Kerry Wilkins, "Negative Capability: Of Provinces and Lands Reserved for the Indians," Indigenous Law Journal 1 (2002): 95–7.

110 See generally James I. Reynolds, "Taking and Enforcing Security under the Indian Act and Self-Government Legislation," Banking and Finance Law Review 18 (2002): 37–65.

111 Dunstan v Dunstan, [2002] BCJ No 433, 2002 BCCS 335, paras 15–24.

112 Kwikwetlem Indian Band v Cunningham, [2009] BCJ No 1523, 2009 BCSC 1032; Skyway Indian Bank v James, [2005] BCJ No 455, 2005 BCCS 300 (as well, when a band member has not complied with "the terms of an agreement surrounding the advance of funds..., the Band is entitled to terminate [the member's] right to use the land whether she be regarded as a tenant at will or a licensee").

possession of an Indian, at the latter's request, without the consent of the band or a formal designation. Corporations have been allowed to enter into a lease under this subsection.[113] As an aside, it should be noted that the discretion of the minister is not absolute. In one case, a lease he approved for development would have allowed non-members to reside on a reserve whose water, sewer, and storm-water systems could not accommodate this expansion. The lease was also retroactive to avoid a band by-law and was strenuously opposed by the band council.[114] The officer who analysed these objections "made a general and condescending statement" and ignored these problems, so the decision of the minister was set aside and the lease was declared void. In any case, section 58 (3) seems to have been used mainly for development purposes; arguably, it could allow the leasing of a family residence. But the *Indian Act* does not regulate this kind of agreement either.

2. INTER-JURISDICTIONAL IMMUNITY

In the absence of some specific provision, it would seem natural to apply provincial or territorial law to define the rights and obligations flowing from "leases."[115] However, because section 91.24 of the *Constitution Act, 1867* grants exclusive jurisdiction to Parliament over "Indians, and Lands reserved for Indians," the extent to which the latter can be subject to provincial law remains unclear. As a general rule, Indian reserves are not considered "enclaves" and provincial laws can apply there.[116] However, the courts have carved out numerous exceptions to this principle, because of "interjurisdictional immunity."

---

113 *Canada v Boyer*, [1986] 2 FC 393 (FCA) 403, leave to appeal refused, (1986) 72 NR 365. See *Opetchesaht Indian Band v Canada*, [1997] 2 SCR 119 (for the right of non-members to enter into a section 58 (3) lease, see the *obiter* of Major J. at para 44). It remains possible that subsection 58 (3) applies only to uncultivated or unused lands, as do the other subsections of section 58.

114 *Tsartlip Indian Band v Canada (Minister of Indian Affairs and Northern Development)*, [1999] FCJ No 1767, [2000] FC 314.

115 See *Interpretation Act*, RSC 1985, c I-21, art 8.1. (Both the common law and the civil law are equally authoritative and recognized sources of the law of property and civil rights in Canada and, unless otherwise provided by law, if in interpreting an enactment it is necessary to refer to a province's rules, principles, or concepts forming part of the law of property and civil rights, reference must be made to the rules, principles, and concepts in force in the province at the time the enactment is being applied.)

116 *Cardinal v Attorney General of Alberta*, [1974] SCR 695; *Kitkatla Band v British Columbia (Minister of Small Business, Tourism and Culture)*, [2002] 2 SCR 146, 2002 SCC 31, paras 74–7.

Most notably, in *Derrickson v Derrickson*, the Supreme Court of Canada held that the "right to possession of lands on an Indian reserve is manifestly of the very essence of the federal exclusive legislative power." This precluded the application of the *Family Relations Act* of British Columbia, inasmuch as it "regulates who may own or possess land" situated on a reserve.[117] This principle applies to all these lands, whether or not they are in the possession of an individual Indian. Chouinard J. added that "orders dealing with ownership, right of possession, transfer of title, partition or sale of property, severance of joint tenancy are ... in 'actual conflict' with ... the Indian Act," but these words could well be used to describe inter-jurisdictional immunity.[118] In *Paul v Paul*, a trial judge relied on the same British Columbia legislation to grant "interim possession of the matrimonial home" on an Indian reserve to the wife, following the separation of the parties. Chouinard J. held that this could not be done, since the provisions "relating to occupancy of the family residence on the reserve" were in "actual conflict" with the provisions of the *Indian Act*; however, he did not discuss inter-jurisdictional immunity.[119] Of course, with the advent of the *Family Homes Act*, or First Nations laws adopted pursuant to its authority, provincial laws can play no role in determining the rights of ex-spouses to reserve lands or to a share of their value.[120]

Since then, the Supreme Court has held that "interjurisdictional immunity is of limited application and should in general be reserved for situations already covered by precedent," since legal vacuums "generally speaking ... are not desirable."[121] Therefore, provincial legislation will be held inapplicable only if it "impairs" the core jurisdiction of Parliament; it is not enough that it will "affect" this legislative power.[122] In the case of Aboriginal peoples, courts have used this reasoning "to

---

117 *Derrickson v Derrickson*, para 296.
118 *Derrickson v Derrickson*, para 302.
119 *Paul v Paul*, para 311.
120 *Tsilhqot'in Nation v British Columbia*, 2014 SCC 44, [2014] 2 SCR 256. The preamble of the Act states that provincial laws pertaining to "certain family law matters" are not applicable on First Nation reserves and that Parliament "wishes to advance the exercise ... of First Nations law-making power over family homes on reserves and matrimonial interest or rights." Provincial laws cannot apply in this context because this would frustrate Parliament's purpose, which is impermissible under the doctrine of paramountcy (at para 130). *Alberta (Attorney General) v Moloney*, 2015 SCC 51, [2015] 3 SCR 327.
121 *Canadian Western Bank v Alberta*, [2007] 2 SCR 3, 2007 SCC 22, paras 77, 44.
122 *Canadian Western Bank v Alberta*, para 48. But see *Quebec (Attorney General) v Canadian Owners and Pilots Association*, [2010] 2 SCR 536, 2010 SCC 39 (see the expansive view of "impairment" of the majority, paras 42–8).

shield Aboriginal peoples and their lands from provincial legislation of general application affecting certain aspects of their special status," notably "relationships within Indian families and reserve communities, matters that could be considered absolutely indispensable and essential to their cultural survival."[123] This seems to refer to issues such as adoption.[124]

Most courts and tribunals have held that since "occupation is part of possession," provincial law cannot govern automatic renewals, eviction orders, and termination of tenancy, as opposed to issues related to rent or claims in damage.[125] Instead, the "common law of landlord and tenant" that preceded modern residential tenancies legislation should be resorted to.[126] Therefore, in the absence of a covenant or condition concerning notice, a band was allowed to terminate a lease unilaterally.[127] This illustrates perfectly the problem raised by an expansive view of inter-jurisdictional immunity: it throws back the parties on outdated rules that have long been discarded by provincial or territorial legislatures. However, Quebec courts have generally applied the rules of the *Civil Code* governing residential leases.[128]

It should be observed that leases entered into with developers create freely transferable interests in lands (through assignments, for instance) or immovable real rights that may be held by non-members. For this reason, the lands in question must be designated (section 37 (2)). Their

---

123 In *Canadian Western Bank v Alberta*, paras 40, 61, the majority writes that *Paul v Paul* held that "provincial family law could not govern disposition of the matrimonial home on a reserve," but the issue concerned the interim possession of a family home (see para 12).

124 *Natural Parents v Superintendent of Child Welfare*, [1976] 2 SCR 751.

125 *Anderson v Triple Creek Estates*, [1990] BCJ No 1754 (BCSC); *Lightfoot v Big Canoe*, [2001] ORHTD No 119; *Little Leaf v Houle*, [2011] AJ No 234, 2011 ABPC 31; *Order under Section 69, Residential Tenancies Act, 2006* [2013] 1 CNLR 345; *Attorney-General for Nova Scotia v Millbrook Indian Band*, (1978) 93 DLR (3d) 230 (NSCA) (note that it often was unclear whether section 28 of the *Indian Act* applied, in which case the court would automatically refuse to enforce the pretended lease); *Nolan v Charlie*, [2002] ORHTD No 71.

126 *Matsqui Indian Band v Bird*, [1992] BCJ No 1887, [1993] 3 CNLR 80.

127 *Matsqui Indian Band v Bird*.

128 *Vollant v Innu Takuaikan Uashat Mak Mani-Utenam*, JE 95-936 (QSC); *Houle St-Aubin c Landry*, [1999] RJQ 605 (CQ), (where the issue was not discussed, because the attorney general had not been given proper notice at 606); *Awashish c Conseil des Atikamekw de Wemotaci*, [2007] JQ No 14936, 2007 QCCS 6194; *Conseil des Montagnais du Lac-Saint-Jean c Cleary*, (Régie du logement, Roberval, no 04-050901 002 P 071207, le 7 juillet 2009, Me Claire Courtemanche, régisseure); David Schulze, "Le droit applicable au bail résidentiel dans les réserves indiennes" (2006) 36 RGD 381–433, at 396–8, 425–6.

regulation is part of the core jurisdiction of Parliament, because a les-see or licensee may deplete the resources or change the features of the land permanently. This is also the case with the cutting of timber or the extraction of minerals. These activities require a designation or the consent of the band and can be regulated by the minister (section 57).[129] In my view, only through federal legislation could provincial or territorial laws apply in such a case.

It seems possible to distinguish between two types of rights recognized by the *Indian Act:* lawful possession of lands, which has an indefinite duration, on the one hand, and occupation for residential purposes during a limited term, on the other. If this is so, the latter situation is not part of the core legislative power over Indian lands, and provincial laws can apply in the absence of federal legislation. There are no lasting consequences for the lands in this case. Nothing prevents band members from entering into such contracts, although they may have to respect the limits imposed by the *Indian Act* on their transfer or their sublease to non-members. It is hard to see how the application of provincial or territorial rules concerning residential tenancies to band members would, in and of themselves, impair the ability of Parliament to exercise its power over Indian lands.[130] Such an intrusion is not "significant or serious."[131] In other words, the total exclusion of laws concerning residential leases would serve no useful purpose and there should be no interjurisdictional immunity in this regard.

However, in 2014 the Supreme Court of Canada decided that "the doctrine of interjurisdictional immunity should not be applied in cases where lands are held under Aboriginal title."[132] Rather, "provincial laws

---

129 See *Indian Mining Regulations*, CRC, c 956, s 4; *Indian Timber Harvesting Regulations*, SOR/2002-109; *Indian Timber Regulations*, CRC, c 961, s 25.

130 See Leclair, "Le droit des successions autochtones"; see also Jean Leclair and Michel Morin, "Peuples autochtones et droit constitutionnel," in *Droit constitutionnel*, ed. Stéphane Beaulac and Jean-François Gaudreault-DesBiens (Montreal: LexisNexis Canada, 2012), 15.

131 *Marine Services International Ltd v Ryan Estate*, 2013 SCC 44, para 64.

132 *Tsilhqot'in Nation v British Columbia*, 2014 SCC 44, [2014] 2 SCR 256, para 151. See Maxime St-Hilaire, "*Nation Tsilhqot'in c. Colombie-Britannique*, bonne décision, mauvaises raisons" (2014) 44 RGD 445; Kent McNeil, "Aboriginal Title and the Provinces after Tsilhqot'in Nation" (2015) 71:1 SCLR (2d) 67; Bruce McIvor and Kate Gunn, "Stepping into Canada's Shoes: *Tsilhqot'in, Grassy Narrows* and the Division of Powers," *University of New Brunswick Law Review* 67 (2016): 146. And see Christian Morey and Sari Graben, "Aboriginal Title in *Tsilhqot'in*: Exploring the Public Power of Private Property at the Supreme Court of Canada," this volume, for a thorough discussion of the case.

of general application, including the *Forest Act*, should apply unless they are unreasonable, impose a hardship or deny the title holders their preferred means of exercising their rights, and such restrictions cannot be justified pursuant to the justification framework" developed by the Court.[133] Thus, provincial residential laws can apply to reserve lands over which a First Nation holds an Aboriginal title. But they obviously deny the preferred means to exercise managerial rights over reserve lands and can conceivably impose a hardship. Therefore, "the government must show: (1) that it discharged its procedural duty to consult and accommodate; (2) that its actions were backed by a compelling and substantial objective; and (3) that the governmental action is consistent with the Crown's fiduciary obligation to the group."[134] To my knowledge, no consultation has ever occurred on this issue. As for a compelling and substantial interest, it must be considered "from the Aboriginal perspective as well as from the perspective of the broader public" and "must further the goal of reconciliation." Interfering with the ability of First Nations to define the terms of residential leases does not meet this objective; it bears no resemblance to the economic or environmental objectives mentioned by the Court.[135] Finally, even if the government pursues a compelling and substantial goal, its fiduciary duty includes an obligation to act in a proportionate manner. A blanket imposition of provincial laws certainly does not qualify.

What about reserve lands over which there is no Aboriginal title?[136] Theoretically, under the pre-2014 approach described above, provincial residential tenancies laws could apply.[137] This may be the kind of situations the Supreme Court had in mind when it stated that for "competing provincial and federal powers," the issue of interjurisdictional immunity could still arise.[138] However, it is well established that "aboriginal interest in reserve land" and "aboriginal title … are fundamentally

---

133 *Tsilhqot'in Nation v British Columbia*, 2014 SCC 44, [2014] 2 SCR 256, para 151.

134 *Tsilhqot'in Nation v British Columbia*, para 77.

135 *Tsilhqot'in Nation v British Columbia*, paras 84–5.

136 *Wewaykum Indian Band v Canada*, [2002] 4 SCR 245, 2002 SCC 79, para 98.

137 See *McCaleb (cob Sylver sage Trailer Park) v Rose*, [2017] BCJ No 1811, 2017 BCCA 318. The British Columbia Court of Appeal has reached the conclusion that *Tsilhqot'in* does not apply in such a context. It therefore followed its prior decision declaring the *Manufactured Home Park Tenancy Act*, SBC 2002, c 77, constitutionally inapplicable to reserve lands.

138 *Tsilhqot'in Nation v British Columbia*, at para 144; *Peter Ballantyne Cree Nation v Canada (Attorney General)*, [2016] SJ No 529, 2016 SKCA 124. According to the Saskatchewan Court of Appeal, there is simply "no room" for inter-jurisdictional immunity when Aboriginal or treaty rights are considered, paras 252–62.

similar."[139] It would certainly be desirable to establish a uniform regime in this instance. If the governance of reserve lands represents the exercise of an Aboriginal or treaty right that is simply regulated by the *Indian Act*, the reasoning would be the same as the one discussed for the infringement of Aboriginal title.[140] Therefore, provincial residential tenancies laws could not apply. But until now, the Supreme Court of Canada has been very reluctant to grant constitutional protection to self-government powers that would supplement or displace the *Indian Act*, and it has imposed a heavy evidentiary burden on First Nations claiming such powers.[141] If the inter-jurisdictional immunity analysis is still relevant, one could reject the distinction between occupation and possession of lands, on the one hand, and the leasing of a dwelling, on the other. If the result is the same for both types of situation, provincial residential tenancies laws could not apply to Indian reserves. Lastly, there remains the possibility that the *Indian Act* implicitly refers to provincial laws. In the discussion that follows, I will assume that these laws could apply to reserve lands over which a First Nation holds an Aboriginal title, but I think the objections already made would be insuperable: the federal government has not consulted First Nations, nor is it pursuing a compelling and substantial objective when it attempts to impose provincial rules on residential leases because of the wording of the *Indian Act*.

3. THE SUPPLEMENTARY ROLE OF PRIVATE LAW

If leases of dwellings in Indian reserves are covered by inter-jurisdictional immunity, Parliament can legislate to the full extent of its competence and grant a supplementary role to provincial law.[142] Precisely, the sections of the *Indian Act* just discussed rely on private law concepts without defining or qualifying them.[143] This throws the readers back

---

139 *Osoyoos Indian Band v Oliver (Town)*, [2001] 3 SCR 746, 2001 SCC 85, para 41.
140 *Grassy Narrows First Nation v Ontario*, 2014 SCC 48, [2014] 2 SCR 447. The Tsilqhot'in approach applies to treaty rights.
141 See John Borrows, "Unextinguished: Rights and the *Indian Act*," *University of New Brunswick Law Journal* 67 (2016): 1.
142 See *Cree-Naskapi (of Quebec) Act*, SC 1984, c 18. For this approach, "unless otherwise provided in the lease, provincial laws relating to the rights and obligations of lessors and lessees do not apply to a lease for residential purposes of a building situated on Category IA or IA-N land," s 131.
143 See Schulze, "Le droit applicable au bail résidentiel dans les réserves indiennes," for a thoughtful analysis of the cases of conflict between the *Indian Act* and the articles of the *Civil Code of Quebec* concerning the contract of lease; *Canadian Western Bank v Alberta*, [2007] 2 SCR 3, 2007 SCC 22, paras 69–75.

on provincial law rules. Therefore, using them cannot be said to create a conflict with the *Indian Act*.[144] This should be distinguished from the situation in *Paul*, where the trial court imposed a temporary restriction on the rights granted by a certificate of possession, which is meant to have an indefinite duration and to give prerogatives akin to those recognized to an owner.

The Federal Court seems to have assumed the applicability of provincial laws to leases of dwellings situated on Indian reserves. In *Gamblin v Norway House Cree Nation (Band Council)*,[145] the plaintiff and his partner had breached a band council resolution denying housing to, and imposing banishment on, anyone trafficking in illegal drugs or alcohol on the reserve. They had signed an undertaking to stop and desist from these illegal activities. Because there was no evidence of a customary rule allowing the imposition of banishment, the applicant was allowed to return to the reserve (but with no housing provided).[146] The Court came to the conclusion that there was no landlord-tenant situation, because no rent was due, nor was a trust created. Nevertheless, a private contract was entered into by Gamblin and the council, including the condition not to exercise illegal activities.[147] Presumably this was made on the basis of provincial law. The Court therefore recognized that housing band policies can be made part of a contract or be considered implied terms. So a band council could provide for the transfer of the lease or similar agreements in case of separation.

According to this view, a decision of a band council not to renew a lease could not be reviewed by the Court, since the power to do so and to "breach an existing contract, did not flow from any grant of authority from any power that is public in nature." It is more accurate to speak of "the First nation's inherent interest in lands and the reservation of its rights to consent [to leases] in Treaty No. 3." This does not preclude the recourse by way of action to private law remedies such as damages and specific performance.[148] The Federal Court came to the same conclusion in the decision to evict a band member from rental accommodations

---

144 *Marine Services International Ltd v Ryan Estate*, 2013 SCC 44.
145 [2002] FCJ No 2132 (TD).
146 *Gamblin v Norway House Cree Nation (Band Council)*, [2002] FCJ No 1411 (FCA). An appeal against that part of the judgment confirming the eviction was dismissed, essentially for the reasons given by the trial judge.
147 [2002] FCJ No 2132 (TD), para 41.
148 *Devil's Gap Cottagers (1982) Ltd v Rat Portage Band No 38B*, [2008] FCJ No 1018, 2008 FC 812, paras 64, 76.

belonging to the band, because no duty of fairness was owed when a party took steps to enforce a private law contract.[149]

The *Indian Act* clearly recognizes the validity of leases between band members or between one of them and the band council, without providing any guidance on the default rules that will define the rights and obligations of the parties. Furthermore, courts have regularly relied on private law in such cases. They seem also willing to recognize that customary rules and band policies can be incorporated in leases and similar agreements or supplement them. This would allow for the creation or recognition of effective and equitable dispute resolution mechanisms, preferably by establishing a process independent from the band council.[150]

Overall, it appears that lawful possession by one spouse represents the most difficult situation for First Nations who wish to regulate the consequences of a breakdown, since courts have analogized it to a right of ownership. This explains why the default regime of the *Family Homes Act* provides for their transfer only in exceptional circumstances. First Nation laws can fill this gap. If they are silent, other provisions can be resorted to, such as a bylaw on the residence of members, their spouses, and their dependent children. Additional restrictions could be imposed in the case of ex-spouses, as long as they are authorized by the Act. This could easily be done for lands held under customary possession, since they are subject to the discretionary powers of the band council, as long as the decision process is fair. In the absence of an Aboriginal title over reserve lands, provincial laws governing the transfer of a residential lease could be resorted to, either because there is no inter-jurisdictional immunity, or because *Indian Act* provisions implicitly refers to them. A band council could develop its own policy or follow traditional rules and incorporate them in a lease, especially when it exercises powers flowing from its Aboriginal title over reserve lands.

IV. Conclusion

It took twenty-seven years for Parliament to remedy the lack of protection of the interest of spouses in immovable or real property located on Indian reserves. This inaction of the federal government and of band councils exemplifies one of the worst aspects of colonialism. Under the

---

149 *Cottrell v Chippewas of Rama Mnjkaning First Nation Band*, [2009] FCJ No 369, 2009 FC 261.

150 Flanagan and Christopher Alcantara, "Customary Land Rights," 156–7; Joseph Thomas Flies Away, Carrie Garrow, and Miriam Jorgensen, "Divorce and Real Property on American Indian Reservations: Lessons for First Nations and Canada," *Atlantis* 29, no. 2 (2005): 81–91.

Indian Act lawful possession of lands on a reserve will come to an end in limited circumstances mentioned in the Act; it cannot be transferred to a non-member (whether through a sale, a gift, or a will, or as part of an estate).[151] Prior to the adoption of *Family Homes Act*, it did not seem possible to order the transfer of such lands to an ex-spouse or survivor who was not a band member. Other reserve lands are said to be regulated by "custom," which the band council has a general residuary power to manage. This allows customs to develop in reserves and even to regulate the rights of family members, including ex-spouses or survivors. Though they are not bound to do so, courts may use administrative law safeguards to annul decisions that refuse to recognize customary interests in lands. Customs may also be invoked in the case of leases. There are several issues that arise in this regard. First, the core jurisdiction of Parliament does not extend to leases of dwellings, as opposed to leases entered into for development, which require a formal designation. In the absence of federal legislation on the subject, provincial law can apply to the first category, except if reserve lands are covered by an Aboriginal title. Although the cases are contradictory, many have applied provincial laws. They have also recognized that customs or band policies can be made part of the leases and that there was no administrative law remedy if the band exercised its rights under a contract.

One possibility for affording greater protection to spouses is the adoption of band by-laws dealing with the residence of members and their spouses. The Department of Indian Affairs and Northern Development seems to have ruled out the possibility of granting rights to the family home in this manner, but with the repeal of the disallowance power of the minister, the courts may revisit the issue. Under this approach, nothing in the *Indian Act* prevents a band council from granting to an ex-spouse the right to live on lands held under customary tenure. However, for lands that are in the lawful possession of an Indian, the situation remains unclear. Though an implausible scenario, the issue may resurface if a First Nation law adopted under *Family Homes Act* is silent on the subject. The latter Act represents the government's attempt to deal with the problems confronting ex-spouses whose family homes are located on a reserve. It was adopted and debated, despite the opposition of the Assembly of First Nations and the Native Women's Association of Canada, who demanded full powers of self-government and financial support to address burning social issues that are the legacy of colonialism. It recognizes the full jurisdiction of First Nations in a limited field, the rights of spouses to the possession or occupation of family homes

---

151   RSC 1985, c I-5.

situated on reserve lands and the division of interests in them, as well as cases of domestic violence, which is a welcome development. Moreover, it leaves them free to deal with some or all of these issues. However, drafting a law in this field and organizing a vote of all members imposes high costs to communities who are often small and impoverished.

The default regime of the Act, which applies in the absence of a First Nation law, is exceedingly complex. It is true that applications for emergency protection orders are made much easier, especially in remote or semi-remote areas. Exclusive occupation orders of the family home for a definite but renewable period of time allows an ex-spouse who has dependent children to remain in the family home for an extended period of time. This fills the gap created by the inapplicability of provincial or territorial legislation to reserve lands. Furthermore, the rights held under a lease may also be transferred. On the other hand, only a superior court may make such orders. This may create accessibility problems, with the risk that non-Aboriginal judges will not be sensitive to the unique circumstances of First Nations communities, although they are required to hear representations made by the band council on such issues.

The rules governing the division of rights in reserve lands are very problematic. They allow the court to order the transfer of lands possessed by an Indian to an ex-spouse in very limited circumstances. This regime also deprives non-member spouses or survivors of any right in the value of lands underlying buildings in a reserve. Provincial laws also apply to personal or movable property situated on reserve, as well as for property located elsewhere. This will create a complex and costly juxtaposition. Finally, enforcement of court orders rendered in favour of non-members will depend on the discretion of the band council or, if it refuses or neglects to act, of the court, which seems to have little means to secure compliance of its orders.

Although discussions of all these issues should take place, first and foremost, at the local level, this does not mean that every community should debate such highly technical issues in depth. It is hoped that the Assembly of First Nations and the Native Women's Association, or a group of First Nation communities that share a common identity (such as the Mohawks, Anishnabe, etc.), will be able to agree on a model law that will facilitate the adoption of a suitable law in each community. Perhaps, after all, this will turn out to be a significant step in the direction of self-government, although it may initially be prompted by the desire to escape the cumbersome default regime put in place by the *Family Homes Act*.[152]

---

152   However, as of 14 February 2020, only 15 First Nations have enacted their own law, https://www.aadnc-aandc.gc.ca/eng/1408981855429/1408981949311.

8 Aboriginal Title in *Tsilhqot'in*: Exploring the Public Power of Private Property at the Supreme Court of Canada

SARI GRABEN AND CHRISTIAN MOREY

I. Introduction

The decision of the Supreme Court of Canada in *Tsilhqot'in Nation v British Columbia*[1] was a watershed in Canadian jurisprudence. It recognized the Aboriginal title of the Tshilhqot'in First Nation on the basis of territorial usage and it ensured that the financial benefits of land and resources will flow to the Tsilhqot'in (rather than the Crown or third parties). The Court recognized that title holders enjoy all of the "incidents" normally associated with fee simple ownership, and limited the Crown's interest in Indigenous lands to a residual form of title (with no beneficial interests). As a result, the Court has forwarded a conception of title that highlights the financial benefits of Aboriginal rights for Aboriginal peoples.[2]

But, what types of benefits does the Court have in mind? In the hope of protecting the integrity of the land for Indigenous peoples, the Court had previously forwarded the benefits of title that is *sui generis* with respect to other types of rights recognized at common law.[3] Literally,

---

1 2014 SCC 44 (*"Tsilhqot'in"*), rev'g 2007 BCSC 1700 (*"Tsilhqot'in BCSC"*), rev'g 2012 BCCA 285 (*sub nom William v British Columbia*) (*"Tsilhqot'in BCCA"*).

2 For a discussion on the progressive shifting of intergovernmental relations from political to proprietary, see P.G. McHugh, "A Common Law Biography of Section 35," in *From Recognition to Reconciliation: Essays on the Constitutional Entrenchment of Aboriginal and Treaty Rights*, ed. Patrick Macklem and Douglas Sanderson, 145–51 (Toronto: University of Toronto Press, 2016). For a discussion of the pragmatics of this shift, see Gordon Christie, "Who Makes Decisions over Aboriginal Title Lands?" *UBC Law Review* 48, no. 3 (2015): 743.

3 *Delgamuukw v British Columbia*, [1997] 3 SCR 1010 (*"Delgamuukw"*), para 190. For redefinition of *sui generis* title, see Sari Graben and Christian Morey, "Aboriginal Title and Controlling Liberalization: Use It Like the Crow," *UBC Law Review* 52, no. 2 (2019): 435.

these rights are "of their own kind." As such, most of the jurisprudence has forwarded benefits that cannot be fully characterized by reference to existing forms of interest, estate, or title recognized in the common law of property. This open definition created a possibility that the claimed authority of Indigenous peoples to govern title lands could be given legal effect. Moreover, the language, rights, and remedies employed by the Court in its construction of title has not drawn exclusively from the realm of property law. Instead, definitions of title have incorporated concepts drawn from equitable "beneficial ownership" as well as procedural remedies akin to those found in the realm of administrative law. This multi-pronged approach to title reflects the Court's confidence that the benefit of Aboriginal title (versus fee simple title) is that it is capable of recognizing and protecting the relationship and rights of Indigenous communities.

However, in reality, the moniker of *sui generis* has so far served to limit the definition and uses of Aboriginal title so that only through negotiation have Aboriginal peoples been able to exercise legislative authority in relation to title lands. Notions of territory have often been ignored in the jurisprudence. Moreover, the *sui generis* descriptor has functionally served to qualify the recognition of Aboriginal rights by limiting protection. Rather than open up the definition, the descriptor has effectively limited Indigenous control over title lands while creating rights for non-owners to participate in decision-making regarding its uses.[4]

In light of these criticisms, it is easy to see *Tsilhqot'in* as an attempt to confer the financial benefits of title without recognizing jurisdictional frameworks necessary for territorial rights. Its reliance on notions of private property could confine the definition of title to a bundle of rights analogous to those held by fee simple owners and ignore the governmental character of title claimed by Aboriginal peoples in Canada. Therefore *Tsilhqot'in* could be seen as a missed opportunity to clarify that the incidents of Aboriginal title include the right to govern.

Despite these limitations, we question whether the Court has a grander agenda in its formulation of property than that of merely ensuring the financial utility of Aboriginal title. While private property ownership certainly does not reflect the territorial nature of Aboriginal title, it is pertinent to ask if the decision aims to satisfy more than the financial goals of ownership. Is it instead possible that the Court in

---

4   Brian Donovan, "The Evolution and Present Status of Common Law Aboriginal Title in Canada: The Law's Crooked Path and the Hollow Promise of *Delgamuukw*," *UBC Law Review* 35 (2001): 69.

Tsilhqot'in is attempting to politically empower Indigenous peoples as collectives by recognizing their private control over vast tracts of lands? The clarity of the Court regarding the beneficial interest in title land, the scope of territory to be included, the commonality of holding, and the right to decide on its uses are key themes that could indicate this intention. Taken together with its trend towards using compensation as a key indicator of consultation, these characteristics authorize title-holders to directly exclude non-consensual users and indirectly impose a cost on government infringement so high as to be prohibitive or, at least a serious disincentive.

If we are correct about the Court's objective, then *Tsilhqot'in* marks the beginning of active judicial engagement with characterizing Indigenous rights to lands as simultaneously public and private, proprietary and jurisdictional, communal and individuated. As Jamie Baxter has illustrated in his chapter on social movements, what is important at this juncture of contestation is how Indigenous legal rights are framed by any actor (judicial, political, or propertied) seeking to operationalize interpretations for particular ends. We take the opportunity here to explore the indicators that the Court has consciously waded into this exercise and flag the pragmatic legal requirements for achieving territorial and jurisdictional control through private property in the final sections of this chapter.

II. *Tsilhqot'in*: Case Summary

The six bands that make up the Tsilhqot'in Nation inhabited their traditional territory – including the Nemiah valley in Northern British Columbia – for hundreds of years prior to their first contact with Europeans. Although the case that eventually became *Tsilhqot'in* began in 1990, the Tsilhqot'in have a long history of conflict with colonial authorities, throughout which they have maintained their insistence that no one should be allowed to enter or conduct development on their lands without their express permission. Like other First Nations of British Columbia, the Tsilhqot'in never signed any treaties with respect to their ancestral lands.

The *Tsilhqot'in* case did not begin with the band's decision to seek a declaration of title.[5] Rather, the case arose out of failed negotiations between the province and the Xeni Gwetin Band regarding the

---

5   Note that Aboriginal groups cannot seek relief in the form of a declaration of title as the sole basis for a court challenge, unless there is some threat to their legal interests involved: *Kaska Dena Council v British Columbia (Attorney General)*, 2008 BCCA 455.

province's plans to begin logging within the Nemiah valley. After refusing to accommodate the Xeni Gwetin's insistence on a right of first refusal for any future logging projects, the Crown elected to move forward with granting timber licences in the absence of consent. This decision led to a blockade of the only bridge into the area, a court challenge seeking to invalidate the timber licence, and ultimately an application for a declaration of title.

The case was litigated over 339 trial days.[6] In order to consider the complete range of evidence relevant to the case, Vickers J. of the Supreme Court of British Columbia travelled to the claim area, heard oral testimony from elders of the Tsilhqot'in Nation, and considered an extensive range of historical and documentary evidence. Ultimately, the judge found that the Tsilhqot'in had exercised territorial control over an area that included most of the area claimed in the pleadings, as well as additional small parcels adjacent to the claimed area. On this basis, the judge found that the Tsilhqot'in were in principle entitled to the declaration of title that they had sought but[7] declined to make a declaration of title as a result of procedural defects in the plaintiffs' pleadings.[8]

The British Columbia Court of Appeal reversed Justice Vickers's findings on evidence of title, primarily on the basis that the judge's findings used a territorial as opposed to a "site-specific" method of identifying the areas of land that were eligible for such a declaration. Drawing on the SCC's decision in *R v Marshall; R v Bernard*,[9] the Court of Appeal held that use of lands must be "intensive and regular."[10] On this view, the Tsilhqot'in would have been eligible to receive a declaration of title over specific sites that had been shown to be regularly used for specific purposes, but could not claim title over the larger network of paths, rivers, and surrounding territory that the Tsilhqot'in had relied upon in making their seasonal rounds.

The SCC decision in *Tsilhqot'in* provided the court with an opportunity to review and consolidate its previous jurisprudence on the subject of Aboriginal title. Although the case for the most part purports to follow the tests set out in *Delgamuukw*, the interpretation given to those principles in this case has significant implications for the questions of how title is to be proven, what rights it entails, when and how these rights may be infringed, and which branches of government have the power to impose such infringements.

---

6 *Tsilhqot'in*, para 97.
7 *Tsilhqot'in* BCSC, paras 959–60.
8 *Tsilhqot'in* BCSC, para 129.
9 2005 SCC 43 ("*Marshall/Bernard*").
10 *Tsilhqot'in* BCCA, paras 172–3.

In *Delgamuukw* the Court held that Aboriginal groups are eligible for a declaration of title if they can satisfy the burden of proving that their use of the land was sufficiently "regular," "continuous" (in cases where present occupation of the land is relied as proof of occupation at the time of contact), and "exclusive." As noted above, the key question distinguishing the conclusions of the trial judge and the Court of Appeal was whether courts should adopt a "site-specific" or "territorial" approach to identifying sufficiently regular use for the purposes of establishing title. In their arguments, the province of B.C. sought to rely on Kent McNeil's comment on the decision in *Marshall/Bernard*, in which he wrote that the Court "appears to have rejected the territorial approach of the Court of Appeal."[11] "In fact," the Court held, "this Court in *Marshall; Bernard* did not reject a territorial approach, but held only (at para. 72) that there must be 'proof of sufficiently regular and exclusive use' of the land in question, a requirement established in *Delgamuukw*."[12]

The province had abandoned its procedural objections in its arguments before the Supreme Court, which meant that the Court's findings constituted a sufficient basis to grant the Tsilhqot'in a declaration of Aboriginal title. Having done so, the Court set out additional principles regarding the content, or "incidents," of Aboriginal title. In the following sections we outline how *these principles* have brought Aboriginal title closer to common-law ownership in regards to proof, benefit, exclusion, alienability, and regulation.

III. The Effect of *Tsilhqot'in*

A. Proof

On the subject of "site-specific" versus "territorial" use of land, the decision in *Tsilhqot'in* purports to apply the same test as in *Marshall/Bernard*; however, the result is strikingly different. In particular, the Court in *Tsilhqot'in* overruled the decision of the Court of Appeal on the grounds that the lower court had applied a "site-specific" test, which would have required that claimants prove that their ancestors "intensively" used the claimed land.[13] In addition, the Court cited with approval Justice Cromwell's decision in *Marshall (NSCA)*, for the proposition that "the sufficiency of occupation required to establish Aboriginal title [is

---

11 *Tsilhqot'in* BCCA, para 43, citing Kent McNeil, "Aboriginal Title and the Supreme Court: What's Happening?" *Saskatchewan Law Review* 60 (2006): 281.
12 *Tsilhqot'in* BCCA, para 43.
13 *Tsilhqot'in* BCCA, para 28.

similar] to the requirements for general occupancy at common law."[14] Interestingly, the outcome and reasoning in this case are consistent with a number of points made by McNeil, who criticized the Court's decision in *Marshall/Bernard*.[15]

In *Delgamuukw*, Lamer CJ defined Aboriginal title as being established where an Aboriginal group demonstrates "sufficient" physical occupation of claimed land.[16] The Court clarified that physical occupation may be established in a variety of ways, ranging from the construction of dwellings through cultivation and enclosure of fields to regular use of definite tracts of land for hunting, fishing, or otherwise exploiting its resources. Moreover, the Court held that the evidence that could be used to establish proof of occupation should be sensitive to the specific characteristics of the First Nation and their territory, including "the group's size, manner of life, material resources, and technological abilities, and the character of the lands claimed."[17] The later cases of *Marshall* and *Bernard* both turned on the question of what constitutes sufficiently regular use for the purposes of this test (in this case, the test was applied to determine whether the claimants enjoyed Aboriginal title over sites in which they had engaged in timber harvesting).

In particular, the majority and the minority decisions differed on the question of whether, as suggested by Cromwell J.A. of the Nova Scotia Court of Appeal, it would be sufficient to demonstrate exclusive occupancy of a well-defined territory that included the cutting sites;[18] the majority characterized this as a test based on "incidental or proximate occupancy."[19] On this view, the majority held that this standard was less onerous than the correct legal standard of "regular and exclusive use."[20] Despite concurring in the result for evidentiary reasons, Lebel and Fish J.J. would have held that the majority's approach was too narrow and ran the risk of effectively ruling out claims of title made by nomadic and semi-nomadic groups.[21] In particular, the minority warned that the majority's test might have the effect of essentially declaring the territories of nomadic groups to be effectively unoccupied, which would be an unacceptable result.[22]

---

14 *Tsilhqot'in* BCCA, para 39.
15 *Tsilhqot'in*, para 43.
16 *Delgamuukw*, para 149.
17 *Delgamuukw*, para 149, quoting Slattery, "Understanding Aboriginal Rights," 758.
18 *R v Marshall*, 2003 NSCA 105, para 5.
19 *R v Marshall*, para 41.
20 *R v Marshall*, para 41.
21 *R v Marshall*, para 126.
22 *R v Marshall*, para 134.

A key difference between the majority and minority opinions in *Marshall/Bernard* was the majority's approach of attempting to translate the pre-sovereignty practices of an Aboriginal group into an appropriate modern Aboriginal right. In particular, this approach drew on the Court's reasoning in *R v Adams*[23] and *R v Coté*[24] to the effect that Aboriginal hunting and fishing rights need not be grounded in an underlying claim of title. On this view, at least some uses of land would give rise to a right that is less than full title. In particular, the majority was critical of the approach taken by Cromwell J.A., which would have held that the identification of Aboriginal title should take into account the lifestyle and cultural practices of the Aboriginal group in question. This approach would have been sensitive to whether the group's use of land was determined in part by a nomadic or semi-nomadic lifestyle. The majority of the Supreme Court held that this approach was "circular," in that it sought to tailor the modern right to fit traditional land use patterns, rather than translating the pre-sovereignty practice into a recognized Aboriginal right. However, the majority left open the possibility that nomadic and semi-nomadic Aboriginal groups could establish title to land in a future case. *Tsilhqot'in* arguably was this case.

The concept of Aboriginal title as articulated in *Delgamuukw* and *Marshall/Bernard* compared unfavourably to common-law ownership in a number of respects. First, by requiring exclusive occupation to be shown from the assertion of sovereignty, Aboriginal claimants were placed at a disadvantage with respect to common-law occupants. As Kent McNeil points out, possession gives rise to a presumption of title at common law[25] and title can be acquired through adverse possession after as little as ten years.[26] McNeil was among the first to point out that the standards of occupation and use sufficient to ground a claim to title at common law should also be sufficient to ground a claim to Aboriginal title.[27] Although the first of these disadvantages remains intact under *Tsilhqot'in*, the Court's quotation of both McNeil and Cromwell J.A. in *Tsilhqot'in* suggests a change in the Court's perspective regarding

---

23 *R v Adams* [1996] 3 SCR 101.
24 [1996] 3 SCR 139 (*"Coté"*).
25 Kent McNeil, "The Onus of Proof of Aboriginal Title," *Osgoode Hall Law Journal* 37 (1999): 793.
26 Kent McNeil, "Aboriginal Title and Aboriginal Rights: What's the Connection?" *Alberta Law Review* 36 (1997): 136; see also Brian Donovan, "The Evolution and Present Status of Common Law Aboriginal Title in Canada: The Law's Crooked Path and the Hollow Promise of *Delgamuukw*," *UBC Law Review* 35 (2001): 88.
27 McNeil, "Aboriginal Title and Aboriginal Rights," 136; see also Donovan, "Evolution and Present Status," 88.

294 Creating Indigenous Property

sufficiency of occupation; in particular, the Court's distinction between "regular use of territory" and "regular presence on or intensive use of particular tracts" shows that territorial control is now sufficient to ground a claim of Aboriginal title.[28]

B. Beneficial Uses

In *Tsilhqot'in* the Court confirmed that "Aboriginal title confers ownership rights similar to those associated with fee simple, including: the right to decide how the land will be used; the right of enjoyment and occupancy of the land; the right to possess the land; the right to the economic benefits of the land; and the right to pro-actively use and manage the land."[29]

This differs significantly from earlier definitions of Aboriginal title, where it was alternatively described as a "personal and usufructuary" right[30] or as a form of beneficial ownership in trust.[31] Usufructuary rights, which originate in the property theory of the civil law tradition, divide full ownership into the subordinate rights of *usus* (the right to use the land), *usus fructus* (the right to enjoy the fruits of the land), and *abusus* (the power to fully exhaust the benefits of the land); significantly, usufructuary rights differ from proprietary ownership (*dominium*) primarily in that they do not confer the power to fundamentally alter the character of the land, or the power to transfer or alienate ownership of the land.[32] Beneficial ownership confers only the entitlement to benefit from the land but not directly control its use. Both limit the decision-making power of the title holder.

In *Delgamuukw* the Court held that Aboriginal title holders may use the land in ways that are not limited to the practice of Aboriginal rights protected under section 35(1), subject only to the inherent limit built into the Court's definition of Aboriginal title.[33]

In addition, "Aboriginal title post-sovereignty reflects the fact of Aboriginal occupancy pre-sovereignty, with all the pre-sovereignty incidents of use and enjoyment that were part of the collective title enjoyed

---

28 *Tsilhqot'in*, para 56.
29 *Tsilhqot'in*, para 73.
30 *St Catharine's Milling and Lumber Co v the Queen* (1887) 13 SCR 577.
31 *Guerin v The Queen*, 382. Note that Justice Dickson's precise words were that Aboriginal title "does not, strictly speaking, amount to beneficial ownership," one key difference being that beneficiaries of trusts can transfer their interests to others.
32 Max Radin, "Fundamental Concepts of the Roman Law," *California Law Review* 13 (1925): 209–13.
33 *Delgamuukw*, para 125; see also "Inherent Limits," below.

by the ancestors of the claimant group – most notably the right to control how the land is used. In Tsilhqot'in, these uses are not confined to the uses and customs of pre-sovereignty times; *like other land-owners,* Aboriginal title holders of modern times can use their land in modern ways, if that is their choice."[34]

It is interesting to compare this language with the Court's other findings in *Delgamuukw* concerning the limits of Aboriginal control over title lands. In particular, the majority found that Aboriginal title was not subject to an "internal limit" and that the Crown's fiduciary duty to Aboriginal title holders would be therefore satisfied by an approach to priority. Specifically, the majority held that control over title lands could be legitimately allocated between Aboriginal and non-Aboriginal stakeholders; under this process, the government need only demonstrate that "'both that the process by which it allocated the resource and the actual allocation of the resource which results from that process reflect the prior interest' of the holders of aboriginal title in the land."[35]

This adoption of "priority" as a model for allocating rights of control over land is not in keeping with the usual common-law rules of property; in particular, while the common law recognizes no private rights of ownership over fisheries, the ownership of land in fee simple is necessarily exclusive of third-party interests. In *Delgamuukw* the majority suggested that the priority requirement might be satisfied by, e.g., "the conferral of fee simple licenses for agriculture."[36] If Aboriginal title holders are truly "like other land-owners," it is not clear why they would require fee simple licences to conduct agriculture on their own land. In light of this history, is notable that the Court in *Tsilhqot'in* describes the participatory requirement of the justification test as being "different" from the test for priority.[37] Nevertheless, it is important to note that the Court in *Tsilhqot'in* reaffirmed that the "compelling and substantial purposes" identified in *Delgamuukw* remained potentially valid causes for the infringement of title rights, subject to the (revised) test for justification.

Tsilhqot'in also establishes that the entire beneficial interest in Aboriginal title lands vests in the Aboriginal right-holders; in particular, this means that Aboriginal title lands are not "vested in the Crown" for legislation such as the B.C. *Forest Act.*[38] This would seem to suggest

---

34 *Delgamuukw*, para 75, emphasis added.
35 *Delgamuukw*, para 167.
36 *Delgamuukw*, para 167.
37 *Tsilhqot'in*, para 16.
38 *Tsilhqot'in*, para 116.

that, in the absence of legislation specifically applying to Aboriginal title lands (as opposed to Crown lands), Aboriginal groups have the right to manage and develop the resources on their own lands on their own behalf. If so, this would mark something of a departure from *Delgamuukw*, in which LaForest J. suggested that the recognition of Aboriginal title should require "that governments accommodate the participation of aboriginal peoples in the development of the resources of British Columbia."[39] However, the Court in *Tsilhqot'in* noted that it would be open to the province to redraft the *Forest Act* to affect title lands, "provided it observes applicable constitutional restraints."[40]

C. Exclusion/Infringement

In *Delgamuukw* the Court established the principle that Aboriginal title is like other Aboriginal rights in that it is capable of being justifiably infringed. The test for justifiable infringement is set out in *Sparrow* and consists of two parts. First, the infringement must be in furtherance of a compelling and substantial legislative objective. For the purposes of this test, an objective is compelling and substantial if it is directed at "the recognition of the prior occupation of North America by aboriginal peoples or ... the reconciliation of aboriginal prior occupation with the assertion of the sovereignty of the Crown."[41] Second, the infringement must be consistent with the Crown's fiduciary duties towards Aboriginal peoples.

In *Tsilhqot'in* the Court considered the question of when and how Aboriginal title may be infringed. The first part of this analysis built on the Court's earlier remarks in *Delgamuukw*; in particular, the Court reaffirmed that the Crown may infringe title for a variety of purposes, including "the development of agriculture, forestry, mining, and hydroelectric power, the general economic development of the interior of British Columbia, protection of the environment or endangered species, the building of infrastructure and the settlement of foreign populations to support those aims."[42]

However, in *Tsilhqot'in* the Court held that infringements of Aboriginal title require that government meet the "different" standard of involving Aboriginal groups in decisions made with respect to their lands.[43]

---

39 *Delgamuukw*, para 167.
40 *Tsilhqot'in*, para 116.
41 *Tsilhqot'in*, para 161.
42 *Tsilhqot'in*, 83, citing *Delgamuukw*, para 165.
43 *Tsilhqot'in*, para 16.

Significantly, the Court held that the Crown's power to infringe on Aboriginal title is bounded by its fiduciary duty to exercise this power in the best interests of Aboriginal title holders.[44] However, the Court also held that the duty to consult and accommodate applies to lands where Aboriginal title has been proven. In such cases, infringement seems to require both deep consultation and accommodation as set out in *Haida Nation*,[45] and justification as set out under the *Sparrow* test.[46]

The second aspect of infringement considered by the Court is the question of whether provincial laws may infringe upon the right of Aboriginal title. Here, unlike the other areas of the decision, the court held that the previous authorities on this point "should no longer be followed."[47] In particular, Aboriginal title is no longer protected from provincial infringement through the doctrine of inter-jurisdictional immunity. Instead, the Court elected to characterize the constitutional protections that attach to Aboriginal rights as a limit that applies equally to both the federal and provincial orders of government.[48] However, despite holding that provincial laws may in principle apply to Aboriginal title lands, the Court held that the Tsilhqot'in's territory did not qualify as "Crown lands" for the purposes of the B.C. *Forestry Act*, as the Crown is not vested with any beneficial interest in lands held under Aboriginal title.[49]

D. Inalienability

Tsilhqot'in clearly states that holders of Aboriginal title may use the land in ways that are not limited to the practice of Aboriginal rights protected under section 35(1) and are subject only to the inherent limit built into the Court's definition of Aboriginal title.[50] Despite this finding, the Court held that the use of Aboriginal title must be subject to certain restrictions in order to ensure the preservation of title land for future generations of Aboriginal beneficiaries. These three restrictions (the "inherent limit," communal ownership, and inalienability other than to the Crown) follow from the Court's earlier decisions regarding Aboriginal title as a form of beneficial ownership.

---

44 *Tsilhqot'in*, para 88.
45 *Tsilhqot'in*, para 79, citing *Haida Nation v BC (Minister of Forests)* 2004 SCC 73 ("*Haida Nation*").
46 *Tsilhqot'in*, para 77. This affirms the same principle stated in *Delgamuukw*, para 168.
47 *Tsilhqot'in*, para 150.
48 *Tsilhqot'in*, para 142.
49 *Tsilhqot'in*, para 115.
50 *Tsilhqot'in*, para 111.

Conceptually, these three requirements are related by being described as sui generis differences between Aboriginal title and fee simple ownership, and by being justified in terms of Aboriginal groups' prior occupation and systems of law. In particular, in Lamer C.J.'s analysis, both the inherent limit and the inalienability condition follow from the fact of communal ownership: because Aboriginal title is held communally, and the community is deemed to include future generations, the right must inure to the benefit of those generations. As such, actions of any party that would deprive those generations of their use of the land are prohibited.[51] This includes both actions that would irreparably alter the character of the land, and the act of alienating the land.[52] While *Tsilhqot'in* does not specifically discuss the inalienability condition, the Court does note that the inherent limit applies to Crown infringements on Aboriginal title; if such an infringement would substantially deprive future generations of the benefit of the land, it cannot be justified.[53]

The Court notes that "the usual remedies are available" for unjustified violations of Aboriginal title. This is a departure from the type of remedies contemplated in earlier cases premised on breach of fiduciary duty.[54] Rosenberg and Woodward take the usual remedies described in *Tsilhqot'in* to be the exercise of the right to ejection for trespass.[55] However, this principle does not address how *Tsilhqot'in* affects past actions that were inconsistent with Aboriginal title, or that have devalued title land in some way. A second possibility would be to interpret this remark as referencing common law remedies for regarding expropriation – in this case, it is worth noting that these rules have been replaced in most jurisdictions by statutes,[56] in which case it is not obvious what the "usual rules" are at this point. The third possibility is that the Court is referring to remedies for interference with property rights in tort.[57] This possibility raises the issue of whether protection in tort law amounts to an equivalent form of protection to that ensured by property law. In particular, where a property right is infringed and

---

51 *Tsilhqot'in*, para 127.
52 *Tsilhqot'in*, para 129.
53 *Tsilhqot'in*, para 86.
54 *Guerin v The Queen*, [1984] 2 SCR 335.
55 David M. Rosenberg and Jack Woodward, "The Tsilhqot'in Case: The Recognition and Affirmation of Aboriginal Title in Canada," *UBC Law Review* 48 (2015): 943.
56 See, e.g., *Expropriations Act*, RSO 1990, c E.26; *Expropriation Act*, RSBC 1996, c 125, etc.
57 For a thorough discussion of valuation of Aboriginal title, see Sam Adkins and Bryn Gray et al. "Calculating the Incalculable Principles for Compensating Impacts to Aboriginal Title," *Alberta Law Review* 54 (2016): 351.

subject to compensation in tort, the value assigned to the property right for the purposes of compensation is the market value, whereas a property right holder is not obligated to value property interest at market rates for the purposes of sale or development.

The most obvious case in which Aboriginal title is vulnerable to past actions is the case in which title lands are subject to conflicting ownership in fee simple. One possible indicator of how such cases may be handled is given by the Ontario case of *Chippewas of Sarnia Band v Canada (AG)*.[58] In that case, the Court of Appeal held that a grant of Crown land that was mistakenly believed to be surrendered was effective in conferring title on a good faith purchaser for value.[59]

According to McNeil, this case is troubling in that it amounts to extinguishment by "judicial discretion."[60] McNeil notes that the Court in that case found that title was not extinguished either by treaty or by explicit legislation, as is generally required.[61] Instead, the Court held that the defective grant of title was valid until challenged at law, which McNeil notes is contrary to precedent.[62] McNeil also notes that the rule that protects good faith purchasers for value is equitable in origin, and historically applied only to trust property. At common law, the traditional rule is *nemo dat quod non habeo* (one cannot give what he does not have).[63] The effect of this decision would be to refute the claim that Aboriginal title lands stand on equal footing with other forms of ownership, as they are vulnerable to defences that do not apply to fee simple properties.[64]

E. Provincial Regulation

One final way in which title holders are more like fee simple owners following the *Tsilhqot'in* decision is that both are now subject to the same powers of provincial regulation. The Court had previously held in *Delgamuukw* that inter-jurisdictional immunity would prevent provinces from extinguishing Aboriginal title, on the grounds that this would "touch the core of Indianness which lies at the heart of s. 91(24)."[65]

---

58   (2000), 51 OR (3d) 641.
59   (2000), 51 OR (3d) 641at para 292.
60   Kent McNeil, "Extinguishment of Aboriginal Title in Canada: Treaties, Legislation, and Judicial Discretion," *Ottawa Law Review* 33 (2002): 303.
61   McNeil, "Extinguishment of Aboriginal Title," 327.
62   McNeil, "Extinguishment of Aboriginal Title," 334.
63   McNeil, "Extinguishment of Aboriginal Title," 329.
64   McNeil, "Extinguishment of Aboriginal Title," 338.
65   *Delgamuukw*, para 178.

However, the Court held that provincial laws of otherwise general application would still apply to Aboriginal title lands.[66]

In *Tsilhqot'in* the Court went further in holding that the doctrine of interjurisdictional immunity has no role to play where provincial regulation of Aboriginal title lands is concerned.[67] Critical opinions as to what effect this ruling may have are mixed. One the one hand, McNeil has expressed considerable astonishment at the fact that the decision in *Delgamuukw* held provincial laws to be applicable to title lands.[68] By contrast, Gordon Christie argues, if the provinces were to have legislative authority over Aboriginal title lands this would not put them in a position to disregard Aboriginal interests in the lands. On the contrary, it would catch provincial governments in a web of responsibilities and duties. The Supreme Court would be, effectively, placing the provinces with such legislative authority in potentially onerous fiduciary positions. The real danger would be that the fiduciary web would be tremendously weakened by a biased or reluctant Court.[69]

IV. Property and Indigenous Empowerment

On the basis of these changed characteristics, it is arguable that the decision in *Tsilhqot'in* removes a number of features that distinguish Aboriginal title holders from other property owners. Even though the Court in *Tsilhqot'in* maintains that title is not equated with fee simple ownership and cannot be described with reference to traditional property law,[70] the net effect is to bring Aboriginal title conceptually closer to the position assigned to private property–owners in the liberal framework. As such, it is clear that the decision reflects an effort by the Court to improve the financial capacities of Indigenous peoples in Canada.

While financial empowerment may be a positive development, *Tsilhqot'in* appears to confer the financial benefits of fee simple on Indigenous peoples, without recognizing their jurisdictional claims to territory.[71]

---

66 *Delgamuukw*, para 179.
67 *Tsilhqot'in*, para 140.
68 See generally Kent McNeil, "Aboriginal Title and the Division of Powers: Rethinking Federal and Provincial Jurisdiction," *Saskatchewan Law Review* 61 (1998): 431; and McNeil, "Aboriginal Title and Section 88 of the *Indian Act*," *UBC Law Review* 34 (2000): 159.
69 Gordon Christie, "Who Makes Decisions over Aboriginal Title Lands?" *UBC Law Review* 48 (2015): 743n47.
70 *Tsilhqot'in*, para. 72.
71 See generally Nicholas Blomley, "The Ties That Blind: Making Fee Simple in the British Columbia Treaty Process," *Transactions of the Institute of British Geographers* 40,

This remains problematic for Aboriginal peoples because it may preclude Aboriginal peoples from managing their societies according to their laws and principles that reflect their relationships to land. In particular, the constraints of the common law might restrict the ways in which Aboriginal governments may divide and share the benefits of title amongst their own people and with third parties. Limiting Aboriginal governments to the role of private property–owner may not reflect the nature of Aboriginal title as a form of communal ownership or the unique ways Indigenous peoples express relationships with land. Communal ownership of this kind necessarily requires some form of communal decision-making on how the land will be used.[72] In order to be legitimate, such decisions will have to represent the will of the people who make up the community in which ownership of the land is vested. Yet, in the current framework, communities are expected to use title to become socially and politically stable as a result of wealth. The risk from using title in this way is what Sarah Carter and Nathalie Kermoal reflect upon in their chapter in this book – that the philosophical influence of Hayek and his version of neoliberalism can have a totalizing effect on other modes of economic organization.[73] This runs against arguments for a pluralist notion of Aboriginal title and instead reflects a more general concern in this book that the imposition of marketized notions of land may represent a threat to collective self-determination.[74]

If there are inherent limitations to *Tsilhqot'in*, what aspects of *the decision* leave room for our interpretation; namely that the Court intends to empower Indigenous governments to use their authority over private lands in a way that meets their own communities' needs? As Gordon Christie has asked, the real question remains what "nature and degree of control an Aboriginal title-holder enjoys over what happens on Aboriginal title lands."[75] Under what conditions does the decision address more than the financial goals that are usually permitted or envisioned for property owners?

---

no. 2 (2015): 168; and Blomley, "Making Space for Property," *Annals of the Association of American Geographers* 104, no. 6 (2014): 1291.
72 *Routledge Handbook of Constitutional Law*, ed. Mark Tushnet, Thomas Fleiner, and Cheryl Saunders (London: Routledge, 2015).
73 Sarah Carter and Nathalie Kermoal, "Property Rights on Reserves: 'New Ideas' from the Nineteenth Century," in this volume.
74 For example, see Shalene Jobin, "Market Citizenship and Indigeneity," in this volume.
75 Gordon Christie, "Who Makes Decisions over Aboriginal Title Lands?" *UBC Law Review* 48 (2015): 743.

It seems to us that, in addition to securing financial benefits, the Court envisioned *Tsilhqot'in* as empowering Aboriginal title holders to *politically* benefit as a collective from the private control of vast tracts of land. Recognition that the entire beneficial ownership in the land and its resources vests in the Indigenous government means that the uses, gains, and profits from the land belong to them alone. The exclusive right to decide how the land is used and the right to benefit from it means that any private party seeking to access the land requires consent. This limitation is concomitant with the authority of any private landowner. However, for Indigenous governments, this right has a political effect. Indigenous governments can use their title lands for communal goals. Moreover, given the size of title territories and the likelihood that title includes subsurface, air, and water resources, this level of control should not be underestimated. The capacity of title holders to make different economic uses of different parts of title lands also means that Indigenous governments can integrate title lands into their economic plans for communities, with certainty that they will receive its full value, are empowered to exclude, and empowered to negotiate the terms upon which they will consent to any development. In this way, Indigenous governments are now significantly more empowered vis-à-vis individuals and corporations.

What remains unknown is whether title holders are in any way empowered vis-à-vis the Crown. It should be said that *Tsilhqot'in* has provided absolute clarity on the legal point that the Crown has no retaining interest in Aboriginal title lands and so may not in any way benefit from the use of title lands, nor confer the right to benefit from those lands on others. Nevertheless, by retaining the potential for infringement, the court has left open the possibility that title lands can be used for large-scale infrastructure or resource development deemed to be in the public interest. So, while the Court has held that the Crown does not enjoy any beneficial interest in title lands, the Court has acted to provide the Crown with a means of asserting ultimate control by grounding the power in the Crown's claim of radical title.[76]

The Court's definition of Aboriginal title includes a "right to encroach" on the part of the Crown, which presents a challenge to Indigenous governments' efforts to exert governmental control over their lands

---

76 For a critique of this grounding of authority over title lands in radical title, see Graben and Morey, "Aboriginal Title and Controlling Liberalization"; Kent McNeil, "Aboriginal Rights, Resource Development, and the Source of the Provincial Duty to Consult in *Haida Nation and Taku River*," *Supreme Court Law Review* (2nd ser.) 29 (2005): 447–53, esp. 451–2.

and communities in opposition to other governments. Here it is analytically useful to understand *encroachment* as including both control of lands by regulation (limiting the scope of potential uses) and control of lands through infringement (transferring some or all of the rights and benefits associated with ownership to the Crown, or to third parties); in particular, the Court's affirmed list of "compelling purposes" for which title can be infringed indicates that the Court still sees the Crown as having the power to transfer some proprietary rights from Aboriginal title-holders to itself or third parties

With this framework in place, the Court continues to work with a vision of a federalist Canada – one in which the planning of economic, political, and social development requires the power to authorize the construction of necessary infrastructure. Even though the Court has not provided legal argument to support the assumption of sovereign authority and radical title by the Crown, it is unlikely to disrupt federal powers aimed at federal and provincial purposes in the absence of an alternative vision of how it will continue to achieve its ends. To remove Aboriginal title lands from this constitutional arrangement would be a radical departure from the method by which Canada has been governed since colonization.

Nevertheless, it is possible to read *Tsilhqot'in* as working to insulate title lands from Crown control by indirect means. Because it will be Indigenous governments that receive the financial benefits of future development on Indigenous lands, the issue of whether and to what extent the Crown will exercise effective control of these lands remains an open question. More specifically, by conferring the entire beneficial value of title lands on title holders, the Court may be attempting to disincentivize infringement by elevating the cost of development for governments and third parties. In this sense, private ownership by Indigenous governments introduces opportunity costs that may deter non-consensual or infringing behaviour and assumes that the Crown would not attempt to approve projects from which neither it nor a third party would receive value.

An effort to disincentivize infringement that is cost prohibitive can be seen as a continuation of the Court's long-term efforts to use rights to encourage the negotiation of proprietary and managerial authority over land use.[77]

---

77 For discussion, see Sari Graben and Abbey Sinclair, "Tribunal Administration and the Duty to Consult," *University of Toronto Law Journal* 65, no. 4 (2015): 419; Dwight G. Newman, *The Duty to Consult: New Relationships with Aboriginal Peoples* (Saskatoon, SK: Purich, 2009), 20–1 (encouraging negotiation of legality); Larry Chartrand, "Agent of Reconciliation: The Supreme Court of Canada and Aboriginal Claims," in *The Judiciary as Third Branch of Government: Manifestations and Challenges*

By tinkering with the relative power of the different governments to promote or hinder resource development, the judgment in *Tsilhqot'in* then becomes part of a larger attempt by the Court to limit the very broad authority it has granted the Crown to infringe Aboriginal rights and title.

Nonetheless, thinking through this intention requires asking whether simple private ownership by Indigenous governments is sufficient to inhibit Crown approvals. The following collateral issues reflect a need for clarity to actually empower Indigenous governments vis-à-vis the Crown and third parties.

A first question of benefit is how to create certainty of ownership for *Indigenous peoples*. If the Court's goal is to confer the financial benefits of title land on title holders, does this intention presume that there are no overlapping proprietary interests by other governments in resources, or differing proprietary interests in different types of resources? Any continuing interest of the Crown (especially the province) in any resources on, under, or above title lands may foreseeably lead to strategic efforts by the federal and provincial government to license those resources and confine financial benefits to those issues related to land access. Clarification that title includes ownership of all related resources (i.e., subsurface, air, and water) would disincentivize Crown behaviour that would seek to obtain value from the land absent consent, and vitiate attempts to limit the scope of compensation for access to particular resources.

What additional benefits run with the land? If the intent is to empower title holders and title cannot be extinguished, then at least a percentage of tolls, taxes, and royalties from infrastructure, such as pipelines, dams, or electrical lines should be directed, as of right, to title holders. Clarification that title confers *all* related benefits on Indigenous governments would disincentivize behaviour that treats Aboriginal title holders as simple individual private land owners, whose land entitlements can be expropriated and/or replaced with statutorily defined compensation. Such clarification would recognize that Indigenous governments hold Aboriginal title lands in perpetuity. Moreover, any other scheme would ultimately require negotiation of these benefits on a case-by-case basis and increase inefficiencies.

Lastly, what happens when Indigenous governments use their Indian Act or treaty governments to pass laws pertaining to their title lands

---

to Legitimacy, ed. M.J. Mossman and Ghislain Otis (Montreal: Canadian Institute for the Administration of Justice, 2000), 104 (court as agent of reconciliation); Mark Walters, "The Jurisprudence of Reconciliation: Aboriginal Rights in Canada," in *The Politics of Reconciliation in Multicultural Societies*, ed. Will Kymlicka and Bashir Bashir (Oxford: Oxford University Press, 2008), 165 (jurisprudence of reconciliation)

in ways that conflict with provincial and federal laws? It is clear that the communal ownership of Aboriginal title lands by an Aboriginal government necessarily implies some form of governmental decision-making in regards to the uses and non-uses of title lands.[78] Numerous contemporary treaties have already established that provincial and federal jurisdiction do not obviate Aboriginal jurisdiction.[79] They have outlined areas of lawmaking in which the treaty governments may exercise concurrent and paramount legislative authority. That power originates from an inherent right to self-government, which must be, by dint of the simplest logic, held by other Aboriginal peoples as well. Similarly, band governments already exercise powers over lands on reserve. It would be ludicrous to assume *Indian Act* band councils can exercise greater powers over reserve lands than over title lands.

Moreover, beyond the formal recognition of jurisdiction is a more fundamental question of how plural legal orders, premised on perhaps incompatible (or at least challenging) compatibility will be reconciled. In principle, the incidents of property might be divided among any number of individuals in any variety of possible configurations. In practice, however, the common law has recognized only a limited number of possible estates and has exhibited a preference for pigeonholing novel arrangements into existing categories.[80] Of these existing categories, fee simple ownership confers the full bundle of rights normally associated with ownership. Owners can potentially occupy and reap the benefits of the land; exclude non-owners, make permanent alterations to it; destroy old features of the land, or create new ones; and may alienate their title (i.e., transfer it to others).[81] It is entirely conceivable that Indigenous legal orders will exercise these sticks in the bundle of rights in unique ways that challenge a more limited definition or that

---

78 Graben and Morey, "Aboriginal Title and Controlling Liberalization."
79 *Campbell et al v AG BC/AG Cda & Nisga'a Nation et al*, 2000 BCSC 1123. For discussion, see Sari Graben, "Nisga'a Final Agreement: Negotiating Federalism," *Indigenous Law Journal* 6, no. 2 (2007): 63; for application to implementation, see Sari Graben and Mathew Mehaffey, "Negotiating Self-Government Over & Over & Over Again: Comparators and Pressure Points in Contemporary Treaties," in *The Right(s) Relationship: Reimagining the Implementation of Historical Treaties*, ed. John Borrows and Michael Coyle, 164–84 (Toronto: University of Toronto Press, 2017).
80 Thomas Merrill and Henry E. Smith, *Property: Principles and Policies* (New York: Foundation, 2007), 1857, refer to this as the *numerus clausus* principle, and they justify this principle on the basis of transactional efficiency; in theory, the law is more likely to lead to its intended outcomes if potential interlopers can make reasonable assumptions regarding how rights to land are held and managed.
81 See, e.g., Felix Cohen, "Dialogue on Private Property," *Rutgers Law Review* 9 (1954): 374.

they will conceive of new definitions of property to be included in that bundle. If so, Aboriginal title will produce new challenges for the common law.

Chapters by Tenile Brown and by Emily Snyder and Valerie Napoleon give substance to these concerns and provide a glimpse into future legal questions related to multi-level governance and gender. Brown's study of pluralism, where there are entitlements to property in Swazi law and custom as well as Dutch common law, illustrates a constant reframing to address gendered impacts in different legal orders. Snyder and Napoleon's critical Indigenous feminist property theory illustrates how fledgling plurality in Canada will have to attend to what political ideologies and assumptions are contained in all ideas about property. In short, Aboriginal title is sure to operate in ways that are compatible with the common law and that may challenge it.

V. Conclusion

Taken together, characteristics of title that authorize title-holders to exclude non-consensual users and impose a prohibitive financial cost on governments that may want to infringe might reflect a fledgling effort by the Court to empower title-holders. While this certainly cannot be construed as veto power vis-à-vis the Crown or clear jurisdictional power over territory, redirecting profit away from the Crown and third parties should affect the frequency of infringement. However, what has been made evident by the above points is that this assumption requires future cases to clarify that this is the intention of the Court. More importantly, it requires the courts to think creatively about how to build up entitlements to related resources and the related legislative jurisdiction of Indigenous governments in order to protect those boundaries from Crown encroachment.[82]

What is clear from the case law predating *Tsilhqot'in* is that jurisprudential reliance on *sui generis* principles is, in one sense, an acknowledgment that Aboriginal rights are grounded in a separate and distinct legal and cultural tradition, and that they constitute a category that is conceptually distinct from common-law rights. However, the differentiation of Aboriginal rights from other types of property rights has meant that the proprietary nature of Aboriginal rights has remained contested. Practically, the term *sui generis* has been used to distinguish specific types of Aboriginal rights from comparable common law

---

82 See the authors' work on this: Graben and Morey, "Aboriginal Title and Controlling Liberalization."

rights. Thus, Aboriginal title has been described as sui generis in order to emphasize that the reasoning and principles that attach to common law property concepts (in particular the concept of ownership in fee simple) do not apply in title cases.

Tsilhqot'in constitutes a shift in thinking because it removes a number of features that distinguish Aboriginal title holders from other property owners. In doing so, it brings Aboriginal title conceptually closer to property–ownership in the liberal framework. The effect may be to increase the financial usefulness of title lands for Aboriginal peoples but it is not entirely clear that financial use is sufficient for their territorial objectives.

While the Court has clearly avoided aligning territorial jurisdiction with territorial title, there may be something more to the use of proprietary language than merely seeking to ensure the financial utility of Aboriginal title. The Court's remarks on the nature of beneficial interest in land, the scope of territory to be included, the commonality of holding, and the right to decide its uses are key themes that could enable more than the strictly financial uses that property law usually permits or envisions. These characteristics authorize title holders to exclude non-consensual users and impose prohibitive costs on other governments for infringement. Taken together with its overall trend towards forwarding reconciliation through negotiation, *Tsilhqot'in* may empower Indigenous peoples as collectives by recognizing their effective control over vast tracts of lands.

If we are right, and this is a fledgling attempt at empowerment, our quick foray into the ways it can be brought asunder predicts that future courts will need to think creatively about how to build up entitlements to related resources and the related legislative jurisdiction of Indigenous governments in order to protect those boundaries from Crown encroachment. Moreover, while the power to regulate land uses, which likely attaches to title, will affect how property is used, there is little question that defining title in line with fee simple ownership predetermines its characteristics. Consequently, finding a path to self-determination under *Tsilhqot'in* will remain a challenge.

PART FOUR

Lessons from the Transnational Context

9 Land, Niger Delta Peoples, and Oil and Gas Decision-Making

IBIRONKE T. ODUMOSU-AYANU*

I. Introduction

Land and land rights in African countries are topical scholarly endeavours and of significant practical relevance due to land acquisition for large-scale projects and natural resource production.[1] Nigeria, Africa's most populous country and the continent's largest oil producer, which is also ranked eleventh-largest oil producer in the world,[2] is home to the Niger Delta. Since oil was discovered in commercial quantities in 1956,[3] revenue from oil and gas production has contributed significantly to the economic well-being of the Nigerian state. However, this economic contribution has not been without its challenges. One of those challenges has been the difficult relationship between Niger Delta peoples and the government and investors that explore and produce oil and gas. Several mechanisms have been adopted to address these challenges, including the establishment of the Niger Delta Development Commission,[4] philanthropic corporate social responsibility (CSR) measures,[5] and industry-community agreements that promise

* Thanks to the Social Sciences and Humanities Research Council for funding and to Benjamin Omoruyi and Sara Hansvall for excellent research assistance.

1 See generally, Sonja Vermeulen and Lorenzo Cotula, "Over the Heads of Local People: Consultation, Consent, and Recompense in Large-Scale Land Deals for Biofuels Projects in Africa," *Journal of Peasant Studies* 37 (2010): 899.

2 United Nations Conference on Trade and Development, *Investment Policy Review: Nigeria* (New York: United Nations, 2009), 14.

3 Martin M. Olisa, *Nigerian Petroleum Law and Practice*, 2nd ed. (Lagos: Jonia Ventures, 1997), 1; G. Etikerentse, *Nigerian Petroleum Law* (London: Macmillan Publishers, 1985), 2.

4 *Niger-Delta Development Commission (Establishment) Act* No. 6 of 2000.

5 Olatoye Ojo, "Nigeria: CSR as a Vehicle for Economic Development," in *Global Practices of Corporate Social Responsibility*, ed. Samuel O. Idowu and Walter Leal

better benefits and development initiatives.[6] In spite of these initiatives many Niger Delta peoples continue to live in poverty, and community agitation for greater voice in oil and gas decision-making persists. The relationship between Niger Delta peoples' real property rights and their ability to contribute to oil and gas decision-making is the focus of this chapter. Here I explore the extent to which real property rights affect the negotiating leverage of Niger Delta peoples in their interactions with oil and gas companies and governments. This question is relevant to communities that host natural resource production around the world, including Indigenous peoples in Canada.

This chapter is part of a series of articles that develop a multi-actor contract framework to address challenges to stakeholders in developing natural resources and other large projects that have serious impacts on host and affected local communities, while simultaneously critiquing industry's engagement with local communities.[7] These contracts are tripartite contractual arrangements among states, industry actors, and local communities that provide directly enforceable obligations that account *inter alia* for the interests of local communities. The challenges of local communities' interactions with other actors in natural resource extraction are beyond the scope of this chapter. Rather, this work focuses on land and land rights as a mechanism to ensure sustained and meaningful interactions among all the relevant actors in natural resource development.

In developing a multi-actor contract framework or other enforceable agreements that involve local communities, help to define the scope of projects, and include concrete protections for communities, one is confronted with the question, What do local communities bring to the

Filho (Berlin: Springer, 2009), 402–9. See also Uwem E. Ite, "Multinationals and Corporate Social Responsibility in Developing Countries: A Case Study of Nigeria," *Corporate Responsibility and Environmental Management* 11 (2004): 1; Ite, "Poverty Reduction in Resource-Rich Developing Countries: What Have Multinational Corporations Got to Do with It?" *Journal of International Development* 17 (2005): 913.

6 See, generally, Ibironke T. Odumosu-Ayanu, "Foreign Direct Investment Catalysts in West Africa: Interactions with Local Content Laws and Industry-Community Agreements," *North Carolina Central Law Review* 35, no. 1 (2012): 65.

7 Ibironke T. Odumosu-Ayanu, "Government, Investors and Local Communities: Analysis of a Multi-Actor Investment Agreement Framework," *Melbourne Journal of International Law* 15 (2014): 473; Odumosu-Ayanu, "Multi-Actor Contracts, Competing Goals and the Regulation of Foreign Investment," *University of New Brunswick Law Journal* 65 (2014): 269; Odumosu-Ayanu, "Foreign Direct Investment Catalysts."

negotiating table?[8] A direct practical response could be "everything," and to an extent such a response would be correct. But for actors that seek tangible contributions or rights to trade in negotiations, this chapter provides an analysis based on land and land rights. Industry actors provide finances and technical expertise and are thus able to negotiate agreements that protect their investments and sometimes even guarantee protection from some risks. Governments provide permission for projects, and in many parts of the world they "own" the resources and sometimes the land under which the resources are located. Governments also have the legislative ability to change laws to favour their position. The third category of important stakeholders is the local communities that host and/or are impacted by these projects. Domestic and international actors are quick to presume that governments represent and protect the interests of their citizens. But peoples such as minorities in extractive industry projects and governments sometimes have fundamentally conflicting interests. Also, these kinds of projects have particular impacts on these minorities that other citizens do not ordinarily share. In addition, (international) law is no longer as state-centric as it used to be. It now, *inter alia*, permits foreign investors to espouse independent claims without the aid of their home governments and recognizes the separate personality of these investors, and it permits non-governmental organizations to act as observers in international organizations. In addition, international law has recognized the human rights claims of individuals against their governments for decades. These factors are among those that compel development of a local community-focused extractive industry regime.

Given the decentring of the state in a globalized world and the challenges that communities face with natural resource extraction, what law-related leverage may local communities exercise in concluding tripartite agreements on projects that affect them? In this chapter, I explore the contributions of one factor: land. In this analysis, I adopt as a case study the relationship between Nigeria's Niger Delta peoples, land, and oil and gas decision-making. This relationship is more complicated than many others because of the legislative provisions that regulate land and oil and gas exploration and production in Nigeria. Given the limited rights attached to land in Nigeria, adopting land as a basis for negotiating better co-existence with oil and gas project proponents involves rereading current initiatives to foster greater leverage for local communities.

---

8   Odumosu-Ayanu, "Governments, Investors and Local Communities."

In part II of this chapter, I introduce the land tenure system in Nigeria and its impacts on oil-bearing communities of the Niger Delta. Part III briefly introduces the multi-actor contract framework and local communities' ability to use land as leverage to conclude such contracts. In this part, I consider three current initiatives with the potential for favourable reading of a limited land tenure system. While they contribute to a land-based negotiation strategy, they all involve substantial challenges. The first initiative focuses on government-led statutory enactments that recognize the importance of peoples' participation in decision-making that affects them. It demonstrates that governments recognize the importance of participation, even if they provide little practical recourse for meaningful local community participation in oil and gas decision-making. Second, I introduce industry-driven initiatives in the form of industry-community agreements. These agreements also rely on interests in land. They demonstrate that agreements that incorporate local communities as parties already exist, albeit with limited focus. Arguments that it is unnecessary or unworkable to include local communities as parties to agreements are untenable. The third initiative is driven by some Niger Delta communities that suggest that they are Indigenous peoples so they are entitled to certain standards of protection of their relationship with land and their interests in land. Part IV concludes. While the land argument as a negotiating tool is not easy to make in light of Nigeria's current land tenure system, it is a plausible (legal entitlement) argument for seriously taking the agency and interests of local communities in the Niger Delta into account in oil and gas decision-making. Ordinarily Niger Delta peoples' moral entitlements should be sufficient, but in a world driven by legal arguments, land rights and other economic interests and rights – including fishing and hunting rights – and possible (international) recognition of Indigenous status become the focus of contestation and negotiation.

II. Niger Delta Peoples and Land Tenure in Nigeria

A. The Land Use Act

The Niger Delta is Nigeria's oil producing region. It spans the states of Akwa Ibom, Baylesa, Cross River, Delta, Edo, Rivers, and others. Communities that inhabit the Niger Delta are diverse, with some of the most widely known being the Ijaw, Urhobo, Itsekiri, and Ogoni.[9]

---

9 See United Nations Development Program, *Niger Delta Human Development Report* (Abuja: UNDP, 2006).

Land occupies an essential position in the Niger Delta. It is "very scarce" and "treasured."[10] Land "forms the very basis – spiritual and material – of life in the peasant communities of the Niger Delta."[11] The Niger Delta region is densely populated; a significant portion of land is dedicated to oil exploitation; people, farms, and rivers co-exist with pipelines; and pollution and other forms of environmental degradation are rife, making land in the Niger Delta even more scarce and a subject of intense contention.[12] These practical realities are compounded by legislative enactments, including the *Land Use Act*.[13]

By virtue of the *Land Use Act*, all land in Nigeria is held by the state.[14] Subsurface rights to natural resources including oil and gas also belong to the federal government.[15] Ownership and control of these subsurface resources without ownership of the surface rights to land is not radical. The piece of legislation that radicalizes the ownership of land (and control of oil and gas) is the *Land Use Act*. Perhaps no other piece of legislation in Nigeria "has elicited so much controversy, so much criticism, so much divergence in the interpretation of its provisions and so much discourse in the academic and business circles as the Land Use Act, 1978."[16] The *Land Use Act* "significantly transformed Nigeria's oil

---

10 Cyril I. Obi, "Globalization and Environmental Conflict in Africa," *African Journal of Political Science* 4 (1999): 50.

11 Obi, "Globalization and Environmental Conflict," 51. Niger Delta peoples' relationship with land is replicated in many parts of the world. In Ako's study of land, natural resources and environmental justice in Nigeria, South Africa, India, and Papua New Guinea, he notes, "Land in these jurisdictions, as with most developing countries in Africa and the Asia-Pacific, has deeper spiritual and cultural connotations. This is not to underestimate the economic importance, as the discussion also highlights the important role traditional land systems play in the determination of access to natural resources ... the underlying trend is that the traditional conception of land ownership dictates the relationship between communities, the state and natural resource exploitation." Rhuks Temitope Ako, *Environmental Justice in Developing Countries: Perspectives from Africa and Asia-Pacific* (London: Routledge, 2013), 98–9.

12 See Obi, "Globalization and Environmental Conflict," 51.

13 *Land Use Act*, Cap. 202, Laws of the Federation of Nigeria 1990.

14 *Land Use Act*, s 1, noting, "Subject to the provisions of this Act, all land comprised of each State in the Federation are hereby vested in the Governor of that State and such land shall be held in trust and administered for the use and common benefit of all Nigerians in accordance with the provisions of this Act."

15 *Petroleum Act*, Cap. 350 Laws of the Federation of Nigeria 1990, s 1.

16 Adefi M.D. Olong, *Land Law in Nigeria*, 2nd ed. (Lagos: Malthouse, 2011), 115, citing A. Nnamani, "The Land Use Act: 12 Years After," *Nigeria Law Journal* 2 (1991): 105.

industry."[17] To some, the Act has become "the fundamental cause of the violence that has become characteristic of the Niger Delta region that hosts upstream oil operations."[18] Ako argues that with the promulgation of the *Land Use Act*,

> the federal military government intended to ensure that the control of oil resources be the absolute and exclusive preserve of the federal government to obviate "minority" agitation over any form of ownership or participatory rights as earlier claimed.... [I]f ownership of land had remained vested in the local communities, they would have maintained some influence over oil exploration and production activities. Therefore, they would have been in a position to dictate the mode and size of operations within their territory as well as the socio-economic and political benefits that must accrue to them. This would have enhanced their political and economic power substantially within a federation that relies extensively on oil revenues to sustain the national economy.[19]

Ako is not alone in arguing that the *Land Use Act* is detrimental to local communities in the Niger Delta. Oronto-Douglas has said, "No single piece of legislation in the country has robbed, in a more vicious manner, the people of the oil bearing Niger-Delta communities of their humanity than the Land Use Act of 1978.[20] Frynas also notes, "The Land Use Act allowed oil companies to gain easier access to the land and to the oil resources through the government. Companies were no longer obliged to negotiate over the sale or allocation of land with the

---

17 Rhuks T. Ako, "Nigeria's Land Use Act: An Anti-Thesis to Environmental Justice," *Journal of African Law* 53 (2009): 294. See page 297, where Ako notes that before the *Land Use Act*, oil communities were not precluded "from having enforceable rights to participate in the oil industry because they owned the land underneath which the oil was exploited. Before the promulgation of the Act, even though ownership of the oil was vested absolutely in the federal government, the communities owned the land beneath which the resource was situated. Therefore, they had to be consulted before oil operations began on that land. However, after the Act became effective, the region's inhabitants were stripped of this right and the federal government became vested with the sole right to determine where and when oil operations could be undertaken."

18 Ako, "Nigeria's Land Use Act," 294.

19 Ako, "Nigeria's Land Use Act," 295.

20 Oronto-Douglas, quoted in Cyril I. Obi, *The Changing Forms of Identity Politics in Nigeria under Economic Adjustment: The Case of the Oil Producing Minorities Movement of the Niger Delta*, Research Report No. 119 (Uppsala: Nordiska Afrikainstitutet, 2001), 26.

customary land owners."[21] He also argues that the Act did not "safe-guard the rights of customary land owners," making it "biased in favour of oil companies at the expense of village communities."[22]

The *Land Use Act* and its effects appear to be unique – legally and in effect. In legal terms, Nigerians no longer have the fee simple absolute that they held before the Act came into effect. Although the effects of the *Land Use Act* are not particularly visible, as people and families continue to occupy and use land as they did before the Act was enacted, by law the extent of land rights has changed, and nowhere is this change more visible than in the Niger Delta. Under the *Land Use Act* land is "held in trust and administered for the use and common benefit" of the people by the government.[23] Some have argued that all land in Nigeria was nationalized[24] or at least expropriated. As Justice Eso noted in the Supreme Court of Nigeria decision in *Nkwocha v Governor of Anambra State & Ors.*, the "tenor" of the *Land Use Act*, "as a single piece of legislation, is the nationalization of all lands in the country by the vesting of its ownership in the state leaving the private individual with an interest in land which is a mere right of occupancy."[25] The Supreme Court was not exaggerating the position under the *Land Use Act* in this statement. By section 5 of the *Land Use Act*, for land in both urban and non-urban areas, the governor may grant a "statutory right of occupancy," and upon such grant, "all existing rights to the use and occupation of the land which is the subject of the statutory right of occupancy shall be extinguished." While the government cannot simply acquire people's land by virtue of the *Land Use Act* without revoking a right of occupancy, what is being revoked is not a right holder's "ownership" rights but the rights of occupancy.[26] In addition, sections 21 and 22 of the Act require the consent of the governor to alienate rights of occupancy. Hence, irrespective of the language used – *nationalization, expropriation*, or another word – the *Land Use Act* vests ultimate title in the governor. It also vests "ownership" rights in all lands in a state in the governor.

---

21 Jedrzej George Frynas, *Oil in Nigeria: Conflict and Litigation between Oil Companies and Village Communities* (Hamburg: LIT, 2000), 80.
22 Frynas, *Oil in Nigeria*, 80.
23 *Land Use Act*, s 1.
24 Ako, "Nigeria's Land Use Act," 294.
25 *Nkwocha v Governor of Anambra State & Ors.* 1984 6 SC 362 at 404; (1984) 1 SCNLR 634 at 652. For a review of alternative views on the impact of section 1 of the *Land Use Act*, see O.O. Sholanke, "The Nigerian Land Use Act – A Volcanic Eruption or a Slight Tremor?: Garuba Abioye v. Saadu Yakubu," *Journal of African Law* 36 (1992): 93.
26 *Land Use Act*, s 28.

Private land owners now have rights of occupancy akin to leasehold interests. This represents a departure from the ownership structures, including customary land tenure, which prevailed in southern Nigeria until the *Land Use Act* was enacted in 1978.

Under customary law, land tenure was based on communal ownership, and "land had economic, social, political, and religious significance."[27] Commentators argue that the customary land tenure systems that applied in other parts of southern Nigeria also applied to several Niger Delta peoples, including the Ijaw, Itsekiri and Urhoro.[28] In the oft-cited Privy Council decision in *Amodu Tijani v The Secretary, Southern Provinces*, Viscount Haldane quoted with approval Chief Justice Rayner's Report on Land Tenure in West Africa:

> The notion of individual ownership is quite foreign to native ideas. Land belongs to the community, the village or the family, never to the individual. All the members of the community, village, or family have an equal right to the land, but in every case the Chief or Headman of the community or village, or head of the family, has charge of the land, and in loose mode of speech is sometimes called the owner. He is to some extent in the position of a trustee, and as such holds the land for the use of the community or family. He has control of it, and any member who wants a piece of it to cultivate or build a house upon, goes to him for it. But the land so given still remains the property of the community or family.[29]

However, the customary land tenure systems that applied in southern Nigeria must not be romanticized. Some commentators argue that the *Land Use Act* was meant to reform the customary land tenure systems

---

27   P. Ehi Oshio, "The Indigenous Land Tenure and Nationalization of Land in Nigeria," *Boston College Third World Law Journal* 10 (1990): 46. On customary law in Nigeria, see, generally, Remigius N. Nwabueze, "The Dynamics and Genius of Nigeria's Indigenous Legal Order," *Indigenous Law Journal* 1 (2002): 153. Questions of customary law are debated in many parts of the world. For African customary law, see Jeanmarie Fenrich, Paolo Galizzi, and Tracy E. Higgins, eds, *The Future of African Customary Law* (New York: Cambridge University Press, 2011). For discussions of customary law and Aboriginal peoples in Canada, see Norman Zlotkin, "From Time Immemorial: The Recognition of Aboriginal Customary Law in Canada," in *Protection of First Nations Cultural Heritage: Laws, Policy and Reform*, ed. Catherine Bell and Robert K. Paterson (Vancouver: UBC Press, 2009), 343.

28   See Onoawarie Edevbie, "Ownership of Pre-Colonial Warri," in *History of the Urhobo People of Niger Delta*, ed. Peter Palmer Ekeh (Lagos: Urhobo Historical Society, 2007), 234–5.

29   *Amodu Tijani v The Secretary, Southern Provinces* [1921] 2 AC 399 at 404.

that some regarded as a "clog to development efforts."[30] While the system generally appeared to work for the people, like other systems, it had some pitfalls, including unscrupulous transfers that occurred when alienation became permitted for political and socio-economic reasons.[31] There was official backlash against the customary system,[32] spurred on by the government's desire to have access to land for oil and gas exploration and production in the Niger Delta region.[33] Agbosu also notes that with the *Land Use Act*, land rights no longer depend on membership in families or communities.[34] He argues that "the hitherto narrow tribal, kinship, family or community membership concept upon which the beneficial enjoyment of landed property was based has been abolished. In its place is established a much broader concept – Nigerian citizenship."[35]

Given the changes adopted in the *Land Use Act*, the extent to which customary land tenure continues is debatable. By virtue of the *Land Use Act*, land is not ultimately vested in communities but in the state governments. Customary law arguably remains relevant for land but not in urban areas in cases of devolution[36] and payment of compensation to communities.[37] In *Abioye v Yakubu*,[38] the Supreme Court of Nigeria affirmed the *dictum* in an earlier decision of the Court in *Ogunola v Eiyekole*,[39] noting, "Land is still held under customary tenure even though dominium is in the Governor. The most pervasive effect of the Land Use Act is the diminution of the plenitude of the powers of the holders of land. The character in which they hold remains substantially the same. Thus, an owner of customary land remains owner all the same even though he no longer is the ultimate owner. The owner of land now requires the consent of the Governor to alienate interests which hitherto he could do without such consent." In addition, such land may be taken without much procedure, since the ultimate title resides in the state governor.

---

30 Kaniye S. Ebeku, *Oil and the Niger Delta People in International Law: The Injustice of the Land Use Act* (Koeln: Rüdiger Köppe, 2006).
31 Oshio, "Indigenous Land Tenure," 48–51.
32 Oshio, "Indigenous Land Tenure," 50.
33 See Ako, "Nigeria's Land Use Act."
34 L.K. Agbosu, "The Land Use Act and the State of Nigerian Land Law," *Journal of African Law* 32 (1988): 5.
35 Agbosu, "Land Use Act," 5.
36 *Land Use Act*, s 24.
37 *Land Use Act*, s 29(3).
38 *Garuba Abioye & Ors. v Sa'adu Yakubu & Ors.* (1991) All NLR 1; (1991) 5 NWLR (Pt 190) 130.
39 *Ogunlola v Eiyekole & Ors.* (1990) 4 NWLR (Pt 146) 632 at 648.

A local government may grant "customary rights of occupancy" over land not in an urban area to persons or organizations for agricultural or grazing purposes.[40] Customary right of occupancy is defined as "the right of a person or community lawfully using or occupying land in accordance with customary law and includes a customary right of occupancy granted by a Local Government" under the Act.[41] The Supreme Court of Nigeria often reiterates the continued relevance of customary law, albeit limited, under the *Land Use Act*. In *Abioye v Yakubu*, the Supreme Court notes, "A person with a customary right of occupancy is entitled to use the land in accordance with customary law. A customary right of occupancy pre-dates the Land Use Act and is intimately linked with the custom of the people of the area. It is a creation of customary law and the fact that it can now be granted by the local government has not taken it out of the realm of customary law. The total quantum of interest contained in the right of occupancy has to be determined by the customary law of the area."[42] Hence for land used for agricultural purposes, some customary law may continue to apply, but customary rights of occupancy cannot be granted for agricultural purposes in land that exceeds 500 hectares.[43] These customary rights may also be expropriated by the local government upon "compensation for the value at the date of revocation of their unexhausted improvements."[44] The challenge with this quantum of compensation is that unexhausted improvements often represent only a fraction of the value of the land. Where land expropriated by the local government was used for agricultural purposes, the local government is to allocate other agricultural land to the holder of the customary right of occupancy.[45]

A state governor may also revoke both statutory and customary rights of occupancy "for overriding public interest," including "the requirement of the land for mining purposes or oil pipelines" or any purposes that are connected with such uses.[46] Compensation is not only

---

40 *Land Use Act*, s 6(1). For the nature of rights of occupancy under the *Land Use Act*, see *Joshua Ogunleye v Babatayo Oni* (1990) All NLR 341.

41 *Land Use Act*, s 51(1).

42 *Abioye v Yakubu*, at 94 (All NLR).

43 *Land Use Act*, s 6(2).

44 *Land Use Act*, s 6(5). For a critique of compensation for acquired land in Nigeria, see Muhammad Bashar Nuhu, "Compulsory Purchase and Payment of Compensation in Nigeria: A Case Study of Federal Capital Territory (FCT) Abuja," *Nordic Journal of Surveying and Real Estate Research* 3 (2008): 102. See also Frynas, *Oil in Nigeria*, 94–8.

45 *Land Use Act*, s 6(6).

46 *Land Use Act*, s 28.

payable to individuals; it may be paid to a community.[47] Revocation of rights of occupancy for public purposes is effective with the giving of notice. The *Land Use Act* does not envisage consultations in the event of planned revocations. Compensation for revoking these rights for mining or oil purposes is based on mining and/or oil legislation.[48]

Situating the *Land Use Act*'s provisions in the context of pre–*Land Use Act* laws better illustrates the radical nature of the Act and the extent to which it contributes to limiting communities' participation in oil and gas decision-making that affects their land rights. Ebeku notes that the ability to grant rights of access to land and to receive compensation for use of land was "a way by which the communities had some sense of participation in oil operations."[49] Before the *Land Use Act* was enacted, oil companies received rights to produce oil and gas from the federal government and negotiated surface rights of access to land with local communities.[50] After the state acquired the right to own natural resources, which it did not have in pre-colonial times, but before the *Land Use Act* was enacted, "there was a tripartite arrangement wherein the state owned the oil resources, the communities owned the land and the oil companies exploited the resource."[51] The loss of radical title to land was effectively the loss of decision-making in the exploitation of oil and gas for Niger Delta communities. Prior to the *Land Use Act*, in order to possess land held by others, the government had to acquire the land and pay compensation to the holders of title to the land. Expropriation had to be for a public purpose and not for a private purpose. Hence in order to expropriate land on behalf of oil companies, the government relied on "eminent domain," arguing that uses by oil companies were in the public interest.[52] At the time, compensation was more robust. In *Nzekwu v Attorney General East Central State*, the Supreme Court of Nigeria expressed the view that compensation evaluation under the *Public Lands Acquisition Law* is based on "open market value."[53]

Essentially, before the *Land Use Act*, peoples and communities had more robust land rights and could negotiate with companies that

47 *Land Use Act*, s 29(3).
48 *Land Use Act*, s 29(2).
49 Ebeku, *Oil and the Niger Delta People*.
50 Ebeku, *Oil and the Niger Delta People*.
51 Ako, *Environmental Justice in Developing Countries*, 29–30.
52 Frynas, *Oil in Nigeria*, 75.
53 *Nzekwu v Attorney General East Central State* (1972) All NLR 543 also citing the *Public Lands Acquisition Law* (Cap 1050, Laws of Eastern Nigeria, 1963).

sought access to subsurface resources on their land. The *Land Use Act* has all but extinguished this land-based negotiating leverage.

B. *Land Tenure and Oil and Gas*

Section 43 of the *Constitution of the Federal Republic of Nigeria*, 1999, guarantees the right of "every citizen of Nigeria" to "acquire and own immovable property anywhere in Nigeria."[54] From the discussion in the preceding section, it is clear that the right to "own" land is limited. That limitation is confirmed by section 315(5)(d) of the Constitution, which provides that some pieces of legislation, including the *Land Use Act*, shall continue to have "full effect."[55] The essence is to make the *Land Use Act* and these other statutes difficult to amend or repeal. Including the *Land Use Act* in the Constitution is an attempt to seal the place of the *Land Use Act* in Nigerian law.

Section 44(3) of the Nigerian Constitution constitutionalizes the right of the federal government to own all oil and gas. The property in – as well as the control of –these natural resources is vested in the federal government. Section 44(3) states, "The entire property in and control of all minerals, mineral oils and natural gas in under or upon any land in Nigeria or in, under or upon the territorial waters and the Exclusive Economic Zone of Nigeria shall vest in the Government of the Federation and shall be managed in such manner as may be prescribed by the National Assembly." Nigeria's *Petroleum Act* also vests the "entire ownership and control of all petroleum" in Nigeria, including the territorial waters and continental shelf in the state.[56]

The combined effect of the *Land Use Act*, the Constitution, and the oil and gas statutes is that the surface and subsurface rights to land and oil and gas respectively are vested in various levels of government. The state governors hold land and grant rights of occupancy to people. Subsurface rights to oil and gas are vested in the federal government, which grants exploration, prospecting, and mining rights to oil companies. Hence the rights to occupy and use land and natural resources are at the pleasure of these levels of government. And these rights may be extinguished. The difference between rights to land and rights to use subsurface resources is that holders of mining rights in subsurface

---

54 *Constitution of the Federal Republic of Nigeria*, 1999, Schedule to the Constitution of the Federal Republic of Nigeria (Promulgation) Decree No. 24 of 1999.

55 For an interpretation of a similar provision in an earlier version of the Constitution, see *Nkwocha v Governor of Anambra State*.

56 *Petroleum Act*, s 1.

natural resources are extensively protected by statutes, treaties, and contracts. While this form of protection is not inherently problematic, the absence of similar protection for holders of limited surface rights of occupancy in land stands out. The balance of this chapter interrogates the extent to which peoples and communities that hold these limited rights of occupancy in land can leverage these limited land rights as socio-legal tools/resources for negotiating better positions in their relationships with governments and oil companies.

III. Land Rights and Oil and Gas Decision-Making

A. Background

> In practice, the legal rights of the public ... do not affect the projects at the initial stages of planning and approval, as they are not really part of the decision-making process at that point. When they are, they operate from a weak bargaining position due to the fact that, at the end of the day, all the "publics" are in favour of the project coming to fruition, irrespective of environmental effects. The inadequacy of the legal rights of the communities, coupled with the lack of basic amenities and low development, had led to their taking the law into their hands by causing disturbances or even taking hostages to impose demands.[57]

Omorogbe's comment above articulates the weak bargaining position of Niger Delta peoples. In other jurisdictions, some "publics" have better bargaining power than Niger Delta peoples. In Canada, Lucas notes that landowners, occupiers, and especially Indigenous peoples have better participation rights in tribunals' natural resource decision-making.[58] From Canada to other parts of the world, local communities' participation in natural resource decision-making is topical. There is no dearth of scholarly and other views on the contributions that participation could make to alleviate the plight of Niger

---

57 Yinka Omorogbe, "The Legal Framework for Public Participation in Decision-Making in Mining and Energy Development in Nigeria: Giving Voices to the Voiceless," in *Human Rights in Natural Resource Development: Public Participation in the Sustainable Development of Mining and Energy Resources*, ed. Donald M. Zillman, Alastair Lucas, and George Pring (Oxford: Oxford University Press, 2002), 583.

58 Alastair R. Lucas, "Canadian Participatory Rights in Mining and Energy Resource Development: The Bridges to Empowerment," in Zillman, Lucas, and Pring, *Human Rights in Natural Resource Development*, 307.

Delta peoples.[59] Kalu specifically considers access to information, access to justice, and participation in decision-making.[60] The Committee on the Elimination of Racial Discrimination also recommends "effective and meaningful consultation" of local communities in the Niger Delta.[61] In spite of the recognition that participation of local communities in decisions that affect them is essential, such participation and consultation in the Niger Delta is almost non-existent. This is partly attributable to land tenure structures that effectively place communities in positions of weakness.

The weak negotiating position of Niger Delta peoples is exacerbated by legislative enactments and government policy that direct more attention to acquiring maximum benefits from the exploitation of oil and gas without requisite attention to the rights and interests of Niger Delta peoples. The inadequacy of legal frameworks adopted primarily to protect foreign investment in oil and gas for protecting host and affected communities is readily apparent. This inadequacy is the impetus for developing what I call a multi-actor contract framework.[62] The framework is a proposed network of agreements that incorporate three major stakeholders – industry, peoples and governments – as parties to multi-stakeholder contracts. These contracts will define contractual rights and responsibilities of the parties in the production of oil and gas and other natural resources. Through these contracts, governments and investors will not only owe obligations and responsibilities to one another; they would also have direct responsibilities to local communities that would have the contractual rights to enforce these obligations. These agreements would define the scope of the projects and not only focus on benefit-sharing. By being foundational instruments, they would ensure local community perspectives on the most definitive parts of projects rather than only on the formation of "benefits" or "development" agreements after projects have been designed, approved, and finalized. The framework is an initiative for direct participation in decision-making that affects local communities. It takes

---

59 See Omorogbe, "Legal Framework for Public Participation"; Victoria E. Kalu, "State Monopoly and Indigenous Participation Rights in Resource Development in Nigeria," *Journal of Energy and Natural Resources Law* 26 (2008): 418.
60 Kalu, "State Monopoly and Indigenous Participation Rights."
61 United Nations Committee on the Elimination of Racial Discrimination, "Concluding Observations of the Committee on the Elimination of Racial Discrimination: Nigeria," Sixty-Seventh Session 2–18 August 2005, CERD/C/NGA/CO/18, para 19.
62 A detailed analysis of the multi-actor contract framework, including its potentials and challenges, is beyond the purview of this chapter. See Odumosu-Ayanu, "Government, Investors and Local Communities."

the concerns of local communities into account while also accounting for governments' concern that projects that may benefit the entire country may be stifled. It is a framework for protecting the interests of host and affected communities through contractually binding obligations that are subject to effective judicial and quasi-judicial enforcement.

In the balance of this chapter, I interrogate land rights as a factor that could compel the conclusion of multi-actor contracts that would take the agency, identity, and interests of Niger Delta peoples into account in oil and gas decision-making. I analyse land as the basis on which host and/or affected communities may insist on contractual arrangements that incorporate their interests. Given the limited rights that the *Land Use Act* and other legislation confer, peaceful popular resistance has been resorted to in asserting rights in the Niger Delta.[63] In discussing popular resistance, I do not address the militant groups that have formed in the Niger Delta. References to popular resistance in this chapter only incorporate peaceful resistance through social movement–like groupings to demand more favourable conditions. Such peaceful popular resistance has defined and could continue to define the relationship between local communities in the Niger Delta and other stakeholders.

Property rights asserted primarily through popular resistance and occasionally through judicial processes are analysed through three initiatives that I discuss in the remaining sections of this part of the chapter: statutory initiatives including statutorily mandated community development agreements, industry-community agreements such as the global memorandum of understanding, and claims to Indigenous status. All these initiatives provide impetus to assess the workability of a framework like the multi-actor contract framework. However, the following discussion extends beyond an assessment of the potential contributions of these initiatives; it offers suggestions for better harnessing each of these initiatives to provide better leverage for local communities. Each initiative will be considered in turn. But first I briefly introduce assertions of (limited) property rights and (or in light of) popular resistance.

Peaceful popular resistance is not an end in itself; it is a means to an end. It is a means by which peoples have highlighted their dissatisfaction with the usurpation of their property rights. But this option might not be sustainable, given the history of the Niger Delta and

---

63 For a discussion of social movements and activism regarding Indigenous peoples' land rights in Canada, see Jamie Baxter, "Indigenous Land Rights and the Politics of Property," in this volume.

governments' means of quelling resistance in that part of Nigeria.[64] In the African Commission on Human and Peoples Rights (ACHPR) case, *The Social and Economic Rights Action Centre and the Centre for Economic and Social Rights v Nigeria* ("*SERAC v Nigeria*"), it was alleged that the "government ... ignored the concerns of Ogoni communities regarding oil development, and ... responded to protests with massive violence and executions of Ogoni leaders."[65] In spite of heavy-handed government responses, popular resistance sometimes yields favourable results for local communities in the Niger Delta. For example, the movement garnered international attention in the 1990s following the work of the leaders of the Ogoni people. The protests of the 1990s also resulted in oil companies making substantial discretionary payments for land use.[66] Frynas also notes that a sub-contractor for the Nigeria Liquefied Natural Gas project "ear-marked US$1 million as the 8-year rent for a piece of land on Bonny Island."[67]

Recourse to popular resistance may also be partly linked to an inability to easily access formal dispute settlement institutions. Speaking about Kenya, Peter Kiplangat Cheruiyot has been quoted as saying, "Our people struggle to even take a single case to the Kenyan courts – the community has to sell the few possessions they have to gather enough money to institute proceedings in court – and have often lost. How can we possibly imagine taking a case to the African Commission on Human and Peoples' Rights all the way in The Gambia – and even if we win it has no meaning in Kenya because no one will ensure it is respected."[68] Hence while Niger Delta peoples have had recourse to

---

64 Omorogbe notes that violent suppression of community resistance is "the normal government reaction under both military and democratic governments. Even the democratic government of President Obasanjo reacted in a very heavy-handed fashion in 1999 against the people of Odi, Rivers State. They sent in soldiers to quell a disturbance. Men were killed, women were raped, and the town was practically razed to the ground. About a year later the President apologized, but the damage had been done." Omorogbe, "Legal Framework for Public Participation," 573.

65 *The Social and Economic Rights Action Centre and Centre for Economic and Social Rights v Nigeria*, (Communication 155/96), African Commission on Human and Peoples Rights, 27 October 2001, https://www.achpr.org/sessions/descions?id=134, para 5 ["*SERAC v Nigeria*"].

66 Frynas, *Oil in Nigeria*, 177.

67 Frynas, *Oil in Nigeria*, 177.

68 George Mukundi Wachira, *African Court on Human and Peoples' Rights: Ten Years and Still No Justice* (London: Minority Rights Group International, 2008), 11, https://minorityrights.org/wp-content/uploads/old-site-downloads/download-540-African-Court-on-Human-and-Peoples-Rights-Ten-years-on-and-still-no-justice.pdf.

judicial and quasi-judicial means of dispute settlement in addition to popular resistance, judicial recourse is limited by at least two major factors. First, a judicial decision will apply the legislative scheme that is being contested in the first place, and second, judicial recourse is often beyond the financial capacities of these communities. Where the purpose of agitation is legal change, the judiciary may resort to judicial activism via ingenious interpretations of the law, but realistically the judiciary cannot change the land tenure system.

As discussed earlier, the *Land Use Act* limits the property rights of Niger Delta peoples, and indeed all Nigerians. This limitation has been recognized outside Nigeria by bodies such as the Committee on the Elimination of Racial Discrimination, which recommends repeal of the *Land Use Act* and the *Petroleum Act*.[69] Given that the legislative scheme under the *Land Use Act* vests ownership of land in the government while granting citizens and communities rights of occupancy, it is difficult to adopt land ownership arguments based on the current land tenure system as leverage in securing favourable (contractual) arrangements with government and investors. Rights of occupancy could, however, offer some relevant, albeit limited, contributions. Based on statute, it is necessary to give notice and to pay compensation before land is acquired for use in oil and gas exploration, production, and other development.[70] Nevertheless, these notice and compensation rights are severely limited. In *Elf Petroleum Nigeria Ltd. v Umah* the respondents initiated legal action on behalf of a community in the Niger Delta because the appellant had acquired their land.[71] The Court of Appeal expressed the view that the appellant was not permitted to enter upon the respondents' land simply by producing an oil mining lease. The Court noted that the community's right of occupancy should have been revoked and compensation paid before the oil mining lease was granted. The fact that the *Land Use Act* permits relatively easy revocation of rights of occupancy does not permit much reliance on rights of occupancy as a significant negotiating leverage.[72]

In light of these limited property rights, popular resistance has gained a heightened position. What follows in this chapter is an analysis of

---

69   Committee on the Elimination of Racial Discrimination, "Concluding Observations," para 19.
70   See Part III B (1) of this chapter.
71   *Elf Petroleum Nigeria Ltd v Umah* (2007) 1 NWLR 44.
72   The land tenure system in other West African countries such as Ghana is different, possibly permitting a more feasible adoption of land ownership as a major negotiating leverage. However, in practice, the situation is not often very different

land-related initiatives upon which more robust and concrete participatory and decision-making mechanisms such as the multi-actor contract framework can be grounded. These initiatives are read in light of (and in spite of) limited real property rights, the challenges of each initiative are identified, and the analysis involves a rereading of these initiatives in order to identify avenues for better and more robust stakeholder engagement in the Niger Delta. The initiatives are grouped according to their major proponents: government, industry, and peoples. All the proponents draw on their rights to land (and resources) – the government on its ownership rights, industry on its licences and leases, and communities on their rights of occupancy. In drawing on their rights to land, each stakeholder, sometimes inadvertently, defines the rights of the other stakeholders.

B. *Locating Law-Related Negotiating Leverage in Land*

1. GOVERNMENT INITIATIVES: STATUTORY MECHANISMS

Clearly governments recognize that host and affected communities are major stakeholders in oil and gas exploration and production. However, many of the statutory initiatives adopted in order to incorporate these communities as active stakeholders are peripheral. They mostly gloss over the communities' major concerns. These initiatives do not grant decision-making power to host and affected communities. Instead, they encourage some consultation as well as the establishment of funds and development projects to alleviate the communities' concerns. They also demonstrate government's recognition that host and affected communities can have a voice in decisions that affect them. However, this recognition has not generated significant practical change.

The *Nigerian Minerals and Mining Act*[73] requires that mining companies and host communities conclude community development agreements (CDAs).[74] While not necessarily a statute regulating oil and gas production, the Act demonstrates the government's realization that

---

from what Nigerian communities encounter. On Ghana, see, generally, George A. Sarpong, "Improving Tenure Security for the Rural Poor: Ghana – Country Case Study (Towards the Improvement of Tenure Security for the Poor in Ghana: Some Thoughts and Observations)," Legal Empowerment of the Poor Working Paper No. 2 (Food and Agriculture Association of the United Nations, 2006). See the discussion of Papua New Guinea's customary land ownership system that differs from the Nigerian system in Ako, *Environmental Justice in Developing Countries*.

73 *Nigerian Minerals and Mining Act*, No. 27 of 2007, ss 116–17.
74 See Odumosu-Ayanu, "Foreign Direct Investment Catalysts."

there is a need to contractually engage local communities in the extractive industries. However, these CDAs are cast in the Act as "development" funding agreements and contribute little to ensuring that
communities participate in decision-making about issues that affect
them significantly. Like the other initiatives discussed in this section,
CDAs depend on title to land, as these agreements apply to host communities and not to all Nigerians, and by definition host communities
have interests in land.

Rights granted under Nigeria's *Oil Pipelines Act* also depend on
rights to and access to land. The minister is entitled to grant permits
for oil pipeline route surveys and licences for the construction, maintenance, and operation of oil pipelines.[75] Upon receipt of a permit to
survey, the permit holder is granted extensive rights to enter upon
lands on or "reasonably close" to the permit route to survey the land,
dig, cut, and remove vegetation, and to "do all other acts necessary to
ascertain the suitability of the land" for oil pipelines.[76] These extensive
rights are subject to the permit holder obtaining the consent of the
owner or occupier of land, or giving fourteen days' notice of the intention to enter the land.[77] It appears that even in the absence of consent,
a permit holder may proceed once the fourteen days' notice is given.
In fact where a person withholds possession of land contrary to the
Act, the holder of a permit or licence may make an *ex parte* application
to the Court for a writ of possession to eject the person withholding
possession.[78] There are also criminal sanctions for hindering possession of land.[79] However, under section 15 of the *Oil Pipelines Act*, a
licensee requires prior consent of the owners, occupiers, or persons
in control of "venerated land" in order to "enter upon, take possession of or use" such lands.[80] In other cases where an application for
an oil pipeline licence has been made, holders of interest in affected
lands may issue objections.[81] Inquiries and hearings follow such
objections, and the minister ultimately decides to grant or withhold
the licence.[82] Persons whose lands or interest in land are "injuriously
affected" by the exercise of rights attached to oil pipelines are entitled

---

75 *Oil Pipelines Act* Cap 338 LFN 1990, s 3.
76 *Oil Pipelines Act* Cap 338 LFN 1990, s 5(1).
77 *Oil Pipelines Act* Cap 338 LFN 1990, s 6(1).
78 *Oil Pipelines Act* Cap 338 LFN 1990, s 24.
79 *Oil Pipelines Act* Cap 338 LFN 1990, s 25.
80 *Oil Pipelines Act* Cap 338 LFN 1990, s 15.
81 *Oil Pipelines Act* Cap 338 LFN 1990, s 9.
82 *Oil Pipelines Act* Cap 338 LFN 1990, s 10.

to compensation.[83] These lands do not have to be land in respect to which a licence is granted, as long as the holders' lands or interests in the lands are "injuriously affected."[84] While the notice and objection process grants some participatory rights to holders of land or interests in land, these persons ultimately have little to contribute where a permit to survey has been granted and where the minister decides to grant an oil pipeline licence notwithstanding objections.

In spite of their limited nature, the legislative provisions discussed in this section are not always adhered to. It is arguable that these provisions are respected more in breach than adherence. The facts of and the celebrated decision in *SERAC v Nigeria* confirms this position.[85] The communication, which relates specifically to Ogoniland in the Niger Delta, alleged *inter alia* that oil reserves were exploited without "regard for the health or environment of the local communities."[86] The communication also alleged that contrary to the *Environmental Impact Assessment Act*, the government did not require the oil companies or government agencies to produce environment and health impact studies.[87] The communication further alleged the destruction of food sources, including the destruction of farmland.[88] More relevant to this chapter is the allegation that the government did not require oil companies "to consult communities before beginning operations, even if the operations pose direct threats to community or individual lands."[89] Apart from occupancy rights, consultations with holders of rights of occupancy where there could be adverse impacts on their rights has been a major feature of legislation. To refuse to abide by this minimal requirement is to completely deprive individuals and communities of the limited rights they have remaining.

The African Commission found the Nigerian government in violation of the socio-economic rights of the Ogoni people enshrined in the

---

83 *Oil Pipelines Act* Cap 338 LFN 1990, s 11(5). For compensation, see section 20 of the *Oil Pipelines Act*. By section 21, "Where the interests injuriously affected are those of a local community, the court may order the compensation to be paid to any chief, headman or member of that community on behalf of such community or that it be paid in accordance with a scheme of distribution approved by the court or that it be paid into a fund to be administered by a person approved by the court on trust for application to the general, social or educational benefit and advancement of that community or any section thereof."

84 *Oil Pipelines Act* Cap 338 LFN 1990, s 11(5).

85 *SERAC v Nigeria*.

86 *SERAC v Nigeria*, para 2.

87 *SERAC v Nigeria*, para 5.

88 *SERAC v Nigeria*, para 9.

89 *Oil Pipelines Act* Cap 338 LFN 1990, para 6.

African Charter on Human and Peoples Rights.[90] Included among the violated rights are the rights to health, clean environment, shelter, food, and life.[91] The African Commission referred to its mission to Nigeria where it witnessed the "deplorable situation in Ogoniland" "first hand."[92] It noted that Ogonis depend on their land and farms for survival, and these were destroyed by pollution and environmental degradation of a "humanly unacceptable" level.[93] The African Commission specifically commented *inter alia* on article 21 of the *African Charter*, which recognizes the rights of peoples to "freely dispose of their 'wealth and natural resources.'" According to article 21, the right is to be "exercised in the exclusive interest of the people," and they shall not be deprived of that right. The African Commission insightfully noted that the "origin" of the provision can "be traced to colonialism, during which the human and material resources of Africa were largely exploited for the benefit of outside powers, creating tragedy for Africans themselves, depriving them of their birthright and alienating them from the land. The aftermath of colonial exploitation has left Africa's precious resources and people still vulnerable to foreign misappropriation. The drafters of the [African] Charter obviously wanted to remind African governments of the continent's painful legacy and restore co-operative economic development to its traditional place at the heart of African Society."[94]

As the *SERAC v Nigeria* case demonstrates, the reality is unfavourable, even in the face of the legislative provisions on consultation, compensation, and development. Hence, before instituting mechanisms such as consultation and compensation, it is pertinent to address the challenges that limited real property rights pose. It is therefore necessary to develop foundational arguments in favour of local communities within this government-led initiative. Two of these arguments are what I call the trust argument and the *African Charter* argument.

First, even though its limitations should be readily conceded, communities may rely on the trust provisions of the *Land Use Act*. The *Land Use Act* states that state governors hold land in trust "for the people," and such land is to be "administered for the use and common benefit of all Nigerians."[95] Drawing insights from trust law, including rules

90 *African Charter on Human and Peoples' Rights*, 27 June 1981, OAU Doc. CAB/
    LEG/67/3/Rev.5, (1982) 21 ILM 58.
91 See, generally, *SERAC v Nigeria*.
92 *SERAC v Nigeria*, para 67.
93 *SERAC v Nigeria*, para 67.
94 *SERAC v Nigeria*, para 56.
95 *Land Use Act*, s 1 and long title.

governing trustee–beneficiary relationships, may be helpful.[96] The trustee – that is, the government – may be charged with trust and fiduciary obligations that favour holders of interest in land. One such obligation would be to ensure that industry actors conclude enforceable agreements, with host or affected communities, that recognize the stake of these communities in land and oil and gas development. One could also imply a duty to consult the beneficiaries based on strict trust law interpretations.

Second, insights from the *African Charter* and interpretations of the charter are helpful. The *African Charter* has been domesticated in Nigeria. In *Abacha v Fawehinmi*, it was held that the *African Charter* is domesticated in Nigerian law by the *African Charter on Human and Peoples Rights (Ratification and Enforcement) Act*,[97] and the Act prevails over local statutory enactments (except the Constitution) in cases of conflict.[98] However, the Act does not affect the validity of other statutes. At paragraph 53 of *SERAC v Nigeria*, the African Commission held that "Government compliance with the spirit of Articles 16 and 24 of the African Charter must also include ... providing meaningful opportunities for individuals to be heard and to participate in the development decisions affecting their communities." This interpretation of the charter to include the right of host and affected communities to participate is important. The *African Charter* argument emphasizes accounting for the broader socio-economic rights of African peoples.

Government-led initiatives can be meaningful mechanisms that provide negotiation voice for Niger Delta communities only if, in the absence of repeal, primary statutes like the *Land Use Act* are read in light of more foundational arguments like trustee–beneficiary relationship and an *African Charter* human rights requirement to ensure that people are able to participate in decisions that affect their communities. Otherwise, the government-led legislative initiatives discussed above will contribute little to communities' land-related negotiating tools, apart from signalling government recognition of peoples' rights without giving these rights much practical effect.

---

96 Nwabueze has considered application of trust law to the *Land Use Act* in the context of null and void transactions. Remigius N. Nwabueze, "Equitable Bases of the Nigerian Land Use Act," *Journal of African Law* 54 (2010): 119.

97 *African Charter on Human and Peoples Rights (Ratification and Enforcement) Act*, Cap 10 LFN 1990. This statute was also favourably considered in *Gbemre v Shell Petroleum Development Company Nigeria Ltd and Others* (2005) AHRLR 151 (Ng. HC 2005).

98 *Abacha v Fawehinmi* (2000) 6 NWLR 228.

2. INDUSTRY INITIATIVES: GLOBAL MEMORANDUM OF UNDERSTANDING AND PROPERTY RIGHTS

All over the world, communities and industry actors involved in the extractive industries have concluded industry-community agreements that promise benefits transfer to communities. While industry-community agreements are supported to varying degrees by different actors, in Nigeria's oil and gas industry, these agreements have been led largely by industry. Hence, this section regards these agreements as industry initiatives and refers to "industry-community agreements" because of industry dominance in these agreements in Nigeria. However, the same level of industry dominance in agreement-making does not apply in every jurisdiction. As a result, this chapter's references to agreements as industry initiatives are specific references to the global memorandum of understanding (GMOUs) formed between industry and communities in the Niger Delta. In Nigeria, both Shell and Chevron have developed the GMOU and have concluded these agreements with communities in the Niger Delta. In Canada, impact benefits agreements have been concluded. These IBAs are not the focus of this discussion, but a brief introduction to IBAs helps situate GMOUs in the context of other agreements with communities in the extractive industries. Gogal, Riegert, and Jamieson argue that there are three sources of the legal requirement for IBAs:[99] "the common law duty to consult and section 35 of the [Canadian] Constitution Act 1982," statutory requirements, including land claim or settlement agreements," and "regulatory requirements." Statutory requirements could be specifically included in oil and gas legislation.[100] Sosa and Keenan also provide a list of legal and other factors that prompt the conclusion of IBAs, including land claim agreements (some of which grant surface and/or subsurface rights to Aboriginal peoples and as a result also confer some control on these peoples), general Aboriginal rights as constitutionally guaranteed, "government policy," and "private sector initiative."[101] Hence,

---

99 Sandra Gogal, Richard Riegert, and Joann Jamieson, "Aboriginal Impact and Benefit Agreements: Practical Considerations," *Alberta Law Review* 43 (2005): 130.

100 See Gogal, Riegert, and Jamieson, "Aboriginal Impact and Benefit Agreements," citing section 5(2) of the *Canadian Oil and Gas Operations Act* on page 138.

101 Irene Sosa and Karyn Keenan, "Impact Benefit Agreements between Aboriginal Communities and Mining Companies: Their Use in Canada" (Canadian Environmental Law Association, 2001), 6–8. For example, the *Nunavut Land Claims Agreement* requires that an impact and benefit agreement should be negotiated between companies and Inuit organizations before a major development project commences. See section 26 of the *Nunavut Land Claims Agreement*, https://www.gov.nu.ca /sites/default/files/Nunavut_Land_Claims_Agreement.pdf. Sosa and Keenan note

Indigenous land rights[102] and legal and policy requirements[103] are relevant to the development of IBAs. Although fraught with challenges beyond the scope of this chapter, many IBAs are, however, more robust than GMOUs in Nigeria.[104]

GMOUs are fairly recent in Nigeria and are significantly limited. They do not purport to address significant decision-making that this chapter addresses. GMOUs are part of industry's initiative to cultivate a relationship with Niger Delta peoples. Because of the recent nature and confidentiality of these agreements, there is a paucity of analysis of GMOUs. Chevron Nigeria Limited introduced the GMOU in 2005,[105] and Shell adopted this form of agreement in 2006.[106] Chevron describes GMOUs as "multiyear agreements between the communities, Chevron and state governments."[107] The GMOUs create regional development committees that work with communities in advocating for their interests and leading decisions regarding spending.[108] According to Chevron, GMOUs "have generated approximately 200 projects in more than 400 communities, villages and chiefdoms and benefited some 600,000 community members."[109] These agreements are largely

the example of the *Nunavut Land Claims Agreement* as well as an instance where the government demanded the conclusion of an IBA. They note that the "negotiation of IBAs is now considered to be a *de facto*, albeit unwritten regulatory requirement in the North." Sosa and Keenan, "Impact Benefit Agreements," 7–8.

102 Steven Kennett, *Issues and Options for a Policy on Impact and Benefit Agreements for the Northern Territories*, prepared for the Mineral Resources Directorate, Department of Indian Affairs and Northern Development (Calgary: Canadian Institute of Resource Law, 1999).

103 Janet Keeping, "The Legal and Constitutional Basis for Benefits Agreements: A Summary," *Northern Perspectives* 25 (1999–2000), http://www.carc.org/wp -content/uploads/2017/10/1999-2000-NP-Impact-Benefit-Agreements.pdf.

104 See Ibironke T. Odumosu-Ayanu, "The (Legal) Nature of Indigenous Peoples' Agreements with Extractive Companies," in *Indigenous-Industry Agreements, Natural Resources and the Law*, ed. Dwight G. Newman and Ibironke T. Odumosu-Ayanu (London: Routledge, forthcoming).

105 Chevron, "Roots of Change: Chevron's Model Community Empowerment Program in the Niger Delta," 2017, https://www.chevron.com/-/media/chevron /stories/documents/nigeria-case-study-GMoU.pdf.

106 Shell, "Global Memorandum of Understanding (GMOU)," https://www.shell .com.ng/sustainability/communities/gmou.html. See also Uwafiokun Idemudia, "Oil Extraction and Poverty Reduction in the Niger Delta: A Critical Examination of Partnership Initiatives," *Journal of Business Ethics* 90 (2009): 91.

107 Chevron, "Empowering Communities."

108 Chevron, "Empowering Communities."

109 Chevron, "Nigeria: In the Community," http://www.chevron.com/countries /nigeria/inthecommunity/.

infrastructure and service provision initiatives that incorporate community decision-making in determining which services will be provided. They do not affect decision-making on the siting of oil and gas projects, the establishment of these projects, their development, or how they proceed. They are essentially means to acquire a social licence to operate in the Niger Delta. Chevron itself notes that the objective of these agreements "is to bring peace and stability to areas where Chevron operates."[110]

For Shell, a "GMoU is a written statement of understanding between SPDC [Shell Petroleum Development Corporation] and a group (or cluster) of several communities detailing the role of all parties in the implementation of community development plans."[111] Shell sets up institutional structures including a community trust, a cluster development board, and a steering committee (that is "chaired by the state government").[112] Like the Chevron GMOUs, the Shell GMOUs facilitate communities' decision-making on the development projects that should be undertaken. According to Shell, by 2011, GMOUs had been concluded with "27 clusters, covering 290 communities, about 30% of the local communities" around Shell's operations in the Niger Delta.[113] Shell reports granting scholarships and providing health care and other services under the GMOU model.

Like the Chevron model, Shell's GMOU is mostly a service and infrastructure provision agreement. Faleti outlines some problems with the GMOU framework, including community factions, absence of environmental issues from the agreements, perceived imposition of the GMOU model ousting "community governance" structures, and problems of classifying communities as host or affected communities.[114] Amidst the challenges of GMOUs, it is argued that they are a response to the events occurring in this oil-producing region. Oil-producing companies provide development funding, and communities respond with "guarantees of uninterrupted operations."[115] GMOUs represent companies' aspiration to acquire a social licence to operate in communities. While GMOUs are essentially responses to the unrest in the Niger Delta,

---

110 Chevron, "Nigeria."
111 Shell, "Shell in Nigeria."
112 Shell, "Shell in Nigeria."
113 Shell, "Shell in Nigeria."
114 See Stephen A. Faleti, "Challenges of Chevron's GMOU Implementation in It-sekiri Communities of Western Niger Delta" (paper, Peace & Conflict Studies Programme, University of Ibadan, 28 December 2010), 21–4, for details of these challenges.
115 Faleti, "Challenges of Chevron's GMOU Implementation," 25.

GMOUs are not divorced from land and land-related issues. Communities that conclude these agreements are holders of rights attached to land. The communities are aware of this fact. In expressing his concern with a GMOU, a Niger Delta resident noted, "The idea of the GMOU is a good intention, but the implementation is faulty. Chevron as a company is our *tenant*. Here we have the *tenant* dictating to us – it is worrisome."[116] The dynamic between communities and industry is partly a creation of statutorily determined land tenure. The *Land Use Act* and other legislative enactments effectively prevent these communities from exercising strong negotiating leverage.

The GMOU is a recent phenomenon that is only slowly capturing the attention of commentators. Clearly, several problems are associated with the conclusion, implementation, and focus of GMOUs, IBAs, and other CDAs. But some of these agreements appear to have stronger legal backgrounds than others. In comparing the IBA and GMOU models, the prospects appear more favourable for IBAs than for GMOUs, as GMOUs and many other CDAs are significantly limited agreements. Two primary factors account for these differences. First, the status of the peoples usually involved in these agreements (at least as recognized by the relevant governments) is different. In Canada, IBAs are usually concluded with Indigenous peoples. However, in Nigeria, the government is reluctant to accept the Indigenous status of any community to the exclusion of others. Second, the laws, especially those related to land tenure, in Canada and Nigeria are different. Notwithstanding challenges and weaker legal backgrounds, GMOUs allow us to observe the potential contributions and challenges of a model where host communities are part of agreements. What is necessary in order to pursue more effective and enforceable multi-actor contracts are stronger real property rights, or, in their absence, the ability to marshal compelling arguments that extend the limited rights granted under the current land tenure system.

3. PEOPLES' INITIATIVES: INDIGENOUS PEOPLES' PROPERTY RIGHTS
Of the three initiatives discussed in this chapter, the peoples' initiative is the most radical. It involves a claim to Indigenous status, which has become topical in some African countries. While not necessarily radical in other parts of the world, the claim to Indigenous status in Africa is not yet mainstream. Like many other countries, the territory known as

---

116 Cited in Faleti, "Challenges of Chevron's GMOU Implementation," 23. Emphasis added.

Nigeria is a creation of the colonial administration. Even though the discussion of Indigenous status in Africa is cast mostly in light of the relationship between marginalized communities and the post-colonial state (and transnational corporations), questions of Indigenous status cannot be separated from colonialism. Nigeria includes many diverse ethnic groups, and the agitation of the minorities is an issue that pre-dates political independence in 1960.

The Commission Appointed to Enquire into the Fears of Minorities and the Means of Allaying Them (the Willink Commission) examined the concerns of minority groups in Nigeria, including in the Niger Delta region.[117] The commission prepared its report before Nigeria's political independence from British rule. With specific reference to the Ijaw of the Niger Delta, the Willink Commission observed that the Niger Delta region was "poor, backward and neglected."[118] As early as this time, the Ijaw expressed the view that the rest of the country did not understand their "difficulties."[119] The commission recommended the "declaration of the Ijaw country as a Special Area" in order to "direct public attention to a neglected tract and give the Ijaws an opportunity of putting forward plans of their own for improvement."[120] In its conclusion and recommendations, the commission found that in all three regions of Nigeria, there was "either a minority or a group of minorities who described fears and grievances which they felt would become more intense when the present restraints were removed and who suggested as a remedy a separate state or states."[121] While several states have been created in the life of the Nigerian federation, the minorities in the Niger Delta did not separately acquire states. Even before the creation of these states, the Willink Commission had expressed the view that "a separate state would not provide a remedy for the fears expressed."[122] "Genuine fears" remained, according to the commission, and in its view, "the future was regarded with real apprehension."[123] That future has arrived. At the time of the Willink Commission's report, oil had just been discovered in commercial quantities. The concerns that the commission observed only worsened with the production of petroleum

117 See *Report of the Commission Appointed to Enquire into the Fears of Minorities and the Means of Allaying Them* (Secretary of State for the Colonies, July 1958).
118 *Report of the Commission*, 96.
119 *Report of the Commission*, 95.
120 *Report of the Commission*, 97.
121 *Report of the Commission*, 88.
122 *Report of the Commission*, 88.
123 *Report of the Commission*, 88.

resources. Several other commissions and panels have been constituted to address the Niger Delta question, and the difficulties only seem to exacerbate.[124]

Nigeria is not alone with the challenges t in navigating the government's relationship with minorities and the land rights of these peoples.[125] Even more challenging is recognizing the Indigenous status of some people in Nigeria and in many other parts of Africa.[126] Some governments in Africa, including the Nigerian government, expressed discomfort with Indigenous rights during discussions on the draft United Nations *Declaration on the Rights of Indigenous Peoples*.[127] Among the concerns were the criteria for determining Indigenous status, self-determination and secession, potential veto through the concept of free prior and informed consent, and control over land and natural resources.[128] Nigeria ultimately abstained from voting.[129]

Like the Nigerian government, Omorogbe argues that "indigenous rights have no place in any sovereign state that did not experience substantial settlement by European and other populations."[130] She contends that adopting Indigenous rights in this context "would create a situation where some groups could claim to be more indigenous

---

124   For a review of the reports of these commissions and panels, see *Report of the Technical Committee on the Niger Delta*, November 2008.

125   For analysis of Indigenous peoples' property rights in Canada, see Val Napoleon, "Looking beyond the Law: Questions about Indigenous Peoples' Tangible and Intangible Property," in *Protection of First Nations Cultural Heritage: Laws, Policy and Reform*, ed. Catherine Bell and Robert K. Paterson (Vancouver: UBC Press, 2009), 370.

126   See S.K. Date-Bah, "Rights of Indigenous People in Relation to Natural Resources Development: An African's Perspective," *Journal of Energy and Natural Resources Law* 16 (1998): 389.

127   *United Nations Declaration on the Rights of Indigenous Peoples* A/RES/61/295, 13 September 2007.

128   "Ogoni: Nigeria Opposes Indigenous Rights Declaration," Unrepresented Nations & Peoples Organization, 26 May 2007, http://www.unpo.org/article/6763. For a discussion of state sovereignty and the rights of Indigenous peoples, see Stefania Errico, "The Controversial Issue of Natural Resources: Balancing States' Sovereignty with Indigenous Peoples' Rights," in *Reflections on the UN Declaration on the Rights of Indigenous Peoples*, ed. Stephen Allen and Alexandra Xanthaki (Oxford: Hart Publishing, 2011), 329.

129   United Nations, "General Assembly Adopts Declaration on Rights of Indigenous Peoples," Sixty-First General Assembly Plenary 107th & 108th Meetings (AM & PM), 13 September 2007, GA/10612, https://www.un.org/press/en/2007/ga10612.doc.htm.

130   Omorogbe, "Legal Framework for Public Participation," 569.

than others."[131] Commentators such as Date-Bah prefer to refer to African peoples as "local people" rather than Indigenous peoples entitled to recognition under international law, for several reasons, including the dangers of perpetuating ethnic conflicts in African countries.[132] For Date-Bah, all Africans should, following the International Labour Organization Convention No. 169 standards, be entitled to enjoy their (cultural and spiritual) relationship with land, enjoy ownership and possession of traditional lands, and have adequate access to resolve land claims through the legal system.[133]

Scholars often discuss Indigenous status in light of colonialism and possession of land for longer periods of time.[134] The more subjective element of self-identification is also becoming accepted as a mode of identifying Indigenous peoples. Article 1(2) of the International Labour Organization's *Convention Concerning Indigenous and Tribal Peoples* (to which Nigeria is not a party) recognizes self-identification as a criterion for determining Indigenous status.[135] The 2006 *Report of the African Commission on Human and Peoples' Rights and the International Work Group for Indigenous Affairs* emphasizes self-identification.[136] Anaya also includes "minority or non-dominant tribal peoples of Africa" among some of

---

131 Omorogbe, "Legal Framework for Public Participation," 569. The African Commission's Working Group of Experts on Indigenous Populations/Communities rebuts arguments of this nature. See African Commission on Human and Peoples' Rights & International Work Group for Indigenous Affairs, *Report of the African Commission's Working Group of Experts on Indigenous Populations/Communities* (adopted by the African Commission on Human and Peoples' Rights at its 28th Ordinary Session) (ACHPR & IWGIA, 2005), 88–9, http://pro169.org/res/materials/en/identification/ACHPR%20Report%20on%20indigenous%20populations-communities.pdf.

132 Date-Bah, "Rights of Indigenous People," 411. On national unity and Indigenous status in parts of Africa, see Omorogbe, "Legal Framework for Public Participation," 571.

133 Date-Bah, "Rights of Indigenous People."

134 See, generally, S. James Anaya, *Indigenous Peoples in International Law*, 2nd ed. (Oxford: Oxford University Press, 2004); James (Sa'ke'j) Youngblood Henderson, *Indigenous Diplomacy and the Rights of Peoples: Achieving UN Recognition* (Saskatoon, SK: Purich, 2008); Steven Curry, *Indigenous Sovereignty and the Democratic Project* (Aldershot, UK: Ashgate, 2004).

135 *Convention Concerning Indigenous and Tribal Peoples in Independent Countries* No. 169, 27 June 1989 (1989) 28 ILM 1382.

136 African Commission on Human and Peoples Rights and the International Work Group for Indigenous Affairs, *Indigenous Peoples in Africa: The Forgotten Peoples? The African Commission's Work on Indigenous Peoples in Africa* (ACHPR and IWGIA, 2006), 10–11, https://www.achpr.org/public/Document/file/Any/achpr_wgip_report_summary_version_eng.pdf [ACHPR and IWGIA, "Forgotten Peoples"].

the peoples that "regard themselves as indigenous."[137] These views are reflections of the position that specific criteria applicable to all Indigenous peoples in all parts of the world may be difficult to achieve.[138]

Some Niger Delta peoples claim Indigenous status. Among these are the Ogonis,[139] who are one of the oldest settlers in the Niger Delta.[140] The claim of the Ogonis and other African peoples to Indigenous status is contrary to the view that "we are all indigenous in Africa."[141] The *Report of the African Commission's Working Group of Experts on Indigenous Populations and Communities* responds to the claim that "all Africans are indigenous to Africa," and without defining the term *Indigenous peoples*,[142] the working group offers criteria that help determine Indigenous status in the African context. The report states,

> It is often being argued that all Africans are indigenous to Africa. Definitely all Africans are indigenous as compared to the European colonialists who left all of black Africa in a subordinate position, which was in many respects similar to the situation of indigenous peoples elsewhere. However, if the concept of *indigenous* is exclusively linked with a colonial situation, it leaves us without a suitable concept for analysing internal structural relationships of inequality that have persisted after liberation from colonial dominance.
>
> We should put much less emphasis on the early definitions focusing on aboriginality, as indeed it is difficult and not very constructive ... to debate

137   Anaya, *Indigenous Peoples in International Law*, 3.

138   See Benedict Kingsbury, "'Indigenous Peoples' in International Law: A Constructivist Approach to the Asian Controversy," *American Journal of International Law* 92 (1998): 414 (suggesting a constructivist approach to analysing Indigenous status).

139   The African Commission on Human and Peoples Rights and the International Work Group for Indigenous Affairs list the Ogoni as an example of African peoples who self-identify as Indigenous peoples. ACHPR and IWGIA, "Forgotten Peoples," 16.

140   Sonpie Kpone-Tonwe, "Property Reckoning and Methods of Accumulating Wealth among the Ogoni of the Eastern Niger Delta," *Journal of the International African Institute* 67 (1997): 130.

141   Dorothy L. Hodgson, "Becoming Indigenous in Africa," *African Studies Review* 52 (2009): 3. On the difficulty of recognizing Indigenous status in Africa, see, generally, Felix Mukwiza Ndahinda, *Indigenousness in Africa: A Contested Legal Framework for Empowerment of "Marginalized" Communities* (The Hague: TMC Asser, 2011); Ndahinda, "Marginality, Disempowerment and Contested Discourses on Indigenousness in Africa," *International Journal on Minority and Group Rights* 18 (2011): 479. For the "Asian controversy," see Kingsbury, "'Indigenous Peoples,'" 147.

142   *Report of the African Commission*, 87, noting, "Other peoples of the world are not required to define themselves in similar ways."

this in the African context. The focus should be more on recent approaches focusing on *self-definition* as indigenous and distinctly different from other groups within a state; on a *special attachment to and use of their traditional land* whereby their ancestral land and territory has a fundamental importance for their collective physical and cultural survival as peoples; on an experience of *subjugation, marginalization, dispossession, exclusion or discrimination* because these peoples have different cultures, ways of life or modes of production than the national hegemonic and dominant model.[143]

Some commentators have proposed minority rights as an alternative, especially in the African context. Article 27 of the *International Covenant on Civil and Political Rights*[144] and the *UN Declaration on the Rights of Persons Belonging to National or Ethnic, Religious and Linguistic Minorities*[145] are international instruments that guarantee the rights of minorities. These instruments address cultural, religious, and language rights. The *African Charter* also guarantees similar rights, including the right to culture, in article 17.[146] The extent to which minority rights are able to address the rights of peoples in the Niger Delta, especially with regard to land, is yet to be seen. However, if the suggestions of scholars are accurate, Indigenous rights appear to currently provide more protection than minority rights.[147]

Although the case law on the property rights of Indigenous peoples before human rights bodies in Africa is not as developed as it is in other jurisdictions,[148] some cases lend credence to the validity of land claims based on Indigenous status in African countries. In *Centre for Minority Rights Development (Kenya) and Minority Rights Group International on Behalf of Endorois Welfare Council v Kenya ("Endorois Case")*, the

---

143 *Report of the African Commission*, 92–3.
144 *International Covenant on Civil and Political Rights*, adopted 16 December 1966, 999 UNTS 171 (entered into force 23 March 1976).
145 *Declaration on the Rights of Persons Belonging to National or Ethnic, Religious and Linguistic Minorities*, adopted 18 December 1992, GA Res. 47/135 Annex, UN Doc. A/Res/47/135/Annex (1992).
146 *African Charter*.
147 Miriam J. Aukerman, "Definitions and Justifications: Minority and Indigenous Rights in a Central/East European Context," *Human Rights Quarterly* 22 (2000): 1013, 1017; Dieter Kugelmann, "The Protection of Minorities and Indigenous Peoples Respecting Cultural Diversity," *Max Planck Yearbook of UN Law* 11 (2007): 233; Will Kymlicka, "Multiculturalism and Minority Rights: West and East," *Journal on Ethnopolitics and Minority Issues in Europe* 4 (2002): 1.
148 See the decisions of the Inter-American Court of Human Rights, for example, *Saramaka People v Suriname* (Inter-American Court of Human Rights Judgment of 28 November 2007).

African Commission addressed a complaint that arose from alleged displacement of the Endorois community from their ancestral lands for tourism.[149] The allegations also included inadequate compensation and absence of proper consultation. The decision is notable for several reasons, including the African Commission's finding on the Indigenous status of the Endorois people and its recognition of the right to development. The African Commission specifically responded to the question of whether the Endorois are "indigenous peoples and thereby needing special protection."[150] The commission noted the contested and ambiguous nature of the terms *peoples* and *Indigenous peoples* or *Indigenous communities*.[151] It expressed the view that "some marginalised and vulnerable groups in Africa are suffering from particular problems.... [M]any of these groups have not been accommodated by dominating development paradigms and in many cases they are being victimised by mainstream development policies and thinking and their basic human rights are violated.... [I]ndigenous peoples have, due to past and ongoing processes, become marginalised in their own country and they need recognition and protection of their basic human rights and fundamental freedoms."[152] For the commission, Indigenous peoples have a recognizable link with land and their culture.[153] In this case, the Endorois community's "culture, religion and traditional way of life are intimately intertwined with their ancestral lands and they also self-identify as Indigenous peoples."[154] The finding of Indigenous status and the right to property guaranteed in article 14 of the *African Charter* led the commission to the view that Indigenous peoples' traditional possession of land is equivalent in effect to "state-granted full property title," and Indigenous peoples are entitled to "demand official recognition and registration of property title."[155] Further, Indigenous status also led to an interpretation of consultation as consent.[156]

In light of the challenges that Niger Delta peoples have encountered, the concerted effort to address Indigenous status through the work of the African Commission, and the decisions that are being rendered on

---

149 *Centre for Minority Rights Development (Kenya) and Minority Rights Group International on Behalf of Endorois Welfare Council v Kenya*, African Commission on Human and Peoples Rights Communication 276/2003.

150 *Centre for Minority Rights Development (Kenya) v Kenya*, para 146.

151 *Centre for Minority Rights Development (Kenya) v Kenya*, para 147.

152 *Centre for Minority Rights Development (Kenya) v Kenya*, para 148.

153 *Centre for Minority Rights Development (Kenya) v Kenya*, para 154.

154 *Centre for Minority Rights Development (Kenya) v Kenya*, para 156–7.

155 *Centre for Minority Rights Development (Kenya) v Kenya*, para 209.

156 *Centre for Minority Rights Development (Kenya) v Kenya*, para 226.

Indigenous status in Africa, the quest for recognition as Indigenous peoples by some Niger Delta peoples is not an empty endeavour. With international recognition as Indigenous peoples comes access to internationally (and domestically) protected rights related to land, natural resources, consultation, and consent.[157] The UN Permanent Forum on Indigenous Issues notes, "Land is the foundation of the lives and cultures of indigenous peoples all over the world. This is why the protection of their right to lands, territories and natural resources is a key demand of the international indigenous peoples' movement and of indigenous peoples and organizations everywhere.... Without access to and respect for their rights over their lands, territories and natural resources, the survival of indigenous peoples' particular distinct culture is threatened."[158] The African Commission also notes that rights to land and natural resources are central to Indigenous rights.[159] Principles enunciated in instruments such as the UN *Declaration on the Rights of Indigenous Peoples* could contribute to alleviating the plight of the peoples of the Niger Delta.[160] However, the question remains whether Niger Delta peoples are recognized as Indigenous peoples under international law and domestically. Perhaps more pertinent questions are whether it matters and why. Irrespective of the finding, peoples like the Ogoni have realized that recognition of Indigenous status would contribute to addressing their land struggles, especially in relation to the Nigerian state and industry actors involved in exploiting oil and gas within their territories.

While Indigenous status is challenged in most parts of Africa, it is not in many parts of the Americas, including Canada. Nevertheless, Canada's Indigenous peoples continue to face significant challenges. Indigenous status comes with Indigenous rights, including rights related to land. Such rights to land should provide the impetus for significant socio-economic rights and negotiating leverage for agreements, if Indigenous peoples wish to conclude such agreements. Canada's Indigenous peoples have concluded several agreements

---

157 James Anaya, "Indigenous Peoples' Participatory Rights in Relation to Decisions about Natural Resource Extraction: The More Fundamental Issue of What Rights Indigenous People Have in Lands and Resources," *Arizona Journal of International and Comparative Law* 22 (2005): 7.

158 United Nations Permanent Forum on Indigenous Issues, *Report on the Sixth Session* (14–15 May 2007), Economic and Social Council Official Records Supplement No. 23, UN Doc. E/2007/43 E/C.19/2007/12, para 5.

159 *Report of the African Commission*, 97.

160 *United Nations Declaration on the Rights of Indigenous Peoples.* See, generally, Allen and Xanthaki, *Reflections on the UN Declaration.*

including impact and benefits agreements, environmental agreements, and other agreements – related to natural resource extraction.[161] These agreements have been based mostly on Indigenous peoples' sui generis relationship with Canada and with land. Eroding these land rights has significant potential harmful effects, including the inability to negotiate terms that are favourable to Indigenous peoples.

Participating as parties in foundational multi-actor oil and gas contracts provides a framework for peoples to negotiate agreements with governments and industry actors, where these peoples choose to engage in such negotiations, on terms agreeable to them. If land rights are eroded because of privatization or other reasons, negotiating leverage that is law-related is reduced or non-existent. Such erosion of land rights may be reminiscent of the Nigeria situation. The legal status of peoples in Nigeria and Canada, including the land tenure system, is somewhat different. First, while Indigenous status is recognized in Canada, it is vigorously contested in Nigeria. Second, customary law applies to communities in Nigeria and Indigenous law to Indigenous communities in Canada, although the contents of the laws are different. However, while it is argued that customary law related to land survived the *Land Use Act*, such customary law has been significantly affected by the Act. Third, and related to the second, is the nature of land-tenure systems applicable in areas that are mostly affected by resource extraction. The *Land Use Act* applies in all parts of Nigeria, whereas Indigenous land tenure systems have endured in many parts of Canada. These differences allow an easier application of multi-actor agreements to Canada's extractive industries. Nevertheless, as this chapter has argued, these agreements could apply in places like Nigeria, notwithstanding the significantly reduced land rights that people have.

The multi-actor agreement framework acknowledges peoples' real property rights, protects their property rights, and acknowledges peoples' agency. While the framework empowers peoples and communities, it also has the potential to contribute to peaceful coexistence between communities, industry, and government based on negotiated terms. It could facilitate conflict resolution via negotiation. It aims to protect actors' interests and expectations via contract and clearly

---

161 See Odumosu-Ayanu, "Governments, Investors and Local Communities"; James Gathii and Ibironke T. Odumosu-Ayanu, "The Turn to Contractual Responsibility in the Global Extractive Industry," *Business and Human Rights Journal* 1 (2015): 69.

identified dispute resolution mechanisms. Where peoples (Indigenous or otherwise) are deprived of land rights that they have traditionally held or where "creeping" deprivation of land rights occurs, there is the potential for conflict, or where such conflict already exists, the potential to aggravate conflict. Participation, dialogue, acknowledgment of peoples' agency, and concrete and enforceable decision-making capabilities are essential for peaceful coexistence among communities, industry actors, and government. Host and affected communities have an entitlement to such decision-making ability. And, in a system that relies heavily on legal rights, stronger land rights are a plausible legal argument for peoples' decision-making abilities. It is true of peoples as diverse as Niger Delta peoples and Canada's Indigenous peoples.

IV. Conclusion

This chapter has explored the argument that negotiating voice in contributing to decision-making that affects host and impacted communities in oil and gas development in Nigeria's Niger Delta depends largely on the land rights that these communities can channel. While this argument would have been rather easy to advance, provisions of Nigeria's statutes, especially the *Land Use Act*, dictate that communities have limited rights to land that can be leveraged in concluding enforceable agreements that ensure that their interests are well protected in developing projects that affect these peoples. Such limitation and its attendant consequences are a useful case study for other resource-rich jurisdictions such as Canada, especially as it plans to embark on land reform in Indigenous territory.

Recognizing that peaceful popular resistance (and some judicial and quasi-judicial action) have been the most prominent mechanisms for advancing their real property interests, I considered three initiatives on which one could draw in arguing for a land-related negotiating voice for Niger Delta peoples. These initiatives include serious challenges but they present potential. First, for the government-led statutory initiatives, trust law principles and fiduciary obligations of the government – which holds land in trust for the people as well as *SERAC v Nigeria*–like *African Charter* interpretations – could enhance the land-based negotiating voice for Niger Delta peoples. Second, I discussed the challenges of industry-driven agreements such as GMOUs, and concluded that while they have serious limitations, these agreements demonstrate the practicality of concluding agreements with communities as a way to protect their interests and respect their agency as stakeholders in oil and gas development. Third, I assessed the people-led Indigenous status argument. While the Nigerian government disagrees with this argument, it has the potential to provide the much-needed land tenure security for Niger Delta peoples.

The quest for asserting agency in the Niger Delta in the development of petroleum resources cannot be separated from land and interests in land. As each of the stakeholders – government, industry actors, and communities – acquires, loses, or asserts interests in land, these acquisitions, losses, and assertions define the rights of the other actors to, and their interests in, land.

10 Locating the Woman: A Note on Customary Law and the Utility of Real Property in the Kingdom of Eswatini (Formerly the Kingdom of Swaziland)*

TENILLE E. BROWN

This chapter looks at women, land, and property law in the Kingdom of Eswatini (Swaziland). In recent years, in common with its southern African neighbours, Eswatini has seen an increased awareness of land and property security as a gendered issue. In Eswatini this has resulted in mobilization of gender activists to support equality claims to real property and land law in the Roman-Dutch system. I observe that although the promotion of the culturally Indigenous has historically been done at the expense of women's experience with land and real property, a core opportunity afforded by relying on the self-governance of Swazi law and custom for promoting security of property rights is its ability to situate the woman's multifaceted relationship to land within her cultural reality. This observation is particularly important in a legally dualistic society such as Eswatini, where judgments from the High Court operate within an Indigenous legal and cultural context. Ultimately the chapter explores the importance of grounded research in the interaction between law and custom and common law in engaging with and realizing rights to property.

In part I I outline the landscape of property and land law. In part II I outline the legal provisions for land and real property in the Indigenous customary system, called Swazi law and custom, and then in part III I out-line provisions of property law in the imported colonial Roman-Dutch civil law, referred to as the common law. The focus here is to look at the processes, rights, and entitlements to land and real property in both legal systems, and to critically understand them from gendered perspectives.

---

* The country name has been changed as of April 2018 (Legal Notice No. 80 of 2018). In this chapter the new name "Kingdom of Eswatini" will be adopted and the word "Swazi" will continue to be used to describe laws, traditions, and people. I will refer to "Swaziland" where required due to its inclusion in existing frameworks and records.

I observe that legal dualism is particularly pronounced in land and property law, whereby land is categorized and then regulated through a corresponding set of rules. Like Morales and Thom, and Napoleon and Snyder in this volume, this chapter identifies land regulation found in both common law and Indigenous law systems. I argue that neither common law nor Swazi customary law is attuned to solving the problem of gender inequity in property ownership in isolation. Instead we must look at these two legal systems together in order to better understand the lived effects of property inequality.

I. Introduction

The Kingdom of Eswatini is a small, land-locked country in southern Africa and the last remaining absolute monarchy in sub-Sahara Africa.[1] In Eswatini the strength of the monarchy and Swazi culture remain strong facets of national identity. Swazi institutions are deeply and intimately tied to family, community, and country. As part of this context the ability to own and control land is a largely contested and highly regulated aspect of Swazi life. The systems for regulation are found in both Swazi law and custom, and the imported common law.

As has been done elsewhere, access to land and real property ownership is increasingly being understood as an issue for the realization of gender equality in Eswatini.[2] In recent years the inequality in security of land tenure enjoyed by women has come under pressure, and there has been increased mobilization around real property ownership rights for women. The route taken to claim women's property and land rights by civil society has been made primarily on the basis of constitutional equality claims

---

1   OECD, "Swaziland," in *OECD Atlas of Gender and Development: How Social Norms Affect Gender Equality in Non-OECD Countries* (Paris: OECD Publishing, 2010), 268–9.

2   Recent literature has begun to look at women's experience with land. See, for example, Hilary Lim and Anne Bottomley, *Feminist Perspectives on Land Law* (Abingdon, UK: Routledge-Cavendish, 2007); Fareda Banda, *Women, Law and Human Rights: An African Perspective* (Oxford: Hart, 2005); Banda, "Women, Law and Human Rights in Southern Africa," *Journal of Southern African Studies* 32, no. 1 (2006): 13; Anne Bottomley, *Feminist Perspectives on the Foundational Subjects of Law* (London: Cavendish Publishing, ca 1996); Sandra F. Joireman, "Entrapment or Freedom: Enforcing Customary Property Rights Regimes in Common-Law Africa," in *The Future of African Customary Law*, ed. Jeanmarie Fenrich, Paolo Galizzi, and Tracy E. Higgins, 295–311 (Cambridge: Cambridge University Press, 2011); Janet L. Banda, "Romancing Customary Tenure: Challenges and Prospects for the Neo-Liberal Suitor," in Fenrich, Galizzi, and Higgins, *Future of African Customary Law*, 312–35; and Sandra F. Joireman, *Where There Is No Government: Enforcing Property Rights in Common Law Africa* (Oxford: Oxford University Press, 2011).

through the transplanted Roman-Dutch legal system. In taking this route, civil society has bypassed challenging the Swazi law and custom system. Reliance upon the common law to ensure equality rights is a bold move in a country in which the strong Swazi cultural tradition means that the protection of the culturally Indigenous enjoys paramount concern.

For recent equality gains, the interaction between common and customary law remains largely unexamined. In particular, the allotment of gender rights in the respective legal regimes is fluid and contested. The property ownership legal scheme highlights the critical challenge in having two living legal systems. A close examination of property, land, allotment of rights, and the gendered nature of the Swazi experience with land provides an opportunity to explore the Swazi legal pluralist reality. In Eswatini the property question can serve as a conduit for meaningful dialogue about what it means to be a Swazi and how the country can balance competing interests codified in Swazi law and custom, the Constitution of Eswatini, and common law. Having this dialogue is essential to any efforts to operationalizing gender equality claims.

A. Part I: The Landscape of Land and Property Law

The law pertaining to real property and land ownership in Eswatini is a complex area of multiple sources of law and competing land interests. For the purposes of legal categorization, Eswatini is divided into three types of land: Crown land, title deed land, and Swazi Nation Land (SNL) or *Umhlaba wakaNgwane* or *Umbhlala weMaswati*.[3] For all three types of land, the king holds the land in trust for the Swazi nation.[4] Underlying this categorization of land types, there are two legal systems: the received colonial Roman-Dutch legal system and the customary system, Swazi law and custom. Both legal systems have provisions for real property use, access, and ownership. To some extent the category of land determines the law governing its use. As such we see that Swazi law and custom largely governs the use of SNL. Likewise a mixture of statutory and case law from the common law tends to govern the title deed land.

However, the reality of the dual legal system in Eswatini does not always lend itself to neat categorization of land types with the

---

3 F.P. van R. Whelpton, "Land Tenure Dealing with Swazi Nation Land in the Kingdom of Swaziland," *Stellenbosch Law Review* 16, no. 1 (2005): 146.

4 Susan Scott, "Some Thoughts on the Law of Property in Swaziland," *Comparative and International Journal of South Africa* 39 (2006): 152. See also Richard Levin, *When the Sleeping Grass Awakens: Land and Power in Swaziland* (Johannesburg: Witwatersrand University Press, 1997), 114–16.

corresponding legal management system. One defining feature of the Swazi legal culture is the pluralism of legal administration. The annexation of Eswatini as a Dutch and then British protectorate[5] resulted in the enforcement of traditional Swazi systems of governance, coinciding with the imposition of British governance and law, which was effectively layered on top of the law and custom regime.[6] The duality of legal systems means that whilst non-Swazis are subjected only to the common law, Swazis find themselves subject to two, sometimes competing, sets of legal rules. The danger posed by this multiplicity of judicial authorities has long been recognized.[7] The existence of two legal systems increases the legal obligations placed on Swazis, as well as increasing the likelihood that people with command of both systems are able to cherry-pick between legal systems in order to achieve policy aims. A compelling example of the way in which dual systems can be taken advantage of can be found in the prosecution of the crime of prostitution in the 1970s.[8] As a lesser criminal offence, prostitution could be tried in either the law and custom courts, or within the

---

5   For a summary of the colonization and subsequent independence of Swaziland, see Hilda Kuper, *The Swazi: A South African Kingdom* (London: Holt, Rinehart & Winston, 1966); Kuper, *An African Aristocracy* (London: Oxford University Press, 1947), 19–33); Levin, *When the Sleeping Grass Awakens*, 84–113.

6   General Law and Administration Proclamation, No. 4 of 1907, s 3(1), which imported Roman-Dutch law into Swaziland. See also the *Constitution Act, 2005*, s 252(1), which states, "The principles and rules that formed, immediately before the 6th September 1968 (Independence Day), the principles and rules of the Roman Dutch Common Law as applicable to Swaziland since 22nd February 1905 are confirmed and shall be applied and enforced as the common law of Swaziland except where and to the extent that those principles are inconsistent with the Constitution of a statute."

   The Constitution of the Kingdom of Swaziland, No. 001/2005, http://www.ilo .org/wcmsp5/groups/public/---ed_protect/---protrav/---ilo_aids/documents /legaldocument/wcms_125409.pdf. See Susan Scott, "Some Thoughts on the Law of Property," 160.

   See also Joireman, "Entrapment of Freedom," 297. Here the author explains that Britain took an indirect rule approach to colonial governance. This meant that British institutions were superimposed on customary systems. Although these customary systems were retained, they were also solidified and enforced in relation to the new British rule.

7   R.T. Nhlapo, "Legal Duality and Multiple Judicial Organisation in Swaziland: An Analysis and a Proposal," in *The Individual under African Law: Proceedings of the First All-Africa Law Conference, October 11–16, 1981, Royal Swazi Spa, Swaziland*, ed. Peter Nanyena Takirambudde (Kwaluseni: University of Swaziland, 1982), 67; and Women and Law in Southern Africa Research and Educational Trust (WLSA), *Inheritance in Swaziland: Law and Practice* (Swaziland: Women and Law in Southern Africa Trust, 1994), 1–2; and Joireman, *Where There Is No Government*, 41.

8   Nhlapo, "Legal Duality and Multiple Judicial Organisation in Swaziland," 68–9.

common law courts.[9] It was reported in national news in 1979 that the Office of the Director of Public Prosecutions made an affirmative choice to prosecute the crime in the customary law system, as the lower evidentiary requirements meant that there would be a higher rate of conviction.[10] Thus whilst the freedom of choice in the legal forum creates the opportunity to further policy aims, it can simultaneously compromise individual rights and decrease judicial safeguards.

There are multiple sources of property and land law, including the Constitution, statutory law, common law judicial decisions, and Swazi law and custom.[11] While the dual legal systems pose uncertainty about which will regulate land or property in question, the three distinct categories of land provide *some* guidance for the applicable legal regulation. The first category of land, Crown land, is the smallest amount of land in Eswatini. Crown land is sold to mostly foreign-owned corporations operating in Eswatini. Since a 1973 decree, the title to this land vests in the king under a ninety-nine year leasehold.[12] Second, there is free-hold title or title deed land, which is available for purchase, historically by non-Swazis, and more recently by a small sector of Swazis who are able to purchase. The regulation of both Crown land and title deed land is governed by the common law. The third and most prevalent category of land tenure is that of SNL. Administratively SNL is governed solely by Swazi law and custom, whereby chiefs and later customary courts regulate access to land and handle disputes. SNL is of most immediate relevance to Swazis. Within Swazi law and custom, land access, and property ownership are connected to many societal rights and obligations. SNL is understood with reference to the greater body of Swazi law and custom, which represents a complex system of duties and responsibilities.

The reality of legal pluralism makes the land and property law landscape difficult to map. Within the duality of the legal systems and the categorization of land, there are continued gender inequalities that have particular impacts upon Swazi women's experience with land. The response to this inequality has been mainly to seek gender equality through the common law, whilst simultaneously attempting to codify Swazi law and custom in ways that take gender into account.

---

9 *Criminal Procedure and Evidence Act*, no. 67 of 1938.
10 Nhlapo, "Legal Duality and Multiple Judicial Organisation in Swaziland," 70.
11 Scott, "Some Thoughts on the Law of Property in Swaziland," 152.
12 Vesting of Land in King, Order 45 of 1973.

B. Part II: Swazi Law and Custom

Central to Swazi identity is Swazi law and custom, which is a living system of law that acts as a daily enforcer of societal regulation.[13] On the one hand Swazi law and custom exists as a formal legal system, with rules, courts, and mechanisms for enforcement. The arbitrators in the customary courts are chiefs appointed within the customary arrangement by the king of Eswatini. In addition, Swazi law and custom operates in a more complex informal pattern governing social and familial relations.[14] It is recognized that "understanding the complex patterns of women's relationship with land requires that land and property systems be situated within a wide ranging set of political, economic, and socio-cultural matrices."[15] An understanding of Swazi law and custom as a nationwide system allows us to appreciate the fluidity between the structural land management systems and the familial interaction with land. The duplication of social regulation at the family and governmental levels means that cultural institutions of management are replicated at multiple levels of Swazi society, which has specific impacts on gender.

At the national land-management level, Swazi law and custom regulates the use of SNL, which is the most prevalent land in country, constituting 74 per cent of land within Eswatini. Of that area, 42 per cent is customary land set aside for domestic use,[16] although the amounts and boundaries of SNL have not been strictly delineated by legislation.[17] SNL is held by the king in trust for Swazis, and in turn the control and management of the land is delegated to a chief, who then manages the land for the people within his chiefdom.[18] Most commonly Swazis will automatically gain the right to live on the land in which they are born through their family. In addition, there is the option of going through

---

13 Anne Griffiths, "Networking Resources: A Gendered Perspective on Kwena Women's Property Rights," in Lim and Bottomley, *Feminist Perspectives on Land Law*, 218. See similarly in the Ugandan context Winnie Bikaako and John Senkumba, "Gender, Land and Rights: Contemporary Contestations in Law, Policy and Practice in Uganda," in *Women and Land in Africa: Culture, Religion, and Realizing Women's Rights*, ed. L. Muthoni Wanyeki (London: Zed Books, 2003), 243–4.

14 WLSA, *Inheritance in Swaziland*, 59.

15 Griffiths, "Networking Resources," 218.

16 B.I. Nyoka, "State of Forest and Tree Genetic Resources in Dry Zone Southern Africa Development Community Countries" (Forestry Department, Food and Agriculture Organisation of the United Nations, February 2003), chap. 5, http://www.fao.org/docrep/005/ac850e/ac850e00.htm#Contents.

17 Whelpton, "Land Tenure Dealing with Swazi Nation Land," 147.

18 Whelpton, "Land Tenure Dealing with Swazi Nation Land," 147.

kukhonta, or swearing allegiance to another chief in order to move to a different chiefdom.[19] In both processes, the right to control land extends to males only. Only a male can *khonta*, or gain an allocation of a family's SNL for his use and control.

The boundaries of land areas are influenced by political organization under the traditional political system called *tinkhundla*. The *tinkhundla* system divides the country into chiefdoms, with the chief of an area having been appointed by the king.[20] The *tinkhundla* system as it exists today is the result of the codification of a Swazi land-management system by the Britain at the time of de-colonization. The *tinkhundla* form of country management uses land in a very specific way: land is both a subject of the customary system and a tool for the continued importance of Swazi law and custom. Even before de-colonization, the British rule over Swazi affairs was minimal, concerned as it was with the affairs of the settler community.[21] The work of Hilda Kuper, a leading Zimbabwean anthropologist, remains one of the most comprehensive accounts of Swazi customary culture.[22] In her work, Kuper describes some of the rules and duties that have arisen as part of the process of maintaining residency in a particular chiefdom. A chief derives his power and prestige from the number of citizens he has living in his chiefdom, and all citizens are required to pay tribute to their chief. Tribute may take the form of assisting in the maintenance of land and property, or through observance of national traditional celebrations, or by supporting the community during death and burial.[23] Similar requirements have arisen in the process of *kukhonta* in recent years.[24] Compared to early in the twentieth century when Swazis had greater freedom of movement, a confluence of factors has made mobility between chiefdoms more difficult. This has accumulated in the modern

---

19 WLSA, *Inheritance in Swaziland*, 51.
20 Levin, *When the Sleeping Grass Awakens*, 105–10. See also Physicians for Human Rights, *Epidemic of Inequality: Women's Rights and HIV/AIDS in Botswana & Swaziland: An Evidence-Based Report on the Effects of Gender Inequity, Stigma, and Discrimination*, 67–77, http://physiciansforhumanrights.org/library/reports/botswana-swaziland -epidemic-of-inequality.html. For a fuller ethnographic account of traditional political structures, see Kuper, *African Aristocracy*; and Brian Allan Marwick, *The Swazi: An Ethnographic Account of the Natives of the Swaziland Protectorate* (Cambridge: Cambridge University Press, 1940).
21 Levin, *When the Sleeping Grass Awakens*, 40; Joireman, *Where There Is No Government*, 27–34.
22 Kuper, *African Aristocracy*.
23 Kuper, *African Aristocracy*, 44–9.
24 Levin, *When the Sleeping Grass Awakens*, 113–44; Kuper, *African Aristocracy*, 44–9.

development of the process of *valelisa*, which is to bid farewell to the chief by presenting a gift.[25] Nowadays it takes the form of cash payment, the *khonta* fees.[26]

The observations made by Kuper in the 1940s about the importance of these laws was reaffirmed in 2002 with countrywide efforts to codify law and custom through a government initiative, the Project for the Recording and Codification of Swazi Law and Custom.[27] The project found that Swazi law and custom is intimately connected to land and it is enforced at both the state and family levels. At the state level, the codification project affirmed that bonding with chiefs through a series of reciprocal rights and duties remains an integral part of the land allotment process.[28] Furthermore it confirmed that these rights and duties are enforced through the customary court system, which is actively used by customary officials.[29] At the more intimate level, Swazi law and custom is upheld by the *lusendvo*, the family council.[30] The *lusendvo* is recognized by Swazi law and custom as a formal institution with powers to decide matters related to the family. The *lusendvo* uses Swazi law and custom rules to settle disputes within the family, to subdivide family land for the use of married sons and returning widowed women, and to assist in the settlement of issues with others in the community. The *lusendvo* is particularly powerful in matters of inheritance for both movable and immovable property, where it governs the dissolution of property upon a family member's death, or to stipulate the land that an adult son may build upon. The head of the family, the *inkhosana*, with the support of the *lusendvo* holds the SNL property in a trust-like system for his family, in the same way the chief does within the chiefdom and the king for the whole of Eswatini. In both the larger political *tinkhundla* system and in the more intimate family system, these key features distinguish them from the imported common law. These features have specific impacts on the gendered experience. The patriarchal

---

25 Kuper, *African Aristocracy*, 49.

26 Levin, *When the Sleeping Grass Awakens*, 139.

27 Whelpton, "Land Tenure Dealing with Swazi Nation Land"; and Scott, "Some Thoughts on the Law of Property in Swaziland."

28 Whelpton, "Land Tenure Dealing with Swazi Nation Land," 147.

29 As well it receives referrals from the non-customary police force. Nhlapo, "Legal Duality and Multiple Judicial Organisation," 71; Scott, "Some Thoughts on the Law of Property in Swaziland."

30 See also Administration Order No. 6 of 1998, section 3, where the *lusendvo* is "an inner council of a family as underscored under customary law." See Maxine Langwenya, "Swaziland Justice Sector and the Rule of Law," 2013, https://www.eldis.org/document/A70410.

and patrilineal nature of the Swazi law and custom regulates the intimate division of SNL in the family and the community relationship
with land within chiefdom. Swazi law and custom is utilized daily to
judge what is "Swazi" and what is "un-Swazi."[31] Within this system,
customary leaders and family members have a vested interest in maintaining traditional Swazi values, for to do otherwise would jeopardize
their control over land. Within this system of land division there are
three features of Swazi law and custom that have a particularly gendered impact.

1. COMMUNAL

First, Swazi law and custom land tenure is communal. With much in
common with other customary law systems, in Africa and elsewhere,[32]
the difficulties of translating customary legal structures into Western legal language are well documented.[33] In the Swazi communal
land ownership system, control and access to resources corresponds
to claims to sovereignty over the land. Being able to access land and
resources within this system depends upon a multiplicity of factors,

---

31 WLSA, *Inheritance in Swaziland*, 20; and Marwick, *Swazi*.
32 Kwame Akuffo, "The Conception of Land Ownership in African Customary Law
    and Its Implications for Development," *African Journal of International and Compar-
    ative Law* 17, no. 1 (2009): 57; Winnie Bikaako and John Ssenkumba, "Gender, Land
    and Rights: Contemporary Contestations in Law, Policy and Practice in Uganda,"
    in *Women and Land in Africa: Culture, Religion, and Realizing Women's Rights*. ed. L.
    Muthoni Wanyeki (London: Zed Books, 2003), 232. See also Abdulmimini A. Oba,
    "The Future of Customary Law in Africa," in Fenrich, Galizzi, and Higgins, *Future of
    African Customary Law*, 58–80.
33 The use of language to accurately describe ownership of land in customary law has
    proven to be particularly complex, and the early debate between two pre-eminent
    Africanists, Max Gluckman and Paul Bohannan, remains relevant. Gluckman car-
    ried out an ethnographic study of the law of the Barotse peoples of Northern Rho-
    desia (Zambia), finding elements of Western legal traditions in the customary law,
    particularly a legal standard of the reasonable man. Gluckman described the system
    of Borotse land use through the language of trusts and estates, though he conceded
    that these phrases do not perfectly capture the customary relationship with land.
    On the other hand, in his work concerning the Tiv of Nigeria, Bohanna rejected the
    practice of searching for Western legal concepts. Instead, he relied upon the use of
    the local language and legal terms of art.
       For more information, see Max Gluckman, "Property Rights and Status in
    African Traditional Law," in *Ideas and Procedure in African Customary Law*, ed. Max
    Gluckman (London: Oxford University Press, 1966), 258–9; Gluckman, *The Judicial
    Process among the Barotse of Northern Rhodesia (Zambia)* (Manchester, UK: Manchester
    University Press, 1966); Paul Bohannan, *Justice and Judgement amongst the Tiv*, 3rd ed.
    (Prospects Heights, IL: Waveland, 1989).

including the intended use of the land, the relationships of the individuals involved, and the traditional use of that land and property area.[34] In Western legal language this is often described as a trust.[35] The utility of the legal concepts of trusts and usufruct (user) rights in Africa has been highly debated. One criticism has been that the trust classification denotes a limited set of rights over land, and the creation of a power relationship with one person (the attributed trustee) having the power of disposition of land, which in turn affects the rights of access for another.[36] Utilizing the trust terminology assists in divorcing of traditionally communally owned land from the corresponding traditional obligations to community members.

In the Swazi context the very parameters of the land areas governed by custom, and therefore communal, is not clear. In addition to the areas governed by custom, there are areas governed by colonial English law, which adopts trust structures in the full meaning of a trust. Together this means that although the areas of SNL are not clearly delineated by statute,[37] by definition title to SNL is vested in the king, who holds it "in trust for the nation."[38] In Eswatini the trusteeship model is particularly pronounced as a result of the pre- and post-colonial objective of the Swazi ruling elite to repurchase partitioned land from the British government. The repurchased land, termed *tibiyo/tisuka* land, is held in trust for the Swazi nation.[39] In common with the accounts of trusteeship-like land identified by early anthropologists, SNL traditionally cannot be bought, mortgaged, leased, or sold (though there are some accounts of the leasing of *tibiyo* land to companies operating in Eswatini).[40]

---

34 H.W.O. Okoth-Ogendo, "Property Systems and Social Organisation in Africa: An Essay on the Relative Position of Women under Indigenous and Received Law," in *The Individual under African Law*, ed. P. Takirambudde (Mbabane: University of Swaziland, 1982), 48.

35 Akuffo, "Conception of Land Ownership."

36 Okoth-Ogendo, "Property Systems and Social Organisation," 49. See also Max Gluckman, "Concepts in the Comparative Study of Tribal Law," in Gluckman, *Judicial Process among the Barotse*, 359.

37 See the Natural Resources Act No. 71 of 1951, which defines "Swazi areas" of the colonial era: "'Swazi area' means any land set apart for the sole and exclusive use and occupation of Africans under the Concessions Partition Act No. 28 of 1907 and land set aside for African land settlement in terms of the Swazi Land Settlement Act No. 2 of 1946, and shall include any land registered in the name of the Ngwenyama in Trust for the Swazi Nation."

38 Levin, *When the Sleeping Grass Awakens*, 115; WLSA, *Inheritance in Swaziland*, 51; and Marwick, *Swazi*, 159.

39 Levin, *When the Sleeping Grass Awakens*, 116–17.

40 Levin, *When the Sleeping Grass Awakens*, 116–17.

2. BROADLY PATRIARCHAL SOCIETY

A second feature of Swazi law and custom is its broadly patriarchal structure.[41] A patriarchal structure traces descent through the male line, and in the Swazi context this process in seen in the immediate family structure, as well as being mirrored in the community and social structure. While land and real property – in the form of homesteads – are not the only manifestations of a patriarchal society, they do act as significant perpetuators in the Swazi context. Land holds a central position in the patriarchal system of Swazi law and custom found in both the family through the *lusendvo*, and through the customary courts. At the intimate level the familial homestead is central to the continuation of Swazi culture. In Swazi law and custom the *inkhosana*, the family head of the *lusendvo* in council, will almost always be a male within the family,[42] and more specifically often the father of the family or, upon his death, the eldest son.[43] Likewise only a married male can inherit land from the family homestead, and *kukhonta* into new chiefdoms. Upon marriage a Swazi woman traditionally lives with her in-laws and has the right to access land through her husband, who will be allocated land from within his extended family's homestead.[44]

In addition to male-dominated decision-making structures regarding control of and access to land, it is also patrilineal, meaning that

---

In addition it is reported that individuals can relinquish customary land rights over SNL and gain rights to a water project, Lower Usuthu Small-Holder Irrigation Project, over the same land. This process is documented through "enhanced chiefs letters." This process allows groups to secure loans; however, it has also created situations in which individuals sought to relinquish land rights over land that is not their own. For more information, see Chisomo Gunda, Janvier Gasasira, Sam Sithole, Harold Liversage, and Steven Jonckheere, "Securing Smallholder Farmers' Land and Water Rights and Promoting Equitable Land Access in Irrigation and Watershed Management in Malawi, Rwanda and Swaziland" (paper presented at the Annual World Bank Conference on Land and Poverty, Washington DC, 8–11 April 2013), 21–3.

41 WLSA, *Inheritance in Swaziland*, 47. See, generally, Lim and Bottomley, *Feminist Perspectives on Land Law*; Banda, *Women, Law and Human Rights*; Banda, "Women, Law and Human Rights in Southern Africa"; and Joirement, *Where There Is No Government*, 45. Concerning Eswatini, see Marmick, *Swazi*, 47; and Kuper, *African Aristocracy*, 89–92.

42 Typically the *inkhosana* will be a male heir, although there are reports of women being appointed the *inkhosana* if they have favourable education and employment. The flexibility of Swazi law and custom equally allows for other males in the family to be appointed or to claim to have the *inkhosana* role. See WLSA, *Inheritance in Swaziland*, 44–5.

43 WLSA, *Inheritance in Swaziland*, 40 and 51.

44 WLSA, *Inheritance in Swaziland*, 40 and 51.

the immediate access or ownership of the land is traced through the male members of the family.[45] Patrilineal land reverts to the male in the family if there is a breakdown of the marital family structure.[46] Traditionally the patrilineal system reflects the desire to protect a given area of land for use by future generations of the family.[47] The patrilineal and patriarchal management of land does not happen in a vacuum; instead management entails a host of reciprocal duties and rights between community members and chiefs. The *inkhosana* holds a host of reciprocal duties and rights for the family on the homestead land,[48] with the emphasis being on the responsibilities of land management for the benefit of the family.[49] The *inkhosana* has the duty to manage the estate for the entire family, ensure the upkeep of buildings for widows still living in the property, and pay for the *lobolo*, bride price, for his male family members.[50]

The intimate experience of male-dominated land is replicated at the national level through the Swazi system of government, the *tinkhundla* system, and ultimately the power that is vested in the king. Recalling that that *tinkhundla* system is a form of political representation, although not directly tied to the system of hereditary chiefs, it is deployed as a facet of royal rule and mirrors the enforcement of Swazi law and custom:[51] the *tinkhundla* system is ruled by male traditional leaders who ensure that Swazi law and custom is maintained at the local level. The patriarchal powers are thus mutually reinforced through cultural reproduction of law and custom within the family setting as reflective of *tinkhundla* management of land and kingship.

In the Swazi context the patriarchal nature of customary law is directly concerned with the division of land, but its impact extends to accessing resources in property beyond real property. Personal movement is monitored, with women having to get the permission of their husbands or male family member to get a passport or open

---

45 Ernest Kofi Abotse and Paolo Galizzi, "Traditional Institutions and Governance in Modern African Democracies: History, Challenges and Opportunities in Ghana," in Fenrich, Galizzi, and Higgins, *Future of African Customary Law*, 26.
46 Abotse and Galizzi, "Traditional Institutions and Governance," 269.
47 Okoth-Ogendo, "Property Systems and Social Organisation," 47–57.
48 WLSA, *Inheritance in Swaziland*, 40–7.
49 WLSA, *Inheritance in Swaziland*, 46.
50 *Lobolo* is the "bride price," paid by the husband's family to the wife's family. This is traditionally in the form of cattle, but it can take the form of cash. See Kuper, *African Aristocracy*, 97–8; and WLSA, *Inheritance in Swaziland*, 42–3.
51 Levin, *When the Sleeping Grass Awakens*,"108.

a bank account,[52] or the colonially enforced requirement whereby women were forbidden to leave the country or work without permission from male family members.[53] Fundamental aspects of freedom of movement and empowerment for women are thus impeded through customary land-management systems.

3. AN INTERLOCKING SYSTEM OF RIGHTS

The regulation of SNL represents a system of complex and interlocking rights. The rights of individuals are tied intimately to the collectively held land system. Land management within chiefdoms emphasizes community responsibilities as essential to daily life, and Swazi law and custom emphasizes the role that land plays in sustaining Swazi culture. The impact on daily life is tangible. For example, swearing allegiance to a chief is essential in order to gain access to land for living and agricultural purposes. A citizen in a community is required to attend to national duties, such as attendance at the national *incwala* ceremony[54] and *Umhlanga*, the reed dance,[55] and to partake in traditional ceremonies for births, deaths, and marriages within the community. For women, the death of a spouse requires them to pay respect by not leaving the house until a new *inkhosana* is appointed to head the *lusendvo*.[56] This requirement is enforced even if the individual has employment obligations, and not leaving the house could put her employment status at risk. The resulting access to land, as distinct from ownership of land, is significant, because it means that a member of society gains the right to use land for a specific purpose, instead of having the right to sole and independent use of land.[57] Thus roaming cattle are a frequent

---

52   WLSA, *Inheritance in Swaziland*, 50; see also Christopher Amherst Byuma Zigira, *Religion, Culture and Gender: A Study of Women's Search for Gender Equality in Swaziland* (Munich: Lincom, 2003), 46.

53   H.S. Simelane, "Sharing My Bed with the Enemy: Wives and Violent Husbands in Post-Colonial Swaziland," *Journal of Contemporary African Studies* 29, no. 4 (2011): 498.

54   Whelpton, "Land Tenure Dealing with Swazi Nation Land," 148. This is the annual ceremony of kingship, entailing a series of rituals in which Swazis show their support for the king. See Kuper, *African Aristocracy*, 223.

55   In this annual ritual, girls and young women collect reeds and bring them to the king's mother, to repair the queen mother's fence. Traditionally this dance was the prequel to the king choosing a future queen from the female youth. Zigira, *Religion, Culture and Gender*, 44.

56   Kuper, *African Aristocracy*.

57   An example is the grazing rights outside planting season over a neighbour's land that is generally used for agriculture. Okoth-Ogendo, "Property Systems and Social Organisation," 48; and Griffiths, "Networking Resources," 229.

sight, even in towns close to the major cities. The process of continually assessing land based upon cultural adherence (amongst other considerations) put women in the precarious situation of proving themselves by Swazi cultural standards.

The patriarchal communally oriented and interconnected nature of Swazi law and custom creates particular challenges for the realization of gender equality. Above we have seen Swazi law and custom defining an individual's rights and responsibilities to the land and equally to fellow members in society, represented through the family structure and mirrored in the chiefdom organization, tightly regulating access to land through a complex system of relationships. The need to improve women's rights to land and property within customary systems is widely recognized.[58] In addition to its patriarchal nature, the communal aspect of land use and role of community-enforced rights and obligations for regulating land use together create an enforceable customary law system. The connection between abuse, patriarchy, and security of land tenure is itself demonstrative of this.[59]

The challenges posed by the confluence of communal property ownership in the patriarchal society found in customary law in Eswatini can be seen in the phenomenon of "property grabbing" – the illegal taking of property from a widow through force or social pressure. The property could be real property built on land, or movable property such as cattle, as well as restricting access to SNL itself.[60] The property can be taken by the in-law family, through the authority of the *lusendvo*, or more informally taken as the result of a breakdown of relationship.[61] As a practice, property grabbing is supported by the male-dominated decision-making process and the stated desire to protect the community's access to land. These claims are then supported by particular interpretations of traditional Swazi law and custom practices, to create a mutually enforcing pattern of deprivation of property through traditional law reinforced with patterns of inequality. Under Swazi law, the patriarchal, marriage-based land-holding system contains reciprocal obligations: a widow *should* be able to retain access to land and

58 See Thea Hilhorst, "Women's Land Rights: Current Developments in Sub-Saharan Africa," in *Evolving Land Rights, Policy and Tenure in Africa*, ed. Camilla Toulmin and Julian Quan (London: DFID/IIED/NRI, 2000), 196.

59 Action Aid International Briefing Paper, "Securing Women's Right to Land and Livelihoods: A Key to Ending Hunger and Fighting AIDS" (Johannesburg: Action-Aid, 2008), https://landportal.org/sites/landportal.info/files/actionaid_womens_right_to_land.pdf.

60 WLSA, *Inheritance in Swaziland*, 84.

61 WLSA, *Inheritance in Swaziland*, 85.

be supported by her spouse's family, even though the land is in control of other male family members. Increasingly this does not happen, Swazi customary law is no longer functioning the way it was originally designed. The Swazi patriarchal system of governance has built-in access to land and support for unmarried women who could not access land via marriage, but that aspect of Swazi land law is breached in a land grab. The result for widows in Eswatini is that the distribution of property acquired through marriage is carried out on an uncertain basis, depending upon the personal relationships involved.

The impact of relying on traditional law and custom is explained by Anne Griffiths in speaking about Botswana. Griffith explains the difference in the manner that women access land: "[A] gendered perspective on property shifts the focus away from formal rights, towards a much more complex pattern of identifying the issues governing women's access to the use and ownership of property."[62]

The concern for women claiming access to SNL within the confines of Swazi law and custom is the extent to which women must navigate patriarchal requirements of Swazi custom in order to gain access to land. Even though hierarchal domination may have been embedded through colonial norms, reciprocal traditional protection of land access afforded to widows, for example, is no longer respected. As early as 1982, in the first All Africa Law Conference, which was held in Eswatini, it was recognized that status and the active membership of an individual within a community played a large role in what form of customary law applied.[63] A key question raised at this conference was who arbitrated Swazi law and custom. The idea on which this question is based is the recognition that in the traditional context land is socially embedded. [64] In the Swazi context it is recognized that the interconnection between societal regulation and land tenure has contributed to the longevity of the customary leaders and authority patterns.[65] Rights activists acknowledge the importance of Swazi law and custom, and there has been a long-standing project to codify the law for certainty, transparency, and fairness; for instance, capturing the aspects of Swazi law that provide unmarried women access to land and economic

---

62 Griffiths, "Networking Resources," 218.
63 Okoth-Ogendo, "Property Systems and Social Organisation," 56–7.
64 Akuffo, "Conception of Land Ownership," 61.
65 Sandra F. Joireman, "Entrapment or Freedom: Enforcing Customary Property Rights Regimes in Common-Law Africa," in Fenrich, Galizzi, and Higgins, *Future of African Customary Law*, 195.

support.[66] Whilst this has been ongoing, there has been a simultaneous push to address property ownership through the common law.

C. Part III: Property Law Claims through Colonial Laws

Alongside the robust Swazi law and custom system there is also the colonial legal system that has been imported into Eswatini. The received common law has jurisdiction over civil and customary issues; as well it acts as a system of appeal for all matters.[67] The division of jurisdiction for a given issue is often unclear. For example, issues of property and inheritance law, which are civil issues, fall under the jurisdiction of the common law, and there are statutory provisions that concern a variety of property issues. The common law operates parallel to the provisions in Swazi law and custom. The response to this duality from gender rights activists has been to opt for the common law system rules in order to claim property rights. In this next section we will look at how human rights claims have been made through the auspices of the imported common law.

1. DOMESTIC LAWS

In recent years gender equality and rights-based legal frameworks have been strengthened substantially. This has been done in an effort to harmonize the common law through updating legislation, and in recent judicial decision-making. As well in 2005 a constitution was adopted for the first time. The *Constitution of the Kingdom of Swaziland*[68] contains a host of provisions that promote human rights, and particularly gender equality. The Constitution seeks to promote freedom to choose to participate in the traditional practices of Swazi law and custom. Thus Article 28 includes the right "not to be compelled to undergo or uphold

---

66 The rules of Swazi law and custom are not recorded, despite attempts made with the support of the UNDP in the Project for the Recording and Codification of Swazi Law and Custom, 2001. Scott, "Some Thoughts on the Law of Property in Swaziland." At the time of writing, the codification project completed February 2015 has not been made public. See Hoole 'Nyane, "A Critique of the Swazi Constitutional Rules on Succession to Kingship," *De Jure* (Preoria) 52, no. 1 (2019). See Welcome Dlamini, "Tikhulu to Have Look at Codified Swazi Law and Custom," *Observer*, 22 February 2015, https://www.pressreader.com/eswatini/sunday-observer/20150222/281522224532868.
67 The Swazi Courts Act of 1950 established jurisdiction over civil and criminal matters: "The hierarchy of the courts is as follows: Swazi courts, Swazi Court of Appeal, Higher Swazi Court of Appeal, High Court and Judicial Commissioner." WLSA, *Inheritance in Swaziland*, 82.
68 *The Constitution of the Kingdom of Swaziland.*

any custom to which she is in conscience opposed." In addition, recognizing the critical importance of property practices in Eswatini, the Constitution highlights the importance of property rights. Article 34 enshrines the property rights of spouses, so that "a surviving spouse is entitled to a reasonable provision out of the estate of the other spouse whether the other spouse died having made a valid will or not and whether the spouses were married by civil or customary rites."[69]

Adopting a constitution is a very significant step towards adopting gender-equality norms in the country. As the same time there has been a push to harmonize legislation to reflect constitutionally protected gender-equality norms. Within the common law, a host of legislation pertains to property issues. Some of these pieces of legislation include the *Age of Majority Act*,[70] the *Wills Act*,[71] the *Intestate Succession Act*,[72] and the *Deed Registry Act*.[73] The utility of common law to create enforceable property rights through such legislation remains limited. This is due in part to largely outdated legislation. As a result, in 2009 the Commonwealth Secretariat identified these legislative pieces for harmonization and provided support for them to be rewritten as part of a push to reflect constitutional provisions.[74]

A key piece of legislation that has been identified as outdated is the *Deeds Registry Act*, which governs the transmission of land classified as "title deed land."[75] Section 16(3), the key part of the *Act*, states,[76] "Immovable property, bonds and other real rights shall not be

---

69 *The Constitution of the Kingdom of Swaziland*, article 34.
70 *Age of Majority Act* No 11 of 1953. In July 2013 the High Court held that marital power is illegal, in *Nombuyiselo Sihlongonyane v Mholi Sihlongonyane High Court Case No. 470/2013 A*. The concept of marital power denies women married under civil rights and in community of property the ability to sue and be sued in their own name.
71 *Wills Act* No. 10/1955.
72 *Intestate Succession Act* No 3/1953.
73 *Deeds Registry Act* No 37/1968.
74 These pieces of legislation were created with the assistance of the Commonwealth Secretariat, who provided provided legislative drafting support from 2006 to 2013 as part of the Secretariat's Rule of Law Programme. See Commonwealth Secretariat, *Evaluation of Commonwealth Secretariat Support to Member Countries on Legislative Drafting* (London: Commonwealth Secretariat, 2015), https://thecommonwealth .org/sites/default/files/inline/97%20-%20Legislative%20Drafting%20Evaluation -Final%20Report.pdf. The Commonwealth Secretariat sent attorneys from neighbouring South Africa and Zambia, for a two-year posting to assist with bringing key legislation in line with the Constitution.
75 Recall that title deed land is distinct from SNL, which is most commonly associated with regulation in Swazi law and custom.
76 *Deeds Registry Act* No 37/1968.

transferred or ceded to, or registered in the name of, a woman married in community of property, save where such property, bond or real rights are by law or by a condition of a bequest or donation excluded from the community." This means that if a married couple are to purchase title deed land, the land will automatically be registered solely in the husband's name, regardless of any monetary or non-monetary contributions made by women. The Act does create the opportunity for a person to opt out of being married in "community of property" which would prevent one's individual property from being considered family property. However, unless one opts out, one is automatically married in community of property. The deeds registry act therefore imparts a burden of legal awareness on individuals before they enter into civil marriage. This has a disproportionate impact on women.

Historically title deed land was transferred amongst non-Swazi transplants, who were subject only to the common law; therefore this land was regulated solely through common law systems. Title deed land is now transmitted amongst the entire population, although largely amongst the more wealthy. It remains in the legal jurisdiction of the common law. The Deeds Registry legislation is recognized as discriminatory, and the *Deeds Registry Act* drafted by the Commonwealth Secretariat removes the discriminatory provisions.[77] The amended Act was finally given royal assent in 2015, a full six years after it was initially drafted.

2. INTERNATIONAL HUMAN RIGHTS EFFORTS

Efforts to promote gender norms domestically are mirrored by the adoption of numerous international and regional treaties and agreements. In particular in 2004 Eswatini began ratifying a number of regional and international human rights documents, so that it is now a party to six of the core international human rights instruments. These are the *Covenants on Economic, Social and Cultural Rights*[78] and on *Political and Economic Rights*[79]; and the *Convention on the Elimination of all Forms of Discrimination against Women*.[80] Eswatini had already become

---

77 The updated legislation, *The Deeds Registry Act* (2009), was created with the assistance of the Commonwealth Secretariat, Commonwealth Fund for Technical Co-operation.
78 *International Covenant on Economic, Social and Cultural Rights*, 19 December (1966), 993 UNTS 3 (Acceded to by Swaziland on 26 March 2004).
79 *International Covenant on Political and Economic Rights*, 19 December (1966), 999 UNTS 171 (Acceded to by Swaziland on 26 March 2004).
80 *Convention on the Elimination of all Forms of Discrimination against Women*, 18 December 1979, 12 UNTS 13 (Acceded to by Swaziland on 26 March 2004).

a signatory to the *Convention on the Elimination of all Forms of Racial Discrimination*[81] and the *Convention on the Rights of the Child*.[82] In addition Eswatini is a party to a number of relevant African Union human rights instruments.[83] Of particular importance, Eswatini is a signatory to the *Protocol to the African Charter on Human and Peoples' Rights on the Rights of Women in Africa*.[84] Finally there are a number of regional human rights instruments through the Southern African Development Community (SADC). One guiding objective of the SADC community is to ensure the "mainstreaming of gender in the process of community building."[85] To implement this goal, SADC has a number of instruments that focus solely on women's rights, including the *SADC Protocol on Gender and Development*, to which Eswatini is a signatory.[86] The protocol contains provisions to end discrimination against women contained in domestic legislation. It also recognizes the importance of ensuring access to property and resources, and it commits states to ensure that women have equal access and rights to different aspects of property security.[87]

Together these instruments are a cohesive body of international human rights norms, including equality rights. In its legal reasoning the judiciary has shown a willingness to refer to regional human rights standards, Eswatini's international legal obligations, and domestic legal obligations alike. See, for example, the recent decision, *Swaziland National Ex-Miners Workers Association and Another v The Minister of Education and Others* Civil Case No. 335/2009. In this case the High Court confirmed the right to free education for primary school children. This finding

81 *The International Convention on the Elimination of All Forms of Racial Discrimination*, 7 March 1966, 660 UNTS 195 (Swaziland ratified on 7 April 1969).
82 *Convention on the Rights of the Child*, New York, 20 November 1989, 1577 UNTS 3 (Ratified by Swaziland on 7 September 1995).
83 Swaziland has ratified the *African Charter on Human and Peoples Rights*, 26 June 1981, OAU Doc. CAB/LEG/67/3REV 5 (Ratified by Swaziland on 15 September 1995); the *African Charter on the Rights and Welfare of the Child*, Addis Ababa, July 1990 (Swaziland became a signatory on 26 June 1992).
      Eswatini is also a signatory to the *Protocol to the African Charter on Human and Peoples' Rights on the Rights of Women in Africa*, 11 July 2003. Assembly/AU/Dec.14(II), though it has not as yet been ratified.
84 *Protocol to the African Charter on Human and Peoples' Rights on the Rights of Women in Africa*, 11 July 2003. Assembly/AU/Dec.14(II).
85 *The Treaty of the Southern African Development Community*, article 5(1)(k).
86 SADC, *Protocol on Gender and Development*, 2008, http://www.sadc.int/files/8713/5292/8364/Protocol_on_Gender_and_Development_2008.pdf.
87 SADC, *Protocol on Gender and Development*, articles 3(b) (concerning property rights on the dissolution of marriage), 10 (concerning widow and widowers rights), and 18 (concerning access to property and resources).

was based on constitutional provisions and international human rights standards, in particular those found in the *Convention on the Rights of the Child*. We will see that the judiciary has similarly relied on international and regional legal norms to secure women's property rights.

3. TEST CASE

In the context of substantive changes to the common law, in recent years Swazi activists have made human rights–based claims through the common law. In 2008 a Swaziland human rights activist Mary Joyce Doo Aphane wanted to purchase a piece of land with her husband. The piece of land was across the road from the family home, an empty lot, which was classified as title deed land – that is, land available for purchase. The purchase and sale of title deed land is recorded in a public registry, according to the provisions of the *Deeds Registry Act*. Doo Aphane had the practical ability to purchase the desired land: she had the financial means, a valid purchase and sale, with a willing seller. However, according to the *Deed Registry Act* a woman married in community of property cannot purchase land and have the land title registered in her name. Furthermore, according to the *Marriage Act*, a couple is automatically married in community of property unless they specifically opt out.[88]

In a bid to purchase the piece of land in her own name, Doo Aphane mounted a legal claim, challenging the offending provisions of the *Deeds Registry Act*. In the case Doo Aphane argued that the *Deeds Registry Act* was discriminatory and she wanted to have the property purchased to be in both her husband's name and her name as equal co-owners. From a rule of law perspective, in *Doo Aphane* the plaintiffs built their case on constitutional rights–based claims. In the statement of claim the plaintiff argued that the *Deeds Registry Act* is at odds with the gender equality provisions contained in Swaziland`s 2005 *Constitution*. Doo Aphane sought a declaration that: "the sections of the Deeds Registry Regulations promulgated under the above Act and the Deeds Office practice which requires that a woman married in community of property assumes her husband's surname in the registration of immovable property are inconsistent with the provisions of Sections 20 and 28 of the Constitution of the Kingdom of Swaziland, No. 001/2005 [and are] null and void."[89]

---

88 *Marriage Act* No. 17 of 1964.
89 Reported in *Attorney General v Mary-Joyce Doo Aphane*, Case No (383/09) [2010] SZHC 29, 11–12. For more information, see Mary-Joyce Doo Aphane, "Justice Denied or Deferred for Swazi Women," *BUWA! Journal on African Women's Experiences* 1 (2010): 39–41; Maxine Langwenya, "Historic Step Towards Equality for Swazi Women: An Analysis of Mary-Joyce Doo Aphane v The Registrar of Deeds," Open Society Initiative for Southern Africa Open Debate (2011), 6.

Article 20 of the *Constitution* states, "20(1) All persons are equal before and under the law in all spheres of political, economic, social and cultural life and in every other respect and shall enjoy equal protections of the law." Section 20(2) then confirms that a person shall not be discriminated against on the grounds of gender. Section 28 of the Constitution contains the most unequivocal promotion of gender equality: "Section 28(1)(i): Women have the right to equal treatment with men and that right shall include equal opportunities in political, economic and social activities." In addition the Constitution protects the property rights of spouses[90] and the right for the High Court to enforce all fundamental human rights as contained in the Constitution.[91]

At first instance in February 2010, the court was overwhelmingly supportive of Doo Aphane's legal claims. The sitting judge, Justice Qinsile Dlamini, held that the *Deeds Registry Act* was unconstitutional, as it did not uphold the right of equality for women. Justice Dlamini made a strong statement by chastising Parliament for taking five years to implement the equality provisions of the Constitution by updating in-force legislation to meet equality based claims.[92]

The attorney general appealed, resulting in the landmark decision *The Attorney General v Mary-Joyce Doo Aphane*, May 2010. Arguing a legal technicality, the attorney general framed the issue as a division of powers, questioning the appropriateness of the court altering the *Deeds Registry Act*, arguing instead for Parliament as the correct forum for harmonizing legislation through the democratic process.

In its judgment the Court of Appeal again considered directly the provisions contained in the *Deeds Registry Act* in light of the relatively new constitutional provisions. In keeping with the spirit of the February 2010 case, the court confirmed that the *Deeds Registry Act* contained unconstitutional provisions that were contrary to the gender equality rights of Doo Aphane and of Swazi women wishing to own property in equality with their husbands. The Court of Appeal recognized the superiority of constitutional provisions when it requested Parliament to harmonize the *Deeds Registry Act* to be in line with constitutional obligations. Furthermore, the court recognized the interconnectedness of women's experience with land, her role in the community and gender equality issues. In *Doo Aphane*, Justice Moore A. Began his *dictum* by stating,

---

90 *Constitution of the Kingdom of Swaziland*, chapter 3, article 34.
91 *Constitution of the Kingdom of Swaziland*, chapter 8, part 2(6), article 151 (2).
92 See IRIN News, "Women's Rights Take One Step Forward, Two Steps Back," 16 June 2010, http://www.irinnews.org/Report/89510/SWAZILAND-Women-s-rights-take-one-step-forward-two-steps-back.

368 Creating Indigenous Property

This case is but the latest in a continuing series brought in many countries of the world by women in their attempts to redress what they claim to be discriminatory laws and practices which operated unfairly against them. These precepts and practices have deprived women of rights which were freely available to men, and keep women in a position of inferiority and inequality, in the various societies in which they live, work, pay their taxes, and raise their families, despite the fact that women contribute substantially to the growth and development of the communities and nations to which they belong.[93]

Ultimately the court agreed that it was a division of powers issue and held that it would be *ultra vires* if the judiciary altered the legislation through the legal acts of severing or reading in. Rather the Court of Appeal referred the matter back to Parliament. The court ordered Parliament to harmonize the *Deeds Registry Act* with the gender equality provisions contained in the Constitution within one year. It also found, "pending the enactment of legislation by Parliament, the Registrar of Deeds is authorized to register immovable property, bonds and other real rights in the joint names of husband and wife, married to each other in community of property." Although the updated version of the *Deeds Registry Act* had already been drafted at the time of the Court of Appeal decision, the one-year time frame for the implementation of harmonized legislation expired in May 2011. Although both houses of Parliament debated and adopted the updated legislation in October 2011, it took another four years for the legislation to be implemented.

For Doo Aphane, the litigant in the case, the emphasis was always on Swazi identity and nationhood, even as she utilized common law legal processes. About the decision, Aphane explains, "For me, this issue is a women's rights issue, it is a Swazi issue, and it is a matter of dignity. We as Swazis, men and women, must work together to develop Swazi land and promote Swazi culture. I have the ability to own and develop the land in equal partnership with my husband, and I will fight until that right is legally protected."[94]

The *Doo Aphane* case is indicative of a growing human rights–based dialogue within Eswatini. From a gender rights perspective it is no surprise that the claims for gender equality in land ownership were made through the colonial common law system in the *Doo Aphane* case. The

---

93 *Attorney General v Mary-Joyce Doo Aphane*, per Moore J.A., 5.
94 Private communication with Mary-Joyce Doo Aphane, September 2010; originally reported in Tenille Brown, *Women's Legal Status under Civil Law and Swazi Law and Custom* (Ottawa: Just Governance Group, 2010).

force of Swazi customs can be particularly and deeply felt in relation to land. A 1962 survey of opinions held by Swazis on the question of land observed, "Traditionally, individual land ownership inevitably destroys and degenerates Swazi social life, and ultimately undermines and invalidates the honour, power and significance of Royalty and chieftainship, with respect to Swazi rule."[95]

With the fluidity of land types and use of legal rules and systems to govern those lands, women's rights must be understood in relation to the complexity of the land arrangement in Eswatini as a whole. If women's equality rights to land are understood as being opposite to the Swazi customs pertaining to land, it is not surprising that there is no evidence that the updated *Title Deeds Act* and other legislation has resulted in increased security of land rights for women.[96] Compared to the strong tradition of Swazi law and custom, land ownership claims made upon a normative human rights framework are a new phenomenon.

II. Conclusion

Eswatini is at the early stages of a well-documented, region-wide process of understanding land as a gendered issue. As a component of ensuring personal security for women as they access land for use, it is clear from the *Doo Aphane* decision that we must also address security of land tenure through the legal protection of ownership rights.[97] The Swazi context, with its living system of law and custom, shows that this must be done with respect for traditional legal systems. In the Swazi context the complicated and often arbitrary nature of categorization into three types of land, and the two living legal systems regulating the same, create uncertainty when claiming and seeking to enforce property rights. The bringing of gender equality claims, through the

---

95 A.J.B. Hughes, "Some Swazi Views on Land Tenure," *Africa: Journal of the International African Institute* 32, no. 3 (1962): 258.

96 Private communication with a representative of the Swaziland Coalition of Concerned Civil Society, 22 February 2013. There is evidence that the ongoing insecurity in land rights extends to weak property rights generally. The 2018 World Report from Human Rights Watch reported on a case in which a married Swazi woman was unable to sell livestock she purchased because she was unable to get the consent of her estranged husband, as is required in Swazi Law and Custom. See Human Rights Watch, "World Report 2018: Reporting on Events of 2017" (Human Rights Watch, 2017).

97 Hughes, "Some Swazi Views on Land Tenure," 275.

common law and international law in the area of land and real property, in a customary law context, is a complex task.

The complexity of understanding these provisions, both customary and common law, in the pursuit of gender equality has not deterred gender rights activists, who have adopted a clear advocacy strategy. The common law contains the hallmarks of a transparent and certain system for the realization of rights, and acts as the gateway to regional and international human rights standards. If the goal is certainty of women's codified ability to own land and real property, then one aspect has been resolved: the Eswatini colonial law courts have expressly mandated that property ownership in Eswatini must prioritize equality and human rights in adjudication. In addition the court has mandated that Parliament expedite the harmonization of legislation. Despite these perceived benefits, the common law does not provide the fix-all solution to achieving gender equality. The *Doo Aphane* decision is just one aspect of the spectrum of possible gender rights claims and available processes to achieve gender equality. Though the claim was clearly made pursuant to title deed land, and it utilized Roman-Dutch legal processes connected to it, Aphane acted as an individual and made claims as a Swazi woman who embraces her cultural identity. Incorporation of both these sides resulted in broad support across civil society working in many different sectors.[98] Therefore the decision contributes to understanding the importance of Swazi law and custom for gender issues. Uncertainties about these legal processes in relation to the application of Swazi law and custom, as both a cultural and legal force, remain. The importance of protecting and promoting Swazi culture is a point of national pride, and it is to be weighed in equal importance to the discourse surrounding women's rights.[99]

---

98 Langwenya, "Historic Step Towards Equality for Swazi Women."

99 Sari Wastell, "Being Swazi, Being Human," in *The Practice of Human Rights: Tracking Law between the Global and the Local*, ed. Mark Goodale and Sally Engle Merry (Cambridge University Press, 2007), 332. Here the author observes, "Swazi is understood to be of the same value magnitude as what is non-Swazi, i.e., rather than Swazis being a small part of the teeming globe, Swazi kingship posits the nation-in-kingship as the coequal counterparts to 'the Globe.'"

   The significance of this observation is in the enforceable value of human rights discourse when making women's rights claims, in the situation where human rights are seen to be a moral judgment system in the same way as Swazi law and custom.

Contributors

Jamie Baxter is an associate professor at the Schulich School of Law, Dalhousie University, where he teaches and writes on land and property, agriculture, food systems, and local government. He studied law at the University of Toronto and Yale, and has been a Canada-U.S. Fulbright Scholar at the Appalachian Center, University of Kentucky.

Tenille E. Brown is an assistant professor in the Bora Laskin Faculty of Law at Lakehead University. Her research examines the intersection between land, property, and geography, with a focus on spatial theory. Tenille is a member of the Human Rights Research and Education Centre at the University of Ottawa, and a barrister and solicitor at the Bar of Ontario. Tenille holds an LLM from the University of Ottawa in the field of Aboriginal law and an LLB (Scots law) from the University of Dundee, Scotland. Prior to her academic work, Tenille worked in the Kingdom of Eswatini (formerly the Kingdom of Swaziland) as a legal officer in a national feminist rights organization, and her research in this volume is based on that experience.

Angela Cameron is an associate professor at the University of Ottawa, where she holds the Greenberg Chair in Women and the Legal Profession. She teaches Property Law; Gender, Sexuality, and the Law; a graduate seminar in contemporary legal issues; and co-teaches Indigenous Legal Advocacy with Dr Tracey Lindberg.

Sarah Carter, FRSC, is a professor and Henry Marshall Tory Chair in the Department of History and Classics, and Faculty of Native Studies of the University of Alberta. From Saskatoon, she studied Canadian history at the University of Saskatchewan (BA Hon, MA) and the University of Manitoba (PhD). Her research focuses on the history of settler colonialism in Canada and in comparative colonial and border-lands perspectives. Her 2016 book *Imperial Plots: Women, Land, and the Spadework of British Colonialism on the Canadian Prairies* won the Governor General's History Award for Scholarly Research. Her book *Ours by Every Law of Right and Justice: Women and the Vote in the Prairie Provinces* will appear in 2020 with the University of British Columbia Press.

Richard Daly is a freelance anthropological researcher who works for First Nations and their legal counsel in British Columbia regarding rights to land and self-governance. After higher degrees in social anthropology (Manchester, Toronto), he conducted ethnographic work with the Royal Ontario Museum and Heritage Ontario.

Karen Drake is an associate professor at Osgoode Hall Law School at York University, a citizen of the Métis Nation of Ontario, and a Commissioner with the Ontario Human Rights Commission. Her teaching and research interests include Canadian law as it affects Indigenous peoples, Anishinaabe law, and Métis law.

Sari Graben is an associate professor at the Faculty of Law, Ryerson University, where she holds the position Associate Dean Academic, Research and Graduate Studies (Interim). Her teaching and research address Indigenous peoples and development, with a special focus on regulatory institutions, emergent property systems, and risk. Her work on the interface between administrative decision-making and private law addresses how Indigenous traditions are incorporated into Canadian law.

Shalene Jobin is an associate professor in the Faculty of Native Studies and director of the Aboriginal Governance and Partnership program at the University of Alberta. She is a member of the Red Pheasant Cree First Nation (Treaty Six). She has published in the edited collection *Living on the Land: Indigenous Women's Understanding of Place* and *Indigenous Identity and Resistance*, and in the journals *American Indian Quarterly*, *Revue Générale de Droit*, and *Native Studies Review*.

Nathalie Kermoal is a Breton (a people whose territory is situated on the west coast of France). She is a full professor in the Faculty of Native Studies at the University of Alberta. She holds a PhD in history from the University of Ottawa. She has published three books and numerous articles in academic journals and collective volumes. Her areas of research interests are Métis studies, Indigenous constitutional issues, urban Indigenous history, and Indigenous women's issues. In 2011–12, she was Interim Dean of the Faculty of Native Studies. In 2013–14, she was special advisor on Aboriginal academic programs with the Provost's office. Since 2009, Professor Kermoal has been the Associate Dean (Academic) of the Faculty of Native Studies. Since January 2016, she is also the director of the Rupertsland Centre for Métis Research at the Faculty of Native Studies.

Sarah Morales is an associate professor at the University of Victoria Faculty of Law. She is Coast Salish and a member of Cowichan Tribes. Her research centres on Indigenous legal traditions, specifically the traditions of the Coast Salish people, Aboriginal law, and human rights. She has been active with Indigenous nations and NGOs across Canada in nation building, inherent rights recognition, and international human rights law.

Christian Morey (BSc, JD, MA, LLM) is a lawyer and economist whose research interests include Indigenous rights, law and development, and access to justice. He currently works as a policy analyst with the Office of International Affairs for the Health Portfolio, Government of Canada.

Michel Morin is a full professor at the Faculty of Law of the Université de Montréal. His research focuses on comparative legal history of public or private law and the evolution of Aboriginal peoples' rights. In 1998, the Humanities and Social Sciences Federation awarded him the Jean-Charles Falardeau prize for his book *L'Usurpation de la souveraineté autochtone (The Usurpation of Aboriginal Sovereignty*, 1997). He has published, in French, a *Historical Introduction to Roman, French, and English Law* (2004) and, with Arnaud Decroix and David Gilles, *Courts and Arbitration in New France and Quebec, 1740–1784* (2012, Rodolphe-Fournier 2013 prize).

Val Napoleon is Cree from Saulteau First Nation and an adopted member of the Gitanyow [Gitxsan] nation. She established the Indigenous Law Research Unit (ILRU) in order to partner with Indigenous communities across Canada to substantively articulate and rebuild Indigenous law. She publishes and teaches in areas of Indigenous legal traditions and methodologies, Indigenous legal theories, Indigenous feminisms and gender, intellectual property and oral histories, restorative justice, legal pluralism, Aboriginal legal issues, citizenship, and governance. She also teaches transsystemic property law (Gitxsan and common law) and property law.

Ibironke T. Odumosu-Ayanu is an associate professor at the College of Law, University of Saskatchewan. She was sessional lecturer at the Faculty of Law, University of British Columbia. She has received several research grants including a Social Sciences and Humanities Research Council (SSHRC) Standard Research Grant, a SSHRC Insight Development Grant, and a SSHRC Connections Grant, and her research has been published in several leading journals. Dr Odumosu-Ayanu has served on boards including in the role of vice president of the Canadian Law and Society Association. She serves on the editorial boards of a number of journals including the *Journal of African Law* and the *Business and Human Rights Journal*.

Emily Snyder is an assistant professor in Indigenous Studies and Women's and Gender Studies at the University of Saskatchewan. Her research interests are in the areas of Indigenous legal issues, Indigenous feminisms, HIV criminalization, and legal education. She is the author of *Gender, Power, and Representations of Cree Law*. Emily completed her PhD in sociology at the University of Alberta and was a Social Sciences and Humanities Research Council of Canada Postdoctoral Fellow at the Indigenous Law Research Unit at the University of Victoria. Emily is a white settler originally from Haudenosaunee and Anishinaabe territories in southern Ontario.

Brian Thom is an associate professor in the Department of Anthropology at the University of Victoria, where in 2010 he founded the Ethnographic Mapping Lab (http://ethnographicmapping.uvic.ca). From 1994 to 1997 and 2000 to 2010 he worked as a researcher, senior advisor, and negotiator for several Coast Salish First Nations (Canada) engaged in treaty, land claims, and self-government negotiations. His research is focused on issues of Indigenous territoriality, knowledge, and governance; revealing contemporary practices of Indigenous law; and clarifying the ontological imperatives behind Indigenous political strategies.